REMAPPING TRAVEL NARRATIVES
(1000–1700)

Connected Histories in the Early Modern World

Connected Histories in the Early Modern World contributes to our growing understanding of the connectedness of the world during a period in history when an unprecedented number of people—Africans, Asians, Americans, and Europeans—made transoceanic or other long-distance journeys. Inspired by Sanjay Subrahmanyam's innovative approach to early modern historical scholarship, it explores topics that highlight the cultural impact of the movement of people, animals, and objects at a global scale. The series editors welcome proposals for monographs and collections of essays in English from literary critics, art historians, and cultural historians that address the changes and cross-fertilizations of cultural practices of specific societies. General topics may concern, among other possibilities: cultural confluences, objects in motion, appropriations of material cultures, cross-cultural exoticization, transcultural identities, religious practices, translations and mistranslations, cultural impacts of trade, discourses of dislocation, globalism in literary/visual arts, and cultural histories of lesser studied regions (such as the Philippines, Macau, African societies).

Series Editors

Christina H. Lee, *Princeton University*
Julia Schleck, *University of Nebraska, Lincoln*

Series Advisory Board

Serge Gruzinski, *CNRS (Centre national de la recherche scientifique), Paris*
Michael Laffan, *Princeton University*
Ricardo Padrón, *University of Virginia*
Elizabeth Rodini, *Johns Hopkins University*
Kaya Şahin, *Indiana University, Bloomington*

REMAPPING TRAVEL NARRATIVES (1000–1700)

TO THE EAST AND BACK AGAIN

Edited by
MONTSERRAT PIERA

British Library Cataloguing in Publication Data

A catalogue record for this book is available from the British Library

ISBN: 9781942401599
e-ISBN: 9781942401605

https://arc-humanities.org

Printed and bound by CPI Group (UK) Ltd, Croydon, CR0 4YY

CONTENTS

PART III. TO THE EAST AND BACK:
EXCHANGING OBJECTS, IDEAS, AND TEXTS

LIST OF FIGURES

LIST OF CONTRIBUTORS

AYGÜL AĞIR is Professor of Architectural History at Istanbul Technical University where she also received her PhD (2001), master's, and bachelor's degrees from the Program in Architecture. Dr. Ağır specializes in the city and architecture of the medieval and early modern periods in comparative perspective. She participated in the International Palladian Architecture Course in Vicenza (1991), and research she conducted (1994–1995) at the Institute of Architecture in Venice (IUAV) focused on the *Fondaco dei Turchi*. Her publications include a wide range of articles and chapters concentrating particularly on Italian-Turkish cultural and architectural transitions. Dr. Ağır is the author of *The Old Venetian Settlement of Istanbul* published by the Istanbul Research Institute (2009 and 2013).

ELIO BRANCAFORTE is Chair and Associate Professor at Tulane University (New Orleans), specializing in sixteenth- and seventeenth-century German literature and culture. His scholarly interests include early modern travel literature, translation, cultural exchange, theories of representation, the history of the book, German baroque drama, and the history of cartography. The relationship between word and image informs his current book project: *Europe Discovers Iran and Azerbaijan: Dutch and German Representations of the Safavid Empire (1635–1712).* He is also organizing an exhibition on Britain and Azerbaijan (1561–1918) that is scheduled to be shown at the Royal Geographical Society in May 2019.

AMBEREEN DADABHOY is an Assistant Professor of literature at Harvey Mudd College. Her teaching and research interests focus on cross-cultural encounters in the early modern Mediterranean, race, and religious difference in early modern English drama. Her research centres on the global and transnational scope of the early modern world and offers a challenge to the positioning of England's centrality to global affairs in the period. In addition, her early modern literature courses interrogate how the English construct themselves and others in their encounters with racially different yet culturally superior civilizations. By using contemporary critical and social justice theory she encourages students to finds ways in which literature has contributed, positively and negatively, to the representations of identity.

ADRIANO DUQUE is an Associate Professor in the Department of Romance Languages and Literatures at Villanova University. In 2009 and 2016, he was awarded two Fulbright Scholarships to study Muslim–Christian relations in Syria and Morocco. He is also the recipient of two NEH Summer Institute Fellowships and research grants from the Spanish Ministry of Culture, and the Dumbarton Oaks Society. He has published several articles on Muslim–Christian relations, the Roman discovery of Africa and the Franciscan Expeditions to Mongolia, such as "The Carpino Mission to Mongolia in 1246," in *Travels and Travelogues in the Middle Ages: Essays on Symbolic Engagement in Early Drama.* Ed. Jean Kosta Théphaine (New York: AMS Press, 2009).

MATTHEW V. DESING is an Associate Professor of medieval and early modern Spanish literature at the University of Texas at El Paso. Dr. Desing's research focuses on travel and gender in early Spanish texts, and most specifically those pertaining to the thirteenth-century *mester de clerecía*. Among others, he has published the article "Luciana's story: Text, Travel, and Interpretation in the *Libro de Apolonio*" (*Hispanic Review*) and his book entitled *Mester de Romería: Travel in the Medieval Spanish Imaginary* is forthcoming. He co-organized the first international meeting of scholars of *mester de clerecía*, a conference entitled "The Cleric's Craft: Crossroads of Medieval Spanish Literature and Modern Critique" in 2015. Dr. Desing teaches undergraduate and graduate courses in both medieval and early modern Spanish literature and is increasingly interested in issues related to social space and borders.

REBECCA GOULD is Professor of Islamic World and Comparative Literature at the University of Birmingham, UK, and Principal Investigator for the European Research Council-funded project "Global Literary Theory: Caucasus Literatures Compared." She is the author of *Writers and Rebels: The Literature of Insurgency in the Caucasus* (New Haven: Yale University Press, 2016), which was awarded the University of Southern California Book Prize in Literary and Cultural Studies and the prize for Best Book by the Association for Women in Slavic Studies. She is also the translator of *After Tomorrow the Days Disappear: Ghazals and Other Poems Hasan Sijzi of Delhi* (Chicago: Northwestern University Press, 2016), and *The Prose of the Mountains: Tales of the Caucasus* (Budapest: Central European University Press, 2015).

GREGORY B. KAPLAN is Professor of Spanish in the Department of Modern Foreign Languages and Literatures at the University of Tennessee, where he is also a Distinguished Professor in the Humanities. His field of specialization is medieval Spanish philology, and his books include *Arguments against the Christian Religion in Amsterdam by Saul Levi Morteira, Spinoza's Rabbi* (Amsterdam: Amsterdam University Press, 2017), *La lingüística transdisciplinaria: El caso del origen del castellano* (Vigo: Editorial Academia del Hispanismo, 2017), *Valderredible, Cantabria (España): La cuna de la lengua española* (Santander: Gobierno de Cantabria, 2009), and *The Evolution of "Converso" Literature: The Writings of the Converted Jews of Medieval Spain* (Gainesville: University Press of Florida, 2002).

NEDDA MEHDIZADEH is a full-time Lecturer in writing programs at the University of California, Los Angeles. She received her MA/PhD in English Language and Literature from The George Washington University in 2013. Her current book project, *Translating Persia: Safavid Iran and Early Modern English Writing*, centres on pre-modern fantasies of Persia within the early modern English imagination.

MONTSERRAT PIERA is Associate Professor of medieval Spanish and Catalan literature at Temple University. Her research is devoted to medieval Iberian literature and culture, particularly chivalry novels, moral treatises and women's texts. Her publications include the book *Curial e Güelfa y las novelas de caballerías españolas* (Madrid: Editorial Pliegos, 1998), two forthcoming monographs (*Spinning the Text: Women's Textualities in Medieval and Early Modern Iberia* and *El texto imaginado*), and four edited volumes as well as numerous scholarly articles. She has completed a critical edition and translation of fifteenth-century Castilian author Juan de Flores's *Crónica incompleta de los Reyes Católicos.* Her current project is a monograph on the ties between the cartographer Abraham Cresques and the royal court of Aragon in the fourteenth century.

MARIA DEL PILAR RYAN retired in 2013 as a Professor of History at the United States Military Academy at West Point, where she was the Chief of the International History Division. Her research and teaching centred around Early Modern Europe, World Religions, and Iberian Colonization. Her published works include *El jesuita secreto: San Francisco de Borja* (Valencia: Biblioteca Valenciana, 2008) and *Francisco de Borja y su tiempo: Política, religión y cultura en la Edad Moderna* (Valencia and Rome: Albatros Ediciones, 2011).

JULIA SCHLECK is Associate Professor of English at the University of Nebraska-Lincoln, specializing in English travel narratives. She received her PhD from New York University in 2006. Her book, *Telling True Tales of Islamic Lands: Forms of Mediation in Early English Travel Writing, 1575–1630,* was published by Susquehanna University Press in 2011. Her work on travel relations to the Near East has appeared in *Renaissance Quarterly, Prose Studies,* and a number of recent essay collections. She is co-editor of the book series Connected Histories in the Early Modern World at ARC Humanities Press. Dr. Schleck's current book project investigates the East India Company archive, reading it as the place where global traders drew on the metaphorical resources of a gendered society to craft their vision of the global corporation and its place in the English nation.

SEZIM SEZER DARNAULT is an art and architectural historian. She received her PhD (1997) from Mimar Sinan Fine Arts University, Istanbul, Turkey and her master's degree from Istanbul Technical University. Her research focuses on cross-cultural artistic encounters/exchanges, with a particular emphasis on the Ottoman Empire and Europe. Dr. Sezer Darnault is the author of *Latin Catholic Buildings in Istanbul: A Historical Perspective (1839–1923)* (Istanbul: Isis Press, 2004) and co-author of *The Missak[ian] Ottoman Archives* ([s.n.], 2003). Dr. Sezer Darnault was a visiting scholar at Cornell University. She also taught at Mimar Sinan Fine Arts University (Assistant Professor) and Benedictine University, Lisle, Illinois. Based in the United States, Dr. Sezer Darnault currently conducts research as an independent scholar.

JANET SORRENTINO is Associate Professor and Chair of the Department of History at Washington College on the Eastern Shore of Maryland. She obtained her PhD in Medieval History at the University of North Carolina-Chapel Hill. Her research explores intersections between ritual, and intellectual and social aspects of medieval civilization. She became fascinated with the way historical groups—whether kingdoms or religious groups—invested the very best of their resources into worship. Those very expressions of worship, however, because they usually represented specific dogmatic beliefs, also became the centre of social conflict with others who did not share those beliefs. Her early publications concentrated on the ritual of European monastic communities, particularly the Order of Sempringham in England, where liturgical innovation combined with an unusual community organization with women and men in the same order. Her research has taken new direction in the writings of medieval and early modern Muslim travel writers in order to examine their observations of ritual spaces and activities in the many countries they visited.

ACKNOWLEDGEMENTS

Editing this volume has indeed been an adventurous journey. It timidly began as a cheerful but small suggestion during a farewell reception at the conclusion of an NEH Summer Seminar at the Center for Renaissance & Baroque Studies at the University of Maryland in 2010 and developed over time into a wondrous and fruitful collaboration among a much wider group of scholars sharing a curiosity and fascination for travel narratives. Thus, we are all indebted to the National Endowment for the Humanities and to the organizers and directors of that stimulating seminar, Professor Adele Seeff and Professor Judith E. Tucker, for providing the opportunity to bring several of us together for enlightening intellectual discussions and a rewarding cooperation.

I also want to express my deepest gratitude to all the contributors for their excellent work, their professionalism and their constant support and good humor throughout the entire editing process. Sincere thanks are equally due to the anonymous reviewers who took the time to read our work carefully and offered enriching and constructive suggestions.

I am deeply appreciative to my institution, Temple University, for providing financial support towards the publication of this book. Moreover, for their kind and tireless encouragement for this project, and their sensible guidance at every step of the process the contributors and I wish to extend our thanks to the superb editors at Arc Humanities Press/Amsterdam University Press, particularly Simon Forde and Erika Gaffney. We are equally indebted to Ruth Kennedy and Catherine Hanley for meticulously steering the book toward its completion and for their careful editing of the text.

Last but not least, I would like to dedicate this book to my constant travel companions, my husband Ronald Webb and my children Jordi and Núria, who have shared with me over the years the travels where my research would take me, but have also patiently and encouragingly accepted the absences from them which the writing and editing of this book often demanded.

INTRODUCTION: TRAVEL AS *EPISTEME*—AN INTRODUCTORY JOURNEY

MONTSERRAT PIERA

Those who go out in search of knowledge
will be in the path of God until they return[1]

PERCEPTIVE READERS WILL no doubt observe that I am, of course, unashamedly borrowing this volume's title from J. R. R.Tolkien's novel *The Hobbit, or There and Back Again* (1937). Bilbo Baggins's quest, as described in Tolkien's book and, within the metafictive diegesis, in the character's own memoirs of that same title, exhibit all the paradigmatic ingredients found in travellers' temperaments: an inquiring and curious mind, a love for adventure, courage and resourcefulness as well as distrust and fear of the unknown. Thus, Bilbo Baggins will endure, in equal measure, all the delights and discomforts that have besought fictional as well as historical travellers through the ages. At the onset of our own exploration into the mysteries of travel narratives it is fitting that we whimsically evoke Bilbo and the emphasis that his title (*There and Back Again*) places not only on the effects of travel itself but on the transformative impressions of the act of travelling on someone's life after his or her return to their point of origin as well as the importance of recording these worthy experiences. The hobbit-turned-writer expressive title equally underscores, as will become palpable in the ensuing studies, not only the reciprocal nature of any contact between the traveller and the peoples he/she encounters but also the inescapable acquisition of knowledge which follows any such interaction.

Scholars of medieval and early modern culture and history are keenly aware of the fact that travel narratives, travelogues and maps provide us with a privileged *locus* of investigation of issues of multiculturalism, nationalism and geopolitics. In spite of the fact that these travel narratives[2] enact intriguing cultural exchanges and transfers of knowledge among disparate ethnic, political and religious groups, they have often been

---

1 These words were uttered by the Prophet Muhammad, according to a *hadith* related by al-Tirmidhi (d. 892).

2 I conceptualize the term "travel narratives" not restrictively but very widely. Thus, it encompasses not only traditional written texts but also a wide array of cultural artifacts: maps, Portolan charts, merchants' journals, ships' logs, and also decorative objects, relics, and visual artifacts which depict either instances of travel or objects of exchange and trade that have been transferred through travel. Thus, the travel narratives we scrutinize serve to illustrate that travel created an opportunity for what in modern usage we would term "multicultural" interaction and exchange which circumvented rigid "national" boundaries and categories.

excluded from the historical or literary canon for their purported lack of objectivity and verisimilitude and the simplicity of their discourse.[3] Meanwhile, the emergence of a new field of Travel Writing studies[4] in the last decades has not only begun to transform our estimation of such narratives and artifacts but has also revealed that travelling and the development of scientific advances aimed at enhancing such travel had a crucial impact on the onset of early modernity.

Missing from this latest repositioning in current scholarship is a conscientious assessment of the role of Islamic and other Eastern cultures in these developments and the pivotal role that a common maritime and mercantile *ethos* had in the forging of interactions between several supposedly inimical traditions. This project seeks to reassess this role. We aim at interrogating how various Islamic and Eastern cultural threads were weaved, through travel and trading networks, into Western European/Christian visual culture and discourse and, ultimately, into the artistic explosion which has been labelled the "Renaissance."[5]

While several laudable projects have begun to turn the scholarly tide by offering a much more nuanced understanding of Asia or the "Orient"'s influence on Europe and the

---

3 Thus, travel accounts have often been neglected if deemed unauthentic but, for our purposes, the most relevant aspect of a travel narrative is not the empiric authenticity of the travel but that the narrative presents itself as a travel account. Moreover, our investigation encompasses not only accounts of actual travel but of imaginary and fictional journeys as well as the travel of ideas.

4 Kim Phillips is careful not to call "Travel Writing studies" a "discipline" yet and suggests that we first attempt to define the subject of such discipline (www.medievaltravel.amdigital.co.uk/essays/philips). Other scholars have also addressed the issue of considering whether or not "travel writing" is a genre: Paul Zumthor, "The Medieval Travel Narrative," *New Literary History* 25 (1994): 809–24; Tim Youngs in *Travellers in Africa: British Travelogues, 1850–1900* (Manchester: Manchester University Press, 1994) and *The Cambridge Introduction to Travel Writing* (Cambridge: Cambridge University Press, 2013); Joan-Pau-Rubiés, "Travel Writing as a Genre: Facts, Fictions and the Invention of a Scientific Discourse in Early Modern Europe," *Journeys* 1 (2000): 5–35; Jan Borm, "Defining Travel: On the Travel Book, Travel Writing and Terminology," in *Perspectives on Travel Writing*, ed. Glenn Hooper and Tim Youngs (Farnham: Ashgate, 2004); and Mary B. Campbell, *The Witness and the Other World: Exotic European Travel Writing, 400–1600* (Ithaca: Cornell University Press, 1988). Extremely useful and informative is Jean Richard, *Les récits de voyages et de pèlerinages* (Turnhout: Brepols, 1981).

5 We are, of course, mindful of the fact that, in the case of the European sources studied here, these "eastern threads" are weaved into Europe through European eyes. Thus, while the premise of cultural and artistic exchanges between East and West can be widely recognized, in scrutinizing European texts we still need to remember that the appropriation by Western travellers and artists of Islamic and eastern motifs does not imply or indicate an active agency on the part of Islamic and eastern writers, artists and subjects. Furthermore, a variety of "encounter studies" have proven what Giancarlo Casale aptly summarizes here: "Europe's interaction with the outside world was, from the European perspective, conditioned by the preexisting intellectual traditions of the medieval and Renaissance West" (*The Ottoman Age of Exploration* (Oxford: Oxford University Press, 2010), 10), which made European sources quite unreliable in assessing Eastern cultures.

Renaissance movement,[6] such as Nabil Matar's *In the Lands of the Christians* and *Europe Through Arab Eyes*; Gerald McLean's edited collection *Re-Orienting the Renaissance*; and Jerry Brotton's *Trading Territories: Mapping the Early Modern World* as well his and Lisa Jardine's *Global Interests: Renaissance Art between East and West*, just to name a few, the same cannot always be said about the medieval era and much remains to be explored in terms of the links between East and West during the purported "Middle Ages," despite the welcome appearance in 2013 of Kim M. Phillips's *Before Orientalism: Asian Peoples and Cultures in European Travel Writing, 1245–1510*[7] as well as Shirin A. Khanmohamadi's *In Light of Another's Word: European Ethnography in the Middle Ages* and Martin Jacobs's *Reorienting the East: Jewish Travelers to the Medieval Muslim World*, both of which were published in 2014. Our project, thus, seeks to bridge the frequently artificial and capricious disjunction that continues to be perceived between the so-called "Middle Ages" and "the Renaissance."[8] Furthermore, since we are reading non-European sources as well as European ones and the articles in our volume describe non-European geographies and cultures, we have opted to try to eschew the very European-minded temporal framework which creates the division between Middle Ages and Renaissance; we will apply instead a chronological characterization that can equally encompass all cultures discussed therein. Consequently, we will study travel narratives composed between 1000 and 1700.

In all chronological periods travel, military conquest and trade through the Mediterranean placed Western European citizens and merchants in contact with Islamic and Eastern technology and culture. Documents and maps which describe such contacts consistently illustrate the converging and pragmatic dynamics of cultural acceptance in the neutral *milieu* of the Mediterranean Sea. Thus, a careful and comparative study of these contacts will make it possible to postulate that the spread of the so-called "Renaissance" values and beliefs might have followed a trajectory the reverse of what is generally assumed, that is, it is conceivable that salient aspects of Renaissance culture travelled from the periphery to the centre, from the fringes of Islamic and eastern

---

6 Naturally we are obliged to mention a much earlier and ambitious multi-volume project begun in 1965 but which still remains the most relevant and exhaustive source on the topic of Asia and its influence on European thought and culture: *Asia in the Making of Europe* by historian Donald Lach.

7 In her monograph Kim A. Phillips revisits both Said's ideas about Orientalism and the assumptions of post-colonialism adopting instead what she terms a "pre-colonial" methodological stance. Phillips finds that medieval travellers were very heterogeneous in their responses to encounters with Eastern cultures and she also postulates that, most of the time, these travellers did not exhibit any of the colonial and imperialistic traits that have often been adscribed to them by post-colonial scholars.

8 I cannot engage here in a thorough discussion of the pitfalls of such periodization and on the various stages of such crucial and contested debate. I refer the reader, among many others to which I cannot do justice here, to the valuable contributions of Jacques LeGoff's last book, translated in 2015 as *Must We Divide History Into Periods?* (New York: Columbia University Press) and to Jennifer Summit and David Wallace's introduction to their edited collection of articles in the *Journal of Medieval and Early Modern Studies* 37 (2007), 447–51, entitled "Rethinking Periodization."

cultures to the midst of hegemonically Christian polities. To put it another way, the Christian polities of the West were not, in fact, the centre of the world, as we still imagine nowadays, but the periphery.[9]

This volume is thus devoted to medieval and early modern travel narratives and travelogues in order to critically engage some of the misconceptions about the onset of modernity and about Islamic and Eastern cultures which still pervade current academic as well as popular discourse. The aim of this collection of essays is to probe into this hitherto neglected subject of the representations of cultural exchange in travel literature and to bring to the fore the relevance of the cultural and commercial imprint of the East in any account of the development of the West.

To be sure, classical and medieval geography did not use the terms "East" and "West" and, in fact, it did not even divide the known world into an Asian Orient and a European Occident but acknowledged instead the existence of three continents: Asia, Europe and Africa.[10] As Plinius had stated: "Terrarum orbis universus in tres dividitur partes" and this idea will prevail thanks to St. Augustine, Paulus Orosius and St. Isidore of Seville.[11] Medieval European terminology about the Orient was highly imprecise, as were geographical demarcations. Generally, Asia was divided into two parts: Asia Major and Minor. Mandeville mentions Asia Minor, Asia Major and Deep Asia. The latter, where Catay would be located, was the most oriental of them.[12]

Thus, since the terms "East/Orient" and "West/Occident" are not only theoretically contested but also difficult to define given their fluidity and imprecision from classical antiquity to the modern period, it will become indispensable in our study to use more

---

9 The myth of Eurocentrism which postulates that the West has been historically hegemonic is still very prevalent, despite its supposed lack of currency in academic discourse. According to Eurocentric views, Europe is the only active shaper of world history. Europe is active, the rest of the world passive. Europe is the center, the rest of the world is its periphery. While most scholars realize that Eurocentrism is an ideology that distorts the truth by viewing history from a European perspective and emphasizes the superiority of Western culture, perhaps the most troubling aspect of it is its epistemological implications, the fact that Eurocentrism is so entrenched in scholarship that it creates a paradigm for interpreting the facts, a set of assumptions of how the world should work and thus we judge any other areas of the world as being determined by the same set of assumptions. See Robert Marks, *The Origins of the Modern World: A Global and Environmental Narrative from the 15th to the 21st century* (London: Rowman & Littlefield, 2015) for a more globally minded master narrative which can contribute to dispelling the myth of Eurocentrism.

10 Suzanne Conklin Akbari postulates, in fact, that the dichotomy of Orient and Occident might have come about after a late medieval move from maps with a traditional eastern orientation to maps with a northern orientation (*Idols in the East: European Representations of Islam and the Orient, 1100–1450* (Ithaca: Cornell University Press, 2009), 20–23).

11 St. Isidore affirms in his *Etimologiae* (XIV, II, 1): "Divisus est autem trifarie: e quibus una pars Asia, altera Europa, tertia Africa nuncupatur" (It is divided in three parts, one part being called Asia, the second Europe, and the third Africa).

12 Aníbal A. Biglieri, *Las ideas geográficas y la imagen del mundo en la literatura española medieval* (Frankfurt: Iberoamericana/Vervuert, 2012), 251–52.

explicit geographical terms.[13] Thus, in the broadest sense, "East" will be defined within our collection as the Islamic lands in North Africa (or Maghreb), central European polities in the Mediterranean, the Middle East and Asia. "West," on the other hand, encompasses all the Christian lands west of Hungary. The essays included therein investigate travel accounts written by authors from both geographical areas, "East" and "West" (as opposed to solely European or Western authors, as has generally been the norm), and who have, thus, traversed both geographical and cultural *loci* in both directions.

Our inquiry will be informed by recent scholarship on cultural and economic history, visual arts, and ethnology, which seek to reassess and critique some post-colonial approaches indebted to Edward Said's *Orientalism*. The volume includes studies by scholars from various disciplines: English Literature, History, Architecture, Ottoman Studies, Iberian Studies, Persian Studies, Jewish Studies and Islamic Religion. The following contributions examine the cross-disciplinary and cross-cultural scholarship on the transfer (or, literally, the *translatio*)[14] through travel of cultural and religious values and artistic and scientific practices from the eleventh to the seventeenth centuries. Thus, while the *topos* of *translatio studii*, clearly formulated in several medieval works (for example in Chrétien de Troyes *Cligès* as well as in Juan Ruiz's "Dispute between the Greeks and the Romans" in his *Libro de buen amor*), is most frequently predicated on the idea of a transfer of knowledge from Greece westward, in this volume, instead, we posit that there was indeed a *translatio* from further East moving westward.

Naturally, espousing this transference requires not only a philosophical repositioning but also a geographical and physical one, which can be easily attained just by carefully contemplating ancient and medieval maps, such as the Hereford Mappa Mundi or the so-called Catalan Atlas, which placed Jerusalem and central Asia as the epicentre of the known world while the western lands were illustrated on the fringes of such world.[15]

---

13 I want to also be very cognizant of the fact that many of the labels or terms that are often applied both when one conceptualizes "Europe" or "Asia" or when we refer to the "East" or to "Eastern cultures" can lead to misinterpretation or can denote "Orientalizing" stances. I will not go into a detailed discussion of this contested and hotly debated topic in here but the various articles will at various junctures engage in a discussion of such debates. As a general rule, however, we will try to avoid using labels such as "Orient" uncritically.

14 The *topoi* of *translatio studii* or transfer of knowledge as well as the concomitant *translatio imperii* or transfer of power, which propounded an unbroken continuity between the Roman Empire and medieval cultural paradigms and polities, thus guaranteeing the legitimacy of sovereignty, were often articulated in medieval texts.

15 Several scholars have discussed the relevance of map projections in understanding historical processes and the importance of reassessing how cartography has been utilized as a site to promote political ends and to enact propagandistic narratives. For excellent studies about the development of cartography historically and its functions and interpretations see Jerry Brotton's *Trading Territories: Mapping the Early Modern World* (Ithaca: Cornell University Press, 1997), his more recent (albeit for a more popular public) *A History of the World in 12 Maps* (New York: Viking, 2013), and his article "A 'Devious Course': Projecting Toleration on Mercator's 'Map of the World', 1569," *The Cartographic Journal* 49 (2012): 101–6; John P. Snyder's *Flattening the Earth: Two Thousand*

While many scholars in several disciplines have actively engaged in a revisionist account of the conventional narrative about the rise and supremacy of the West and the foundational attributes of Graeco-Roman civilization, perhaps one of the most widely known among lay audiences is anthropologist Eric Wolf's *Europe and the People without History* (1982). Wolf, and by now many others, have not only made considerable inroads in our appreciation of the ways in which societies that had been disregarded in hegemonic European historical narratives were and are profoundly implicated in global historical systems and changes, but have also contributed to enhancing our understanding of the centrality of the Eastern lands and cultures on global affairs in the past as well as the present.

After all, as the historian Peter Frankopan has recently put it in reference to the centre of Asia, "it was in this bridge between east and west that great metropolises were established nearly 5000 years ago, when the cities of Harappa and Mohenjo-daro in the Indus Valley were wonders of the ancient world [...] where the world's great religions burst into life,"[16] where cities exhibited grandiose buildings as well as sophisticated sewage systems unseen in Europe and where, according to a Chinese geographer, markets bought and sold an enormous range of products, brought from all the corners of the world.[17] It was, in sum, a land "where empires were made."[18]

The German geologist Ferdinand von Richthofen had already described and aptly named this extensive network of routes which served to connect distant peoples and places: the Silk Roads, or *Seidenstraßen*.[19] The peoples who circulated along these roads traded and exchanged not only goods but also ideas, customs and beliefs. They learned from each other thus contributing to further expansions in the sciences, philosophy, language and religion.

Thus, the world of antiquity was more complex and interconnected than conventionally thought. In spite of seemingly unsurmountable obstacles there existed a vibrant and efficient network of transference and exchange crisscrossing the landscape through the Silk Roads. The Greeks and Romans were expanding east but the Chinese were also expanding west.

Years of Map Projection (Chicago: University of Chicago Press, 1993); Frank Lestringant's *Mapping the Renaissance World: The Geographical Imagination in the Age of Discovery* (Oxford: Oxford University Press, 1994); Denis Cosgrove's *Apollo's Eye: A Cartographic Genealogy of the Earth in the Western Imagination* (Baltimore: Johns Hopkins University Press, 2003); and Alison Sandman's contributions, particularly "Mirroring the World: Sea Charts, Navigation, and Territorial Claims in Sixteenth-Century Spain," in *Merchants and Marvels: Commerce, Science, and Art in Early Modern Europe*, ed. Pamela Smith and Paula Findlen (New York: Routledge, 2002), 83–108.

16 Peter Frankopan, *The Silk Roads: A New History of the World* (London: Bloomsbury, 2015; repr., New York: Knopf, 2016), xv.

17 *Records of the Grand Historian by Sima Qian, Han Dynasty*, trans. B. Watson, vol. 2. (rev. ed. New York: Colombia University Press, 1971), 234–35.

18 Frankopan, *Silk Roads*, 3.

19 Ferdinand von Richthofen, "Über die zentralasiatischen Seidenstrassen bis zum 2. Jahrhundert. N. Chr.," *Verhandlungen der Gesellschaft für Erdkunde zu Berlin* 4 (1877): 96–122. According to some scholars, however, von Richthofen's initial formulation of the term he coined does not always coincide with subsequent interpretations offered by later historians and geographers.

Therefore, traders' and travellers' horizons broadened significantly many centuries before the Age of Discovery. The geographer Strabo, for example, affirms that within a few years of Rome's occupation of Egypt, 120 merchant ships were sailing for India each year from the Red Sea.[20] Commercial exchange in Indian ports, nonetheless, was not restricted to merchandise that originated in the subcontinent. A large variety of goods from distant locations such as Vietnam and Java were brought to the Mediterranean via India and Persia:

> Ports on both the western and eastern coasts of India served as emporia for goods brought from all over eastern and south-eastern Asia ready to be shipped west. Then there were the goods and produce of the Red Sea, a vibrant commercial zone in its own right as well as linking the Mediterranean with the Indian Ocean and beyond.[21]

Simultaneously, the Chinese were heading west and establishing regular and intensive trading with Persia, sending as many as ten trading missions a year, often with the purpose of selling their famed silk and acquiring goods as variegated as pearls from the Red Sea, cucumbers, apricots, myrrh from Yemen and even peaches from Samarkand.[22] Chinese silk, in turn, made its way to Rome, where it not only became one of the most expensive and sought-after commodities but also contributed to a revolution in cultural mores and, if we are to believe some moralists like Seneca,[23] to a cataclysmic undermining of traditional Roman rules of decency.

Two intertwined impulses are, hence, at the root of every instance of travel: curiosity and necessity. All throughout history these two impulses have informed the experiences of every traveller: the pilgrim, the conqueror, the adventurer, the merchant, the missionary, the explorer and the diplomat. In whichever guise we find them, travellers set out on a journey to learn new things and acquire knowledge about themselves or their surroundings or with the purpose of acquiring the goods and supplies needed for their subsistence. The act of travelling is always, consequently, an epistemological enterprise.

Travel becomes, thus, *episteme* not in Foucauldian terms but in a purely Platonic sense, that is, "knowledge," in contrast to the concept of *doxa*, which signifies common belief or opinion.[24] The *motif* of travel was omnipresent in the medieval and early

---

20 Strabo, *The Geography of Strabo*, ed. and trans. H. Jones, vol. 1. (Cambridge, MA: Harvard University Press, 1917), 454.

21 Frankopan, *Silk Roads*, 17–18.

22 B. Laufer, *Sino-Iranica: Chinese Contributions to the History of Civilization in Ancient Iran* (Chicago: Chicago University Press, 1919); Edward H. Schafer, *The Golden Peaches of Samarkand: A Study of T'ang Exotics* (Berkeley: University of California Press, 1985), 1.

23 Seneca, *Moral Essays*, ed. and trans. J. Basore, vol. 3. (Cambridge, MA: Harvard University Press, 1935), 478.

24 In *The Order of Things* (New York: Pantheon Books, 1971), Michel Foucault used the term *épistème* to refer to the historical *a priori* that grounds knowledge and its discourses and thus represents the condition of their possibility within a particular epoch. According to Foucault several *epistemes* may co-exist and interact at the same time.

modern imaginary.[25] It was not always regarded as an exciting experience as the etymological meaning of the English word for travel, *travail* (effort), attests. It always included,
nevertheless, an epistemological dimension. To travel was to acquire knowledge and to
know oneself, to grow. Although all monotheistic religions agreed on the importance of
pilgrimage and travel as a symbol of religious experience (*hegira*, *peregrinatio*) this is
particularly true in the Islamic tradition where travel, as attested by the hadith quoted at
the beginning of this introduction, is conceived as a praiseworthy enterprise whose goal
is the search for knowledge:

> Travel in all its myriad forms—pilgrimage, trade, scholarship, adventure-
> expanded the mental and physical limits of the Muslim world [...] Travel as a
> meritorious activity is endowed with an ancient pedigree in the Muslim tradi-
> tion. A rich vocabulary of words related in one way or another to travel is found
> in the Qur'an.[26]

And many Qur'anic verses encouraged Muslims to "travel on the earth and see" (3:137;
6:11; 12:109; 16:36; 29:20; 30:9; 30:42).[27]

This quest for knowledge, nevertheless, is equally present in all traditions, from biblical times to classical antiquity to medieval and early modern Christianity. From the
wandering Moses to Ulysses in Homer's *Odyssey* the *topos* of the traveller has been fundamental and very prolific in the Graeco-Roman tradition. As Jas Elsner and Joan-Pau
Rubiés observe in their introduction to *Voyages and Visions: Toward a Cultural History of
Travel*, the paradigm of the Christian pilgrim of the Middle Ages is derived "from ancient
myths such as Apollonius [of Tyre], who travelled himself into sainthood, or the allegorical Odysseus, whose journey became a metaphor for the spiritual progress of his readers'
lives."[28] From these beginnings there evolved two patterns of travel as pilgrimage in the
Christian tradition: visiting the Holy Land and the veneration of sacred relics. These two
patterns will even merge in the case of some individual travellers, such as the remarkable Egeria, who left us an early and informative travelogue of her explorations. During
her pilgrimage to the Holy Land in the fourth century CE (381–384), she eagerly visited all those places mentioned in the Bible as well as several *martyria* which contained
sacred relics.[29] And these two types of religious quests will in time coalesce fictionally in

---

25 One of the most famous medieval travel narratives was the *Book of John of Mandeville,* a highly
popular book which, although fictional, was believed to be an actual eyewitness account. This work
encompasses the most salient characteristics of the quintessential medieval travel narrative: long
and arduous voyages, assortments of marvels and fantastical tales, exotic creatures and monsters
and ethnographic observations about distant lands and peoples.

26 Dale F. Eickelman and James P. Piscatori, *Muslim Travellers: Pilgrimage, Migration, and the
Religious Imagination* (Berkeley: University of California Press, 1990), 51 and 53.

27 Roxanne L. Euben, *Journeys to the Other Shore: Muslim and Western Travelers in Search of
Knowledge* (Princeton: Princeton Univeristy Press, 2006), 35.

28 Jas Elsner and Joan Pau Rubiés, *Voyages and Visions: Toward a Cultural History of Travel* (London:
Reaktion Books, 1999), 15.

29 Egeria, who was most probably a nun from Spain or France, visited the Holy Land only a few
years after the death of Constantine and, thus, her work is one of the earliest extant descriptions of

the adventures of errant knights in search of the Holy Grail in the popular romances of the Arthurian tradition and historically, in the crusades.

Due to the crusades, Oleb Grabar asserts, "there occurred, in particular in the twelfth century, an extraordinary increase in the number of 'points of access', that is, of places where contacts [between East and West] could and were made, as well as in the variety of these contacts."[30] While this is true, crusaders were nevertheless remarkably bereft of ethnographic curiosity for the people they met along their travels. This lack of interest of the crusaders, despite this opening of "points of contact," illustrates well the "non-fraternization attitude" of the crusader towards the surrounding culture and the clearly colonizing stance of the crusades, discussed by Joshua Prawer in "The Roots of Medieval Colonialism."[31] Oleg Grabar also pointedly remarks that two centuries of contact did not really produce any deep cultural and artistic impacts between the East and the West.[32]

With the sole exception of the Jewish Benjamin of Tudela's *Sefer ha-Masa'ot* (*The Book of Travels*) in the twelfth century, we do not find many documents that describe ethnographic observations about Muslims and other Eastern peoples until the thirteenth century.[33] One example would be the detailed ethnographic narrative of the missionary trip to Mongolia by the Franciscan friars John of Plan Carpini (1245–1247)[34] and William of Rubruck (1252–1255): "In effect the late Middle Ages are characterized by the growth of ethnography within the related genres of geographical literature, ambassadorial reports, mission and even pilgrimage itself."[35] The travel narratives written or dictated by Carpini, William of Rubruck, Marco Polo and the fictional John of Mandeville have in common an attention to practical knowledge and empirical observation, in partic- ular of human subjects. Elsner and Rubiés see this shift as "the ultimate relocation of the paradigm of travel from the ideal of pilgrimage to those of empirical curiosity and practical science" which results from "the transformation of the traditional ideologies of pilgrimage, crusade and chivalry under the impact of new religious, political and social concerns."[36]

---

the area. Her portrayal of the sacred places in the Holy Land and the life of the ascetic desert hermits make of her travel account one of the most informative sources of early Christian ritual and worship (*Egeria's Travels*, ed. John Wilkinson (Liverpool: Liverpool University Press, 1999)).

30 Oleb Grabar "Patterns and Ways of Cultural Exchange," in *The Meeting of Two Worlds: Cultural Exchange between East and West during the Period of the Crusades*, ed. Vladimir P. Goss (Kalamazoo: Medieval Institute Publications 1986), 441–554 and 442.

31 Joshua Prawer, "The Roots of Colonialism," in *The Meeting of Two Worlds: Cultural Exchange between East and West during the Period of the Crusades,* ed. Vladimir P. Goss (Kalamazoo: Medieval Institute Publications, 1986), 23–38.

32 Grabar, "Patterns and Ways of Cultural Exchange," 444.

33 See Kaplan's (Chapter 9) and Piera's (Chapter 3) contributions in this volume for more informa- tion about Benjamin of Tudela and his travel narrative, the *Sefer ha-Masa'ot* (*The Book of Travels*).

34 Adriano Duque's chapter (Chapter 8) in this volume is devoted to this expedition.

35 Elsner and Rubiés, *Voyages*, 31.

36 Elsner and Rubiés, *Voyages*, 31.

It can be posited, however, that the tradition of written traveller's accounts was always shaped by empirical curiosity and pragmatic needs, even more than by religious fervour. It began with seafarers' logs and these logs were probably the origin of the *periplous*,[37] an ancient genre of texts describing coastlines, such as the Carthaginian Hanno's account of his travels along the African coast (early fifth century BCE) and Pytheas and Massalia's *Peri tou Okeanou* (*On the Ocean*) around 320 BCE.[38] And not only the Greeks but all previous and subsequent traditions and cultures produced these types of documents.

Although maritime travel was precarious it was still the fastest and most convenient means of transportation and centuries of seafarers' experience was poured out on to ceaselessly evolving captains' logs, navigational and Portolan charts, atlases and *mappa mundi* which outlined the major sailing routes and the coastal landmarks.[39] The Mediterranean sea was crowded with Arab and Jewish traders as well as Byzantine and Western merchants, predominantly from Italian and Catalan cities but also from Hanseatic cities and the British Isles, to such an extent that a common language of the sea developed:

> The little ships of small traders with local knowledge could follow a myriad of less frequented ways so that, in effect, the whole coastline of the Mediterranean was alive with maritime traffic linking peoples and places together [...] Few embarked on a sea voyage without a degree of apprehension. It did mean entering a world with its own technical language, its own laws and customs. It was, however, also a way to new experiences and possible riches.[40]

The prospect of riches and profit was thus one of the driving forces of travellers, but profit was always intertwined with beauty and the desire for the exotic. Medieval and early modern society, not unlike our own, was attracted to beautiful, luxurious and rare objects and artifacts.

Paul Freedman has brilliantly depicted and analyzed the medieval fascination with spices in *Out of the East: Spices in the Medieval Imagination*. And Anne Goldgar demonstrates on her study on the cultivation of the tulip in Holland in the sixteenth century that "rarity, beauty and profit thus go together; what is rare is beautiful, and what is

---

37 A Greek word still used in some modern languages, for example Spanish ("periplo"), to indicate a long journey.

38 Maria Pretzler, *Pausanias: Travel Writing in Ancient Greece* (London: Duckworth, 2007), 20.

39 Medieval maps are truly not maps as we conceive them in modern times. Medieval *mappa mundi* were more accurately "diagrams" of the world. As P. D. A. Harvey states, medieval maps "are best understood as an open framework where all kinds of information might be placed in the relevant spatial position, not unlike a chronicle or narrative in which information would be arranged chronologically" (*Medieval Maps* (London: University of Toronto Press, 1991), 19). These earlier maps included and conveyed not only geographical information but also zoological, anthropological, moral, theological and historical information (19).

40 Susan Rose, *The Medieval Sea* (London: Continuum, 2007), 11–12.

beautiful is profitable."[41] Tulips, as spices, were brought from the East and were considered very exotic: "The special excitement generated by tulips stemmed first from their foreign nature [...] But tulips were particularly valued because of their unpredictable and exciting capacities for variation."[42] Their arrival in Europe in the sixteenth century is attributed to the imperial envoy Ogier Ghislain de Busbecq, although it is also possible that they were introduced into European markets through trade between Turkey and Italy, France and the Low Countries.[43]

This fascination with exotic objects such as the tulip can be equally applied to many other material luxury goods that Western merchants found in Eastern markets and brought back to Europe. A variety of Islamic material goods (ceramics, glassware, silks, rugs, metalwork) became markers of luxury, social status as well as artisanal skill in Western society. Evidence of the deep influence of Islamic trade and exchange of luxury goods is furnished in Western Renaissance paintings of the period. As Western artisans and artists sought to emulate their counterparts in Persia, Arabia and Syria, they used travel as a means to reach and learn from technical masters in the Islamic world,[44] thereby developing their craftmanship as well as a new understanding or, at times, a misunderstanding of Islamic culture.

The field of Renaissance Studies has been a pioneer in the development of theories of consumption[45] which shift the emphasis from the provenance and actual value of an object of exchange to its perceived significance to consumers, as Patricia Fortini Brown claims: "The exotic and the unfamiliar count for as much as the cost"[46] and objects that came from the Orient or "looked" oriental were eagerly sought after or emulated. At the same time, however, the Ottomans were also looking to the West for artistic inspiration and exotic objects. Lisa Jardine and Jerry Brotton are illustrative examples of the type of Renaissance scholarship that seeks to illuminate the "pragmatic engagement between

---

41 Paul Freedman, *Out of the East: Spices and the Medieval Imagination* (New Haven: Yale University Press, 2008); Anne Goldgar, "Nature as Art: The Case of the Tulip" in *Merchants & Marvels: Commerce, Science, and Art in Early Modern Europe*, ed. Pamela H. Smith and Paula Findlen (London: Routledge, 2002), 324–46 and 338. Goldgar quotes a 1618 commentator on Dodonaeus's *Cruydt-Boeck* as saying about tulips: "In this country men [...] will pay the most, not for the most beautiful [tulip] or the finest, but for the rarest to be found" (337).

42 Goldgar, "Nature as Art: The Case of the Tulip," 326.

43 Goldgar, "Nature as Art: The Case of the Tulip," 326.

44 Perhaps one of the most often cited examples of this type of travel, to perfect an artist's craftmanship, is the case of the Venetian painter Gentile Bellini, who travelled to Istanbul to learn from Ottoman artists.

45 Approaches that support a consumption model of analysis can be found in Daniel Miller's introduction (1–50) to his book *Materiality: Politics, History, and Culture* (Durham: Duke University Press, 2005). These approaches are based on Mary Douglas and Baron Isherwood's understanding of "consumption as a form of cultural production" (*The World of Goods: Towards an Anthropology of Consumption* (New York: Basic Books, 1979)).

46 Patricia Fortini Brown, *Private Lives in Renaissance Venice: Art, Architecture, and the Family* (New Haven: Yale University Press, 2004), 84.

East and West in which each fully acknowledged the participation of the other and negotiated workable relationships"[47] by analyzing sixteenth century art-based transactions
and luxury objects of exchange within their appropriate historical context.[48]

Their findings have served not only to undermine "the Burckhardtian (and with it
the new historicist) view of emerging Western European selfhood in the Renaissance"[49]
but also to counteract Edward Said's "version of Western Europe's construction of the
Orient as an alien, displaced other, positioned in opposition to a confident, imperialist
Eurocentrism."[50] These exchanges, stimulated more by curiosity than necessity, brought
about a reciprocal transfer of cultural values and artistic and scientific practices. As
Gaston Bachelard argued, "the conquest of the superfluous is more spiritually exciting
than the conquest of what is necessary. Man is a creature of desire, not a being motivated
by necessity."[51]

These voyages of commercial exchange had been extremely important all throughout
the medieval period for the development of cartography and to acquire a better knowledge about geography and the world in general. Thus, the considerable advances in
map-making in the fifteenth century which would eventually bring about the Portuguese
and Castilian travels to the New World were indebted not to the work of theoretical
geographers but to the empirical knowledge gained by actual and constant maritime
expeditions. One of the first maps to incorporate the evidence garnered by travel experience was Abraham Cresques's Catalan Atlas[52] compiled between 1375 and 1377
and presented in 1381 as a gift to the king of France by the king of Aragon, Joan I. As
a matter of fact, the Majorcan Jewish school of cartography represented by Cresques
was the first to innovatively integrate inland features in Portolan charts.[53] It is certainly
not a coincidence that such school should be located on the island of Majorca, only
recently reconquered by the Christian army of the Aragonese king, Jaume I, in 1229.
It was precisely because of the Muslim past of Majorca that the island had become not

---

47 Lisa Jardine and Jerry Brotton, *Global Interests: Renaissance Art between East and West* (London:
Reaktion Books, 2005), 61.

48 Particularly enlightening in this regard are their analysis of the significance of Benozzo Gozzoli's
frescoes at the Medici Chapel of the Magi in Florence, Carpaccio's depiction of the St. George cycle
in the Scuola Dalmata in Venice, Holbein's painting "The Ambassadors," and the portrait medals
executed by Constanzo de Ferrara and Antonio Pisanello.

49 Naturally their approach also disavows Stephen Greenblatt's notions of a characteristically
unique "Renaissance self-fashioning," which has also been problematized in the field of Medieval
Studies; see, for instance, the collection of articles in *Self-Fashioning and Assumptions of Identity in
Medieval and Early Modern Iberia*, ed. Laura Delbrugge (Leiden: Brill, 2015).

50 Jardine and Brotton, *Global Interests*, 61.

51 Quoted in Freedman, *Out of the East: Spices and the Medieval Imagination*, 6.

52 Harvey, *Medieval Maps*, 60.

53 See Pinhas Yoeli, "Abraham and Yehuda Cresques and the Catalan Atlas," *Cartographic Journal*
7 (1970): 17–27, for detailed information about the Catalan Atlas and the Cresques family and
workshop. Upon receiving the map, the king of Aragon was so enthusiastic that he named Abraham
Cresques "magister mappamundorum et bruxolarum" (master maker of world maps and compasses).

only a relatively tolerant and thriving multicultural society but also "a world center of commerce" in the fourteenth century:

> In its ports and harbours anchored hundreds of ships and within the walls of the city of Majorca, later named Palma, lived thirty thousand sailors. It was also a center of learning and culture. Astronomy, astrology, mathematics, medicine, philosophy, jurisprudence and the natural sciences in general were highly developed.[54]

It is believed that the Cresques family arrived in Majorca after 1229 from the north of Africa. Emigration of Jews from North Africa to Majorca was robust and they maintained very strong family ties with North Africa: "These connections contributed no doubt to the relatively-detailed geographical information which the Jewish Cartographers of Majorca had of North Africa."[55]

By way of the north of Africa another traveller who was to have an immense influence on the cultural imprint of the West came to the lands of the Iberian Peninsula from Damascus. As Maria Rosa Menocal more poetically relates it:

> Once upon a time in the mid eighth-century, an intrepid young man called Abd al-Rahman abandoned his home in Damascus, the Near Eastern heartland of Islam, and set out across the North African desert in search of a place of refuge. Damascus had become a slaughterhouse for his family, the ruling Umayyads, who had first led the Muslims out of the desert of Arabia into the high cultures of the Fertile Crescent. With the exception of Abd al-Rahman, the Umayyads were eradicated by the rival Abbasids, who seized control of the great empire called the "House of Islam."[56]

This young survivor fled westward to the lands of his Berber mother (in today's Morocco). Once he arrived in the north of Africa he found most of his Berber kinsmen had themselves emigrated to the Iberian Peninsula: "Abd al-Rahman followed their trail and crossed the narrow strait at the western edge of the world. In Iberia, a place they were calling al-Andalus in Arabic, the language of the new Muslim colonizers, he found a thriving and expansive Islamic settlement."[57]

---

54 Yoeli, "Abraham and Yehuda Cresques," 25.

55 Yoeli, "Abraham and Yehuda Cresques," 26. In addition to their contacts with North African Muslims, there is also evidence that Jewish merchants travelled and traded with Muslims as far as Timbuktu.

56 María Rosa Menocal, *The Ornament of the World: How Muslims, Jews and Christians Created a Culture of Tolerance in Medieval Spain* (Boston: Little, Brown and Company, 2002), 3. It should be noted however, that Menocal's and other scholars highly favorable view of "convivencia" in the Iberian Peninsula during that period has ben subsequently nuanced and critiqued. I do not have space here to address that still ongoing debate but suffices to say that what is undoubtable is that there was constant interaction between Muslims, Jews and Christians. What remains controversial is to determine how convivial that interaction truly was in any given historical juncture.

57 Menocal, *Ornament of the World*, 3.

Within two centuries the city where he now arrived, Cordoba, would be called "the ornament of the world," one of his descendants would become the caliph and for seven hundred years there would be a Muslim presence in Europe and al-Andalus's cultural achievements would reverberate all over Christian Europe for centuries to come.[58] Abd al-Rahman's *rihla* transformed him as much as every traveller transforms the worlds with which he or she comes in contact. Every travel brings us closer to *episteme*.

The ensuing articles seek to illuminate the different manifestations of epistemological discovery rendered through travel and its inherent contradictions. The collection is divided thematically in three parts. The first will be devoted to the examination of a variety of travel narratives (penned by Muslim, Jewish, and Christian travellers) which creatively and critically destabilize the boundaries of the *rihla* tradition. The second part considers how Eastern cultures and, in particular, eastern *loci* (Egypt, Persia, and Istanbul), were conceptualized, comprehended, and, especially, imagined (in both an intellectual and a visual sense) by Christian travellers and writers from 1000 to 1700. The third and last part analyzes the relevance of material and intellectual exchange and reciprocal circulation within the dynamics of commercial and political interaction between the East and the West.

The first three essays in this collection focus on the Islamic *rihla* tradition from three different perspectives and three different geographic areas. Rebecca Gould introduces in "From Pious Journeys to the Critique of Sovereignty: Khaqani Shirvani's Persianate Poetics of Pilgrimage," one of the most important and least-studied Persian travel narratives, *Khaqani Shirwani's Tuhfat al-Iraqayn (Gift from the Two Iraqs)*, composed in the middle of the twelfth century while Janet Sorrentino describes pre-modern Muslim ritual by scrutinizing the travel accounts of two Muslim authors, Ibn Jubayr and Ibn Battuta. Montserrat Piera compares and contrasts three travel narratives, spanning from the twelfth to the sixteenth centuries, which were composed by Iberian subjects (Benjamin of Tudela, Pero Tafur and Leo Africanus/al-Wazzan) from each of the three monotheistic traditions.

Rebecca Gould begins her essay by contextualizing Khaqani's text within a larger discussion of the travel narrative genre and the culture of pilgrimage in medieval Persian (and more broadly Islamic) literary culture, and examines the links between these texts and an emerging discourse of autobiographical reflection on the poetic self. Gould explores Khaqani's memorable renderings of his journeys through Baghdad and other cities of Iraq on his way to Mecca, focusing in particular on the rich metaphors through which the itinerant traveller genders the landscape through which he passes, and on the political implications of his poetic critiques of the sultan from whose grasp he escaped when he departed Azerbaijan. Gould's analysis ultimately demonstrates that the Persianate literature of travel substantially deviates from its Arabic counterpart by exerting a narrative shift from piety to political insubordination.

---

58 As Alexander E. Elison reminds us in *Looking Back at al-Andalus* (Leiden: Brill, 2009) one can argue that al-Andalus is a construct created to satisfy contemporary needs for a nostalgic past: "Whether it is viewed as a lost paradise of cultural splendor, a symbol of displacement and exile, a site of religious tolerance, or a past to be embraced and learned from, al-Andalus has proven to be a highly evocative site of nostalgic expression" (2).

In "Observing Ziyara in Two Medieval Muslim Travel Accounts," Janet Sorrentino discusses Muslim travel literature of the medieval and early modern period but focuses not only on their observations about scientific and artistic exchange, but particularly on the ways these travellers articulated their observations about worship and ritual. Sorrentino's essay examines the writings of two such travel writers: Ibn Jubayr (sixth/ twelfth centuries) and Ibn Battuta (eighth/fourteenth centuries),[59] who carefully surveyed religious observances performed wherever they travelled and who did not distinguish or disparage sectarian identity in what they observed. Their observations and attitudes, derived in general from direct experience, open a window to the broader Islamicate religious culture of the post-classical period.

The third chapter in the first part of the collection delves into Iberian travellers' experiences of Eastern cultures. For medieval subjects the act of travelling was a very unpredictable and dangerous endeavour which could render the traveller vulnerable to violence, abuse, warfare and misfortune, among other perils. Montserrat Piera's article explores both the actual (or physical) and figurative vulnerabilities expressed and enacted by three early modern Iberian travellers: one Jewish (Benjamin of Tudela, twelfth century, d. 1173), one Christian (Pero Tafur, 1410–1484), and one Muslim (al-Hassan al-Wazzan, known as Leo Africanus, 1486/88–1554?) who engaged in long voyages throughout Europe, Asia and the Maghreb and wrote in detail about their experiences. In these three writers, vulnerability is inextricably connected not only to their travels but also to their geographical origins and their particular historical circumstances.

Our exploration of how the East was imagined by early modern travellers and readers in Part II begins with the article " 'Tierras de Egipto': Imagined Journeys to the East in the Early Vernacular Literature of Medieval Iberia." In it Matthew V. Desing tells us about the Apollonius of Tyre legend, a tale of nautical adventures set in the eastern Mediterranean and one of the most popular narratives in Europe from the eleventh to the sixteenth centuries. The mid-thirteenth-century Spanish version, the *Libro de Apolonio*, provides a fascinating locus for the study of portrayals of travel in the Near East, and particularly in Egypt, not only because of the content of the narrative itself but because of its manuscript context as well. Within the narrative, the author constructs Egypt as an imaginary landscape for the protagonist's purifying pilgrimage. Egypt is, thus, not a specific place in this text, but rather a general locale for the purification of sins. Approximately a century after the *Libro de Apolonio*'s composition, the text was copied and included in the manuscript Escorial III-K-4 and Desing argues that this new context casts the function of Egypt in a different light. Egypt strikingly appears in all three poems of the manuscript: the *Libro de Apolonio*, the *Vida de Santa María Egipciaca*, and the *Adoración de los Reyes*. When placed into this expanded context, the *Libro de Apolonio*'s Egypt ceases to be an abstract place, and becomes fixed through its connections to a geographical web of places familiarly imagined, not only because of the audience's experience with biblical and hagiographical narratives that deal with such locales, but also because of the expanding gaze of the Christian Iberian kingdoms beyond the peninsula during the century between the poem's original composition and its inclusion in the manuscript.

---

59 Where dual dates are given in this volume, the first relates to the Muslim calendar, and the second to the Christian calendar.

In the next contribution, "The Petrification of Rostam: Thomas Herbert's re-vision of Persia in *A Relation of Some Yeares Travaile*," Nedda Mehdizadeh follows the English East India Company's 1626 expedition to Persia through Thomas Herbert's popular travelogue, *A Relation of Some Yeares Travaile*. Like many travellers to Persia, Herbert finds himself at the crossroads of two very different chronological periods: the memory of Persia's ancient past under the Achaemenids, which he had learned about through translation of texts like Herodotus's *Histories* or Xenophon's *Cyropedia*, and the present moment of growth and prosperity of the Safavid Empire he witnesses during the expedition. Despite the expedition's goal to improve mercantile and diplomatic relations between England and Persia, Herbert finds himself travelling between these two different times, transposing the past onto the present. Indeed, he continues this process well into the future as he revisits Persia with each subsequent revision of his travel narrative—four in total. Each subsequent edition expands dramatically with inclusions of classical stories, biblical narratives, and faded memories. Despite the fact that each section of his travelogue experiences massive changes, his account of the empire's capital, Isfahan, experiences only modest changes. A vibrant metropolis, Isfahan invites travellers from all over to do trade; rather than offering discussions of the comings and goings of the city, Herbert gives details about the architecture as well as a short discussion of the death of Iran's most prominent literary figure, Rostam from Abolqasem Ferdowsi's medieval epic poem, *Shahnameh*. "The Petrification of Rostam" begins by questioning Herbert's intention for including a re-narration of the hero's death. Why does Herbert include this story at all? Why does he omit the well-known details of Rostam's life? And how does this discussion reveal Herbert's own desires about his re-vision of Persia?

Elio Brancaforte delves, in his article entitled "Between Word and Image: Representations of Shiʻite Rituals in Safavid Iran from Early Modern European Travel Accounts," into the way early modern European travellers to the Ottoman and Safavid Empires reimagine the East. This contribution considers examples, both visual and textual, from early modern European travellers and chroniclers—such as Thévenot, Pietro Della Valle, Adam Olearius, and John Ogilby—and their attempts to explain the Sunni–Shiʻite confessional divide for Catholic and Protestant readers in Europe, readers who were all too familiar with the troubles associated with divergent religious beliefs and their impact on the secular world.

In "Visions and Transitions of a Pilgrimage of Curiosity: Pietro Della Valle's Travel to Istanbul," Sezim Sezer Darnault and Aygül Ağır describe Pietro Della Valle's encounter with the Ottoman Empire's capital. Sezer Darnault and Agir's study focuses on Pietro Della Valle's perception and interpretation of Constantinople's visual culture within the frame of European–Ottoman encounters. The Roman aristocrat spent one year in Constantinople between 1614 and 1615 during his voyage to the Ottoman Empire, Persia, and India. Published in the 1650s, Della Valle's detailed letters illustrating his travels were widely disseminated throughout Europe. Unlike his predecessors, he was neither a missionary nor a tradesman; as has been noted, "Della Valle styled himself as the 'pilgrim' and his pilgrimage was, "decidedly a pilgrimage of curiosity". His observations as a self-fashioned nobleman reflect a search for identity and self-fulfillment. His narratives of Turkey reveal the Ottoman Empire during the reign of Sultan

Ahmed I (1603–1617), a period, as Sezer Darnault and Ağır argue, when the Ottoman Empire and Europe were redefining their relationships.

With Adriano Duque's contribution, "Gift-giving in the Carpini Expedition to Mongolia (1246–1248 CE)," we begin the third thematic section in the collection (Exchanging Objects, Ideas and Texts) and we travel farther east in our exploration, to the lands of the Mongols. In 1246, Pope Innocent II sent out an expedition to Mongolia, with the two-fold objective of converting the Mongols and gathering information about their warfare and social organization. Composed of three Franciscan friars, the expedition managed to reach the central camp of the Mongols, where they witnessed the coronation of the great khan. In their travels, the Franciscan friars had to cross numerous territories and follow a series of ritual salutations involving the exchange of letters and presents.

During the European Middle Ages, gift exchanges nourished an immense variety of public and personal experiences. They played a vital economic role in ensuring not only the good relations between peoples but also their social and political recognition. Drawing on previous scholarship on gift-giving by Marcel Mauss, Jacques Derrida, and John Milbank, Adriano Duque's essay addresses questions such as what constitutes a gift and what sorts of objects and texts circulated in late medieval gift exchanges. More importantly, the essay examines the kind of social, political, and/or cultural inferences that the exchanges and the objects themselves acquired during this expedition. Duque concludes that gift-giving in the Carpini expedition provides important insights into the development of Christian–Mongol relations in the mid-thirteenth century and a useful tool to channel social and diplomatic relations.

Gregory Kaplan illustrates not commercial or diplomatic exchanges but intellectual interactions. In his article "The East–West Trajectory of Sephardic Sectarianism: From Ibn Daud to Spinoza" Kaplan discusses how Muslim hegemony in Al-Andalus during the medieval period had exposed Jewish thought to Middle Eastern schools of thought that eventually encouraged Jewish defiance of traditional rabbinical authority. This cross-cultural contact created a lasting effect on the movement called Karaism, which travelled and expanded, by means of the Sephardic diaspora expelled from Spain after 1492, to seventeenth-century Amsterdam and to the writings of Baruch Spinoza. Kaplan studies the evolution of Karaism, which had spread to Iberia from the Middle East and had already been observed by the Jewish traveller Benjamin of Tudela in his *Sefer ha-Masa'ot* (*Book of Travels*), which documents his journey through the Middle East between 1169 and 1171.

The next article does not deal with the travel and exchange of ideas but rather with the travel of material objects. On this occasion, the object, a saint's arm, acquires sacred connotations. In "Piety and Piracy: Repatriating the Arm of St. Francis Xavier" Pilar Ryan studies the circumstances surrounding the voyage of the fleet that was returning St. Francis Xavier's arm to Europe from the Far East via Goa, India. An epigram in a 1695 book describes the threats that pirates posed to the expedition. Through this epigram, we catch a glimpse of the functional agreements and practices between military men, merchants, and missionaries during the age of exploration. Ryan examines how sacred objects were protected from pirates in the Mediterranean Sea and Atlantic and Indian Oceans, the role the ship's chaplain played in this specific defensive mission, and how the rhetoric about the threat of pirates paralleled the rhetoric about the danger of Protestants.

The last two contributions in Part III centre on the theme of early modern English interpretations of the Eastern subject and of their interactions with Western subjects. Ambereen Dadabhoy examines the topic of Muslim conversion and the problematization of the notion of "turning Turk" through the modalities of gender and race in "The Other Woman: The Geography of Exclusion in *The Kight of Malta*." Dadabhoy seeks to find out how the "turned Turk" became such a popular figure on the early modern English stage and a key player in the imaginative geography of the English in their constructions of the "Islamic world." According to Dadabhoy *The Knight of Malta* imbricates, through the use of the generic architecture of romance, categories of difference, such as gender, race, and religion, in its construction of nation and community. She argues that the play offers an innovative lens through which questions of encounter and traffic with Muslim regimes can be framed and answered. By tracing the circulation of women in the play, Dadabhoy reveals the affective and symbolic roles they occupy in addition to the suspicion they engender and claims that the dramatization of the national and imperial triumph of Malta (and Christendom) over the Ottoman Empire (and Islam) is achieved through the simultaneous absorption and exclusion of radical difference. Exploring the intertextual links between *The Knight of Malta* and other late sixteenth- and early seventeenth-century Mediterranean plays topically engaged with Moors and Turks (such as Robert Daborne's 1609 *A Christian Turned Turk* and Philip Massinger's 1624 *The Renegado*) highlights the interest of English dramatists in that locale and the audience's cultural fascination with multiple forms of difference.

The danger of the Barbary Corsairs, the North African pirates operating out of the Ottoman regencies of Algiers, Tunis, and Salee was twofold: in their piratical operations they captured hundreds of English and European men, women, and children, selling them in the slave markets of Algiers and Constantinople; and more terrifyingly, many were English and European by birth but had vouchsafed God, king, and country and now swore allegiance to a foreign emperor and a heretical religion. As Dadabhoy demonstrates, travel accounts and captivity narratives, which enjoyed wide circulation in the period, undergirded the epistemological construction of Anglo-Ottoman encounter. Such narratives provided the raw material for the plots of these plays, but they also contributed the symbolic and affective registers of meaning and difference these representations exposed and emphasized. The author argues that even as these texts demonize the geographies and peoples of Islam, there remains a strain of ambivalence that destabilizes such totalizing constructions and forces us to reconsider moments of encounter through new theoretical frameworks that move away from conflict and toward transaction and contingency.

Although significant knowledge of the Islamic world came to Christendom through the transmission and translation of written works, the eyewitnesses' accounts of European travellers and seemingly uninteresting documents such as merchants' logs served as another major source of information about contemporary Muslim societies. Julia Schleck analyzes this topic in the next contribution, "Experiential Knowledge and the Limits of Merchant Credit," but she cautions us that the transmission and reception of such knowledge was notoriously problematic because travellers were routinely accused of being exaggerators or "travel liars." Schleck declares that some experiential knowledge was valued while some was derided, depending largely on the source of the account and his or her standing in the home community.

This article explores the credence given to one of the most organized and experienced set of travellers from early modern England to the Ottoman, Persian, and Mughal Empires: the English merchants of the nascent Levant and East India Companies. Despite the growing wealth and influence of these merchants in English society, their status as commoners and their devotion to business served to diminish the epistemological value of their knowledge claims. These same traits thus ironically served to enhance their knowledge base, and degrade its reception as truth in England. By focusing on an offer made to King James in 1622 for a direct trade in silks with Shah Abbas I of Persia, Julia Schleck's article will evince the paradoxical role that the experiential knowledge of merchants played in the development of English familiarity with Islamic lands and peoples.

While each essay in our volume focuses on different travel narratives and travel and commercial experiences one can still infer, despite the disparity of disciplines, methodologies and critical approaches utilized by the authors, that there are many points of convergence and shared conclusions among the different essays. A comparative study of the many manifestations of cultural exchanges between West and East will yield intriguing discernments about cross-cultural interaction. Such investigation, however, brings very forcefully to the forefront as well the inherent hindrances that imperil the process of exchange itself, which is never neutral and is always replete with cultural significance and the possibility for misinterpretation. As post-colonial studies as well as some critiques to their formulations have shown us, and the discussions in the following articles will illustrate, contacts and interactions between cultures are never entirely harmonious but decidedly contested instead. This is even more markedly the case in interactions between medieval and early modern Christians and other religious or ethnic groups: Muslims, Jews, Mongols, Persians, Ottoman Turks.[60] Postulating that these groups engaged in constant hostility or warfare, however, is equally inaccurate.

The medieval historian Brian Catlos suggests an alternative to such dichotomy while discussing the construct of medieval Iberian so-called "convivencia" and offers a paradigm of interaction that is more realistic. According to him, disparate communities operated under a "hierarchy of social formality."[61] Thus, some activities (trade, agriculture)

---

60 European travellers and merchants who first came in contact with Eastern populations exhibited much more markedly than native groups every cultural "symptom of colonialism," as Robert Bartlett puts it: they were generally members of "immigrant elites with close ties to the metropolis" and a contemptuous disregard of native customs and controlled or interacted with large disaffected populations with a different language and religion (*The Making of Europe: Conquest, Colonization and Cultural Change 950–1350* (Princeton: Princeton University Press, 1993), 185).

61 Brian Catlos, *The Victors and the Vanquished: Christians and Muslims of Catalonia and Aragon, 1050–1300* (Cambridge: Cambridge University Press, 2004), 397. See also David Nirenberg's

were invested with little religious or ideological importance, so interchange occurred easily in these areas; in other more formal situations (marriages, religious debates) the groups would endeavour vigorously to protect their social boundaries.

The instances of exchanges depicted in this volume elucidate and demonstrate the validity of this theoretical model. Our project has sought to illuminate the processes by which missionaries, ambassadors, merchants and explorers established fruitful and pragmatic ties with their neighbours and hosts for the purpose of religious fulfillment and commercial and political expansion. Ultimately, however, our vision will always be slightly distorted and unsettling because the subjects studied by our travel narratives' narrators are always concealed behind a mask of "sly civility" in Homi Bhabha's words,[62] but also because our travelling narrators' gazes are always informed by their own belief systems.

Consequently, our impression of our topic of study will be indeed very similar to that experienced by Jeffrey Jerome Cohen when reading that most celebrated of travel narratives, the *Book of John Mandeville:*

> Unflaggingly congenial yet quietly treacherous, the *Book of John Mandeville* masks its recalcitrance beneath what postcolonial theory calls a "sly civility". Bearing a reassuring resemblance to traditional accounts of pilgrimage and travel, as well as to classical ethnography, the text seems companionable enough. Its easygoing narrative of foreign marvels and distant travels lure readers into enthusiastic encounter [...] but then leaves them to wonder if the motion-filled and unsettled world it brings into being won't erode the stability of their own. The *Book of John Mandeville* is, in a word, unsettling.[63]

Travel and the epistemological and ethnographic learning of other cultures which travelling provides always erodes the stability and the identity of the traveller and encounters among peoples from different cultures are always both congenial and treacherous. Unsettling yes, but wondrous and worthwhile nonetheless as attested both by all the travel writers studied in this collection and by the scholars who study them. The thirteen scholars here included are daringly debunking several old paradigms in their novel interpretations of historical documents, travelogues, material objects, visual artifacts, and literary texts. It is fitting, thus, to end this introduction by summarizing the elements which we believe make this a distinctive volume.

First, this collection is truly comparative, in that it draws on not only a variety of Islamic and Jewish writings, but also Spanish, Italian, and English works. This

---

"Religious & Sexual Boundaries in the Medieval Crown of Aragon", in *Christians, Muslims, and Jews in Medieval and Early Modern Spain: Interaction and Cultural Change*, ed. Mark Meyerson and E. English (South Bend: Notre Dame University Press, 1999), 141–60, and his book *Communities of Violence* (Princeton: Princeton University Press, 1996).

62 Homi Bhabha, *The Location of Culture* (London: Routledge, 1994), 93.

63 Jeffrey Jerome Cohen, "Pilgrimages, Travel Writing and the Medieval Exotic," in *The Oxford Handbook of Medieval Literature in English*, ed. Elaine Treharne and Greg Walker (Oxford: Oxford University Press, 2010), 611–28 and 611–12.

differentiates our enterprise from previous, more rigidly focused and nationalistically organized collections, which by nature of their rigidity were unable to engage in fruitful comparisons across national traditions and histories and, therefore, neglected to assess contested collectivities like "West" or "Europe" (or "Christendom"). Similarly, our collection features essays that go well beyond the conventional focus on the Ottomans, including a number of essays examining travel narratives to geographical areas not so frequently studied, such as Safavid Persia or Mongolia. Such geographical breadth is, perhaps, only comparable to Nabil Matar's collection featuring essays analyzing travel accounts of Jerusalem by travellers throughout Western and Eastern Europe, Russia, and the Near East.[64]

Furthermore, this collection is also singular in that it encompasses wide fields of inquiry, ranging from examinations of Muslim travel writings to Sephardic Jewish philosophy. This remains quite unusual in the literature on travel writing (particularly the examination of the *rihla* genre) which, despite repeated calls for work from non-European authors, remains, for the most part, resolutely Eurocentric. It is our hope that the inclusion in our collection of several essays devoted to non-European travel topics will bolster and validate work done recently by scholars such as Nabil Matar, Giancarlo Casale,[65] and others which aims to refute long-standing misconceptions in our field, namely, that the "Age of Discovery" was marked by an upsurge in European travel alone, and that Muslims rarely "travelled."

Lastly, the collection indisputably concentrates on travel narratives.[66] While there have been a high number of publications in the last decade[67]—particularly collections, but also monographs—on East–West exchange and/or European depictions of the "East" (usually defined as the Ottoman Empire and Morocco, with occasional attention to the Safavid Empire), the fact remains that, with some notable exceptions, the majority of them focus on European literary representations, with reference to

---

64 Nabil Matar is, perhaps, the scholar who has most contributed to expanding our knowledge of the Arab perception of "Western cultures" in the early modern period, thanks to his frequent editions of travel accounts written by Arabic travellers: *In the Lands of the Christians* (New York: Routlege, 2003); *Europe Through Arab Eyes, 1578–1727* (New York: Columbia University Press, 2009); and *An Arab Ambassador in the Mediterranean World: The Travels of Muhammad ibn 'Uthmān al-Miknāsī, 1779–1788* (New York: Routledge, 2015), among other worthwhile publications. Matar's work has also served to counteract the prevailing Eurocentric emphasis in Travel Writing studies.

65 Giancarlo Casale, for example, rightly decries in his book *The Ottoman Age of Exploration* that no serious attempts have been made by scholars "to portray Ottoman achievements as part of the larger story of physical expansion abroad and intellectual ferment at home that characterized Western European history during precisely the same period" (4) and concludes that the so-called "Age of Exploration" cannot truly be called solely "European."

66 That is the case of most of the articles, with only one exception, Chapter 11, which deals more specifically with a literary representation of travel. Even in this case, however, the emphasis is still on travel and on issues of encounter and traffic in the Mediterranean Sea.

67 See pp. 2 and 3 of this introduction and corresponding footnotes for copious bibliographical references to many of these publications.

other European prose documents, including travel narratives, only to help forward more detailed analyses of literature (romances and dramatic works in particular). This is especially the case within English Studies, where the interest in Anglo-Islamic exchange has been particularly keen. The focus of our collection, on the contrary, is on travel narratives and their genuine enactment of intriguing cultural exchanges and transfers of knowledge among disparate ethnic, political, and religious groups.

The ensuing articles analyzing such travel narratives and their authors' collective perceptions have fashioned a unique navigational charting of what we envision will be a remapping of our assumptions about the emergence of modernity and subjectivity, about the transference of knowledge and the establishment of bonds between peoples of disparate origins through global travel and about the interaction between Eastern and Western cultural modes in the period before the onset of the so-called "Renaissance" and "the Age of Discovery" as well as during that era and beyond.

Part I

Transforming the *rihla* Tradition: The Search for Knowledge in Jewish, Muslim, and Christian Travellers

Chapter 1

FROM PIOUS JOURNEYS TO THE CRITIQUE OF SOVEREIGNTY: KHAQANI SHIRVANI'S PERSIANATE POETICS OF PILGRIMAGE[1]

REBECCA GOULD[2]

ABSTRACT

Like most world literatures, the Islamic world generated many different types of travel writing. While the trope of the Islamic pilgrimage (*ḥajj*) is well known, the impact of the imagery and concept of travel on poetic production from the Islamic world, particularly in Persian, has not merited the same scrutiny. Countering this tradition of neglect, this chapter introduces one of the most important and yet least-studied Persian travel narratives to an interdisciplinary readership: the *Gift from the Two Iraqs* (*Tuhfat al-'Iraqayn*), composed in the middle of the twelfth century by the Persian poet Khāqānī Shirwānī. I examine this work's contribution to world literature and global poetics by documenting its deployment of key tropes from a longer tradition of thinking about mobility within Persian and Islamic poetics. Of particular interest is Khāqānī's method of transforming the *riḥla*, a discourse known for celebrating migration as a pious act, into a means of critiquing sovereign power.

Keywords: travel, *riḥla*, journey, Persian poetry, medieval Islam, sovereignty, poetic critique

"BECAUSE TRAVEL BROUGHT them, through suffering, into learning as a way of life," writes Houari Touati in his recent intellectual history of travel in the medieval Islamic world, "Muslims saw [travel] as a figure for metamorphosis, coupled with the experience of pain."[3] The medieval Islamic understanding of travel as a stage of self-transformation, a horizon of new experience, and a harbinger of a new epistemology has many parallels in world history. The conceptual and practical centrality of travel

---

1 I would like to thank Elizabeth Gould for her editorial support.

2 This publication has received funding from the European Union's Horizon 2020 Research and Innovation Programme under ERC-2017-STG Grant Agreement No 759346.

3 Houari Touati, *Islam et voyage au Moyen Age: histoire et anthropologie d'une pratique lettrée* (Paris: Seuil, 2000), 2.

to the historical formation of Islamic law and related Islamic disciplines, however, conferred on it a unique, and arguably unparalleled, importance in the world of Islam. Known in Arabic as *riḥla* (from the same root that generated "camel saddle"), soon after its institutionalization within Islamic culture, this journey subsequently also came to signify a literary genre.[4]

The *riḥla* genre (which I refer to here also as the travel narrative) has been richly studied by many generations of Arabist scholarship, particularly with reference to its contribution to the consolidation of Islamic thought and doctrine. This chapter considers how this tradition relates to classical Persian texts that made travel into a metaphor. I show, not only how Persian literature drew on core Islamic traditions, but also how this poetry transformed Islam from within. I thereby supplement the narrative of Islamic pilgrimage with a Persianate inflection that transfers the physical journey of *riḥla* to the realm of the imagination, where Persian poetics found its fullest expression. Given that Persian poetics is not traditionally dominated by narrative form, the role of narrative in shaping this aspect of the tradition is worth noting.

My analysis documents how this literature differed from its counterpart in Arabic prose, in part by plotting a trajectory from travel as an act of piety to travel as an act of rebellion against sovereign power. In part because the shift from piety to the critique of sovereignty is most apparent in the oeuvre of the poet Khāqānī of Shirwān (d. 1199), this poet's oeuvre dominates this discussion. At the same time, I integrate several of the precedents and intertexts for Khāqānī's aesthetic into a larger conversation concerning the many ways in which travel signified to medieval Persian readers and writers. Tropes pertaining to mobility converge among three overlapping genres in classical Persian literature: the literature of exile, the literature of imprisonment, and the literature of travel.[5] Before exploring these intersections in greater detail, I will dwell on the meanings that were attached to the *riḥla* in Arabic, prior to its New Persian transformation.

Both as a practice and as a mode of reflection, the *riḥla* generated a highly sophisticated repertoire for conceiving travel's uses and aims. Central among these were the obligation to undertake the pilgrimage to Mecca and to migrate away from lands that had fallen under infidel rule and which thereby had to be classified as belonging to the abode of war (*dār al-ḥarb*).[6] With the rise of Islamic empires across central and western Asia, the *riḥla* came to signify a means of clarifying the territorial, and hence, the conceptual

---

4 For a brief overview, see Ian Netton, "Riḥla," *The Encyclopedia of Islam²* [henceforth abbreviated as *EI²*], ed. E. Bosworth et al. (Leiden: Brill, 1961–2004), 8:528.

5 Of these three, only the literature of imprisonment is clearly delineated as a genre in Persian literature, as shown in my PhD dissertation on the prison poem (*ḥabsiyyāt*), "The Political Aesthetic of the Medieval Persian Prison Poem, 1100–1200" (Columbia University, 2013), currently under revision under the title *The Persian Genre of Incarceration: Prisons and the Literary Imagination*.

6 For two collections on these topics, see Dale F. Eickelman and James Piscatori, eds. *Muslim Travellers: Pilgrimage, Migration, and the Religious Imagination* (New York: Social Science Research Council, 1990) and Ian Netton, ed., *Golden Roads: Migration, Pilgrimage and Travel in Medieval and Modern Islam* (London: Routledge, 2005).

and doctrinal borders of the space known in Islamic sources as *dār al-islām*, the abode (*dār*) of Islam.

As a genre, the travel narrative traverses disciplines, and epistemologies, as diverse as ethnography, history, and geography. Somewhat more peripheral to the *riḥla* tradition, although crucial for grasping Islamic perceptions of the spatial and cultural differences that are traversed by many forms of travel, is *ʿajāʾib* ("wonders"), the literary genre that describes the marvels of far-off lands, and which has a medieval European counterpart in *mirabilia*.[7] Although *ʿajāʾib* texts purport to represent the outermost regions of the world, they are based in explicitly imaginary texts. This representational tradition figures into Arabic travel literature, particularly in the late medieval period, but is not strongly represented in the Persian corpus, with a few important exceptions.[8] To venture a sweeping generalization that nonetheless will help to situate the analysis of poetic traditions that follow, we might venture to describe Dante's *Inferno* as a text wherein diverse strands of influence stemming from the *riḥla* tradition on the one hand and *ajāʾib* tradition on the other, converge.

As a practice, the *riḥla*'s deepest importance to the history of Islam lies in the role played by the "search for knowledge" (*ṭalab al-ʿilm*) in the collection and organization of the corpus of *ḥadīth* (sayings of the prophet and his companions) that, alongside the Qurʾan, constituted the *sunna*, from which subsequent jurists deduced Islamic teachings. In the late nineteenth century, Orientalist Ignaz Goldziher connected the development of the *riḥla* genre in the early eighth century to the consolidation of the *ḥadīth*, which was in turn instrumental in helping to form the major schools of Islamic law.[9] Goldziher's account was nuanced in subsequent decades, but his general argument represents the prevailing view.[10] The eighth-century Islamic scholar Ziyād b. Maymūn treated the search for knowledge as a secondary obligation (*ṭalab al-ʿilm farīḍa*) incumbent on all Muslims.[11] Three centuries later, Khaṭīb al-Baghdādī composed an entire book, *Travel in Search of Ḥadīth* (*Al-riḥla fī ṭalab al-ḥadīth*), reporting on scholars who had journeyed across the abode of Islam for the sake of gathering and refining oral traditions related to the Prophet.[12]

---

7 For the literature of *ʿajāʾib*, see Syrinx von Hees, "The Astonishing: A Critique and Re-reading of ʿAǧāʾib Literature," *Middle Eastern Literatures* 8 (2005): 101–20, and C. E. Dubler, "Adjāʾib," *EI²* 1:203–4.

8 Exceptions include Naghmeh Sohrabi, *Taken for Wonder: Nineteenth Century Travel Accounts from Iran to Europe* (Oxford: Oxford University Press, 2012), 21–46, and the texts discussed in Rebecca Gould, "Cosmopolitical Genres and Geographies: Poetry and History in the Nineteenth Century Caucasus," *Comparative Literature* (forthcoming).

9 Ignaz Goldziher, *Muhammedanische Studien* (Halle: Niemeyer, 1889–90), 2:33–34, 176–80.

10 See G. H. A. Juynboll, *Muslim Tradition: Studies in Chronology, Provenance and Authorship of Early Hadith* (Cambridge: Cambridge University Press, 2008 [1983]), 66–70, and Nadia Abbott, *Studies in Arabic Literary Papyri II: Quranic Commentary and Tradition* (Chicago: University of Chicago, 1967), 2:40.

11 Aḥmad ibn ʿAlī ibn Ḥajar al-ʿAsqalānī, *Kitāb tahdhib al-tahdhīb* (Beirut: Dār al-Fikr, 1984 [reprint of Hyderabad ed., 1325–1327]), 5:102ff.

12 Abū Bakr Aḥmad ibn ʿAlī ibn Thābit al-Khaṭīb al-Baghdādī, *al-Riḥla fī ṭalab al-ḥadīth*, ed. Nūr al-Dīn ʿIṭr (Beirut: Dār al-Kutub al-ʿIlmīyah, 1975).

Riḥla as a Spiritual Quest

Also related to the *riḥla* is the institution of the *ḥajj*, the pilgrimage to Mecca that able Muslims are required to perform at least once in their lives. The poem around which this chapter turns, the *Gift from Two Iraqs* (*Tuḥfat al-ʿIraqayn*), owes its genesis to the institution of the *ḥajj*. The geographic denominator in the text, "*Two Iraqs*" references (and in one word, the dual plural *ʿIraqayn*, hence less anomalously than in English) both Persian and Arab Iraq, specifically the region of Basra, where the Tigris and the Euphrates met, and Kufa, on the Euphrates near the terminus of the ancient caravan route from the Hijaz. Its author, Khāqānī Shirwānī, performed the *ḥajj* twice, and this narrative, completed in 1157–1158, appears to date to the period of his first pilgrimage.[13] However, as will be seen, the *Gift from Two Iraqs* is much more than a record of a journey, even once as fraught with a sense of mission as was the *ḥajj*. The complexity of the text's relationship to the world it claims to represent is attested by the fact that, according to the conceit of the text, the poet remains enchained at home for the entire course of his "journey."

Alongside its nominal association with Islamic pilgrimage, *Gift from Two Iraqs* exemplifies a broader tradition, which is deeply rooted in Islamic culture yet also distinct from the pilgrimage tradition, of journeying for the sake of knowledge. Touati's argument that the journey for the sake of knowledge was "constructed as a break" with the *ḥajj* and in the belief that travel anywhere in the world for the sake of increasing one's knowledge was as praiseworthy as the pilgrimage is borne out by a cursory review of medieval Persian travel literature.[14] Even poets like Khāqānī, whose travel narratives originated in the practice of *ḥajj*, filled their narratives with eulogies to many other cities, such as Baghdad, and reserved only a few verses for Mecca and Medina. This disjuncture between the stated purpose and the literary form taken by its representation reverberates across Persian literature. As Khāqānī scholar Beelaert notes, "pilgrimage itself is not an important subject in Persian literature—or indeed in Islamic literatures as a whole—even if it is a very important event in the life of a Muslim."[15] Hence, the split between the pious purpose of the pilgrimage and the genres that were concerned with its (partial) representation is intrinsic to Islamic culture. As I will argue, however, Khāqānī took this disjuncture further than any poet prior to him had done.

------

13 The dates of Khāqānī's pilgrimage have not been established and the question of the relation of *Tuḥfat* to this journey remains unsettled. For further discussion, see Ḥusayn Āmūzgār, *Muqaddamah-i tuḥfat al-khavāṭir* (Tehran: Intisharat-i Ruznama-i Zindagi, 1955), 26–30.

14 Houari Touati, *Islam and Travel in the Middle Ages*, "Preface to the English-Language Edition," trans. Lydia Cochrane (Chicago: University of Chicago Press, 2010), xiii.

15 A. L. F. A. Beelaert, *A Cure for the Grieving: Studies on the Poetry of the 12th Century Persian Court Poet Khāqānī Širwānī* (Brill: Leiden, 1996), 37. One exception is the nineteenth century travelogue *Safarnāmah-ʾi Farhād Mīrzā, Muʿtamad al-Dawlah*, ed. Ismāʿīl Navvāb Ṣafā (Tehran: Zawwār, 1366/1987). For further on Persian pilgrimage poems, see Henri Massé, "Aspects du pélerinage à la Mecque dans la poésie persane," *Melanges Franz Cumont* (Bruxelles: Annuaire de l'Institut de Philosophie, 1936), 859–65.

While the vast majority of *riḥla* narratives are in Arabic and in prose, there is growing recognition of the Persian contribution to this literary corpus, particularly for the early modern and modern periods.[16] Like many of its Arabic predecessors, the earliest extant Persian travel narrative, Nāṣir Khusrow's *Book of Travel* (*Safarnāma*), conjoins the search for knowledge with a religious pilgrimage, in this case to Shī'a-ruled Fatimid Cairo, at that time a political centre for the Ismāʿīli faith.[17] The author, Nāṣir Khusrow (1004–1088), was a poet and philosopher from Qubādyān, in the Marv District of north-eastern Khorasan. Over the course of his journey, he converted to the Ismāʿīli branch of Shī'a Islam. The instigation for Nāṣir's journey was a dream he had in 1045, while he was serving as a "wine-loving bureaucrat in the Seljuq administration."[18] During this dream, a voice reproached the poet for wasting his life in drink, and asked him why he did not remain sober. Nāṣir Khusrow replied that drinking is the only solution that "the wise [*ḥukuma*] have devised to alleviate this world's grief [*andūh-i dunyā*]" (2). The voice enigmatically replied, "seek and you shall find [*jūyand yābandeh bāshad*]" and then pointed towards the *qibla*, the direction of the Ka'ba towards which Muslims pray.

As the direction in which Muslim prayers are pointed, the *qibla* visually entails a mental peregrination to Mecca on the part of every believer; hence pilgrimage is inscribed into every act of prayer in the Islamic tradition. Taking this symbolic linkage of pilgrimage and prayer literally, Nāṣir immediately set about making preparations for his journey. A few days later, he travelled to Faryāb and Marv. Announcing that he had decided to travel in the direction of the *qibla*, Nāṣir quit his job, settled his debts, renounced every-thing worldly (*az dunyā anche bud tark kardam*), and began his journey to the western lands under Ismāʿili rule. As he later recalled, the dream had revealed to him that, unless he changed all his ways and actions, he would never find happiness (*farrukh*, 2). Hence, Nāṣir's westward pilgrimage was a concrete endeavour to implement such change.

Although the *qibla* that instigated Nāṣir's journey points to Mecca, the author had another, equally important, destination in mind when he embarked on his journey: Fatimid-ruled Cairo, a city that, since 969, had been the political centre of Ismāʿīli Shī'ism. While Mecca was Nāṣir's nominal destination, reaching Cairo was argu-ably his ultimate goal. Although he includes valuable descriptions of both cities, it was in Cairo that Nāṣir stayed the longest from the year 1046 to 1052. It was also in Cairo

---

16 Most notably in recent years, see Muzaffar Alam and Sanjay Subrahmanyam, *Indo-Persian Travels in the Age of Discoveries, 1400–1800* (Cambridge: Cambridge University Press, 2007); Roberta Micallef and Sunil Sharma, eds., *On the Wonders of Land and Sea: Persianate Travel Writing* (Cambridge, MA: Harvard University Press, 2013); Sohrabi, *Taken for Wonder*, and Nile Green, ed., *Writing Travel in Central Asian History* (Bloomington: Indiana University Press, 2013). Notably, and partly due to the paucity of sources, these works do not treat the medieval period.

17 *Safarnāma-i Abū-Muʿīn Ḥamīd-ad-Dīn Nāṣir Ibn-Khusrau Qubādyānī Marwazī*, ed. Muḥammad Dabīr Sīyāqī (Tehran: Zawwār, 1956/1335). Future citations are from this edition and given parenthetically.

18 The citation is from Ehsan Yarshater's preface to the English translation of the *Safarnāma* by Wheeler Thackston, *The Book of Travels=(Safarnāma)* (Albany: Bibliotheca Persica, 1986), vii.

that Nāṣir became formally initiated into the Ismāʿili creed and rose to the rank of *ḥujjat*, a religious leader charged with overseeing one of the twelve regions (*jazāʾir*) where Ismāʿilis lived but which was not controlled by the Fatimids.[19]

Although his *Safarnāma* chronicles what he saw as he passed through Mecca, Cairo, and Jerusalem, Nāṣir traversed a geography that was in many substantive empirical senses similar to what Khāqānī saw a century later when he journeyed from Azerbaijan to Diyār Bakr. The cities of Darband (Daghestan), Qazvin, Rayy, and the topography of Mount Damavand and the Caspian Sea, all of which are mentioned by Nāṣir, also comprise the figurative geography for Khāqānī's masterwork. The *Safarnāma* thus set an important precedent for subsequent Persian travel literature, and provided a countertext against which the later Persian travellers could fashion their narratives that often differed radically from this initial example. Although he does not mention the *Safarnāma* by name, Khāqānī was familiar with Nāṣir's poetry. As will be seen below, he incorporates many of his literary devices into his poetry, particularly when Nāṣir touches on the topoi of exile, travel, and imprisonment.

As the first Persian travel narrative in verse, and possibly the first text of this genre in any Islamic language, Khāqānī's *Gift from Two Iraqs* (1157) differs from its Persian and Arabic predecessors in many crucial respects.[20] First and foremost, this is due to its status as poetry. The difficulty of situating the text in relation to the precise dates of the poet's travels attests to the complex relation between this Persian travel narrative the world it proposed to represent, for in this verse narrative, the sun, not the poet, "is the traveler."[21] Much more than a documentation of an empirical sequence of events, *Gift from Two Iraqs* is a fictional journey grounded in historical fact. Its intimate relation with other poetic genres, in particular the poetry of exile and imprisonment (explored in greater detail below), further complicate the text's relationship to the world it represents. *Gift from Two Iraqs* is a travel narrative that uses the topos of travel in the same way that prior Persian poets had used the topos of exile: as a means of arriving at a new relation to the poet's self. Hence the striking preponderance of autobiographical material in the text, including, famously, the poet's eulogies to his grandfather, father, mother, and uncle, which take the form of celebrations of their professional activities, and which he links to his poetic vocation (*Tuḥfat*, 198).

In contrast to the literature of wonders (*ajāʾib*), much travel writing in the Islamic world assumed an empirical, rather than a fantastical, trajectory for the traveller.

---

19 As noted by V. Ivanov, *jazāʾir* typically means islands in Arabic and Persian, but in this context it refers to "the Ismaili community in a country which politically was not under Fatimid sovereignty" (Ivanov, "The Organization of the Fatimid Propaganda," *Journal of the Royal Asiatic Society* 15 (1939): 12).

20 For the claim to primacy for this text, see J. Rypka, *History of Iranian Literature* (Dordrecht: D. Reidel, 1956), 204. Beelaert lists later Persian travel narratives that reference *Tuḥfat*, as well as a manuscript held in the Leiden University Library (Or. 1620), by the poet Sāʾī, that narrates the author's journey from Shirwān to Ṣafavīd-ruled Isfahan (*A Cure*, 11n53).

21 Beelaert, *A Cure*, 10.

Khāqānī's *Gift from Two Iraqs* instead develops an elaborate poetic tropology. It announces its foreignness to the *riḥla* canon through its extended metaphors and similes (particularly comparisons to the sun), its autobiographical reflection, and its rhetorical engagements with objects and persons that, outside of poetry, would have called for a more inhibited imagination. Even as it parts ways with normative pilgrimage narrative conventions, however, *Gift* competes with and imitates the best travel narratives, not least through the author's division of his text into seven *maqāla* (chapters), a taxonomy that was reserved for non-fictional treatises, histories, and other avowedly documentary genres.[22]

Persianizing the *Riḥla* Narrative

Even as Khāqānī inflects his narrative with his poetic consciousness, he uses the empirically oriented *riḥla* tradition to introduce new narrative strategies for evoking the physical world, and which prior to him were marginalized by a Persian poetic tradition that made "the literary imagination [...] paramount, autonomous, and even sovereign."[23] After he returned from his pilgrimage, Khāqānī's predecessor in Persian travel narrative, Nāṣir Khusrow, began to compose the poems that would be included in the complete version of his collected poems (*dīwān*). Many of these texts were written in the remote village of Yumgān in Afghanistan, to which Nāṣir had been exiled following his return, and where he remained in hiding until the end of his life, fearing persecution from those hostile to the Ismāʿili faith.[24] One *qaṣīda* (ode) composed during this period resonates particularly powerfully with the pathos of exile, while also incorporating a device that was to profoundly inflect Khāqānī's *Gift*: the trope of the messenger who travels to places that the poet himself cannot reach. The poet addresses the wind:

سلام کن ز من ای باد مر خراسان را

مر اهل فضل و خرد را نه عام نادان را

خبر بیاور از ایشان به من چو داده بوی

ز حال من به حقیقت خبر مر ایشان ر[25]

[Say my hello, O wind, to Khorasan,
to the virtuous and wise among them, not to the vulgar and ignorant ones.
Bring back from them the news to me
as you have taken the truthful news of my situation to them.]

---

22 For a Persian text divided into four *maqālas* that was almost exactly contemporaneous with Khāqānī's *Tuḥfat*, see Niẓāmī ʿArūḍī, *Chahār maqāla*, ed. Muḥammad Muʿīn (Tehran: Zawwār, 1957).

23 Hamid Dabashi, *The World of Persian Literary Humanism* (Cambridge, MA: Harvard University Press, 2013), 53.

24 For Nāṣir Khusraw's exile in Yumgān, see Manūchihr Ātishī, *Nāṣir-i Khusraw: sargashtah-'i jahān va tabʿīdī-i Yumgān* (Tehran: Muʾassasah-i Intishārātī-i Āhang-i Dīgar, 2009/1388).

25 *Dīvān-i ashʿār-i Ḥakīm Abu Muʿīn Ḥamīd al-Dīn Nāṣir ibn Khusraw Qubādīyānī* (Isfahan: Intishārāt-i Kitābʿfurūshī-yi Taʾyīd, 1956–1957/1335), 10 (*qaṣīda* 4, vv. 3–4).

Whereas Nāṣir made the wind into the bearer of his grief in his poems, Khāqānī developed the image of the sun in the same way in *Gift*.

Alongside Nāṣir, Khāqānī had a second major predecessor in his efforts to narrate a journey in verse. This was Sanā'ī of Ghazna (d. 1131), a poet with whom Khāqānī shared a similarly exalted sense of his vocation. For most of his career, Sanā'ī was based at the court of Mas'ūd III (r. 1099–1115) in Herat. Tense poet–patron relations are evident in the work of this poet, who, similarly to Khāqānī, conceived of himself as "the master of the world of words [...] and yet a servile slave to his brutal masters."[26] Khāqānī connected his own entry into the world with Sanā'ī's death, as the following self-referential verses attest:

بدل من آمدم اندر جهان سنایی را

بدین دلیل پدر نام من بدیل نهاد[27]

[I entered the world as a replacement [*badal*] to Sanā'ī.
For this reason my father gave me the name Badīl.]

Sanā'ī completed the *ḥajj* in 1130, but, significantly, did not commemorate this event with a poem.[28] His contribution to the Persian literature of travel veered more toward polemics, and was more suffused with satire than spiritual uplift. The most notable work in this regard is Sanā'ī's *Chronicle of Balkh* (*Kārnāmah-yi Balkh*). Although occasioned by his departure from Ghazna to Balkh, where he sojourned during the years 1109–1114, the text is primarily engaged with historical personalities from Ghazna.[29] Both *Gift* and *Chronicle of Balkh* belong formally to the most important Persian narrative verse form, called the *mathnawī* genre. This form consists of rhyming couplets with ten to eleven syllables per hemistich. Its recitation creates a sense of forward narrative movement in a way that other verse forms such as the *qaṣīda*, lack. Also like *Gift*, Sanā'ī's text is structured topographically and addressed to multiple patrons. The setting moves from Ghazna, where the poet had been based at the Ghaznavid court, to Balkh, which at that time was, like the "two Iraqs" of Khāqānī's text, under Saljuq rule.[30] It is not surprising therefore to see Khāqānī refer to Sanā'ī's text in the pages of his own *Gift* (28, v. 11).

---

26 Dabashi, *The World of Persian Literary Humanism*, 145.

27 *Dīvān-i Afẓal al-Dīn Badīl ibn 'Alī Najjār Khāqānī Shirvānī*, ed. Ẓiyā' al-Dīn Sajjādī (Tehran: Zawwār, 1960), 850.

28 For Sanā'ī's *ḥajj*, see J. Stephenson's introduction to *The First Book of the Hadiqatu'l-haqīqat; or, The Enclosed Garden of the Truth* (Calcutta: Baptist Mission Press, 1910), viii. Sanā'ī did complete his major work, *Ḥadīqa al-ḥaqīqa*, soon after completing the *ḥajj*, but this text does not dwell on any physical journey.

29 *Kārnāmah-i Balkh* is included in *Maṣnavīhā-yi Ḥakīm Sanā'ī: bi-inẓimām-i Sharḥ-i sayr al-'ibād ilá al-ma'ād*, ed. Mudarris Raẓavī (Tehran: Dānishgāh-i Tihrān, 1348/1969), 142–78. For further intertexts with Sanā'ī's travel narrative, see Sunil Sharma, *Persian Poetry at the Indian Frontier* (Delhi: Permanent Black, 2000), 57, and Matthew Chaffee Smith, "Literary Courage Language, Land, and the Nation in the Works of Malik al-Shu'ara Bahar" (PhD dissertation, Harvard University, 2006), 28.

30 For *Kārnāmah-i Balkh* in the context of Sanā'ī's biography, see J. T. P. de Bruijn, *Of Piety and Poetry: The Interaction of Religion and Literature in the Life and Works of Hakīm Sanā'ī of Ghazna*

As Khāqānī was later to do with unparalleled mastery, *Chronicle of Balkh* combines Persian rhetorical devices pertaining to the many varieties of complaint (*ḥasb-i ḥāl, shikwa*) with social satire of a world from which the poet was alienated.[31] Sanā'ī's tense relationship to Ghazna in many respects parallels Khāqānī's complicated relationship to his native Shirwān, which permeates his oeuvre, from his prison poetry to his ghazals and his *Tuḥfat*.[32] Both poets were deeply attached to their places of origin, and both were equally haunted by the desire to escape from their native lands through travel. Their feelings of confinement generated a new literary idiom, which was multivalently expressed in the literatures of exile, travel, and incarceration (each of which frequently overlapped). Sanā'ī condenses these idioms into verses that insist on the futility of travel even when engaging in this practice:[33]

مرد در شهر خویش با نیروست

دیده هم بر میان چشم نکوست

خاک در ساکنی پسندیدست

چون بجمبید آفت دیدهست

نه بهر شهر تازهتر فلکیست

رازق هر چه کشور است یکیست

سفر و خانه ژاژ دان و هوس

کار لطف خدای داند و بس

[A man is powerful [only] in his own city.
The pupil is confident [only] in the center of the eye.
Dust is pleasant when it is motionless.
When it stirs, it is a calamity for the eye.
One cannot find a new fortune in every city.
The giver of sustenance in every country is the same.
Journeying and staying at home alike are nonsense.
God's beneficence alone knows what will come.]

Even as they pursued similar themes, Khāqānī and Sanā'ī relied on the same poetic device: that of the messenger who serves as an alter ego for the poet's self. Throughout *Gift*, Khāqānī turns to the sun, addressing it as a friend, a prophet, and a patron.[34] The sun is Khāqānī's interlocutor destined for geographies he cannot himself travel to, trapped as he is in the "sublunary world" of Shirwān, imprisoned (fictionally) beneath the ground. As he laments:[35]

(Leiden: Brill, 1983), 39–56, and de Bruijn, "Kār-Nāma-ye Balk," *Encyclopedia Iranica* (Costa Mesa: Mazda Publishers, 1991–), 15(6): 585.

31 For varying formulations of this device, see Sharma, *Persian Poetry*, 54, and Beelaert, *A Cure*, 35.

32 For Khāqānī's *ghazals*, see Alireza Korangy, *Development of the Ghazal and Khaqani's Contribution. A Study of the Development of Ghazal and a Literary Exegesis of a 12th c. Poetic Harbinger* (Wiesbaden: Harrassowitz Verlag, 2013).

33 *Maṣnavīhā-yi Ḥakīm Sanā'ī*, 177. This translation modifies that in Sharma, *Persian Poetry*, 55.

34 Khāqānī's sun imagery is most thoroughly discussed in Beelaert, *A Cure*, 29–114.

35 Beelaert, *A Cure*, 31.

از دهر خط امانم آری

پس گوش سوی دهانم آری

کز سستی دل نمی‌توانم

کاواز بتو بلند رانم   ³⁶

[[To bring me a safety guarantee from fate.
tilt your ear towards my mouth.
With a weak heart I cannot
raise my voice to you.]

Having established a relationship with the sun as his messenger, Khāqānī instructs the sun to journey to Iraq on his behalf

طوبی لک اگر کنی تجشم

زی روضه کشور چهارم

مه قعده فلک جنیبه سازی

دو اسبه سوی عراق تازی

(*Tuḥfat*, 84, vv. 1–2)
[Lucky you if you depart
to the garden in the fourth clime,
if you make the moon and the sky companion-mounts
and rush to Iraq riding the two horses.]

Thus *Gift* is structured by the sun's journey through Iraq, all the way to Mecca, all the while serving as a proxy for the poet, metaphorically enchained in Shirwān. Given its status as one of the inaugural texts in the Persian *riḥla* tradition, the fictional conceit that lies at this tradition's inauguration foundation tells a broader story of the importance of the imagination to Persian poetics. The increasing autonomy of the Persian literary imagination in relation to the literature of travel was also accompanied by an increased capacity to develop and deliver a critique of worldly powers, as will be seen below.

Among the many Persian poets who used the messenger trope as a device to envision the circulation of their verse was Sanāʾī, who in his *Chronicle of Balkh* addresses the wind as a traveller who traverses spaces vaster and more rapidly than the poet himself:

ویحک ای نقشبند بی‌خامه

قاصد رایگان بی نامه

فلک از بهر ناخوشی و خوشی

کرده بر نام تو خریطه‌کشی³⁷

[Oh fortunate painter without a brush,
free messenger without a letter,
fate has inscribed its designs
in your name, for better or worse.]

---

36 *Maṣnavī-i tuḥfat al-ʿIrāqayn*, ed. Yaḥyā Qarib (Tehran: Shirkat-i Sahāmī-i Kitābhā-yi Jībī bā hamkārī-i Muʾassasah-ʾi Intishārāt-i Amīr Kabīr, 1978–1979/1357), 80, v. 13; 81, v. 1. Future citations from *Tuḥfat* are from this edition and are given parenthetically.

37 *Maṣnavīhā-yi Ḥakīm Sanāʾī*, 142.

As with Nāṣir's verses above, the wind is figured in these verses as an artist gifted with the miraculous ability to move through space. Unnamed as such, this "painter without a brush" spreads the poet's words across the vast spaces of Ghaznavid dominion. Beyond the congruence between Khāqānī's sun and Sanā'ī's wind, both verse narratives include a panegyrics to a multitude of patrons. Such formal parallels suggest the importance of Sanā'ī's precedent for Khāqānī's Persianate poetics of pilgrimage.

Although it nominally reproduces the narrative structure of the Islamic pilgrimage, *Gift* participates in the poetry of exile and imprisonment (while extending its formal range and thematic scope) by thematizing the difficulty of reaching Mecca and Medina. Midway through his text, and not in any particularly chronological sequence, the poet eulogizes the Kaʿba:

مانی بعروس حجلهبسته

در حجله چارسو نشسته

حوری بمثال عبقریپوش

شاهی بمثل دواج بر دوش

(*Tuḥfat*, 133, vv. 6–7)
[You are a bride behind a veil,
seated in the bride's rectangular chamber.
You are a *houri* in glorious garments.
You are a shah with a mantle on his shoulders.]

Although the sun, and with it, Khāqānī's imagination, dwells briefly in Mecca, the core of this narrative transpires in other geographies. To this extent, it ceases to wholly belong to the *riḥla* genre, even while partaking of its core features. Khāqānī dedicated his text to Jamāl al-Dīn Mawṣilī (of Mosul in Iraq), a vizier who never made the pilgrimage during his lifetime, although he was said to have funded the construction of walls around Medina and the repair of the Prophet's mosque.[38] Due to such acts of patronage, Jamāl al-Dīn attained fame as a generous patron within Mecca. The Andalusian traveller Ibn Jubayr noted during his visit to the city from 1183–1185 that Jamāl al-Dīn had endowed the bath (*ḥammān*) in Mecca, arranged for the construction of stairs leading up to Mount Arafat, restored houses that had fallen into disrepair, and constructed an elegant grave for himself in Medina, next to the Prophet.[39] Known during his lifetime as al-Jawād ("generous one") in recognition of his beneficence, Jamāl al-Dīn was imprisoned in 1163 by the Zangi ruler Quṭb al-Dīn Mawdūd, who perhaps had grown jealous of and come to fear his vizier's wealth.[40] Jamāl al-Dīn died in prison the following year. These final tragic episodes in the life of the patron pertain to a period after Khāqānī's sojourn in Mosul, yet his text seems to anticipate such a turn of events.

In addition to looking after the welfare of travellers to Mecca and Medina and sharing his wealth with the poor, Jamāl al-Dīn was a patron of Arabic as well as Persian literature.

---

38 Osman Latiff, *The Cutting Edge of the Poet's Sword: Muslim Poetic Responses to the Crusades* (Leiden: Brill, 2017), 86.

39 Ibn Jubayr, *Riḥla*, ed. William Wright (Leiden: Brill, 1907), 124–27, 167–96.

40 See Carla Klausner, *The Seljuk Vezirate: A Study of Civil Administration, 1055–1194* (Cambridge, MA: Center for Middle Eastern Studies of Harvard University, 1973), 67–68, 73.

His material support for poets earned him a special place in Khāqānī's narrative. While Jamāl al-Dīn was but one of the many patrons eulogized in Khāqānī's *Gift*, he is praised at greatest length and most frequently. Khāqānī makes Jamāl al-Dīn's legendary generosity into a metaphor for the ideal poet–patron relation.

Instructing the Sovereign

Having followed Persian adaptations of the *riḥla* through narrative form, the remainder of this chapter shifts towards a more lyric-epic mode in order to consider how the Persian transformation of the *riḥla* generated a critique of sovereignty among Persian poets such as Khāqānī. In particular, I focus on a poem known as "Īwān-i Madā'in," due to its being set near the ancient, pre-Islamic, site known in Arabic sources as al-Madā'in ("the two cities") and which lay between the ancient royal centres of Ctesiphon and Seleucia. By the time of Khāqānī's sojourn to Iraq, and indeed in a figurative sense since the beginning of Islam, al-Madā'in had become a ruin and ceased to command its former regal glory. Whereas *The Gift from Two Iraqs* straddled the dual identity of Persian and Arab Iraq, the Madā'in qaṣīda encompassed a similarly multifarious geography of Persian kings and their Muslim conquerors.

Khāqānī conceived the Madā'in qaṣīda during his return from the *ḥajj*, on his way to Shirwān, during the same years that *Gift* was composed. The poem traverses a geography similar to that of the *Gift*, but unlike this lengthier text, the journey in this lyrical poem (technically not a lyric *ghazal*, but rather a *qaṣīda*) is undertaken in the poet's own name, and the speaker is the traveller who directly observes what is described. No sun serves as cosmic mediator or as allegorical trope. The voice of the poet is emphatically in the first person mode. With respect to the relation between the literary imagination and the world it references, this poem approximates more closely to the traditional understanding of travel literature than does *Gift*, in that a journey undertaken by the poet unambiguously founds the poem. The narrative of this poem, which describes the poet wandering amid sovereign ruins, offers a biographical, documentary counterpart to the imaginary journey performed by the sun in *Gift*. Also in sharp contrast to *Gift*, this poem, although technically belonging to genre of the Islamic ode, is more an anti-panegyric than a panegyric, and more inclined to question than to praise sovereign power.

For these reasons, the Madā'in qaṣīda is central to the Persian transformation of the *riḥla* tradition, particularly through its influential evocation of Sasanian ruins in an era of declining Saljuq sovereignty. Khāqānī's anti-panegyric *qaṣīda* also elucidates the intertextual relation between the poetry of exile, to which Nāṣir Khusrow contributed substantially, and the literature of imprisonment that was Khāqānī's greatest contribution to Persian literature.[41] That the convergence between the poetry of exile and the literature of imprisonment took place in a text that played a role in transforming, the *riḥla* tradition attests to the productivity of the literary imagination in Persian literary culture.

---

41 For further on the conjuncture between the literature of exile and imprisonment, see Aḥmad Reḍā Sayyādī and ʿAlī Reḍā Nūrī, "Gham-i ghurbat dar ashʿar-i Nāṣir Khusrow, Sanāʾī o Khāqānī," *Majalle-i Keyhāneh Farhangī* 468 (1387/2008–2009): 46–51.

The most important figure in the literary critique of sovereignty in the classical Persian tradition is Khāqānī.[42] Following on the exilic poetry of Nāṣir Khusrow that was in turn inspired by the practice of travel, the poet who nourished himself on the dust (khāk) and oppression (ẓulm) of Shirwān made of prison a metonym for the poet's vocation. Just as he dwelled on the poetic possibilities of a signless Ka'ba, the sky arching over Khāqānī's head could neither absorb nor address the poet's demand for cogent speech, so too were the Saljūqs and their minions deaf to poets who demanded justice. Khāqānī's silent sky captures the paradoxes of twelfth-century Islamic sovereignty. From the tension between the sultanate's discretionary power and the poet's vocation arose a literary voice that argued for poetry's sovereignty by revealing the precarious foundations of the king's sovereign power.

A few words are in order about the historical site that gave rise to Khāqānī's poem on Madā'in. Built during the reign of Khusrow Nushīrwān (r. 531–579), the Īwān (palace) of Ctesiphon, a mud brick vault "thirty-five meters high covering an audience hall eleven hundred square meters in area" is still regarded as a "crowning achievement of ancient architecture."[43] Still standing, albeit in ruins, the original parameters of this palace complex are known primarily through the recollections of poets and other travellers who made their way to Baghdad's environs. Among eighteenth century Persephone travellers, such as the Qajar migrant to India Mīr 'Abd al-Laṭīf Khan Shūshtarī, the encounter with Sasanian ruins was often mediated by Khāqānī's poem.[44]

Madā'in, the Arabic word by which Ctesiphon is known, is the dual plural form of the word for city (madīna). Madā'in refers to the two Sāsānian cities on the banks of the Tigris: Ctesiphon and Seleucia. Together, these cities constituted a bishopric of the Nestorian Church. Ctesiphon itself dates back to the Arsacid dynasty (247 BCE–228 CE), during which period it became the major administrative centre in Semitic Mesopotamia.[45] Edward Gibbon considered Ctesiphon the rightful successor to Babylon as "one of the great capitals of the East."[46] Although the famed Sasanian ruler Nushīrwān did not found Ctesiphon, the city with which he is associated through his palace, he did augment the city architecturally, most notably by infusing it with the iconology of royal sovereignty. This architectural transformation in turn set the stage for the city's

---

42 Karamī, "Nagāhī be maḍāmīn-i Musawī o zībāīhāyī ān dar dīwān-i Khāqānī," 182, connects the poet's new design (ṭarḥī nū) to his appropriation of sovereign metonyms.

43 Scott John McDonough, "Power by Negotiation: Institutional Reform in the Fifth Century Sasanian Empire" (PhD dissertation, University of California Los Angeles, 2005), 3.

44 Mīr 'Abd al-Laṭīf Khan Shūshtarī, Tuḥfah al-'ālam va zayl al-tuḥfa [ca. 1799], ed. S. Muvaḥid (Tehran: Ṭahūrī, 1984), 76–81. For Shūshtarī and other Qajar-era travellers, see Abbas Amanat, "Through the Persian Eye: Anglophilia and Anglophobia in Modern Iranian History," Iran Facing Others: Identity Boundaries in a Historical Perspective, ed. Abbas Amanat and Farzin Vejdani (New York: Palgrave, 2011), 136–37, and Mana Kia, "Contours of Persianate Community, 1722–1835" (PhD dissertation, Harvard University, 2011), 132.

45 V. Minorsky, "Geographical Factors in Persian Art," BSOAS 9 (1938): 624.

46 Edward Gibbon, The History of the Decline and Fall of the Roman Empire (Philadelphia: B. F. French, 1830), 4:78.

Figure 1.1. Depiction of Madā'in-Ctesiphon in *Aiwān-i Madā'in, Iranschähr*, 41.

post-Sasanian appropriation as Madā'in, the preeminent symbol of regal glory from a pre-Islamic civilization.

One particularly striking evocation of these ruins occurs in a book-length collection of poems and reflections on Khāqānī's text published in 1924 by the Berlin-based journal *Iranshahr* (Figure 1.1). Partially translating Reḍa Tawfīq's 1912 Turkish-language edition of Khāqānī's Madā'in qaṣīda, this publication uses lines from the text as envois to new poetic creations. The unsigned editorial preface also not incidentally inaugurates the nationalist reading of the Madā'in qaṣīda that was to frame many subsequent renderings of Khāqānī's poem by locating the text within a long genealogy of appeals to Sasanian regal glory as against the Arab invaders. According to this modern reading, Khāqānī is among those poets who, like Ferdowsī, stands among the ruins (*dar jolū-yi kharābeh'hāyi*) that frame his poetry and gazes with tearful eyes at the little that has remained (*bāqī mondeh*) from the days of Iran's glory (*sar bolandi-yi īrān*).[47] While the readings on the pages of *Iranshahr* yield new poetic reflections concerning the inevitable demise of nation-states suited to a modern age, particularly in the aftermath of World War I, even in the hands of modern Iran's most visionary critics, the proto-nationalist reading that has dominated the text's recent reception has done little to elucidate its contribution to the Persian critique of sovereignty.

---

47 *Aiwān-i Madā'in: tasdīs-i qaṣīda-i Khāqānī, bi qalam-i chand nafar az fuḍalā' wa shu'arā'-i Īrān=Aïwan-i-Medâin: un poème de Khâgâni (1606), adapté et augmenté par quelques poêtes contemporains* (Berlin-Wilmersdorf: Iranschähr, 1343). This text includes a translation of Reḍa Tawfīq's Turkish introduction to his translation of Khāqānī's poem, published under the title *Medayin haraberleri* (Istanbul: Cem'i Kütüphanesi, 1912).

More even than as a result of its own glory, poet travellers including al-Buḥturī (d. 897), Omar Khayyām (1048–1131), Maʿrūf al-Raṣāfī (1875–1945), and historian-chroniclers including al-Masʿūdī and al-Ṭabarī inscribed the ruins of Nushīrwān's palace on Islamic cultural memory both before and after Khāqānī set himself to the task.[48] In many respects, Khāqānī's elegy is continuous with its predecessors. Al-Buḥturī anticipated Khāqānī when he glorified the "generals and troops, / as far as the eye can see" in his homage to the Īwān.[49] Although al-Buḥturī had already noted on gazing at the palace and imagining its inhabitants that "It was built up for joy forever, but / their domain is for condolence and consolation now," Khayyām went even further in locating this chain of references within the discourse of what in medieval European literature is referred to as *ubi sunt*, an abbreviation of "ubi sunt qui ante nos in mundo fuere?" (where are those who, before us, existed in the world?), the question the served as a refrain for many poems emphasizing the fleetingness of world existence. Within medieval Europe, *ubi sunt* came to reference a literary genre (or, as I prefer to term it, a discourse) that foregrounded the transience of life as against the permanence of mortality.[50] As a genre that relies, almost by definition, on the poet's encounter with ruins during the course of his journey, *ubi sunt* too merit inclusion in any taxonomy of Persianate critiques of power through the medium of the journey narrative.

A quatrain (*rubāʿī*) by Omar Khayyām in the *ubi sunt* mode plays on the multivalent meanings attached to the name of the king Bahrām Gūr, whose second appellation alluded to his fondness for hunting the onager (*gūr*), a term that also coincides with the Persian word for grave:

آن قصر که بهرام درو جام گرفت
روبه بچه کرد و شیر آرام گرفت
بهرام که گور می‌گرفتی دایم
امروز نگر که گور بهرام گرفت[51]

[The palace where Bahrām raised his cup,
where lions rested and foxes propagated,
and Bahrām, who used so easily to capture prey [*gūr*],
is taken captive by the grave [*gūr*] today.]

---

48 For an overview of Persian and Arabic poets who have composed elegies to Madāʾin, see Sayyid Aḥmad Pārsā, "Derangī bar Īwān-i Madāʾin-i Khāqānī," *Majallah-yi Dānishkada-yi Adabīyāt-i Tehrān* 41/54–5 (2006–2007/1385): 5–18. For comparisons of Buḥturī and Khāqānī's poems on Madāʾin, see Amīr Maḥmūd Anvār, *Aiwān-i Madāʾin* (Tehrān: Dānishgāh-i Tehrān, 1383/2004) and Jerome W. Clinton, "The *Madāʾen Qaṣida* of Xāqāni Sharvāni, II: Xāqāni and al-Buḥturī," *Edebiyât* 2 (1977): 191–206.

49 *Dīwān al-Buḥturī*, ed. Ḥasan Kāmil Ṣayrafī (Cairo: Dār al-Maʿārif, 1963), 2:1152–62. On al-Buḥturī's sympathetic representation of the Sāsānians, see Samer M. Ali, "Reinterpreting Al-Buḥturī's Īwān Kisrā Ode," *Journal of Arabic Literature* 37 (2006): 58.

50 The *ubi sunt* was a fertile ground of reflection in medieval Persian and Arabic literary culture as well as in the Latinate world. For the Arabic *ubi sunt*, see Carl Becker, "*Ubi sunt qui ante nos in mundo fuere*," in *Aufsätze zur Kultur- und Sprachgeschichte vornehmlich des Orients* (Breslau: Marcus, 1916), 87–105, and Ibrahim al-Sinjilawi, "The Lament for Fallen Cities" (PhD dissertation, University of Chicago, 1983). For *ubi sunt* in European literature, see Mary Ellen Becker, "The Ubi Sunt: Form, Theme, and Tradition" (PhD dissertation, Arizona State University, 1981).

51 *Tarānehayi Khayyām*, ed. Ṣādeq Hedāyat (Tehrān: Jāvīdān, 1352), 71, *rubāʿī* 74.

In the poet's present, the palace [*qaṣr*] where Bahrām raised his sceptre [*jām*], or more precisely his cup, the Iranian symbol of sovereignty, has now become a grave for the much-revered king. Khayyām's *ubi sunt* extends across three temporalities: first, the temporality of Bahrām's reign, when the Sasanian king excelled in capturing onagers and displaying his sovereign power; second, the intermediate temporality when the palace was reduced to ruins, and became a place of habitation for lions (*shīr*) and of propagation for foxes (*rūbahān*); third, the temporality of the poet who gazes on the past as a traveller gazes on a foreign country. This third temporality accomplishes the poet's task by burying the great king Bahrām Gūr, slayer of onagers (*gūr*), now taken captive by a very different kind of *gūr*. Omar Khayyām's *ubi sunt* is but one of many texts in this genre that relies for its meaning on an interplay of homonyms, a poetic device known in Arabo-Persian rhetoric as *jinās* (paronomasia), and which heavily characterizes Khāqānī's poetics generally, and especially his critique of sovereignty. That this mode of verbal opposition occurs in so many *ubi sunt* texts indicates how the discursive world of the *ubi sunt* is premised on a linguistic opposition that is given spatial as well as temporal expression.

Even before poets turned their mind to the task of representing the ruins of Ctesiphon, orators such as the famous Muʿtazilī leader Wāṣil b. ʿAṭāʾ (d. 748) had already engaged with this image to suggest the fleetingness of worldly power. "Where are the kings," asked Wāṣil b. ʿAṭāʾ, "who built Madāʾin?" Typically for the *ubi sunt*, Wāṣil b. ʿAṭāʾ's list of these king's accomplishments contrasts royal sovereignty, which is subject to decay, with the orator's temporality, which is not subject to the decay induced by time:

> And strengthened palaces and fortified gates? [...] And trained purebred horses?
> And possessed all the lands? [...] This world [...] crushed them with its breast, it
> chomped on them with its canines. It gave them in exchange for vast space,
> narrow confines; for might, humility; for life, perishing. They went to reside
> in graves. Maggots ate them. They became such that you see only their
> abodes [*masākanahum*], and you find only their signposts [*maʿalimahum*] [...]
> You do not hear a single sound from them.[52]

The Persian poet Ferdowsī (d. 1025) recycled Wāṣil b. ʿAṭāʾ's oratory of sovereign power's demise in a speech delivered by the Sāsānian king Ardashir (r. 379–383) to the Persian ruling elite:

کجا آن بزرگان با تاج و تخت

کجا آن سواران پیروزبخت

کجا آن خردمند کندآوران

کجا آن سرافراز و جنگی سران

---

52 I cite, with minor modifications, from the translation of Tahera Qutbuddin, "Khutba," in *Classical Arabic Humanities in Their Own Terms*, ed. Beatrice Gruendler and Michael Cooperson (Leiden: Brill, 2008), 267. For the Arabic text, see Aḥmad Zakī Ṣafwat, *Jamharat khuṭab al-ʿarab fī l-ʿuṣūr al-ʿarabiyya al-zāhira* (Beirut: Dar al-Matbuʿat al-ʿArabiyah, 1933), 2:501–3, No. 475.

کجا آن گزیده نیاکان ما

کجا آن دلیران و پاکان ما

همه خاک دارند بالین و خشت

خنک آنک جز تخم نیکی نکشت ⁵³

[Where are the mighty ones with their thrones and crowns?
Where are the horsemen elated with victory?
Where are the wise brave ones?
Where are the proud warriors?
Where are our exalted ancestors?
Where are our valiant servants?
Now their pillow is dust and brick
Lucky he who did not grow but the seed of goodness.]

Ferdowsī's text corresponds precisely to its Latin counterpart in offering a Persian parallel, at the opening of each hemistich, to the *ubi sunt* refrain: "where?" (*kojā*). Ferdowsī deploys anaphora rather than epistrophe, but the effect is the same. From the reflections of Wāṣil b. ʿAṭāʾ to al-Buḥturī to Khayyām and Ferdowsī, one theme is consistently reinforced: the sovereignty of kings, these authors intimate in anticipation of Khāqānī's more forthright declarations, yields to poetry's more permanent sovereignty. The difference between worldly and poetic power is temporally exposed through the discourse of the *ubi sunt*. Spatially it is exposed as the poets gaze on ruins, through the topos of travel. The contrast between worldly and poetic sovereignty leads al-Buḥturī to conclude his poem on Madāʾin by insisting on the equality of races and peoples. "I find myself thereafter in love with noble," states al-Buḥturī, "men of every race [*sinkhin*] and origin [*issī*]" (v. 56). While of course not equivalent to a modern theory of human equality, al-Buḥturī's insistence on the proximity of all peoples to his understanding of greatness constitutes a challenge to the hierarchal discourses on which the prerogative of royal sovereignty is founded, including those that inform Sasanian kingship.

The equalizations inflicted by these poet's *ubi sunt* discourse onto the passage of time through the medium of ruins (as well as spatially through the travel narrative) were fully absorbed in Khāqānī's poem. As the poet who, more than any of his contemporaries, used topoi pertaining to exile and complaint to extend the authority of poetry, Khāqānī also drew on the medieval discourse of *ubi sunt* to contest sovereign power. When Khāqānī set out to compose his *qaṣīda* on the ruins of Nushīrwān's palace in 1156, he had already composed the six prison poems that refashioned his poetic persona within a prophetic lineage and which created the foundation for his understanding of poetry's discursive sovereignty.[54] For Khaqani, poetry vatic utterance had already been infused with sovereignty by the topos of incarceration.

---

53 *Shāhnāma*, ed. Djalal Khaleghi-Motlagh, Mahmoud Omidsalar, and Abū al-Faẓl Khaṭībī (New York: Bibliotheca Persica, 1987–2008), 1504.

54 These poems are included in the appendix to Gould, "The Political Aesthetic."

Khāqānī's Madā'in *qaṣīda* moves wholly within the temporalizing aesthetics of the *ubi sunt*. As Johannes Huizinga argued a century ago, this discourse is inflected by the "ever present theme of death" characteristic of the Middle Ages globally, and pertains well beyond the tradition of any single literature.[55] Yet whereas Huizinga treated the *ubi sunt* as a pan-European phenomenon, there is a case to be made that this discourse was intrinsic to the global Middle Ages, particularly across the Islamic world. Khāqānī pays homage to the temporal contrasts intrinsic to the *ubi sunt* when he asks in v. 13 "What is there to be surprised about [*che ʿajab dārī*]? In the world's garden / the owl follows the nightingale [*bulbul*] just as a lament [*nūḥeh*] follows a sweet song [*alḥān*]." The poet moves beyond the standard emphasis on the fleetingness of worldly power and the eternal cycle of birth and death, anticipating and indeed superseding later poets, when in the second section (vv. 26–35) he turns to ekphrasis, and carries the *riḥla* genre one step further towards the critique of sovereign power. In these verses, the poet evokes a panorama of ruins, on to which is projected a tableau of images from Iran's now distant past.[56]

Khāqānī's poetic discourse differs from other genres of travel literature in that the poet's evocation of the past is not fashioned in response to a royal mandate. There is no patron for this poem: the poet speaks in his own voice. Instead of chronicling the achievements of Sasanian kings, but in keeping with the aesthetics of rebellion that the Madā'in *qaṣīda* seeks to cultivate, Khāqānī exposes the founding violence of royal sovereignty. Here and elsewhere, the conceptual severance of power from glory is one consequence of the Khāqānīan aesthetic mode. The opening hemistich of the Madā'in *qaṣīda* entail a discursive transformation of sovereignty. The lesson (*'ibrat*) Khāqānī instructs the reader to learn from the ruins is the text of his own poem, a mirror (*āyineh*) to the passage of time:

هان ای دل عبرت بین از دیده نظر کن هان
ایوان مدائن را آیینهی عبرت دان [57]

[Behold! O heart willing to take lessons, Take a look!
Know that the ruins of Madā'in are a mirror that gives lessons.]

This distich simultaneously addresses the poet and the regime that limits (and constrains) the poet's vocation. This duality of address is a hallmark of the classical Persian aesthetics, wherein unmitigated calls for revolution would have possessed little cogency, and the most effective political critiques employed a poetics of indirection.

---

55 J. Huizinga, *The Waning of the Middle Ages* (Garden City: Anchor-Doubleday, 1954), 139.

56 As Clinton has noted, most readings of Khāqānī's Madā'in qaṣīda (including that proposed by the editors of *Irānshahr*) end here, causing readers to forget the powerful critique of sovereign power that transpires over the rest of the poem and impoverishing this text's reception history. For a recent example of how the Madā'in qaṣīda is treated in modern Iranian historiography as a proto-nationalist appeal to lost Sasanian glory, see Mehdī Ma'khūzī, *Ātash andar chang* (Tehran: Sukhan, 1388).

57 *Dīvān-i Afżal al-Dīn Badīl ibn 'Alī Najjār Khāqānī Shirvānī* ed. Sajjādī, 358–60. The remaining Persian quotations in this chapter are from this poem.

With his repertoire enriched by his experience of travel, Khāqānī inverted, subverted, parodied and transformed the panegyric genres that structure his *Gift*. Duality of address—whether through apostrophe, *īhām* (simulation in the sense of double entendre), *jinas*, or other forms of allusiveness—is the basic strategy through which such poetry comes to life.

From the hemistich "The earth is drunk. It has drunken deep" (v. 26) onwards, the text's otherworldly temporalizing discourse becomes increasingly inflected by this-worldly critique, which brings it into proximity with the *riḥla* tradition. This poem is less concerned with the fleetingness of time than with the corruptibility of worldly power, yet it uses time as well as space to reinforce this theme. Instead of merely recognizing human mortality, the poet states that the earth is drunk (*mast*) with the blood of Nushīrwān that flows from his son's cup (*kās*). Cups, particularly in Sasanian iconography, are bearers of regal power and not vessels for mortality. The double entendre on *pand* (meaning both advice, and the species of bird known as a kite, translated below as "hawk," given the latter's association with royalty) that follows generates a startling contrast that anticipates the king's eventual fall:

بس پند که بود آنگه بر تاج سرش پیدا

صد پند نوست اکنون در مغز سرش پنهان

So many hawks shined on his crown.
Now much more new counsel is hidden in his brain.

The sovereign power delineated here is fraught with mortality. Nothing will remain, and we know this due to the very position of the speaker, gazing on ruins of what used to be. Sasanian power in Khaqani's rendering breeds death. Khāqānī's pun exposes the entire social order on which medieval kingship is founded.

In v. 30, there is a brief return to the temporalizing *ubi sunt* with the rhetorical question "where have they gone (*kojā raftand*)?" Unusually, the poet answers his rhetorical question. When kings die, their bodies depart, but not to heaven: the earth's belly, the poet says is pregnant (*abestān*) with the flesh of the royal deceased. A series of observations follow that fulfill Walter Benjamin's insight that genres are only realized in the act of their transgression. Whereas Samuel Johnson argued that every new innovation "subverts the rules which the practice of foregoing authors had established," Benjamin went further, pointing out that all major literary works transgress the boundaries of genre. And yet, a text that has transgressed a genre remains accountable to it. "A major work either establishes a genre [*Gattung*] or abolishes it," argued Benjamin. "A perfect work does both."[58] As an exemplar of a range of genres, discourses, and forms (the narrative of mobility and confinement, the *ubi sunt*, and the *qaṣīda*) and as the antithesis of these modes, written after Khāqānī has been freed from prison, the Madā'in qaṣīda fulfills the Benjaminian vision of a work that shapes a genre by violating its norms.

"Giving birth [*zāyīdan*] is difficult," the poet continues, "but sowing seed [*notfeh setadan*] is easy." These words at once transgress the temporalizing focus of the *ubi sunt*,

---

58 Walter Benjamin, *Ursprung des deutschen Trauerspiels*, ed. Rolf Tiedemann (Berlin: Suhrkamp, 2000), 27.

as exemplified by al-Buḥturī, Ferdowsī, and Omar Khayyām, and alter its substance. Suddenly, the poet's subject is less the fleetingness of earthly existence than poetry's perpetual sovereignty. Those who give their bodies to the earth, including the deceased kings Nushīrwān and Hormuz, are performing the imperfect, masculine, labour of sowing seeds that culminates in aborted births, or in death. By contrast with the kings who indiscriminately sow their sperm, Khāqānī aligns the poet's task with the more creative work of giving birth. Rather than feed his body to the earth by lusting after worldly glory, Khāqānī vows with his verse to create sovereignty from poetry. Echoing the medieval discourse of the *ubi sunt*, the qaṣīda's final apostrophe—"How many tyrants' bodies [*tan-i jabbārān*] has the earth eaten so far?" (v. 34)—signals its apotheosis. It also extends poetry's discursive sovereignty, for the cycle that cannibalizes the king's power knows no end. The voracious earth will never be satiated (*sīr nashod*) by human blood.

Whereas other poets deploy the temporalizing discourse of *ubi sunt* to place a cosmic valuation on the fleetingness of worldly power and to suggest that nothing on earth is permanent, Khāqānī offers a counterweight to the emptiness of the worldly sovereign. Pace Clinton, who counts among the most astute readers of this poem to date, Khāqānī is more inspired by poetry's discursive sovereignty than by religious piety. Inaugurating section three (vv. 36–42) with an apostrophe to himself, the poet instructs himself to learn the lesson (*ʿibrat*) of Nushīrwān's court, in the expectation that the balance of power between the poet and his patron awaits imminent reversal. The verse that follows even more explicitly reverses the balance of power between poet and ruler:

امروز گر از سلطان رندی طلبد توشه

فردا ز در رندی توشه طلبد سلطان

Though today the beggar seeks food from the sultan,
tomorrow the sultan will beg from the hungry one.

This prophecy of a new social order in the near future is immediately followed by a verse that draws a decisive link between *Gift* and this *qaṣīda*, composed during the same years. In this verse, Khāqānī provides the name of the text on which he was working at the time, *Tuḥfat al-ʿIraqayn* (Gift from the Two Iraqs), and indicates that it is destined for the court in Shirwān:

گر زاد ره مکه توشهست به هر شهری

تو زاد مداین بر تحفه ز پی شروان

If provisions for Mecca can be taken as a souvenir to every city,
Then take this gift, born in Madāʾin, as a souvenir to Shirwan

This verse signals a remarkable moment of intertextuality, for in this and subsequent verses Khāqānī presents his entire poetic output as a gift (*tuḥfeh*) comparable to the pious offerings that spot the road to Mecca, an Islamic equivalent to Latinate *viaticum*.[59] Does this make the Madāʾin *qaṣīda* is an offering to God? While there is no single answer to that question, it is clear what this poem is not, notwithstanding the qaṣīda's formal status as a panegyric. Khāqānī verses are neither an offering nor an homage; rather they are an admonition (*ʿibrat*) to the sultan to follow the path of justice. In terms of the Persian transformation of the *riḥla*, Khāqānī's comparison is also significant inasmuch as it compares the performance of the *ḥajj* to the writing of poetry. Both the *ḥajj* and the writing of poetry are driven by spiritual values that give these activities an authority that the mere exercise of sovereign power lacks. Hence the Persian transformation of the *riḥla* from an act of piety to an act of rebellion comes full circle in this verse.

Calling his *qaṣīda* a fragment (*qīṭʿeh*), Khāqānī figures himself as a miracle worker:

بنگر که در این قطعه چه سحر همی راند

مهتوک مسیحا دل، دیوانهی عاقل خوان

Observe in this *qīṭʿeh* what magic is performed
by a dead man, with the heart of Christ, a madman with a wise mind.

While other poems by Khāqānī, most notably the Christian qaṣīda, define the political terms of the prison poem through an oppositional aesthetics, the Madāʾin qaṣīda reconfigures space and time to channel the politics of ruins.[60] Like Khāqānī's other works, the Madāʾin qaṣīda sets forth a conception of poetry's sovereignty. Poetry is the court from which the sultan will seek the nourishment (*tūshe*) and counsel of those he is mandated to protect (v. 37–38). The legitimacy of the sultan's sovereignty is contingent on his ability to heed his poets' admonitions. Just as mirrors-for-princes across the medieval world instructed princes to heed the lessons of others in order to maintain their hold on power, here the poet proposes to learn how the poet can emerge triumphant over the worldly sovereign.

The Madāʾin qaṣīda revises elegant tales of kingly glory, including those found in the *Shāhnāma*, to develop an aesthetics that treats poetry, rather than kingship, as the pinnacle of power. Khāqānī was keenly aware of his dependency on patronage networks, and therefore of the pressure to praise the sultan. At the same time, he also perceived that the path to worldly power was paved with hypocrisy at best and bloodshed at worst. The poet's twilight vision of a rapacious earth pregnant with a blood-drenched Sasanian dynastic genealogy initiates a dialectic between worldly power and poetry's sovereignty.

---

59 This reading is not universally attested in all manuscripts, some of which give *tūsha* ("provision"). It is however the variant accepted by Meisami in her important contributions to *Qasida poetry in Islamic Asia and Africa*, ed. Stefan Sperl and Christopher Shackle (Leiden: Brill, 1996), 1:137–82 ("Poetic Microcosms: The Persian Qaṣīda to the End of the Twelfth Century"); 2:162–69, 431–35 (annotated translation of the Madāʾin qaṣīda).

60 For the Christian qaṣīda, Khāqānī's most important prison poem, see Rebecca Gould, "Wearing the Belt of Oppression: Khāqānī's Christian Qaṣīda and the Prison Poetry of Medieval Shirvān," *Journal of Persianate Studies* 9 (2016): 19–44.

Rather than renouncing power, or yielding it to the ruler, the poet appropriates the mantle of sovereignty. Sacralized Persian kingship *and* the sultan's discretionary power are equally challenged by poetry's prophetic utterance.

Al-Buḥturī excused the travesties promulgated at Madā'in by invading Arab armies in 637 CE with reference to the fallibility of human nature. He shed "tears of affection for the cycles of history" with seeking an alternative to this tale of woe.[61] Khāqānī shed no tears. Contrary to the still prevalent nationalist reading of this text, the Madā'in qaṣīda does not weep for the Sasanian kings, the Arab dynasties that followed, or even for the poet's incarcerated self. Building on both the literature of pilgrimage and the poetry of imprisonment, the Madā'in qaṣīda's poetics of ruins offers a uniquely Persian take on the sovereignty of poetic discourse that lurks beneath the façade of worldly power.

---

61 Ali, "Reinterpreting Al-Buḥturī's Īwān Kisrā Ode".

Chapter 2

OBSERVING *ZIYARA* IN TWO MEDIEVAL MUSLIM TRAVEL ACCOUNTS

JANET SORRENTINO

ABSTRACT

Muslim travel literature is rich with observations about worship in the pre-modern era as it took place in mosques, madrasas, shrines, tombs, and other spaces considered holy by devotees; the accounts include records of ritual—whether prayer, posture, or action—offered by believers. In addition to descriptions of *hajj*, one finds accounts by travellers who observed and/or participated in *ziyara*, i.e., visits to tombs and shrines of Muslim saints. The travel writers observed pilgrims who participated in rituals honouring the Prophet's family or Sufi holy men and women. This essay explores the writings of two such travel writers: Ibn Jubayr and Ibn Battuta, sixth/twelfth and eighth/fourteenth centuries, respectively, who paid close attention to religious observances—their own and others—and who did not distinguish sectarian identity in what they observed. The records demonstrate an inter-sectarian devotion to saints, mediated by popular Sufi spirituality, which characterized the middle period.

Keywords: *ziyara*, Ibn Jubayr, Ibn Battuta, *rihla*, al-Qarafa (or 'City of the Dead')

MUSLIM TRAVEL LITERATURE of the medieval and early modern periods is rich with observations about political and economic realities of the pre-modern era, as well as scientific and artistic exchange. The accounts, called *rihla*, also provide precious information about worship spaces in the pre-modern era as it took place in mosques, madrasas, shrines, tombs, and other spaces considered holy by devotees; they furthermore include records of ritual—whether prayer, posture, or action—offered by believers. Modern representations of ritual (worship, liturgy) often portray it as static, popularly illustrated by the monophonic sound of chant in medieval Christian worship and the voice of the *muezzin* in the *adhan*. On the contrary, ritual is dynamic, diverse between regions, and revealing human concerns at their most vulnerable. Moreover, the *shahada* among Muslims, the *shema* among the Jews, and the Nicene Creed for Christians, all possess doctrinal and social significance as well as liturgical. In order to enhance worship while striving to keep it within the limits of doctrinal correctness, believers among all three Abrahamic faiths have created new musical forms, drama, poetry, and public processions. In the political arena, liturgical rituals confirmed the accession of rulers; scholars regularly consult ritual texts for ideas about the nature of kingship and the state.[1] The *rihla* provide first-hand accounts of direct experience with worship and ritual.

There has been growing interest in Muslim sacred places and devotions, in particular *ziyara* or visits to shrines and tombs.[2] Among the recent scholarship, one study in particular examined the place of pilgrimage and worship as evidence of Shiʻi sectarian identity, arguing that particularly in Kufa and Karbala, participation in public ritual, including visits to the shrines of ʻAli ibn Abu Talib and al-Husayn ibn ʻAli demonstrated community identity and sectarian loyalty.[3] Haidar importantly observes how participation in public rituals not only indicated an individual's "communal membership," but also that such participation was a better indicator of sectarian identity than theological orthodoxy.[4] Still, through a close reading of the *rihlas* of the twelfth and fourteenth centuries, one finds a class of travellers who observed and/or participated in *ziyaras* with little concern over the strict sectarian identity among the pilgrims they observed, whether those pilgrims participated in rituals honouring Shiʻite imams or Sufi holy men. Instead, the records demonstrate an inter-sectarian devotion to saints, mediated by popular Sufi spirituality, which characterized the middle period.

This essay explores the writings of two such travel writers: Ibn Jubayr and Ibn Battuta, sixth/twelfth and eighth/fourteenth centuries respectively, who paid close attention to religious observances—their own and others—and who did not distinguish or disparage sectarian identity in what they observed.[5] Their observations and attitudes,

---

1 On the use of liturgical texts and coronations, see Ernst H. Kantorowicz, *The King's Two Bodies: A Study in Mediaeval Political Theology,* 2nd ed. (Princeton: Princeton University Press, 1985). There are a number of works devoted to Turkish imperial circumcision festivals and ceremonies. See Derin Terzioglu, "The Imperial Circumcision Festival of 1582: An Interpretation," *Muqarnas* 12 (1990): 84–100; Dana Sajdi, ed., *Ottoman Tulips, Ottoman Coffee: Leisure and Lifestyle in the Eighteenth Century* (London: I. B. Tauris, 2014), 94–95. See also Carl W. Ernst, *Eternal Gardens, Mysticism, History, and Politics at a South Asian Sufi Center* (Minneapolis: Lerner 2003), 203.

2 Excellent treatments of the topic can be read in Amikam Elad, *Medieval Jerusalem and Islamic Worship: Holy Places, Ceremonies, Pilgrimage* (Leiden: Brill, 1995); Josef W. Meri, *The Cult of Saints among Muslims and Jews in Medieval Syria* (Oxford: Oxford University Press, 2002); Christopher S. Taylor, *In the Vicinity of the Righteous: Ziyara and the Veneration of Muslim Saints in Late Medieval Egypt* (Leiden: Brill, 1999). For a comprehensive and intelligent study of the urban settings in which early Muslims worshipped, see Paul Wheatley, *The Places Where Men Pray Together: Cities in Islamic Lands, Seventh through the Tenth Centuries* (Chicago: University of Chicago Press, 2001).

3 Najam Haider, "Prayer, Mosque, and Pilgrimage: Mapping Shiʻi Sectarian Identity in 2nd/8th-Century Kufa," *Islamic Law and Society* 16 (2009), 151–74.

4 Haidar, "Shiʻi Sectarian Identity," 154–5.

5 One must say "generally" because travel writers borrowed from one another. Ibn Battuta's travel account, for example, dictated after his travels, included portions of Ibn Jubayr's account. Moreover, even among his early readers, there was some doubt about how much of his account dealing with

derived in general from direct experience, open a window to the broader Islamicate religious culture of the post-classical period.[6]

Why did they travel and why did they pay attention to ritual and worship? They had their personal reasons owing to their individual circumstances, as will be shown below, yet these united with an intellectual and spiritual climate which encouraged travel for knowledge. One Muslim tradition bids believers to seek knowledge 'even as far as China,' that is, to seek knowledge even in pagan lands through travel.[7] Although this particular hadith is classed as fair and by some as possibly fabricated, the principle—that God encourages believers to seek knowledge—can be found in the Qur'an and in much stronger traditions.[8] *Talab al-ʿilm*, travel for the sake of gaining religious knowledge, reflects this ethos. Like Ibn Jubayr and Ibn Battuta, the voyagers who left written accounts usually possessed some elevated social standing—a *qadi*, cleric, or court officer, for instance—and they undertook their travels for a variety of reasons, but their accounts, or *rihla*, reflected this deeper spiritual purpose, an intention to observe and consider all aspects of the world as a part of their obedience to God. Scholar-travellers recorded discussions with believers from diverse faiths and backgrounds, a kind of intellectual and spiritual investigation—done as part of their belief that knowledge, especially religious knowledge, is one of the privileges that God has given to humanity. The *rihla* or travel account, therefore, constituted a type of scholarship and a shared literary culture across the multiplicity of Muslim states throughout the middle period.

Travel, knowledge, and ritual acts of devotion and piety bear an intimate connection in the Islamic tradition, and that connection is expressed in the language and in the literature. *Hijra* evokes literally departure, emigration, abandonment, or renunciation. In early Muslim history, several events harnessed the term *hijra* and similar terms deriving from the same root, giving them meaning for Muslim community and worship. For example, in the early period of Muhammad's prophetic ministry, many converts, particularly converted slaves who had been persecuted by Muhammad's opponents in Mecca, including women and children, migrated to Abyssinia during 615–622 CE where the Christian Abyssinian king offered them refuge.[9] Most important in this context was

---

China was drawn from personal experience. He also borrowed from Muhammad al-Abdari al-Hihi, a thirteenth-century Moroccan *qadi* and *haji*. On these points, see Ross Dunn, *The Adventures of Ibn Battuta, A Muslim Traveler of the Fourteenth Century* (Berkeley: University of California Press, 1986), 63–64 and 313–14; and Tabish Khair et al., eds. *Other Routes: 1500 Years of African and Asian Travel Writing* (Bloomington: Indiana University Press, 2005), 290.

6 Marshall Hodgson, *The Venture of Islam: Conscience and History in a World Civilization*, vol. 2. (Chicago: University of Chicago Press, 1974), 220–21, 255.

7 Although in hadith scholarship, this particular tradition is classed among the weaker, the principle of the value of seeking knowledge is affirmed in the Qur'an and in the practice of *talab al-ʿilm*.

8 "Are those who know equal to those who know not?" Qur'an 39:39. A hadith also addresses the issue. "Abu Huraira reported Allah's Messenger—may God's peace be upon him—as saying, 'and he who treads the path in search of knowledge, Allah would make that path easy, leading to Paradise.'" Muslim ibn al Hajjaj al-Naysaburi, *Sahih Muslim* 2699a, trans. Abdul Hamid Siddiqui. https://sunnah.com.

9 Hodgson, *Venture of Islam,* 1:170–71.

the migration of the Prophet with early companions to Medina 622 CE.[10] The obligation to migrate, to break ties, and reject (the local Meccan idolatry) was profound, and
formative for the emerging *umma*.[11] Muhammad connected worship with the obligation to migrate from unbelief to belief, from doing what was forbidden to doing good
by establishing the *ḥajj* as one of the central ritual acts of believers to be performed
once if at all possible. Furthermore, the pilgrimage ritual itself encompasses more than
a singular visit to Mecca and to the central sanctuary of the Ka'bah. It includes, rather,
multiple migrations, i.e., visits to several locations which hold historical significance in
the Qur'anic revelation, and so an itinerary of visits occur throughout the observance of
the larger pilgrimage.[12] Thus to migrate, to travel, implied an obligation to physically and
spiritually move consonant with Muslim religious ethos in society, and become part of
the new community.[13] Seeking knowledge (*talab al-'ilm*) through travel was therefore an
honourable enterprise and a source of blessing (*baraka*), leading to the expectation that
God would aid the seeker in the way to heaven.[14]

The rulers of Muslim states competed with one another to attract such scholar-
travellers. Furthermore, the contact between the travellers and the regions, mediated
by the courts they visited, served to strengthen common Muslim culture as well as to
highlight local diversity. Gellens called this phenomenon a "shifting hierarchy of learning
centers" where political and economic fortunes could make them more or less attractive
to travellers.[15]

There was good reason, therefore, for the voyagers to record their journeys in travel
accounts known as *rihla*. Scholars have identified essentially three kinds: *rihla* (simple)
within one's own region or state; *rihla hijaziyya*, a journey taken primarily to make the
ḥajj but which could incorporate also travel beyond the *ḥajj*; and *rihla sifariyya* in which
a writer reports on travels to foreign lands. Among the latter group, the journey could
be undertaken as an embassy, a mission, or diplomatic commission. These same travel
writers might also perform a pilgrimage during their journey, combining several types.[16]

---

10 Hodgson, *Venture of Islam*, 1:171–72.

11 See Muhammad Khalid Masud, "The Obligation to Migrate: The Doctrine of *hijra* in Islamic Law,"
in *Muslim Travellers: Pilgrimage, Migration and the Religious Imagination*, ed. Dale F. Eickelman and
James Piscatori (Berkeley: University of California Press, 1990), 29–49, at 30–32.

12 The itinerary includes, for example, circumambulation of the Ka'bah, running between the hills
Safa and Marwah, travel to and encampment in the Plain of Mina, the Plain of Arafat, and a return
to Mecca.

13 Masud, "The Obligation to Migrate," 31. One must remember that the *Hijra* of Muhammad is
considered unique and fundamental to the establishment of the *umma*. "The Prophet said, 'There
is no migration after the Conquest of Mecca, but I will take his pledge of allegiance for Islam.' "
Muhammad al-Bukhari, *Sahih al-Bukhari* 3078–79, trans. M. Muhsin Khan.

14 Gellens, "The Search for Knowledge in Medieval Muslim Societies: A Comparative Approach," in
Eickelman, *Muslim Travellers*, 50–65, at 53–55.

15 Gellens, "Search for Knowledge," 55.

16 Abd-er-Rahman El Moudden, "The Ambivalence of *rihla*: Community Integration and Self-
Definition in Moroccan Travel Accounts, 1300–1800," in Eickelman, *Muslim Travellers*, 69–84 at 70;

The style of a *rihla* as a text will fit within a broad range among other travel accounts. Some authors wrote them nearly like daily travel logs or journals, with records of notes and observations taken while still travelling. Others, like that of Ibn Battuta, are composed as literature.[17] By the sixth AH/twelfth century CE, the association of *rihla* and *hajj* converged, with *rihla* as a record of *hajj* such as in the cases of the travels of Ibn Battuta and Ibn Jubayr, and *talab al-ʿilm* remained a journey for the sake of acquiring religious knowledge. The *rihla* provide a record of the activities and observations made by a Muslim traveller as part of his obedience to God to acquire—and pass on—knowledge, both religious and secular. Gellens points out the convergence may reflect the reality that many of the isolated spaces where holy saints had dwelled had become formal shrines, *khanqahs*, or colleges (*madrasas*) with institutional character, or sometimes sacred spaces where a saint had lived and prayed.[18]

These writers of the *rihla* noticed and described formal, architectural monuments such as mosques, churches, tombs, and monumental shrines. They also noticed spaces where dwelled holy men and the communities of disciples who followed them. Ultimately, the descriptions of ritual—whether spaces or actions or prayers—demonstrate an understanding of worship that is of necessity expressed in the labour of the praying believer in posture, words, and obedient attendance, in the praise and appreciation for the art—broadly understood to include architecture, furnishings, colour, music and poetry, etc.—created to honour God, and in the reverent and intentional articulation of holy words from the Qur'an. Therefore, even as the travel writer rehearsed in words descriptions of ritual spaces and actions, he was thereby giving a form of praise. This is demonstrated by the fact that those passages end with a thanksgiving for the experience. Indeed, one aspect of worship includes rehearsing and reiterating the excellencies of God and the response of the believer to those excellencies.

This perspective of worship as the expression of the total being in response to the observed and manifested greatness and goodness of God informed the experience and written record of the Muslim travel writers. For most, it is an unanalyzed predisposition to focus on things religious; for others, for example al-Biruni, the concept of worship within the totality of the Muslim obedience was analyzed and articulated.[19] Nevertheless, Ibn Jubayr and Ibn Battuta demonstrated an intense interest in the rituals they observed and identified themselves with the piety reflected therein. Both travellers left a *rihla*, or travel account, of their journeys, and both participated not only in the *hajj* but in a number of other devotional activities, and in the case of Ibn Jubayr, he visited Shiʿite

---

the tripartite definition from Muhammad al-Manuni, *Al-Masadir al-ʿArabiyya li-Tar'ikh al-Maghrib* (Rabat: Mohammad V University, 1983), 186–92.

17 Dunn, *Adventures of Ibn Battuta*, 253.

18 Gellens, "Search for Knowledge," 53.

19 Al-Ghazzali, *The Mysteries of Worship in Islam*, trans. from *Book of the Ihya*, Edwin Elliot Calverley (Lahore: Sh. Muhammad Ashraf, 1925; repr. 1977); Al-Biruni, *The Chronology of Ancient Nations, an English Version of the Arabic Text of the Athár-ul-Bákiya of al-Biruni or Vestiges of the Past, A.H. 390–1, A.D. 1000*, ed. and trans. C. Edward Sachau (London, 1879; repr. Frankfurt: Minerva, 1969).

shrines in the newly conquered Ayyubid sultanate of Salah ad-Din (Saladin), a champion of Sunni orthodoxy. Their accounts provide information about actual ritual practices and their attitudes about the devotional acts they observed.

Among the rituals they observed were the *ziyara*, visits made by pilgrims to tombs of prophets, including the tombs of Abraham and the Prophet Muhammad.[20] The *ahl al-Bayt*, the family of the Prophet, attracted devotees; the tombs of `Ali ibn Abu Talib, and his sons Hasan and Husayn, the latter and his family and supporters, as the victims and martyrs of the Ummayad massacre at Karbala. Pilgrims, moreover, made *ziyara* to the tombs of revered Sufi masters. By the time Ibn Jubayr and Ibn Battuta travelled, the multiplication of monuments and spaces associated with Sufi *tariqahs* made it possible for medieval Muslims throughout *dar al-Islam*—the poor and uneducated as well as the gentlemanly, literary classes—nearly universal, allowing them to, as Shahab Ahmed expressed it, "benefit from the cosmic economy of the Sufi's *barakah* or spiritual power."[21] Hence, a traveller and author of a *rihla* was at once the recipient of blessings from his own enterprise, and also broadcaster about the "cosmic economy of blessings" received by pilgrims making *ziyara*.

The *rihla hijaziyyah* of Abu al-Husayn Muhammad ibn Ahmad Jubayr al-Kinan, author of *Tadhkirat al-akhbar 'an ittifaqat al-asfar* [*Relation of Events that Befell upon Certain Journeys*], is frequently given as *The Travels of Ibn Jubayr*.[22] Ibn Jubayr was an officer in the court of the Almohad dynasty in Ceuta and Granada. After being coerced to drink wine by his lord, he travelled for expiation of his unintentional sin as a pilgrim to Mecca and Medina, AH 578–582/ 1183–1185 CE, including Sardinia, Crete and Cairo in his travels. He returned to Granada, then he travelled twice more: 585–587/1189–1191 and 614/1217. During the final journey, he again travelled to Mecca, and also to Jerusalem, ultimately dying in Alexandria, Egypt. Because he travelled so much by sea, his chronicle is an important source for sea travel, ports, navigation and shipping practices in the Mediterranean in the twelfth century. His travels took him through Ayyubid territory, in particular Egypt and Syria, where he wrote accounts rich in descriptions of urban architecture, including religious monuments and shrines. Ibn Jubayr focused on Muslim sites, but he also gave attention to monuments and shrines which belonged to the era

---

20 The practice of *ziyara* generated a separate genre of literature: manuals written to guide pilgrims in their itineraries to and through holy sites. The guidebooks instructed the pilgrims about recommended prayers and postures, about the sacred biographies of the holy men and women whose tombs they visited, and what blessings to expect. Aliaa Ezzeldin Ismail El Sandouby, "The *Ahl al-Bayt* in Cairo and Damascus: the Dynamics of Making Shrines for the Family of the Prophet," PhD dissertation, University of California-Los Angeles, 2008, 22.

21 Shahab Ahmed, *What is Islam? The Importance of Being Islamic* (Princeton: Princeton University Press, 2016), 78.

22 Ibn Jubayr, *The Travels of Ibn Jubayr from a MS in the University Library of Leyden*, ed. William Wright (Leyden, 1852); rev. ed. M. J. de Goeje (Leiden: Brill, 1907; Ibn Jubayr, *The Travels of Ibn Jubayr*, trans. R. J. C. Broadhurst (London: Jonathan Cape, 1952). Excerpts can also be found in *Voyageurs Arabes: Ibn Fadlan, Ibn Jubayr, Ibn Battuta et un auteur anonyme*, trans. Paule Charles-Dominique, 1995. Though the term *rihla* does not occur in Ibn Jubayr's title, his account is normally discussed as such in scholarship.

before Muslim conquest of Egypt. Although he always extolled the superiority of Muslim sacred art and architecture, and the creative power of God in nature, he nevertheless expressed his wonder and admiration for the local natural landscape and secular art.[23] After he left Ayyubid territory, he travelled through the Latin Crusader states, including Acre, Sicily, Messina. He wrote significant descriptions of the kingdoms in those territories, and about how Muslims fared in crusader territories.[24]

Even though his pilgrimage to Mecca remained his primary goal, Ibn Jubayr participated in and observed *ziyara* and, like other pilgrims, sought blessings by visiting the shrines of revered members of the Prophet's family—women as well as men—imams, and early companions. The presence of so many tombs in Egypt which belonged to members of the Prophet's family encouraged pilgrimages as part of his full itinerary. For Ibn Jubayr, his *ḥajj* represented a significant period of time when he put aside his courtly career to devote himself to God, and to rehearse the history of God's favour upon believers; consequently, visits to shrines became part of this longer itinerary.

Few territories offered as much opportunity to remember the saints of the Prophet's family in as condensed an area as al-Qarafa in Egypt. The so-called 'City of the Dead' contained mausoleums for al-Husayn, Sayyida Zaynab, Sayyida Nafisa, and imam al-Shafiʿi, among many others.[25] Multiple stages of construction exist at al-Qarafa, beginning as early as the garrison city of al-Fustat, originally divided into sectors, with a living population and cemeteries in close proximity. First the governor Ahmad ibn Tulun built an aquaduct to allow greater expansion; the Fatimids in the tenth and eleventh centuries CE initiated a third great period of construction with secular and religious monuments as well as more aquaducts. Under the Ayyubids, construction continued, especially toward the north, bounded by the Citadel, and another stage of construction under the Mamluk regime, especially sponsored by al-Nasir Muhammad ibn Qalaywun (1309–1340) who turned a stadium into an expansion of cemetery space. Within this ongoing construction of mausoleums, living populations shared space with the dead, as well as with *khanqahs*, *madrasas*, mosques, palaces, and streets.[26]

Ibn Jubayr's stay in Cairo took place in the month of Dhu al-Hijjah, AH 578 (March 28–April 25, 1183 CE).[27] During his time there, he visited the tomb of the head of Husayn ibn ʿAli and recorded what he saw among the other pilgrims who visited the shrine.

---

23 See F. Gabriel, *La literatura árabe* (Buenos Aires: Editorial Losada, 1971), 216. Cf. Carmen Carriazo Rubio, "La Visión del Antiguo Egipto en la *Rihla* de Ibn Yubayr," *Philologia Hispalensis* 14 (2000): 157–66, at 158.

24 Yehoshua Frenkel, "Ibn Jubayr," *Literature of Travel and Exploration: an Encyclopedia*, ed. Jennifer Speake, vol. 2. (New York: Fitzroy Dearborn, 2003), 580–81.

25 Galila El Kadi and Alain Bonnamy, *Architecture for the Dead: Cairo's Medieval Necropolis* (Cairo: American University in Cairo Press, 2007), 297–98.

26 El Kadi and Bonnamy, *Architecture for the Dead*, 297–99; See also Christopher S. Taylor, *In the Vicinity of the Righteous: Ziyara and the Veneration of Muslim Saints in Late Medieval Egypt* (Leiden: Brill, 1999).

27 Broadhurst, *Travels*, 31. In his translation, Broadhurst substitutes 'l for the article *al*; in the quotations here included, I have retained his transliteration, but in the main essay, I have not.

We shall begin by mentioning the monuments and blessed shrines, which for their beneficence are preserved by Great and Glorious God. Of such is the great tomb in Cairo in which is kept the head of Husayn, the son of 'Ali ibn Abi Talib, may God hold them in favour. It is in a silver casket and over it has been built a mausoleum so superb as to be beyond description and beyond the powers of the mind to comprehend. It is covered with various kinds of brocades, and surrounded by white candles that are like large columns; smaller ones are placed for the most part, in candlesticks of pure silver and of gilt. Silver lamps are hung from it and its whole upper part is encircled with golden spheres like apples, skillfully executed to resemble a garden and holding our eyes in spell by its beauty. There too are various kinds of marble tessellated with coloured mosaics of rare and exquisite workmanship such as one cannot imagine nor come near to describing. The entrance to this garden is by a mosque like to it in grace and elegance, with walls that are all marble in the style we have just described. To the right and left of the mausoleum are two chambers of exactly the same style and both leading into it. A brocade covering of exquisite workmanship is hung over all.

We observed men kissing the blessed tomb, surrounding it, throwing themselves upon it. Smoothing with their hands the *kiswah* (drape) that was over it, moving round it in a surging throng, calling out invocations, weeping and entreating Glorious God to bless the hallowed dust, and offering up humble supplications such as would melt the heart and split the hardest flint."[28]

In the passage quoted above, Ibn Jubayr extolls the excellence of the space and the providence of God connected to it and then showed pilgrims showering it with their warm response of reverence and affection. The same pattern appeared when Ibn Jubayr recounted his visit to the tomb of the Prophet, which took place in the month of Dhu al-Qa'dah, AH 579 (February 15–March 15, CE 1184).

On Monday the 13th of the month we entered the birthplace of the Prophet—may God bless and preserve him. It is now a superbly built mosque, and had been the house of 'Abdullah ibn 'Abd al-Muttalib, the father of the Prophet-may God bless and preserve him—of which we have already spoken. The actual spot of his nativity has the likeness of a small basin in the floor, three spans wide, with in its centre a green marble tablet, two-thirds of a span wide, and encircled by silver so that with this attached silver its width is one span.

We smoothed our cheeks on this holy spot which was the place of delivery for the most illustrious child in the world, and which was touched by the purest and most noble of offspring—may God bless and preserve him, and advantage us with the blessings of visiting the place of his birth.[29]

---

28 Broadhurst, *Travels*, 36–37.

29 Broadhurst, *Travels*, 166–67.

Another key component in the travel writing of Ibn Jubayr, a characteristic even more clearly present in the writing of al-Biruni, is the connection between time, the created cosmos, and worship.[30] Each section of his *rihla* begins with a short description of the appearance of the new moon which signals the beginning of the month, and often includes also a rationale or purpose of that month. The appearance of the new moon needed to be witnessed, and for liturgical activities to commence, its appearance needed to be authenticated by a person of stature. Ibn Jubayr had travelled first and foremost to participate in the *hajj*, for him the culminating experience of his travels, so when a discrepancy arose in the sighting of the new moon and the commencement of his pilgrimage, he recorded what he observed.

For the Month of Dhu 'l-Qa'dah, AH 579

The new moon of this month rose on the night of Wednesday, corresponding with the 14th of February, and the testimony of its observation was proved before the Qadi. The greater part of the people in the sacred Mosque saw nothing of it, although they stayed there watching until the end of the sunset prayers. There were those among them who imagined that they observed it and who pointed towards it, but when their claim was examined, the vision disappeared and their information was proved false. God best knows the truth of the matter. This blessed month is the second of the sacred months and the second of the months of the pilgrimage.[31]

Nevertheless, Ibn Jubayr did not believe that God—or His praise—was ultimately dependent on the calendar and astronomy, for that would place the creator below the creation. In the passage below, he addressed the serious discrepancy over the appearance of the new moon in the very month when the central rituals of the *hajj* should take place.

The Month of Dhu 'l-Hijjah, AH 579

The new moon of this month rose on the night of Thursday, corresponding with the 15th of March. In the watching for it the people were involved in a strange circumstance, and a remarkable fabrication; and a false utterance almost provoked the stones, not to mention else, to rebut and deny it.

[Ibn Jubayr then described at length some confusion about the sighting of the new moon; because it was believed that special blessings attended the pilgrims should the *hajj* begin on a Friday, many insisted they had seen it, and the confusion required intervention.]

On the night of this Friday the new moon appeared during a break in the clouds, clothed in the radiance of the thirtieth night. The crowds then raised

---

30 Al-Biruni, *Vestiges of the Past*, 321–25.

31 Broadhurst, *Travels*, 166.

tremendous shouts and proclaimed that the 'standing (on Mount Arafat) would take place on Friday, crying, "Praise be to God who did not render vain our efforts or bring to naught our proposals," as if it were a truth with them that if the standing did not fall upon a Friday it would not be acceptable to God, nor could God's mercy be hoped for or expected. But God is above that. [32]

Probably the best-known Muslim travel writer among Western readers is Abu Abdallah Muhammad ibn Abdallah ibn Muhammad ibn Ibrahim al-Lawati al-Tanji, also known as Shams al-Din ibn Battuta. Born in Tangier, Morocco, and educated as a *qadi*, he began his journeys in 1325 CE and travelled thereafter for nearly thirty years across three continents. His role as *qadi* gave him a significant place in the various courts he visited. He most particularly wished to visit the court of a Dehli sultan who had a reputation for welcoming scholars and jurists from outside his regime. It was this Muhammad ibn Tughluq who commissioned ibn Battuta as an ambassador to the court of China in 1342. His eastern journeys included the Malabar coast, Maldive Islands, Ceylon, Bengal, Assam, China, Sumatra, and Malaya. After he returned to Tangier in 1348, he travelled to Granada in 1350, and again acted as a diplomat, this time for the sultan of Morocco to Timbuktu in 1352. He returned again to Morocco in 1353, and dictated his *rihla* to ibn Juzayy as *Tuhfat al-Nuzzár fí Ghará'ib al-Amsár wa 'Ajá'ib al-Asfár* [*A Feast for the Eyes Exotic Places and Marvelous Travels*]. He continued as a *qadi* in Morocco until his death, exact time unknown.[33] His account was not widely known, even within the Muslim world, until the early 1800s when extracts were published in German and English based on manuscripts discovered in the Middle East containing abridged versions of Ibn Juzayy's Arabic text. Eventually five manuscripts were uncovered and were brought back to the Bibliothèque Nationale in Paris. In 1853, French scholars Charles Defremery and Beniamino Sanguinetti edited the Arabic text and translated it into French.[34] Additionally, there do exist a couple of extra-*rihla* notices of Ibn Battuta's work. In his foreword, the translator of the modern critical edition of Ibn Battuta's account, H. A. R. Gibb, tells us about several pre-modern writers who mentioned the travel account of Ibn Battuta. The first of these derives from *al-Durar al-Kamina, The Concealed Pearls*, a dictionary of eminent persons compiled in the fifteenth century CE by Ibn Hajar of Ascalon. The fifteenth-century dictionary draws on reports given by two fourteenth-century men who lived contemporary with Ibn Battuta. The first was Ibn al-Khatib, vizier of Granada (fl. 1374), and the second, a scholar named Ibn Marzuq from the Tlemcen region of Algeria who became a *qadi* in Cairo, who also died ca. 1370s.[35]

Like Ibn Jubayr, Ibn Battuta wished to make pilgrimage to Mecca and visit the burial place of the Prophet at Medina, "swayed by an overmastering impulse within me and a

---

32 Broadhurst, *Travels*, 172–73.

33 Mohammad Asfour, "Ibn Battuta," in Speake, *Literature of Travel and Exploration* 2:577–78.

34 Dunn, *Ibn Battuta*, 4–5.

35 Ibn Battuta, *The Travels of Ibn Battuta, A.D. 1325–1354*, trans. with revisions and notes from the Arabic text edited by C. Defrémery and B. R. Sanguinetti (London: Hakluyt Society, 1994), ix–x. It would be a *rihla* of a different kind to track and source the manuscript copies, editions, and extra-*rihla* notices of the travel writers, but no doubt a rewarding one.

desire long-cherished in my bosom to visit these illustrious sanctuaries."[36] His secretary Ibn Juzayy included a preface stating that ibn Battuta was asked to record his travels by their ruler Sultan of Morocco, especially to record what he saw in the cities, memorable events, rules of countries, "distinguished men," and pious saints. His scribe confirmed the final composition contained a plethora of marvellous and curious accounts.[37] Ibn Battuta's own resolve to complete the *hajj* appeared early in the account when he came down with a fever. A companion advised him to delay his travels, to which advice he responded, "If God decrees my death, then my death shall be on the road, with my face set towards the land of the Hijaz."[38]

Like Ibn Jubayr, Ibn Battuta visited mausoleums in al-Qarafa during his time in Egypt. He described what he saw as follows:

> At Old Cairo too is the cemetery called al-Qarafah, a place of vast repute for blessed power, for it is a part of the mount of al-Muqattam, of which God has promised that it shall be one of the gardens of Paradise. These people build in the Qarafah beautiful domed chapels and surround them by walls, so that they look like houses, and they construct chambers in them and hire the services of Qur'an readers, who recited night and day in beautiful voices. There are some of them who build a religious house or a madrasah by the side of the mausoleum. They go out every Thursday evening to spend the night there with their children and womenfolk and make a circuit of the famous sanctuaries. They go out also to spend the night there on the night of the mid-Sha'ban, and the market people take out all kinds of eatables. Among the celebrated sanctuaries in the city of Cairo is the imposing holy shrine where rests the head of al-Husayn ibn `Ali (On both be peace). Beside it is a vast convent, of wonderful workmanship, on the doors of which there are silver rings, and plates also on them of the same metal. This shrine is paid its full meed of respect and veneration.[39]

Ibn Battuta was devoted to learning about Sufism, intellectually and experientially, and therefore participated in the pious custom of visiting renowned holy men in their dwellings to learn from them as a visiting disciple. For example, he related his enthusiasm for the *tariqa* of Abu'l-Hasan al-Shadhili as below:

> Another of the religious at Alexandria was the Shaikh Yaqut al-Habashi (the Ethiopian), a man of outstanding gifts, who had been the pupil of Abu `l-Abbas of Murcia, who in his turn was the pupil of the famous saint Abu al-Hasan al-Shadhili, noted for his great miracles and his high degrees of mystical attainment.

Ibn Battuta continued his story with an account of a miracle related by Yaqut. According to Yaqut, Abu al-Hasan al-Shadhili went on pilgrimage every year, travelling through

---

36 Ibn Battuta, *The Travels of Ibn Battutah*, abridged from H. A. R. Gibb's translation by Tim Mackintosh-Smith (London: Picador, 1958; repr. 2003), 3.

37 Mackintosh-Smith, *Travels of Ibn Battuta*, 1.

38 Mackintosh-Smith, *Travels of Ibn Battuta*, 4.

39 Mackintosh-Smith, *Travels of Ibn Battuta,* 16–17.

upper Egypt, staying in Mecca, fasting, and performing other pious exercises, as well as visiting Muhammad's tomb.

> One year he instructed his servant to bring a pickaxe, a basket, aromatics for embalming and "all that is necessary for burying the dead." The servant asked "Why so, O my master?" and the Shaikh answered, "In Humaithira, you shall see." [...] When they reached Humaithira, the Shaikh Abu al-Hasan made a complete ablution, and said a prayer of two prostrations. At the final prostration in his prayers God (Great and Mighty is He) took him and he was buried there.[40]

Ibn Battuta tells his reader that he visited the tomb of al-Shadhili, and remarked especially how the tombstone inscribed the lineage of the saint tracing back to al-Hasan, the son of 'Ali ibn 'Abu Talib. Here, as with Ibn Jubayr's observations of *ziyara* to the mausoleum containing the head of al-Husayn, one sees the reverence for the family of the prophet, the sanctity of 'Ali and his descendants, but no mention of sectarianism associated with the latter.

Ibn Battuta's spiritual affinity for Sufism and Sufi saints did not just encompass visits to tombs or histories of the dead. He also visited the living and recorded the rituals of the Shadhili *tariqa*. In his *rihla*, Ibn Battuta recorded at great length a prayer recited by the disciples of al-Shadhili. What is quoted below significantly truncates the text of the prayer, which contains many quotations from the Qur'an. It evidently struck Ibn Battuta as important that the text of the prayer had been passed down through the generations to his own day.

> In his [al-Shadhili's] annual journey through Upper Egypt he would cross the sea of Juddah (Red Sea) and recite this litany every day. His disciples still recite it every day. "O God, O Exalted, O Mighty, O Forbearing, O all-knowing, Thou art my Lord and Thy knowledge is my Sufficiency. How excellent a lord is my Lord, how excellent a sufficiency my sufficiency. Thou aidest whom Thou wilt, for Thou art the Powerful, the compassionate. We pray Thee to guard us from sin in our movements and stillnesses, our words and designs, and in the stirring of doubts, of unworthy suggestions and of vain imaginings that veil from our hearts the perception of things unseen."[41]

Ibn Battuta shared with other Muslim travellers the characteristics of a literary class. He was a *qadi*, a member of that class of scholars, *'alim*, learned in the Qur'an, hadith, and law, and therefore a desirable person who would be welcomed in courts of Muslim rulers for administration. In Ibn Battuta's case, he was a scholar of the Maliki *madhhab*. In social class, he was a gentleman, a middle-class, literate, cosmopolitan person to whom travel was a pleasant opportunity to explore the world, and gain knowledge, as well as receive welcome and hospitality and honours, what Dunn calls a "literate frontiersman."[42]

---

40 Mackintosh-Smith, *The Travels of Ibn Battuta*, 9. Al-Shadhili died in 1258 CE.

41 Mackintosh-Smith, *The Travels of Ibn Battuta*, 10–11.

42 Ross E. Dunn, "International Migrations of Literate Muslims in the Later Middle Period: The Case of Ibn Battuta," in *Golden Roads: Migration, Pilgrimage and Travel in Medieval and Modern*

Like Ibn Jubayr, Ibn Battuta showed special reverence for the tomb of the head of al-Husayn, although he mentions the services there only in generalities. His account gives us a better picture of the social importance of the great cemetery where living and dead mixed side by side. Neither Ibn Jubayr nor Ibn Battuta explicitly associated their visit to the shrine of the head of al-Husayn with Shi'i sectarianism. In fact, Ibn Jubayr only used the occasion to praise Salah al-Din's generous contributions for new construction and pious endowments (*awqaf*) to the entire *al-Qarafa* district. Rather, both travel writers demonstrate "tourist *adab*," that is, proper respect, behaviour, and enthusiasm for the opportunity to visit the shrine, observe the rituals, and receive blessings for their participation.[43]

Between the two writers of *rihla* here surveyed, the attention the travellers paid to ritual worship accords well with their purposes of travel. For Ibn Jubayr, the pilgrimage fulfilled his purpose to do penance for his unintentional sin, and we are fortunate that he chose to record so much detail about worship. For Ibn Battuta, he tells the reader he wished most of all to participate in the *hajj*; nevertheless, he travelled also for knowledge, experience, and professional opportunity. His reverence for Sufi saints—living and deceased—shows a longing to enter into a deeper spirituality, one he yearned for, but for which he was not fully suited. Their contributions about religious ritual are uneven, but immensely valuable, as they can be compared to records unearthed by archaeologists, pilgrimage guides, prayer books, and other sources to provide a more comprehensive historical understanding of pre-modern Muslim worship.

In many ways, Ibn Jubayr presents the clearest example of the writer of a *rihla* as a "liturgical person."[44] Netton's analysis of Ibn Jubayr's *rihla* identified a structure he called "a trinity of time, place and purpose as expressed in (a) the author's precise, almost neurotic, use of the Islamic calendar, (b) the travel or *rihla* impulse and associated 'sense of place' which imbues the entire narrative, and (c) the primary orientation towards, or focus on Mecca."[45] Furthermore, he rightly noted how Ibn Jubayr's constant use of the Islamic calendar as his principle of organization, and his exuberant admiration for much of what he sees, makes his narrative more plodding than Ibn Battuta's.[46] If, however, one looks at Ibn Jubayr's work through the lens of the writer as a liturgical person, some of the more redundant or effusive aspects of his writing—while no less irritating at times—signify a different purpose, and seem to do so successfully.

In most instances, Ibn Jubayr's record of a liturgical event includes a description of the ritual space, its workmanship when relevant, or God's creation of the space when it is not the result of the art of humans, furnishings, and so forth. The record then presents

Islam, ed. Ian Richard Netton (Richmond: Curzon Press, 1993); also Netton, *The Adventures of Ibn Battuta*, 11.

43 Ian Richard Netton, *Seek Knowledge: Thought and Travel in the House of Islam* (London: Routledge Curzon, 1996), 145–54.

44 For this expression, see Richard W. Pfaff, "St Hugh as a Liturgical Person," in *De Cella in Saeculum*, ed. M. G. Sargent (Woodbridge: Brewer, 1989), 17–27.

45 Ian Richard Netton, "Basic Structures and Signs of Alienation in the *Rihla* of Ibn Jubayr," in *Seek Knowledge*, 127–44, at 128–29.

46 Netton, "Basic Structures," 130–31.

the actions and prayers of persons. These two form a regular bond of description and response analogous to antiphonal singing. The excerpt from his visit to al-Qarafa given above illustrates the point.

His positive and sympathetic representation of the pilgrims at al-Husayn's shrine confirms the universal reverence accorded to Husayn and his own acceptance of the *ziyara* or pilgrimages to the tombs of imams who profoundly shaped belief and practice. Naturally, neither Ibn Jubayr nor Ibn Battuta explicitly associated their visit to the shrine of the head of al-Husayn, grandson of the Prophet and revered as such by the Sunni, with Shi'i sectarianism. What disapproval for *ziyara* was registered by their contemporaries came from scholars and it focused more on the aspects of *ziyara* that, like other popular religious practices, tread dangerously into the area of *bid'ah*, or innovation.

Innovation in religious practice carries with it the potential danger of heresy. Treatises by such scholars as Ibn Taymiyya and Ibn al-Hajj, for example, expressed concern about a number of aspects of popular celebrations. The extra-Qur'anic celebrations, such as the *mawlid* of the Prophet, provided occasions for inappropriate behaviour in the people's revelry. They also challenged the authority of the consensus that defined Islam for those scholars. In their role as guardians of the faith, the scholars needed to assess to what extent did veneration of holy men and women of Islam go beyond the scope of *sunna* as understood and analyzed by the scholars.[47]

Popular religious piety in the medieval Muslim regimes included veneration for holy individuals—whether respected scholars, Sufi *shaykhs*, or local mystics. The tendency to revere a respected master or scholar, moreover, grew with a more widespread presence of Sufi institutions, giving large numbers of people at least superficial familiarity with Sufi practices and goals. Many might not enter into the full spiritual discipline to attain mystical experience of God, but they could hear, see, watch, and revere from the sidelines. Moreover, pilgrims could visit local *shaykhs* attached to *zawiyas*, which were not full *khanqahs* but smaller institutions in a village or town where the *shayhk* would be a source of preaching and guidance.

In those circumstances, the chances were greater for participation in another characteristic of popular piety, that is, syncretism with other local, sometimes ancient, practices. Pious, but uneducated Muslims, could not always distinguish Muslim festivals from Christian or Jewish festivals, or superstitious tokenism such as the "evil-eye" or the use of amulets to drive off bad luck.[48] The resistance to such popular religion, then, came primarily from the *ulama*, but at least in the Middle Ages, was not a serious concern in the minds of the literary travelling class or the secular leadership. On the contrary, for these travel writers, pious visits to graves of Shi'ite imams, as well as visits to living and deceased *shaykhs* of Sufi organizations, rather reflected their sense of shared heritage of Prophet, his family, and early companions.[49]

---

47 Jonathan P. Berkey, *The Formation of Islam: Religion and Society in the Near East 600–1800* (Cambridge: Cambridge University Press, 2003), 248–50.

48 Berkey, *Formation of Islam*, 250–51.

49 Ahmed, *What is Islam?*, 93.

Chapter 3

VULNERABLE MEDIEVAL IBERIAN TRAVELLERS: BENJAMIN OF TUDELA'S *SEFER HA-MASSA'OT*, PERO TAFUR'S *ANDANÇAS E VIAJES*, AND AHMAD AL-WAZZAN'S *LIBRO DE LA COSMOGROPHIA ET GEOGRAPHIA DE AFRICA*

MONTSERRAT PIERA

ABSTRACT

This article explores both the actual (or physical) and figurative vulnerabilities expressed and enacted by three early modern Iberian travellers: one Jewish (Benjamin of Tudela, twelfth century, died in 1173), one Christian (Pero Tafur, 1410–1484), and one Muslim (al-Hassan al-Wazzan, known as Leo Africanus, 1486/88–1554?) who engaged in long voyages throughout Europe, Asia and the Maghreb and wrote in detail about their experiences. In these three writers, vulnerability is inextricably connected not only to their travels but also to their geographical origins and their particular historical circumstances.

Keywords: Benjamin of Tudela, *Sefer ha-Massa'ot*, Pero Tafur, vulnerability, Iberian travelers, Leo Africanus, *Geography of Africa*, Ahmad al-Wazzan

ON THE MARGINS of what doubly constitutes the fourteenth century known world and its physical or pictorial rendering, the magnificent Cresques or Catalan Atlas,[1] the attentive viewer can set eyes on a fragile vessel displaying an Aragonese flag, whose sail is strongly swollen by a favourable wind. One of its four occupants is Jaucme Ferrer or Ferrar, a sailor-merchant very actively involved in trade during the period who is

---

[1] I refer the reader to the introductory essay for more information about the Catalan Atlas and the Majorcan Jewish cartographic school. According to Gabriel Llompart the map of Abraham and Jehuda Cresques from 1375 is based in part on a previous map by Angelí Dulcert signed in Majorca in 1339. Llompart has found documentary evidence of the cartographer Dulcert in Majorca around 1340. He concludes that both Dulcert and the sailor Jaume Ferrer were possibly Genoese immigrants to Mallorca (Gabriel Llompart, "La Identitat de Jaume Ferrer, El Navegant (1346)," *Memòries de L'Acadèmia Mallorquina d'Estudis Genealògics, Heràldics i Històrics* 10 (2000): 7–20.

now, presumably, in search of gold. The rubric displayed right below the illumination describes it thus: "The ship of Jaume Ferrer departed for the River of Gold on the 10th of August of 1350, feast of St. Lawrence."

Poised precariously at the edge of our field of vision, right above the line where the parchment and, thus, the world ends[2] this miniature manages to manifestly allude to Jaucme Ferrer's mysterious vanishing from the historical record since neither the intrepid traveller nor his "coca" (merchant trading vessel) came back from the trip. The illumination serves to tellingly illustrate the dangers and vicissitudes of travelling and exploring in the early modern period.

The Mediterranean was a world in constant motion during that era and the *motif* of travel was ubiquitous in the medieval and early modern imaginary[3] but travel was also a very unpredictable and dangerous endeavour, which could render the traveller vulnerable to violence, abuse, warfare and misfortune, among other perils.[4] This chapter explores the actual (or physical) as well as the imagined and figurative vulnerabilities expressed and enacted by three early modern Iberian travellers who, unlike Jaucme Ferrer, were able to return and tell the tale: one Jewish (Benjamin of Tudela, died in 1173), one Christian (Pero Tafur, 1410–1484), and one Muslim (al-Hassan al-Wazzan, known as Leo Africanus, 1486/88–1554?) who engaged in long voyages throughout Europe and Asia and wrote in detail about their experiences: what happened to them in their contacts with others, what they witnessed, what they heard and what they interpreted based on their particular assumptions and their personal background. Vulnerability in these three writers is inextricably connected not only to their travels, but to their particular historical circumstances.

These three travellers share some commonalities: they were all born and raised in the Iberian Peninsula during the extended period of the so-called *convivencia* between the three monotheistic religions: Islam, Christianity and Judaism; they travelled to what

---

2 This is the place which medieval people considered *terra incognita*, or what Mary B. Campbell defines as "the limits of geographical knowledge – on the borders of the map" (Mary B. Campbell, *The Witness and the Other World: Exotic European Travel Writing, 400–1600* (Ithaca: Cornell University Press, 1998), 50).

3 Two of the most popular medieval books were, as a matter of fact, travel accounts: Marco Polo's account of his travels and the fictional book known as the *Book of John of Mandeville*, which was believed to be an actual eyewitness account. Both texts were favoured by readers for their exciting retelling of perilous and arduous voyages to faraway lands and their description of marvellous and exotic creatures and races, unknown to Westerners.

4 All these dangers, naturally, engendered a certain degree of fear in prospective travellers. This fear was minimized or exacerbated depending on the particular historical context and it distressed all Mediterranean travellers, and not only Christians fearful of Muslim pirates, as it is often held. Nabil Matar, for example, affirms that in the seventeenth century fear of the Christians' ruthless piracy and religious persecution "was a powerful deterrent to travel into the lands of Christians." *In the Lands of the Christians: Arabic Travel Writing in the Seventeenth Century* (New York: Routlege, 2003), xxvii.

we have geographically conceptualized in this collection (see the Introduction) as the "East;"[5] they wrote a travel narrative that detailed their adventures and their contacts with other cultures and, lastly, they all experienced vulnerability.

In reading these travel narratives three types of vulnerability can be articulated: physical, cultural, and transformative vulnerability. A physical vulnerability is the one most widely understood and universally experienced; it is caused by aspects totally beyond the traveller's control: on one hand, the vicissitudes caused by the elements (storms at sea, and general perils of the road faced by travellers) and, on the other hand, physical illness or impairing accidents that compromise the mobility of the traveller. Our travellers experienced all of these hardships; Tafur, for instance, was ill in Genoa, was wounded by an arrow in battle, was pursued by Genoese and Muslims at sea, and endured frightful storms which ended in a shipwreck at the island of Chios; the latter experience was so harrowing that he pronounced that "had I been on the mainland I would never have put to sea again."

As for the second type, cultural vulnerability is experienced when the subject is faced with unknown cultures that act, feel, eat and speak differently than the traveller. This cultural contact causes an "unsettling" of the set of beliefs each traveller stores. Such set of beliefs or ideology are directly influenced by what is often termed as "civil society," particularly in the formulation of the Italian Marxist thinker Antonio Gramsci. In his *Prison Notebooks* he distinguishes between "civil society" (school, church, cultural media), the mechanism of domination which functions through "consensus" and "political society" (government, army, police, courts, prisons) which functions through "force."[6]

Gramsci illustrated the concept of ideology as an array of representations or mental images of reality that are unconsciously extrapolated by any subject from a given culture's legal, religious and economic systems, as well as art and other forms of community expression. For Gramsci, this concept of the world also included codes for social behaviour and action.[7] A traveller had acquired those set of values and conducts by

---

5 It is worth noting that, when the terms "East" and "West" appear in Hebrew (*mizrah* and *ma'arav*) and in Arabic (*mashriq* and *maghrib*) in these texts, they are not employed in the sense of our modern Occident versus Orient dichotomy. The Christian Pero Tafur, on the other hand, uses in his account the terms "Oriente" and "Poniente." My own use in this chapter of such disputed terms as "East" and "West" could be interpreted as an acritical move that only serves to perpetuate colonialist and Orientalist dichotomies which did not exist at the time of our travellers. Nothing is further from my intention, however, so I refer the reader to the introduction for a discussion of the contested nature of the categories "East and "West" and my own stance in that debate. I am, thus, resorting to such contingent names in my argumentation solely on account of their usefulness as geographical markers and taxonomic labels.

6 Asli Daldal, "Power and Ideology in Michel Foucault and Antonio Gramsci: A Comparative Analysis," *Review of History and Political Science* 2 (2014): 149–67, at 157.

7 Antonio Gramsci discusses these issues when speaking, not of civil society *per se*, but about ideology and about hegemony. While Antonio Gramsci was not the first person to speak about

consent[8] with his society and now is faced with the realization that in order to fit in the new foreign environment or to achieve *episteme* he must also "consent" or be permeable to acquiring a different set of values and to behaving in an alien manner. This constitutes a sort of double vulnerability since a failure to achieve this permeability can bring about not only a rejection by the other culture but, perhaps, even a retaliation that could cause the first type of physical or violent vulnerability.

Lastly, the traveller in contact with this "Other" is vulnerable as well in another sense: as he/she is exposed to a different way of living the traveller engages in a transformative move by gazing back to his own set of beliefs and behaviour but this time more critically and subversively, which, in turn, "wounds" his world, in the etymological sense of "vulnerare" (in Latin "vulnus" means wound); that is, he hurts, injures his world, makes it *vulnerable*, not as perfect and wholesome and satisfactory anymore.

This type of vulnerability is, however, not a negative trait.[9] In fact, the capacity to be vulnerable is inherent in human embodiment. To be vulnerable is to be fragile, to be susceptible to wounding and to suffering; this susceptibility is an ontological condition of our humanity, "a universal, inevitable, enduring aspect of the human condition that must be at the heart of our concept of social and state responsibility" as legal theorist Martha Fineman points out.[10] But as Martha Nussbaum and Alasdair MacIntyre underscore, our corporeal vulnerability is also linked to the inherent sociality of human life: "as embodied, social beings, we are both vulnerable to the actions of others and

---

hegemony, he was the one who broadened the idea of hegemony. Previously other philosophers and political theorists declared that hegemony was established to gain political power but Gramsci was the first thinker to articulate the idea that hegemony is an essential element for a ruling class of people to maintain its authority and power. As Roger Simon affirms: "The starting point of hegemony is that a class and its representatives exercise power over subordinate classes by means of a combination of coercion and persuasion." Roger Simon, *Gramsci's Political Thought: An Introduction* (London: Lawrence and Wishart, 1991), 22. When a given group's ideology was pervasive then that ideology had "hegemony." Travellers are, by nature of their transfer from a familiar to an unfamiliar terrain (both physically and culturally) constantly exposed to diverse ideologies and to the instability of shifting hegemonies.

8 This consent is illustrated in Gramsci's definition of the state as "the entire complex of practical and theoretical activities with which the ruling class not only justifies and maintains it dominance, but manages to win the active consent of those over whom it rules." Antonio Gramsci, *Selections from the Prison Notebooks* (London: Wishart, 1980), 244; Martin Carnoy, *The State and Political Theory* (Cambridge: Cambridge University Press, 1986), 65.

9 In fact, feminist theorists have pioneered a move to cease conceptualizing vulnerability as precariousness. They, together with other scholars studying marginalized and subaltern groups, contend that recognizing the vulnerabilities suffered historically by such groups should not imply a theorization of such marginal constituencies as weak or inferior. These scholars envision vulnerability instead as "a space for engagement and resistance emerging from a sense of fundamental openness" (as formulated in the Modern Language Association 2014 Presidential theme, entitled "Vulnerable Times").

10 Martha A. Fineman, "The Vulnerable Subject: Anchoring Equality in the Human Condition," *Yale Journal of Law & Feminism* 20 (2008): 1–23, at 8.

dependent on the care and support of other people."[11] Vulnerability and dependency are, thus, intertwined and nowhere is this link more salient than in travel narratives.

Descriptions of travel to unfamiliar lands and "eastern journeys" that precisely enact the types of vulnerabilities defined above have, for centuries, held a great appeal for European readers in general and Iberian readers in particular, and much before the Age of Discovery and the marvellous travels of the Spanish *conquistadores*, as attested by the number of medieval texts that illustrate the topic.[12] As it was discussed in the Introduction, every traveller's personal *rihla* transforms him or her as much as every traveller transforms the worlds with which he or she comes in contact. Every travel brings us close to *episteme*. The same process can be surmised from the reading of Benjamin of Tudela, Pero Tafur, and al-Wazzan's narratives. My analysis of these three Iberian travellers' texts seek to illuminate the different manifestations of epistemological discovery rendered through travel and its inherent contradictions. Moreover, the justification for analyzing these three particular travellers lies in two factors: first, they each epitomize one of the three monotheistic religions sharing a cultural space in the Iberian Peninsula during the medieval period and secondly, they were raised and acculturated in the unique *milieu* that has been defined by historians as the society of "convivencia."[13]

After intense Visigothic religious intransigence, the Muslim dominance of the Iberian Peninsula ushered in a period of relative religious and social tolerance. Thus, relations between Jews, Christians and Muslims were largely peaceable. The experience of comparatively co-operative relationships during a time of intense diversity of thought and behaviour facilitated the integration and acculturation, if not toleration, of cultures throughout Muslim al-Andalus. That these three travellers who happen to exhibit

---

11 Martha Nussbaum, *Frontiers of Justice: Disability, Nationality, Species Membership* (Cambridge: Harvard University Press, 2006); Alasdair MacIntyre, *Dependent Rational Animals: Why Human Beings Need the Virtues* (Chicago: Open Court, 1999); Catriona Mackenzie, Wendy Rogers, and Susan Dodds, eds., *Vulnerability: New Essays in Ethics and Feminist Philosophy* (Oxford: Oxford University Press, 2014), 4.

12 Some of the Iberian travel narratives are literary fictions which narrate such travels while others are various historical travellers' eyewitness accounts or ambassadorial reports. In the first group we can mention the *Libro del conoscimiento del mundo* and three texts from the first half of the thirteenth century: the *Libro de Apolonio*, the *Vida de madona Santa María Egipciaqua*, and the *Libre dels tres reys d'Orient*. In the second group we can list Benjamin de Tudela's *Sefer ha-Masa'ot* or *Itinerary*, Ramon Muntaner's *Chronicle*, Ruy Clavijo's *Embajada a Tamorlan*, the famous *Catalan Atlas* by Abraham Cresques and the *Andanças e viajes* de Pero Tafur. See the article by Mathew Desing in this volume (Chapter 4) for a detailed discussion of the three thirteenth-century Iberian texts. I refer the reader to his article as well for an assessment on the scholarly literature on travel in the Iberian Peninsula.

13 It could be argued that this factor is debatable in the case of al-Wazzan, since although he was born in Granada, he grew up and received his education in Fez, Morocco. However, I include him here because he visibly grew up in a community in Fez where he was surrounded by exiles who had fled Granada at various times in the recent past and who steadfastly clung to their Iberian (or "andalusí") heritage. Thus, his upbringing was very much influenced by his family and his neighbours' past in Granada and the constant nostalgia at their loss of their ancestral land.

marks of an unaffected and respectful openness towards other cultures originate from the Iberian Peninsula during that historical period is surely not fortuitous. Perhaps the suggestion could be brought forth that Benjamin of Tudela, Pero Tarfur and al-Wazzan are, at least, better disposed ethnographers than the crusaders that Oleb Grab discusses because they came from an Iberian cultural environment where they had already experienced interaction with other cultures and religions. Be that as it may, these three travellers tender to the reader a tangible account of how individuals from the three competing monotheistic religions confronted and resolved the vulnerabilities encountered through their travels.[14]

The first of these Iberian travellers, Rabbi Benjamin ben Jonah (1130–1173) of Tudela in Navarre was the most famous of Jewish travellers: "reckoned one of the greatest travellers that ever lived," in the words of Purchas, who published an English translation of his *Sefer ha-Massa'ot* (*The Book of Travels*), usually called *Itinerary*, in 1625.[15] In 1119, the Christian kingdom of Navarre captured Tudela (Arabic: al-Tutila), which had been ruled by Muslims since the eighth century. This relatively recent change of power enables us to assume that Benjamin had enjoyed a hybrid cultural background. In fact, the co-existence of different cultures in the city is reflected on Tudela's reputation for generating or stimulating important medieval writers such as al-A'mā al-Tuṭīlī, a famous classical poet[16] or Robert Ketton, the English scholar who first translated the Qur'an into Latin and who became a canon of Tudela in 1157.[17]

---

14 Since these three travellers have been widely studied there exists a sizable amount of scholarship devoted to their experiences and, furthermore, in the case of Benjamin and al-Wazzan there is a vast body of literature on them in Arabic and Hebrew. In the interest of time and space and given the fact that my discussion here focuses solely on the issue of vulnerability as related to these three travellers, my use of critical references will not be exhaustive.

15 Benjamin of Tudela, *The Itinerary of Benjamin of Tudela: Travels in the Middle Ages*, trans. Marcus Nathan Adler, with an introduction by Michael A. Signer, Marcus Nathan Adler, and A. Asher (Malibu: Joseph Simon, 1983), "Introduction," xv.

16 Abu 'l-'abbās (or abū dja'far) aḥmad b. 'abd allāh b. hurayra al-'utbī (or al-ḳaysī), "the blind man of Tudela" was a Hispano-Arabic poet (d. 525/1130–1131). His fame derives from being one of the great masters of muwashshaḥ poetry. Manuscripts of his dīwān, containing classical poetry, are to be found in London and Cairo (S. M. Stern, "al-A'mā al-Tuṭīlī," in *Encyclopaedia of Islam, Second Edition*, ed. P. Bearman, Th. Bianquis, C. E. Bosworth, E. van Donzel, and W.P. Heinrichs, http://dx.doi.org/10.1163/1573-3912_islam_SIM_0574).

17 Charles J. Bishko, *Spanish and Portuguese Monastic History 600–1300*, 167, http://libro.uca.edu/monastic/monastic12.htm; *Bibl. Clun.* 1109; Charles H. Haskins, *Studies in the History of Mediaeval Science*, 2nd ed. (Cambridge, MA: Harvard University Press, 1924), 120. Peter the Venerable commissioned translations of several Islamic texts during his travels (around 1142–1143) *circa Iberum*, as he puts it, in his *Liber de miraculis* (*Patrologia Latina* 189, 650). Robert Ketton, who was in charge of translating the Qur'an, was one of the members of a team of translators employed by Peter the Venerable, the others being Herman of Dalmatia, Master Peter of Toledo and a Muslim "called Mohammed." The encounter and the commissioning of the translations most likely took place, as Lacarra suggests, in the vicinity of the monastery of Santa María de Nájera, on the road from Toledo to Pamplona (José M. Lacarra, "Una aparición de ultratumba en Estella," *Príncipe de Viana*

The city of Tudela on the banks of the river Ebro had great strategic value at the beginning of the ninth century. The town had become the power base of the Banu Qasi family, local magnates converted to Islam who managed to stay independent of the emirs by establishing alliances with the kings of Pamplona. Their power, however, waned at the beginning of the tenth century and Tudela fell under the influence of the rising caliphate of Córdoba. From then on, the Muslims used the city as a base to fight against the expanding Christian kingdom of Navarre. When Alfonso el Batallador conquered Tudela in 1119, three different religious communities had been co-existing there (the Muslims, the Mozarabs, and the Jews) but after the Christian victory, community interactions appear to have been severely strained and, while Jews continued to live inside the walls, Muslims were forced to reside outside the town walls.

This is the intellectual, political and social framework into which Benjamin of Tudela was born in 1130. Little is known about his life and occupations before his travels, and the scant information we have of him can only be surmised from his travelogue. Cecil Roth has suggested that he might have been a gem merchant since he often shows an interest not only in mercantile exchanges in general, but in the coral trade in particular.[18] Benjamin's journey has also been categorized as a religious pilgrimage[19] or as a trip undertaken with the objective of locating and describing hospitable Jewish communities on the road to Israel.[20] Marcus Nathan Adler argues that Benjamin's travels "were too extensive to be those of a mere merchant" and,

> inasmuch as the hitherto prosperous Jewish communities, along the Rhine and the route to Palestine, had been dispersed by the fanaticism aroused by the Crusaders, and as, even in the Caliphate of Cordova, his coreligionist were being bitterly persecuted, it is probable that Benjamin's object was to discover where his expatriated brethren might find asylum.[21]

He finished the travels he describes in 1173:

> The said Rabbi Benjamin set forth from Tudela, his native city, and passed through many remote countries, as is related in his book. In every place which he entered he made a record of all that he saw or was told of by trustworthy persons—matters not previously heard in the land of Sepharad (Spain).[22]

---

5 (1944): 173–84). See also James A. Kritzeck, *Peter the Venerable and Islam* (Princeton: Princeton University Press, 1964).

18 Cecil Roth, "Benjamin (Ben Jonah) of Tudela," *Encyclopedia Judaica* (New York: Macmillan, 1972), 4:535–38.

19 Joseph Shatzmiller, "Jews, Pilgrimage, and the Christian Cult of Saints: Benjamin of Tudela and His Contemporaries," in *After Rome's Fall: Narrators and Sources of Early Medieval History*, ed. Walter A. Goffart and Alexander C. Murray (Toronto: University of Toronto Press, 1998), 337–47, at 338.

20 Shatzmiller, "Jews, Pilgrimage," 347.

21 Adler, *The Itinerary of Benjamin of Tudela*, 43.

22 Benjamin of Tudela, *Itinerary*, 55.

In spite of the fact that his is one of the earliest travel accounts, Benjamin of Tudela's work has not been extensively studied. Perhaps due to the fact that the account was written in Hebrew the text, while very well known by Jewish scholars, has attracted little attention among other scholars. This state of affairs is unfortunate because this account, while not as colourful as Marco Polo's or John of Mandeville's, is highly relevant for two reasons: first, it describes the East from a non-Christian perspective; and, secondly, it provides a reversed paradigm to the binary discussed in the Introduction with regard to pilgrimage literature.

It was stated there that the paradigm of the medieval "Christian pilgrim" stemmed from ancient myths such as Apollonius of Tyre and Odysseus, and that their journey became a metaphor for the spiritual progress of his readers' lives. Additionally, Elsner and Rubiés argued that from these myths two patterns of travel as pilgrimage in the Christian tradition developed: visiting the Holy Land and the veneration of sacred relics. Benjamin de Tudela's journey and the tale that emanates from it embryonically share the same traits but its manifestation has shed all Christian underpinnings.

Benjamin's travel is a pilgrimage also since his desire is to visit the biblical land of Israel and all the sacred *loci* of Judaism. In that sense his account is not very different from the Christian pilgrim Egeria's account.[23] He lists the names of the towns he visits and describes holy places that are relevant to the Jewish religion, for example, the grave of Esther and Mordecai in Media.[24] But, unlike Egeria, Benjamin refers as well to the importance of some of the sites he visits to Muslims and Christians. His two other interests in his travel account seem to be more pragmatic: on one hand, he attentively describes the various mercantile products that can be found in each city, for instance, spices; on the other hand, he documents every Jewish community he comes in contact with and he lists the numbers of Jews inhabiting every city he visits as well as the names of some of the most illustrious members of the Jewish community.[25]

---

23 Egeria's *Itinerarium Egeriae* (*Travels of Egeria*) (referred to also as either *Peregrinatio Aetheriae* (*The Pilgrimage of Aetheria*) or *Peregrinatio ad Loca Sancta* (*Pilgrimage to the Holy Lands*)) is one of the earliest extant pilgrimage travelogues to the Holy Land. Egeria visited the most important destinations of pilgrimage in the eastern Mediterranean between 381 and 384 CE (although some scholars dispute that dating). Not much is known about the identity of Egeria. It is believed she most likely lived in the western part of the Roman Empire, perhaps in the region of Gallaecia (Galicia, in modern Spain) although some scholars argue that she could have been from the southern region of modern France. Another interesting pilgrim to the Holy Land who left an account of his travels during the same period as Benjamin, was Daniel of Kiev (possibly Daniel, Bishop of Suriev in Ukraine from 1115 CE to 1122 CE). He travelled in the early twelfth century from his monastery in Ukraine to Constantinople and the Holy Land; his account is the first extant travelogue written in Russian (Charles Raymond Beazley, "Daniel of Kiev," in *Encyclopedia Britannica*, 11th ed. (Cambridge: Cambridge University Press, 1911), 7:808).

24 Benjamin of Tudela, *Itinerary*, 113.

25 In one particular instance, he even describes a Jewish polity located in the Horn of Africa which will turn out to be spurious: "The country is mountainous. There are many Israelites here and they are not under the yoke of the Gentiles, but possess cities and castles on the summits of the mountains." In fact, François-Xavier Fauvelle-Aymas has persuasively suggested that Benjamin was

On closer scrutiny, however, the latter task can be defined as a pilgrimage as well. Benjamin's careful accounting of the Jewish communities goes beyond a mere arithmetical compilation. He is not only looking for these communities as a temporary and personal refuge from danger and starvation during his travels; he is also registering how strong these communities are and how they are faring in their particular social environment and political configuration as if Benjamin were considering a permanent relocation for himself or for his community back in Sepharad (Spain). Consequently, travelling through Europe and the East Benjamin of Tudela faces a double vulnerability: as a lone traveller and as a lone Jewish traveller. His mission, which appears to be rooted on an epistemological desire to acquire knowledge of the world, is also one that confronts vulnerability head on since his aim is to explore the situation of Jewish communities abroad and these communities are constantly assailed by danger and the threat of violence, destruction or exile. One appreciates a certain degree of urgency in the way he attempts to document as dispassionately as possible the constant liminality and precariousness of Jewish communities. This, for instance, is how he describes the situation of his Jewish brethren in Constantinople:

> No Jews live in the city, for they have been placed behind an inlet of the sea. An arm of the sea of Marmora shuts them in on the one side, and they are unable to go out except by way of the sea, when they want to do business with the inhabitants [...] No Jew there is allowed to ride on horseback. The one exception is R. Solomon Hamitsri, who is the king's physician, and through whom the Jews enjoy considerable alleviation of their oppression. For their condition is very low, and there is much hatred against them, which is fostered by tanners, who throw out their dirty water in the streets before the doors of the Jewish houses and defile the Jews' quarter. So the Greeks hate the Jews, good and bad alike, and subject them to great oppression, and beat them in the streets, and in every way threat them with rigor. Yet the Jews are rich and good, kindly and charitable, and bear their lot with cheerfulness.[26]

On the other hand, the city of Bagdad, a much more welcoming environment for the Jews, is clearly contrasted to Constantinople: "In Bagdad there are about 40,000 Jews and they dwell in security, prosperity and honour under the great Caliph, and amongst them are great sages, the heads of Academies engaged in the study of the law."[27]

---

probably referring not to a Jewish kingdom of Ethiopia, which some scholars have equated to the Falasha, but to an Ethiopian Christian community, which exhibited various traits that linked it to Judaism, including the legend of a reigning Solomonic dynasty ("Desperately Seeking the Jewish Kingdom of Ethiopia: Benjamin of Tudela and the Horn of Africa (12th Century)," *Speculum* 88 (2013): 383–404, at 399–400).

26 Benjamin of Tudela, *Itinerary*, 72; *Jewish Travelers*, ed. Elkan Nathan (Adler: RoutledgeCurzon, 1930; repr. 2005), 41.

27 Benjamin of Tudela, *Itinerary*, 99. Benjamin's extolling depiction of the city markedly contrasts, in fact, with another Iberian traveller's account, that of the Muslim Ibn Jubayr, who in 1184 decries the decline of the city which he likens to "an effaced ruin, a remain washed out, or the statue of

In fact, Benjamin devotes many more pages to the description of the main city of Islam and its caliph than to any other city through his travels. He begins by introducing the Abbasid caliph al-Mustanjid (1124–1170, caliph [Khalīfa] from 1160 to 1170) who, in addition to being the temporal ruler of Bagdad was also, as a descendant of the prophet Muhammad (Hebrew: ha-meshuga', "the madman"), the amīr al-mu'minīn, or Commander of the Faithful and thus had nominal religious authority over all Muslims from Spain to India. Very aptly, Benjamin states that "he occupies a similar position to that held by the pope over the Christians."[28]

In addition, Benjamin declares that "he is kind unto Israel, and many belonging to the people of Israel are his attendants: he knows all languages and is well versed in the law of Israel. He reads and writes the holy language (Hebrew)". He also describes the caliph (hafiz) as a "great king," "a benevolent man," or "a righteous man."[29] To illustrate his benevolence Benjamin explains that the caliph built a hospital to take care of the sick poor and another for demented people, where "they chain each of them in iron chains until their reason becomes restored to them."[30] According to Benjamin of Tudela, the patients at these institutions are maintained at the caliph's expense and the caliph does it out of charity.[31]

This flattering characterization markedly contrasts, notwithstanding, with the Jewish traveller's own account of the caliph's brutality and tyrannical rule which, curiously, mirrors the previous comment about chaining the demented patients. Thus, the caliph does not extend his munificence and charitable compassion to his relatives, whom he keeps under chains:

> Each of his brothers and the members of his family has an abode in his palace, but they are all fettered in chains of iron, and guards are placed over each of their houses so that they may not rise against the great Caliph. For once it happened to a predecessor that his brothers rose up against him and proclaimed one of themselves as Caliph; then it was decreed that all members of his family should be bound, that they might not rise up against the ruling Caliph.[32]

---

a ghost." (Muhammad ibn Ahmad Ibn Jubayr, *The Travels of Ibn Jubayr, being the Chronicles of a Mediaeval Spanish Moor Concerning His Journey to the Egypt of Saladin, the Holy Cities of Arabia*, trans. Ronald J. C. Broadhurst (London: Jonathan Cape, 1952), 226).

28 Benjamin of Tudela, *Itinerary*, 98. Martin Jacobs, however, rightly argues that Benjamin's assertion is anachronistic when related to the twelfth century since "the Abbasid caliphate had appreciably declined since the 8th century and their supremacy over the entire Muslim community (Arabic: *umma*) was called into question by rival caliphates" (*Reorienting the East: Jewish Travelers to the Medieval Muslim World* (Philadelphia: University of Pennsylvania Press, 2014), 126). Despite this, Jacobs notes that from Benjamin's perspective the Abbasid Baghdad he encounters is "the capital of the Islamic world" (126).

29 Benjamin of Tudela, *Itinerary*, 96, 98, and 99.

30 Benjamin of Tudela, *Itinerary*, 98.

31 Benjamin of Tudela, *Itinerary*, 98–99.

32 Benjamin of Tudela, *Itinerary*, 96–97.

Benjamin goes on to add that, in spite of their captivity, they are maintained in great luxury and they all "eat and drink and rejoice all the days of their life."[33] An oblique parallel between the living arrangements of the demented people and the caliph's family can be discerned. The implication is, thus, that the caliph is an all-powerful figure who capriciously arbitrates the fate and welfare of his subjects, allowing them to adore him but treating them like little children, as can be seen in the Tudelan's description of the caliph's procession through the streets during El-id-bed Ramazan, the only time of the year when he deigns to come out from his palace and let his subjects see him and kiss his robe.[34]

Benjamin of Tudela, however, finishes his ambiguous description of the caliph with the unequivocal affirmation that "all his actions are for good,"[35] the reason becoming apparent as we progress to the next paragraph (cited above), which states that the Jews dwell in security and prosperity under this caliph. The reader understands now that the caliph's possible shortcomings are altogether compensated by the benevolent way in which he treats his Jewish subjects. Furthermore, this section continues explaining, in an unusually long passage, the role, at the caliph's court, of Daniel, the "Head of the Captivity of all Israel" or exilarch, that is the chief sovereign of the Jewish community under the caliphate.

Our Jewish traveller makes it a point to contrast the singular yearly visit that the caliph bestows upon his subjects to the visit he receives from the Jewish exilarch every five days, underscoring the high place the Jewish authority holds in the caliph's court. As Benjamin describes and Michael Signer summarizes in his introduction to the text, the exilarch was formally invested with authority and had to be saluted by both Muslims and Jews:

> A triumphal march through the streets of Baghdad each Thursday precedes his meeting with the caliph at the royal palace. This pomp and glory demonstrates to Benjamin's satisfaction that the biblical prophecy, "The scepter shall not depart from Judah, nor the ruler's staff between his feet; so that tribute shall come to him and the homage of peoples be his" (Gen. 49:10). The Head of the Exile, like the Caliph, is a man of property, and bestows charity and benevolence upon his people.[36]

Benjamin's magnified and always laudatory sketches of the Jewish communities he encounters, in general, and of the exilarch of Bagdad's excelling attributes, in particular, would seem to evidence an Orientalist perspective, as Edward Said would argue:

> Orientalism depends for its strategy on the flexible positional superiority, which puts the Westerner in a whole series of possible relationships with the Orient without ever losing him the relative upper hand. The scientist, the

---

33 Benjamin of Tudela, *Itinerary*, 97.

34 Benjamin of Tudela, *Itinerary*, 96–97.

35 Benjamin of Tudela, *Itinerary*, 99.

36 Benjamin of Tudela, *Itinerary*, 99–102 and 25.

scholar, the missionary, the soldier [...] was in, or thought about the Orient because *he could be there*, or could think about it, with very little resistance on the Orient's part.[37]

This statement, however, presupposes that the Westerner's intellectual apprehending of what he was seeing operated under an umbrella of Western hegemony over the "Orient."

This, nevertheless, is not the case with Benjamin of Tudela, a vulnerable, marginalized and non-hegemonic subject himself.[38] His account instead, demonstrates that he is able to document, define and distinguish between a beneficial and a prejudicial predicament for the Jews by comparing what he saw through his travels with his own circumstances, with the reality that he knew. He does not need to "create" or invent a discourse to describe what he sees (unlike what the New World Spanish *conquistadores* would have to resort to later in the sixteenth century to express the unknown). He can avail himself of what he has already seen in his own Western and, in Christian eyes, supposedly superior, hegemonic world. Consequently, Benjamin's eyewitness account of the East does, in fact, transport the reader's gaze back to the West, where Jews also live in repressive communities such as that of Constantinople. The account renders an incriminatory and obvious conclusion: Jews suffer under Christian rule, while they thrive under Muslim rule.

As if to make this realization even more patent to the reader Benjamin spins a narrative that emphasizes the point. It is an interesting sort of, as Martin Jacobs affirms, "medieval science-fiction thriller" in which a Christian saboteur causes irreparable damage to the glass mirror mounted on top of the famous and legendary Alexandria lighthouse or "Pharos" and which served as a sort of sophisticated telescope:[39]

> It happened once, many years after the death of Alexander, that a ship came from the land of Greece, and the name of the captain was Theodoros, a Greek of great cleverness. The Greeks at the time were under the yoke of Egypt. The captain brought great gifts in silver and gold and garments of silk to the King of Egypt, and he moored his ship in front of the lighthouse, as was the custom

---

37 Edward W. Said, "Orientalism," in *The Edward Said Reader*, ed. Edward W. Said, Moustafa Bayoumi, and Andrew Rubin (New York: Vintage, 2000), 73–74.

38 In addition to not enjoying a "positional superiority" and being a non-hegemonic subject, Benjamin most certainly observed the East through a different lens than an European Christian. Martin Jacobs claims that Jewish travellers, in fact, even challenged the idea of Europe or the West as home and the Middle East as exile and they deliberately "reoriented the East and decentered Europe" in their accounts (*Reorienting the East*, 3).

39 Alexander of Macedon erected the large tower or lighthouse called in Arabic *Manar al Iskandriyyah*: "On top of the tower there is a glass mirror. Any ships that attempted to attack or molest the city, coming from Greece or from the Western Lands, could be seen by means of this mirror of glass at a distance of twenty days' journey, and the inhabitants could thereupon put themselves on their guard" (Benjamin of Tudela, *Itinerary*, 133). Ibn Jubayr admiringly refers to the tower as well in his rihla (*The Travels of Ibn Jubayr*, trans. Roland J. C. Broadhurst (London: Jonathan Cape, 1952), 33).

of all merchants. Every day the guardian of the lighthouse and his servants had their meals with him, until the captain came to be on such friendly terms with the keeper that he could go in and out at all times. And one day he gave a banquet, and caused the keeper and all his servants to drink a great deal of wine. When they were all asleep, the captain and his servants arose and broke the mirror and departed that very night [...] Ever since then, the men of the King of Egypt have been unable to prevail over the Greeks.[40]

This tale, which Benjamin probably learned or heard from oral sources, is undoubtedly intended to explain why the lighthouse fell into disuse. It also, presents, however, a polemical bent against Christianity since it is a Byzantine spy who destroyed the mirror for the purpose of ending Muslim domination over the Mediterranean. Thus, Benjamin of Tudela seems "to identify with Muslim anxieties over potential Byzantine expansion. Whatever the source, in the context of the *Massa'ot*, the story allows him to depict Christianity as a barbaric force that destroyed one of the great wonders of Antiquity. Similar to his chapter on Bagdad mentioned earlier, Benjamin's account of Alexandria bolsters his hypothesis that the Islamicate world is culturally superior to Christendom,"[41] and thus Muslim hegemony is preferable to Christian hegemony.

This *excursus* on the destruction of the lighthouse can be chiasmatically compared to Benjamin's impressions when he visits Rome. He indirectly alludes to a monument that evokes very painful memories for him and for his co-religionists: the Arch of Titus, which commemorates the second destruction of the Temple of Jerusalem.[42] Benjamin does not mention the arch itself but his selection of the details he describes show that the image of the Arch is foremost in his mind. Benjamin refers to Titus with a sort of incriminating comment (that he was ill-treated by the senators because it took Titus three years to take Jerusalem instead of two)[43] which has the effect of undermining Titus and glorifying instead the fierce Jewish resistance in that battle. In addition, Benjamin injects haphazardly in his narration several clear references to the destruction depicted in the actual arch:

> In the church of St. John in the Lateran there are two bronze columns taken from the Temple, the handiwork of King Solomon, each column being engraved "Solomon the son of David". The Jews of Rome told me that every year upon the

---

40 Benjamin of Tudela, *Itinerary*, 133.

41 Jacobs, *Reorienting the East*, 145–46.

42 The Arch of Titus is a Roman honorific arch erected by Domitian in ca. 81 CE on the Via Sacra in the Forum in Rome. It commemorates the victories of his father Vespasian and brother Titus in the Jewish War in Judea (70–71 CE) when the city of Jerusalem was sacked, and the vast riches of its temple looted. The sculptural relief in the arch shows Titus's 71 CE victory triumph procession as it passes through the Porta Triumphalis to the Forum with the participants carrying booty from the Temple of Jerusalem after the sacking of the city. The loot includes a menorah, silver trumpets, and the Table of Shew bread (Paul Artus, *Art and Architecture of the Roman Empire* (Tauranga: Bellona Books, 2006), 45–48).

43 Benjamin of Tudela, *Itinerary*, 63.

9th of Av they found the columns exuding moisture like water. There is also a cave where Titus the son of Vespasianus stored the Temple vessels which he brought from Jerusalem.[44]

For centuries, Jews have refused to walk under it and thus to give honour to Titus, the destroyer of Jerusalem. Consequently, Benjamin most likely did not walk under the arch while he visited Rome and he purposefully does not directly allude to it in his travelogue, but clearly describes instead the details that evoke the arch itself as well as the dishonour it represents for the Jews, including the explicit reference to the date of 9th Av (Tisha b'Av), considered by the Jews as a day of ignominy since it marks not one but several historical calamities, namely, the first and second destruction of the Temple of Jerusalem, the expulsion of the Jews from England in 1290 as well as the date when Jews were no longer allowed to remain in the country after their expulsion from Spain in 1492.

Therefore, in this case the monument is not destroyed or in the process of being destroyed as was the case with the Alexandrian lighthouse; on the contrary, it is the arch itself that infinitely reenacts and dramatizes another destruction of an equally legendary monument, the Temple of Jerusalem. The messages to derive from the reference to the monuments, however, do coincide: a beacon of civilization behaves in a very uncivilized way. In one case, a Christian Greek tries to destroy a symbol of an enlightened pagan civilization (Ptolemaic Alexandria) now controlled by Muslims; in the other case, the Roman legions destroyed the Temple of Jerusalem in one of the most barbaric wars in antiquity.[45] Benjamin is tacitly contesting the concept of "civilization" and underscoring the fact that the Jews are always defenceless and vulnerable when facing such misguided imperialistic and fanatic forces.

More than two centuries after Benjamin of Tudela's pilgrimage, another Iberian traveller, Pero Tafur, would journey to the East and write an account of his experiences there. The *Andanças e viaje de Pero Tafur por diversas partes del mundo avidos* (*Travels and voyages of Pero Tafur through various parts of the world*),[46] probably composed around 1457, is an autobiographical account of the extensive journeys undertaken by the narrator between 1437 and 1439.[47] Born in Cordoba between 1405 and 1410, and raised in the

---

44 Benjamin of Tudela, *Itinerary*, 64.

45 Hershel Shanks, ed., *Ancient Israel: From Abraham to the Roman Destruction of the Temple* (Prentice Hall: Biblical Archeology Society, 2011); see also Flavius Josephus, *The Jewish Wars*, 7 vols. (Bury St. Edmunds: Loeb Classical Library, 1927); or the more recent edition *The Jewish War: Revised Edition*, ed. Betty Radice and E. Mary Smallwood, trans. G. A. Williamson (London: Penguin Classics, 1981).

46 There is only one extant eighteenth-century manuscript of this text, currently housed at the Biblioteca Universitaria de Salamanca (Ms. 1985). The first modern edition of the manuscript was prepared in 1874 by Marcos Jiménez de la Espada: *Andanças e viajes de Pero Tafur por diversas partes del mundo avidos (1435–1439)* (Madrid: Colección de Libros Españoles Raros y Curiosos, VIII, 1874).

47 E. Michael Gerli, "Pero Tafur," in *Medieval Iberia: An Encyclopedia*, ed. E. Michael Gerli (New York: Routledge, 2003), 767.

household of the master of the chivalric Order of Calatrava,[48] this Andalusian adventurer produces an account remarkable for the number and geographical scope of the areas visited and the vivacious, often touristic style of the author's detailed commentary. Pero Tafur's travel account departs from earlier travelogues which relied on "zoomorphic and anthropomorphic fantasies of Classical *auctoritas*"[49] and it has been categorized as pragmatic and realistic[50] while the Andalusian traveller has been described as an unprejudiced eyewitness.[51]

Margaret W. Labarge suggests that Tafur must have been a member of the urban oligarchy (she adduces as evidence his position among the "venticuatro" or City Hall *regidores* of Córdoba in 1479).[52] Given his keen and frequent observations about markets, exchange commodities, trading caravans and technology it is quite probable that he was from a merchant family, and a wealthy one no doubt since his family was prosperous enough to indulge his taste for travel and adventure. The narrator himself repeatedly alludes to the bill of exchanges he carries and to his interactions with merchants and correspondents anywhere he goes and we know, for instance, that he stayed with the Morosinis in Venice at the outset of his travels.

Tafur provides a wealth of information regarding local customs, politics, commerce, and industry, but he does not do so detachedly; on the contrary, he actively seeks to engage with this "alien other" with whom he is confronted through his travels and exhibits a great eagerness to interact with locals. His contacts include not only prominent personages and dignitaries but also humbler folk. Additionally, he reveals an interest in natural history, paying particular attention to phenomena considered exotic from the European perspective: "A combination of religious pilgrimage, business trip, social promenade, and sightseeing excursion, his narrative expresses both inquisitive ethnographic curiosity and touristic fervor with regard to both European and non-European places and peoples."[53] Thus, he not merely opens up to "vulnerability" but he gladly embraces it as well.

Pero Tafur's stimulus in writing about his travels could be what he sees as a terrible blow for Christendom, the fall of Constantinople to the Turks in 1453. *Andanças e viajes*

---

48 M. A. Pérez Priego, "Introducción," in *Viajes medievales* (Madrid: Fundación José Antonio de Castro, 2006), xx; see also J. Rubio Tovar, *Libros españoles de viajes medievales* (Madrid: Taurus, 1986).

49 Karen M. Daly, "Here there Be No Dragons: *Maravilla* in Two Fifteenth-Century Spanish *libros de viajes*," *Notandum* 29 (2012): 25–34, at 26.

50 Miguel Angel Priego, "Maravillas en los libros de viajes medievales," *Compás de Letras* 7 (1995): 65–78, at 69.

51 Francisco López Estrada, "Viajeros españoles en Asia: la embajada de Enrique III a Tamorlán (1403–1406)," *Revista Universidad Complutense* 3 (1981): 227–46.

52 Margaret Wade Labarge, "Pero Tafur: A Fifteenth-Century Spaniard," *Florilegium* 5 (1983): 237–46. Sofía Carrizo Rueda (*Poética del relato de viajes* (Kassel: Edition Reichenberger, 1997): 111–12) and Filomena Liberatori ("Ideale cavalleresco e mercantilismo nelle 'Andancas' di Pero Tafur," *Studi di Iberistiche* 9 (1987): 109–38, at 138) also examine Tafur's links to the mercantile class.

53 Michael Harney, *Race, Caste, and Indigeneity in Medieval Spanish Travel Literature* (London: Palgrave Macmillan, 2015), 109.

endeavours to recover the link between Western Christendom and the East so forcibly severed by the Ottoman Turks' victory and in order to do so he hyperbolically describes and exalts all those places that he visited during his travels and that are now lost to Christians. His strategy is to mend the fissure by recreating the lost world, by presenting as whole what was broken but, paradoxically, by doing so he starkly exposes the vulnerability of the Christian world and Tafur's own vulnerability.

After all, Tafur is deemed to be the last European traveller to visit and describe Constantinople before the Ottomans' conquest.[54] Thus, his detailed descriptions of Constantinople, Caffa and Trebizond nostalgically and elegiacally conjure up a magnificent but lost world, which is, nevertheless, already imagined or fashioned in his writing as a decaying world. Despite the fact that he admits to being quite enthralled with the magnificent encircling walls and the marvellous monuments of the city, Tafur also reveals that he was already well aware of the weaknesses and the deterioration of Constantinople during his visit. He mentions the depopulation of the city and the state of general poverty and wretchedness observed in the remaining inhabitants' clothes as well as in their incessant wailing, and the visible state of disarray and neglect of the imperial palace:

> La cibdad es mal poblada e han mengua de buenas gentes de armas [...] La casa del emperador muestra aver sido magnífica, pero agora no está así, que ella e la cibdad bien parece el mal que han pasado e pasan de cada dia [...] La gente no bien vestidos, mas triste e pobre, mostrando el mal que tienen [...] Continuamente están dando aullidos como de llanto e por toda la cibdad.[55]

> [The city is severely depopulated and they lack good men of arms [...] The emperor's palace shows traces of having been magnificent but it is no longer so, and in both the palace and the city it is apparent how badly they have fared [...] People are not only badly dressed but they are sad and poor, clearly showing their anguish [...] They are constantly howling and crying all over the city.]

Even when describing his wonderment at the magnificence of Hagia Sofia, Tafur obliquely alludes, through the pointed use of the imperfect verbal tense in Spanish, to that vanished, more splendorous time: "la qual [Hagia Sofia] es tan grande que dizen que, cuando Constantinopla prosperava, avíe en ella seis mil clérigos."[56] (It is indeed so big that they claim that, when Constantinople used to be prosperous, there used to be six thousand priests in charge of it.)

Furthermore, in his travel account he contrasts several times the Byzantine city and its citizens' malaise to the magnificence and orderliness observed among their rivals, the Turks. Tafur is clearly mesmerized by the power and magnificence of the enemy. When the Byzantine emperor asks Tafur to accompany him to Italy as a member of his

---

54 Karen M. Daly, "Here Be No Dragons," 33.

55 Pero Tafur, *Andanças e viajes de Pero Tafur* in *Viajes medievales*, 211–379, at 296 and 313; my translation.

56 Pero Tafur, 308.

entourage for a strategically important meeting with the pope, Tafur declines and sets out instead to visit the Turkish headquarters at Adrianople and see the Grand Turk, Murat II (r. 1421–1444).

In addition, he refers to the Turks as "a noble people" (noble gente en quien se falla mucha verdad)[57] and generally esteems their abilities more than the Byzantines. On one instance, he sees the Ottoman army marching by the mighty walls of Constantinople and the Spanish traveller comments that it was a wonder to behold. He unapologetically praises their elegance, their weapons, liveries and horses and he further adds that he has no doubt that the Turks would have won the battle, had they attacked the city on that day.[58] His *admiratio* of the Turks and other Muslims from a Christian, detached and contrary position will metamorphose into a symbolic arrogation and performative stance at one point in the narrative where Pero Tafur dresses in Muslim garb in order to be able to penetrate, disguised and undeterred, into the Temple of Solomon or Mosque of Omar, at the time a site prohibited to Christians on pain of death:

> E aquella noche yo rogué a un moro renegado, que fue natural de Portugal, que le daría dos ducados e me metiese aquella noche a ver el templo de Salomón. E fízolo así, e a una ora de la noche yo entré con él vestido de su ropa e vi todo el templo, el cual es una sola nave toda de oro musaico labrada, e el suelo e paredes de muy fermosas losas blancas [...] Si yo allí fuera conocido por cristiano, luego fuera muerto.

> [And that night I implored a Moorish renegade, a native of Portugal, to sneak me into the Temple of Solomon in exchange for two ducats, and he did. I entered with him dressed in his clothing and saw all of the temple, which consists of one nave, all decorated with gold mosaic work and the floors and walls made of beautiful white flagstones [...] Had I been recognized as a Christian there, I would have been killed.][59]

By this seemingly innocuous (although defiant and highly dangerous) act of cross-dressing the Westerner has come closer to becoming the "alien other" himself.

In this unprejudiced or "vulnerable" spirit, Pero Tafur highlights through his travels the peaceful co-existence of the many different nationalities and denominations of his fellow pilgrims, including Catholics, Greeks, Jacobites, Armenians, Indians and Copts.[60] Evincing an open-mindedness akin to that expressed by Mandeville in the *Marvels*, he

---

57 Pero Tafur, 300.

58 "Yo ove en dicha de verlo [the Turk] en el campo, e ver su manera como andan en el campo é en la guerra e sus armas e cavallos e atavios; bien creo si con la gente del Poniente se fallasen, non avrie en ellos registençia no porque de la persona no son Buenos, mas falléceles mucho de los necesario a la guerra" (Pero Tafur, *Andanças e viajes por diversas partes del mundo avidos (1435–1439)* (Madrid: Imprenta de Miguel Ginesta, 1874) 184; Perez-Priego, *Viajes medievales*, 315.

59 Pero Tafur (2006), 251. English translation of passage taken from Shayne Aaron Legassie's *The Medieval Invention of Travel* (Chicago: Universty of Chicago Press, 2017), 206.

60 Michael Harney, *Race, Caste, and Indigeneity*, 246; Pero Tafur, 303.

remarks, in a passage describing a visit to Bethlehem, that even the Muslims are capable of piety: "Alli los moros fecieron tanta reverencia como nosotros" (There the Moors showed as much reverence as we do).[61] Later, in the long digression conveying his friend Niccolo de' Conti's account of his travels, the Eastern Christians ruled by Prester John are described as being as Catholic and devoutly Christian as one could want, save for their absolute ignorance of the church of Rome.[62]

Nevertheless, his forbearance is challenged when he finds himself in need of describing the Black Sea trading city of Kaffa. Tafur now criticizes and loathes the practices he beholds ("Tanta es la bestialidat e deformidat de aquesta gente" (These people's bestiality and deformity is enormous))[63] but he also excuses at times and, to a certain degree, he gives in and assimilates and, eventually, no matter how briefly, adopts the other culture's behaviour. He notes the city's extreme exoticism, describing its profusion of things "muy estrañas a los de nuestra nación" (quite alien to those of our nation); the great diversity of its population, including Christians, both Catholic and Greek, and members of all the world's nations. The town's polyglot inhabitants constantly engage in "grandes travesuras" (great abuses) such as fathers selling sons or brothers selling sisters.[64]

Tafur also indicates a certain degree of amazement and voyeuristic pleasure in his eyewitness account of the distasteful procedures of the great slave market of Kaffa. Surprisingly, however, he then engages in the distasteful activity himself, "prefiguring the flirtation with going native that is one of modern tourism's favorite constructed scenarios."[65] Here, in the world's greatest slave market, a papal bull is cited encouraging Christians to purchase Christian slaves of all nations,[66] for fear that they fall into Muslim hands and renounce their faith. Pero Tafur buys two female slaves and one male, informing his readers that they remain with him yet, years later in Córdoba. Showing sympathy for the slaves on the block, he describes the market's harsh procedures, whereby all slaves, males and females alike, are made to strip down to the skin, then paraded naked before prospective buyers. His subsequent hyperbolic reiteration of the astonishing diversity and strangeness of this foreign environment can be read, according to Michael Harney, "as an exculpatory disclaimer regarding his fleeting involvement in alien ways, among a motley horde of races people [sic] with whom he has nothing in common."[67]

---

61 Pero Tafur, *Travels and Adventures, 1435–1439*, ed. and trans. Malcolm Lett (London: Routledge, 1926), 248. Although "moro" [Moor] actually originated from the Latin word for "black" (*maurus*) and referred to inhabitants of Mauretania in North Africa (the actual Mahgreb), Pero Tafur uses the term "Moor" in his account indistinctly to refer to all Muslims, as was the usage among inhabitats of the Iberian Peninsula during the medieval and early modern period.

62 Tafur, *Travels and Adventures*, 274.

63 Tafur, *Andanças e viajes*, 2006, 169.

64 Harney, *Race, Caste, and Indigeneity*, 303.

65 Harney, *Race, Caste, and Indigeneity*, 303.

66 Harney, *Race, Caste, and Indigeneity*, 110.

67 Harney, *Race, Caste, and Indigeneity*, 304.

Ciertamente si no fuera por los ginoveses que alli estan, no parece que los otros no tienen parte con nuestra naturaleza tantas e tan diversas naciones e tantos trajes en el vestir e en el comer e en el uso de las mujeres, que acaeçie en la posada donde estavamos traernos las moças virgenes por un açumbre de vino, de que ellos han carestia, e de toda fruta e aun de pan, aunque alli en la cibdad se falla porque lo llevan los mercaderes, pero caro e por esto se fazen los furtos.

[If it were not for the Genovese, no one here looks close to our nature since there are people from all nations and so much variety in the clothes and the food and the way with women, as for example when we were at the inn and they would bring to us some virgin maidens and offered them to us in exchange for some wine, which they lacked, as well as fruit and even bread, even though one can find those things in the city because the merchants bring them but they are expensive and for this reason people steal.]

And he follows with an anecdote to describe perhaps the most alien or strange of all the groups he is encountering, the Tartars, who are tough, bellicose and strong and since they are constantly ready to fight and mounted on their horses they put their meat between the side of the horse and the seat and that is how they cook their meat.[68] Tafur is visibly fascinated with the Tartars, so much so that he actively tries to arrange to travel further into their country: "Yo trabajé cuanto pude por ir por la Tartaria, pero fui consejado que no lo devia fazer, porque no sería seguro de las gentes que andan por los campos, sueltos, sin obediencia de sennor"[69] (I tried very hard to arrange for travel to the Tartar lands but they advised me not to do it because I would be in danger from the people roaming the countryside, bereft of obeisance to any lord). Here Tafur would like to know more about other cultures but the fear of physical vulnerability on the road dissuades him from his plan to travel. Other times, however, he seems to wish to encounter such dangers as when he wishes that the Turks had attacked so that he could have fought them,[70] and goes so far as to express a yearning for religious persecution. For instance, in Pero Tafur's second-hand report of the experiences of the Italian traveller Niccolò de Conti, whose long sojourn in the East is summarized by our Spanish traveller in an extensive digression, Tafur asserts: "Yo dispuesto estava para rescebir el martirio"[71] (I was very willing to endure martyrdom).

Thus, by the end of his voyage Tafur had not only experienced physical vulnerabilities (which included a shipwreck and an arrow wound to the foot) but had also been transformed ("wounded") by the Eastern cultures with which he had come in contact and his beliefs had been unsettled. Furthermore, his gaze back to his own culture revealed that the West or "Poniente," as he calls it, had lost its ascendancy in all spheres

---

68 "E bien que yo quisiera, aunque teniamos pocas gentes, que nos provara a fazer alguna fuerça." Pero Tafur, 304.

69 Pero Tafur, 305.

70 Pero Tafur, 315.

71 Pero Tafur, 269.

(commercially, socially, politically, and militarily) and that Christian polities were more vulnerable than the ones in the East.

In the "Prologue" to his travel account Pero Tafur had explained the purpose of his journey:

> Es visitar tierras estrañas, porque de tal visitación razonablemente se pueden conseguir provechos cercanos a lo que proeza require, así engrandeciendo los fijosdalgo sus corazones donde sin ser primero conocidos los intervienen trabajos y priesas, como deseando mostrar por obras quién fueron sus antecesores, cuando solamente por propias façañas puede ser de ellos conocedora la gente estrangera.

> [From the practice of travelling into foreign lands a man may reasonably hope to attain proficiency in that which prowess demands. Thus *hidalgos* (knights) may grow stout-hearted where, being unknown, they are beset by hardship and peril, striving to show themselves worthy of their ancestors, and by their own deeds to make their virtues known to strangers.][72]

Pero Tafur's written account of his adventures are exemplary not only of the physical "hardships I have suffered in various parts of the world," as he tellingly puts it,[73] but of the other types of vulnerabilities outlined above. Little did he realize that through the process of transformation effected by the "practice of travelling" he was, in fact, acting as a Muslim and unknowingly following a Muslim mandate, which inspired people to travel and achieve knowledge of themselves and others.

Our third Iberian traveller experienced a similar but reversed and coerced transformation. He was named at birth al-Ḥasan ibn Muḥammad al-Wazzān al-Zayyātī or al-Fāsī, but he became better known among Christian Europeans as Leo Africanus. He was a Berber diplomat and author born in Granada, best known for writing the *Cosmogrophia* [sic] *e Geographia de Affrica*, which describes the geography of the Maghreb and the Nile Valley.[74] At the time of its publication, the book was deemed the most authoritative treatise on the subject of the geography of Africa among the learned in Europe, and it continued to be so at least until the modern exploration of Africa.[75]

Although the writer Amin Maalouf paints a wonderfully detailed picture of the eponymous hero in his 1986 *Leo Africanus* novel, only sparse details are known about al-Hassan al-Wazzan's life. Natalie Zemon-Davies's compelling study *Trickster Travels: A*

---

72 Pero Tafur, ed. Pérez Priego, 2006, 215; Pero Tafur, *Travels and Adventures*, 19.

73 Pero Tafur, *Travels and Adventures*, 20.

74 Al-Hassan al Wazzan/Leo Africanus, *Libro de la Cosmogrophia et Geographia de Affrica*, MS V.E. 953, Biblioteca Nazionale Centrale, Rome.

75 Pekka Masonen, "Leo Africanus: the Man with Many Names," *Al-Andalus Magreb* 8–9 (2001): 115–43; Dietrich Rauchenberger, *Johannes Leo der Afrikaner: seine Beschreibung des Raumes zwischen Nil und Niger nach dem Urtext*, (Wiesbaden: Harrassowitz, 1999), 27–28. Rauchenberger suggests that Sebastiano del Piombo's 1520 portrait of an anonymous humanist probably depicts Leo Africanus (78–79).

Sixteenth-Century Muslim between Worlds does an excellent job at filling in the substantial gaps in our knowledge of Leo Africanus's life, motivations and interests but much remains speculative.[76] Akin to Pero Tafur, Leo did lead, however, an adventurous and perilous existence. As his translator John Pory claims, Leo escaped from "so manie thousands of inminent dangers."[77] During his travels through the Atlas Mountains he endured a severe snowstorm which killed all his caravan companions, and some Arab horsemen attempted to rob him by stripping him in the cold. While travelling in Nubian lands his caravan's guide lost his way in the desert and they wandered for ten days with very little water. Moreover, not only did he suffer kidnapping and enslavement by pirates, imprisonment in Rome and a subsequent forced conversion to Christianity, but he had also experienced the fate of an exile when he and his family fled from Granada right before or soon after the fall of the city to the Christian armies of the Catholic monarchs in 1492.

In spite of the fact that many scholars proposed 1491 as the date of his birth, it is more likely that al-Wazzan was born later, between 1494 and 1495, in the city of Granada. He came from a privileged background. It appears that his father owned lands and the family must have been well to do judging by the distinguished position his exiled relatives occupied in Morocco: his uncle was an ambassador. Al-Wazzan did not live long in Granada although he always proudly attached the demonym "al-Gharnati" (the Granadan) to his name.[78] His family moved to Fez probably only a few years after he was born. The actual reason for the move is unknown, although it has been frequently reasoned that they must have been escaping religious persecution by the new Christian rulers of Granada. Around those years, however, the predicament of the Muslim population had not become desperate yet. In fact, one of the conditions of the surrender of Granada was the granting of religious freedom for the Muslims. Unlike what had happened with the Jews in 1492, the Muslims of Granada had apparently received very tolerant and benign terms of surrender from the Catholic kings. [79]

Notwithstanding, even if al-Wazzan's family had predicted what was to come, perhaps their departure can be better explicated by remembering the Islamic mandate to emigrate from infidel lands. Islamic law required Muslims to break ties with idolatry by

---

76 Natalie Zemon Davies, *Trickster Travels: A Sixteenth-Century Muslim Between Worlds* (New York: Hill and Wang, 2006). Davies herself admits to it and envisions her book's hypotheses as an invitation to the reader "to follow a plausible life story from materials of the time" (13). I refer the reader to her book for extensive information about most of what is known about Leo Africanus, including bibliographical references. For the purposes of my study I will concentrate solely on the issue of vulnerability.

77 Leo Africanus, *A Geographical Historie of Africa, written in Arabicke and Italian by John Leo, a More borne in Granada and brought up in Barbarie*, trans. and collected by J. Pory (London: George Bishop, 1600).

78 As a matter of fact, even after he converted to Catholicism and was baptized by Pope Leo X, al-Wazzan chose as his new name Yuhanna al-Asad al-Gharnati, which translates as John the Lion of Granada.

79 This state of affairs, however, would dramatically change just a few years later when the Catholic kings reneged on their earlier promises and forced all Granadan Muslims to convert.

moving from the lands of Christians or *Dar al-Harb* (territory of war).[80] It is, therefore, very likely that Leo's parents simply followed the example set by most members of the highest echelon of Granadan society, including the defeated king, Boabdil, who himself emigrated to Morocco in 1493.

Thus, although forced conversions did not start until 1499 when the archbishop of Toledo, Francisco Ximénez de Cisneros, was sent to Granada to substitute the more tolerant Hernando de Talavera, many of the richest and most influential Muslims had already left and resettled across the Strait of Gibraltar. They were no doubt escaping what many saw as inevitable, which tragically and promptly came to pass in 1502, when those Muslims left in Granada who had refused to convert to Christianity were finally deported to North Africa in 1502, after their unsuccessful revolt.[81]

In Fez, young al-Hasan Ibn Muhammad al-Wazzan received a good education at the reputable Islamic university of al-Qarawiyyin. While studying, he worked for two years as a secretary in the "bimaristan"[82] of Fez, a hospital for sick foreigners and poor combined with a lunatic asylum. Then after becoming a *faqih* he initiated his life of adventure by travelling first with his uncle the ambassador in some of his missions, and later on his own on a variety of commercial and diplomatic expeditions. His life of travels, nevertheless, was abruptly truncated when the ship in which he was sailing back to Fez from Cairo was seized by Spanish pirate Pedro Cabrera y Bobadilla in 1518. The ruthless captor must have appreciated the value of this diplomat and scholar because he sent al-Wazzan to Rome to be presented as a gift to Pope Leo X. The Moroccan diplomat spent more than a year (1518–1519) in Rome as a prisoner in Castel Sant'Angelo.

---

80 See a more thorough explanation of this obligation in the chapters by Gould (Chapter 1) and Sorrentino (Chapter 2) in this volume. *Dar al-harb* "denotes the territory bordering on dar al-Islam (territory of Islam) whose leaders are called up to convert to Islam" (John L. Esposito, *Oxford Dictionary of Islam*, 62). While a highly contested term, according to the majority of jurists "an Islamic territory taken by non-Muslims" (such as the case of Granada in 1492) "becomes *dar al-harb* when Islamic law is replaced" (62). Tahanawi defined it as "an area in which the writ of the infidel ruler runs" (cited in "Dar al-Islam and dar al-harb in Modern Indian Muslim Thought" in *Dar al-Islam / dar al-harb: Territories, Peoples, Identities*, ed. Giovanna Calasso (Leiden: Brill, 2017), 344). See also in same edited volume the article by Maribel Fierro and Luis Molina, "Some Notes on *dar al-harb* in Early al-Andalus," 205–34.

81 The final expulsion of the remaining converted Muslims or *Moriscos* did not take place until 1609, during the reign of Philip III.

82 A "bimaristan" was "in medieval Islam, a hospital; in modern usage, this Persian appellation is applied especially to a mental hospital. One of the greatest and original institutional achievements of classical Islamic society, the *bimaristan* provided a wide range of services, sometimes without fee, and also functioned as a medical research and teaching school. The first *bimaristan* was established in Baghdad under Harun al-Rashid (r. 786–809). Among the most illustrious were the twelfth-century Adudi hospital in Baghdad and the Mansuri hospital in Cairo, completed in 1284." (www.oxfordislamicstudies.com/article/opr/t125/e352). The institution where al-Wazzan worked reminds us of the hospital created by the caliph of Baghdad and described by Benjamin in his travelogue.

Pope Leo X, however, had shrewdly recognized the benefits that could derive from al-Wazzan's presence in Rome.[83] On one hand, the captive was not only a seasoned diplomat privy to advantageous information about the church's enemies but also an erudite Muslim scholar who could prove useful in deciphering Arabic documents and in instructing Christians on Muslim culture, language and attitudes. Conversely, there was considerable symbolic value to be earned by holding al-Wazzan captive as an archetype of the defeated and humiliated enemy and, later on, by exhibiting al-Wazzan not only as the vanquished enemy but also as an enemy divested of its Muslim ways, now donning Christian attire by virtue of al-Wazzan's conversion to Christianity. In an elaborate and ostentatious ceremony, Pope Leo X himself baptized al-Wazzan in the Basilica of St. Peter in 1520. Pope Leo X's manoeuvres in his treatment of his slave embody well the process of establishing hegemony as outlined by Gramsci: he has managed through coercion (the threat of slavery or death) and persuasion (appealing to al-Wazzan's interest in learning and intellectual sophistication) to exert his power over his vulnerable subordinate and to bring about his conversion. The diplomat/slave now turned Christian took the Latin name Johannes Leo de Medicis (Giovanni Leone in Italian), presumably in honour of his benefactor. In Arabic, however, he chose to append to the translation of his name a reference to his native Granada, in itself an act of resistance: Yuhanna al-Asad al-Gharnati (John the Lion of Granada).

He was, thus, very much a traveller between two worlds, Christian and Muslim, and he was quite aware of the fact that his position as a bridge between the two was quite unstable and dangerous. Our diplomat, however, cleverly understood as well that in order to escape this estate of constant vulnerability and survive one must adapt and assimilate. He illustrates this lesson in the *Geographia* when narrating a tale perhaps recast from the *Kalila wa Dimna* or from the *Kitab al-Hayawan*, that of the amphibious bird which can opportunistically change allegiance or identity. When the king of the birds appears demanding his taxes, the bird declares itself a fish; when the king of the fish wants tribute, the amphibious creature declares he is a bird again. While depicting the virtues and vices of the Africans, al-Wazzan feels remorseful about criticizing the people from the lands where he was brought up, thus appearing ungrateful. It is as he reflects on this dilemma of his task as a truthful historian that al-Wazzan announces that he will do like the bird: "For mine owne part when I heare the Africans evill spoken of I will affirme my self to be one of Granada; and when I perceive the nation of Granada to be discommended then I will professe my selfe to be an African."[84]

Hence, al-Wazzan/Leo Africanus's unconventional *rihla*,[85] the *Geographia*, is very illustrative of his precarious and ambiguous position between two inimical worlds and of the erosion of his cultural and religious identity through the contact with the Western world, while living in *Dar al-Harb*, the Land of War. First, the *Libro de Cosmographia*

---

83 Pope Leo X, born Giovanni di Medici, was the second son of Lorenzo, il Magnifico, and he was a highly learned man, educated in humanistic studies and a significant patron of the arts.

84 Africanus, *A Geographical Historie*, 190.

85 Unconventional in the sense that it is not *sensu strictu* a travel account or *rihla* but can be conceptualized as such.

et Geographia de Affrica does not follow the established patterns of an Arabic travel account since al-Wazzan's adventures "as recounted in his *Geography* are not consecutive, as in a *rihla*. They weave in and out of his narrative," as Natalie Zemon-Davies rightly notes.[86] Secondly, he did not write it in his native language, Arabic, but in a language, Italian, which he had imperfectly learned while in prison and through his new life in Italy. And lastly his cultural and linguistic identity was further eroded in the process of dissemination and publication of his work. Al-Hasan Ibn Muhammad al-Wazzan finished his book in 1526 but in 1550 the Venetian Giovanni Battista Ramusio published it and modified it considerably.[87] In addition to changing the syntax and vocabulary to fit into a more elevated language, Ramusio rearranged materials, omitted many sections of the book, particularly those that alluded to aspects of Islam or Muslim culture, and modified al-Wazzan's use of the third person (more akin to Arabic modes of discourse) by inserting the pronoun "I" and first-person verbs wherever al-Wazzan had consciously, detachedly and humbly referred to himself in the third person.[88]

A further vulnerability made tangible by the *Geographia* and explicitly acknowledged by Leo Africanus within his discourse is his inadequacy in his task as a historian:[89] "Whereas in his book of biographies, he concealed his vulnerability, in the *Geography* he confesses to it—'I haven't seen a history book for ten years'—[90] and explains that he must rely on his 'weak memory'"[91] since he has no access to many of the authoritative sources (Arabic manuscripts not abounding in Rome at the time) he needs as references for his work. This vulnerability can also operate, however, as a formulaic *captatio benevolentia* to forestall any possible objections arising from his actual, intended Christian readers but also among his foreseeable future Muslim readers with regard to the content and tone of his descriptions. Al-Wazzan had to write taking care "to placate the Christians while not defaming Islam."[92] By putting on a mask of inability and humility he succeeds in appeasing both worlds and, in the process, he learns to discern the deficiencies and the merits of the lands of the Christians and the land of Islam. It is because of this acquired knowledge that he neither fully rejects nor fully embraces one or the other in his enigmatic *Geographia*.

---

86 Davies, *Trickster Travels*, 103.

87 Giovanni Battista Ramusio, ed. *Primo volume et Seconda edition delle Navigationi et Viaggi ... nelle quale si contengono La Descrittione dell' Africa* (Venice: Giunti, 1554).

88 Natalie Zemon-Davies suggests that al-Wazzan used the third person and fashioned himself as "el Compositore" to gain distance, "distance from Italian life and from his life as a Muslim in the Maghreb; a provisional distance, allowing him to play the Christian for time, to reflect on his Muslim identity, and then, when ready, return safe and sound to North Africa" (*Trickster Travels*, 232).

89 To be exact, however, al-Wazzan did not identify himself as a historian *per se* but as a composer or compiler.

90 The editor Giovanni Battista Ramusio certainly considered this a vulnerability since he omitted this admission from his refashioning of al-Wazzan's *Geographia* (Ramusio, *La descrizione dell'Africa*, f. 2r, 39–40).

91 Davies, *Trickster Travels*, 105.

92 Davies, *Trickster Travels*, 266.

It is exceedingly ironic that this journey that began for him as a child fleeing a Granada which had forcibly become a *bilad al-nasara* (lands of the Christians) brought him back, albeit in a circumvented way, to the *dar al- harb*, "the house of war," usually seen as Christian territory. The result of his travels was, thus, not an epistemological triumph but a surrendering to a different type of epistemological certainty: that he was terribly vulnerable and that in order for him to survive he had to divest himself of his culture and religion and convert to the faith of the same people that had caused his first vulnerability and his first exile. Al-Wazzan/Leo Africanus's *Libro de la Cosmogrophia et Geographia de Affrica* is also perhaps not only a way for him to enlighten Christians about this culture he had to leave behind but also a strategy for him to remain tied to it now that he has been coerced to abjure it.

While I cannot do justice here to these three fascinating travel accounts I can offer some overarching conclusions as a way to bring attention to all these texts and their peculiarities. Each of them has a different purpose and focuses on different narrative strategies and different travel and commercial experiences but one can still infer, despite the disparity of exemplars, that there are many points of convergence between these documents.

The instances of exchanges depicted in the narratives of Benjamin of Tudela, Pero Tafur and al-Wazzan elucidate and demonstrate the validity of the theoretical model proposed by Brian Catlos, as discussed in the introductory essay. This comparative project has sought to illuminate the processes by which these early Iberian travellers established fruitful and pragmatic ties with their neighbours and hosts for the purpose of religious and intellectual fulfillment and commercial and political expansion. Homi Bhabha would have us believe that our vision will always be slightly distorted and unsettling because the subjects studied by our travel narrative authors are always concealed behind a mask of "sly civility," as he puts it, [93] but I would add that this distortion occurs more pointedly because our travelling authors/narrators' gazes are not only informed by their own belief systems and prejudices but also because their contact with new cultures forces them to gaze back at those belief systems or ideologies, to critique them and expose them as not as absolute, fixed and unyielding as first thought and certainly not as blameless or infallible.

Travel and the epistemological and ethnographic learning of other cultures which travelling provides makes us very vulnerable, it always erodes the stability and the identity of the traveller and encounters among peoples from different cultures are always both congenial and treacherous. As travellers in search of *episteme* we are indeed vulnerable but never victims if we are open to vulnerability and thus, transformation.

---

93 Homi Bhabha, *The Location of Culture* (London: Routledge, 1994), 93.

Part II

**Imagining the East:
Egypt, Persia, and Istanbul in My Mind**

Chapter 4

"TIERRAS DE EGIPTO": IMAGINED JOURNEYS TO THE EAST IN THE EARLY VERNACULAR LITERATURE OF MEDIEVAL IBERIA

MATTHEW V. DESING

ABSTRACT

This article focuses on portrayals of imagined eastward journeys, specifically those in Egypt, in the three poems that make up Manuscript K-III-4 of the Royal Library of San Lorenzo de El Escorial: the *Libro de Apolonio* (a romance of nautical adventures in the Eastern Mediterranean), the *Vida de madona Santa María Egipciaqua* (the hagiography of a sixth-century "holy harlot"), and the *Libre dels tres reys d'Orient* (a tale whose central focus is the Holy Family's flight to Egypt). This article seeks to untangle the web of signification that produced these imagined Egyptian journeys in the period of the composition of the poems in the mid-thirteenth century and in the period of their compilation into a single manuscript in the late fourteenth century. The historical reality and literary landscape of Iberia changed much in the intervening period and so the reception of the poems would have changed as well. This article contrasts the original place of eastern journeys in the individual poems with their increased importance due to their later interrelation in the context of an Iberian imaginary in which the place of Egypt and the Levant had dramatically expanded.

Keywords: Escorial Manuscript K-III-4, *Libro de Apolonio, Vida de Santa María Egipciaca, Libre dels tres reys d'Orient*, St. Mary of Egypt, Aragon

TALES OF TRAVEL to unfamiliar lands have captured the imaginations of Spanish-language readers for centuries. While "eastern" journeys (those in the Eastern Mediterranean, North Africa, and the Far and Middle East) in late medieval and early modern Spanish literature have been an *in vogue* topic in criticism since the beginning of the new millennium, such journeys imagined prior to the late fourteenth century have remained in relative obscurity. In order to begin to remedy this situation, this article focuses on portrayals of eastward journeys, specifically those in Egypt, in the three poems that make up Manuscript K-III-4 of the Royal Library of San Lorenzo de El Escorial: the *Libro de Apolonio* (a romance of nautical adventures in the Eastern Mediterranean), the *Vida de madona Santa María Egipciaqua* (the hagiography of a sixth-century "holy harlot"), and the *Libre dels tres reys d'Orient* (a tale whose central focus is the Holy Family's flight to Egypt). Journeys in Egypt play a role in each of the three poems, but this is an imagined Egypt based on received knowledge rather than an understanding drawn from direct experience. This article seeks to untangle the web of signification that produced these imagined Egyptian journeys in the periods of the composition of the poems and the reception of the manuscript as a literary compilation.

The complicating factor of this analysis is that the periods of the composition of the three poems and their subsequent compilation into a single manuscript are separated by more than a century. Scholars believe that the three poems were composed independently in the early to mid-thirteenth century, but were compiled, copied, and bound together in a single surviving manuscript more than a hundred years later in the late fourteenth century. The role that Egypt played in the medieval Iberian imaginary was much changed between those two periods, and examining such changes underlines the importance of Egyptian journeys, especially for the later reception of the manuscript as a whole. In order to show how this is the case, this article begins with an overview of Iberian literary portrayals of eastern journeys prior to the thirteenth century, and then moves on to a close analysis of the Egyptian and Levantine journeys in the three individual poems of Manuscript K-III-4. Next, the examination turns to the changes in the historical and literary landscapes of medieval Iberia between the two periods under consideration. Finally, the materiality of the manuscript is examined in the historical context of its composition in order to propose that eastern journeys, and particularly those in Egypt, could have been one possible motivation for the combination of these three specific poems. This analysis will shed new light on the understudied place of eastern travels broadly, and specifically those in Egypt and the Levant, in the medieval Iberian imagination prior to the famous travels of the late fourteenth century.

Early modern travel, especially in the "Age of Discovery" of the late fifteenth and early sixteenth centuries, has long eclipsed medieval travel in Iberian studies. Despite this, the antiquated view of the Middle Ages as a static time has in recent decades given way to increased study of medieval travel, both within the Iberian Peninsula primarily in the form of pilgrimage to Santiago de Compostela from the eleventh century on,[1] and outside of the Iberian kingdoms primarily to the Levant and beyond in the late fourteenth and early fifteenth centuries. Academic attention given to travels to the East in this later period has largely focused on the separate journeys of two diplomats. At the turn of the fifteenth century, Ruy González de Clavijo, ambassador at the court of Enrique III of Castile, undertook his famous diplomatic journey to the court of Timur in Samarqand, which he recounted in his *Embajada a Tamorlán*. Several decades later, another Spanish

---

[1] A few prominent examples of scholarship on pilgrimage in Iberia include the following: Maryjane Dunn and Linda K. Davidson's collection *The Pilgrimage to Compostela in the Middle Ages* (New York: Routledge, 2000); Thomas D. Spaccarelli's *A Medieval Pilgrim's Companion: Reassessing El Libro de los huéspedes (Escorial Ms. H.i.13)* (Chapel Hill: U.N.C. Dept. of Romance Languages, 1998); and the critical cluster on the topic of pilgrimage to Santiago de Compostela co-edited by John K. Moore, Jr. and Thomas D. Spaccarelli in the journal *La corónica*: "The Road to Santiago and Pilgrimage," *La corónica: A Journal of Medieval Hispanic Languages, Literatures, and Cultures* 36 (2008): 5–14.

traveller, Pero Tafur, travelled through North Africa, the Mediterranean, the Holy Land, Trebizond, Constantinople, and back through central Europe; he later recounted these journeys in *Andanças e viajes de Pero Tafur por diversas partes del mundo avidos*. Both of these travel narratives received little attention prior to the late 1990s, but since that time, these two texts, along with the late fourteenth-century imaginary travelogue *Libro del conoscimiento de todos los reinos* and the roughly contemporary Aragonese translation of *Mandeville's Travels*, have become fashionable objects of literary inquiry.[2]

The previously mentioned narratives, however, were far from the first instances of medieval authors from the Iberian Peninsula imagining travel outside of Europe. Reaching back into late antiquity, one finds the famous example of the Latin *Travels of Egeria* (*Itinerarium Egeriae*), which tells of the pilgrimage of a fourth-century Galician woman (possibly a nun) who visits locales described in biblical narratives, including long periods in Egypt. While expanding the focus of this study to include such Latin texts of the early Middle Ages would yield a project too broad for the aims of this article, it is of note that the elapsed period between late antiquity and the thirteenth century brought societal shifts that would render actual journeys through North Africa and the Levant more difficult for Iberian Christians. The invasions of Germanic peoples from Eastern Europe and the subsequent sacks of the city of Rome led to the fall of the Roman Empire in the west and the end of the political and economic unity of much of the territory previously held together by it, including the Iberian Peninsula. Of the various powers that sought control of the Peninsula throughout the fifth and sixth centuries, it was the Visigoths who established the most lasting power. However, that fragile political unity would last for little over a century before the invasion of the Iberian Peninsula by Muslim forces in 711. By this time, most of the Levant and North Africa was already under Muslim military control, and from this point much of Iberia would be brought into this new political, religious, and cultural sphere. The Christians of what is now Spain and Portugal who did not convert would live either in subjugation to or in conflict with Muslim powers for the next five centuries.

By the close of twelfth century, the tide was turning in favour of the military and political power of the Christian kingdoms of the Iberian Peninsula, and the imaginary of the northern kingdoms again turned outward. In the late twelfth or early thirteenth century, another pilgrimage guide to the Holy Land surfaces, but now in the vernacular. The *Fazienda de ultramar* presents an itinerary for Holy Land journeys along with abundant biblical material, much of which was translated into an Iberian vernacular for the first time in this manuscript.[3] Egypt naturally plays an important role in the document in

---

2 Recent work on these fourteenth- and fifteenth-century texts include the following: Francisco López Estrada's edition of Clavijo's *Embajada a Tamorlán* (Madrid: Editorial Castalia, 1999); Aníbal A. Biglieri's article "Jerusalén: de *La gran conquista de Ultramar* a Pero Tafur," *La corónica: A Journal Of Medieval Spanish Language, Literature, And Cultural Studies* 36 (2008): 59–73; Benjamin Liu's article "Re-Orienting Medieval Spanish Travel Narratives," *Yearbook of Comparative And General Literature* 52 (2005): 19–30.

3 It is of note that these are some of the first vernacular translations of the Bible in the Iberian Peninsula.

the telling of the Old Testament narratives of Joseph's sale into slavery in Egypt and the Israelites' subsequent escape from subjugation there.

Another vernacular work of the early thirteenth century, a Castilian version of the legends surrounding Alexander the Great, the *Libro de Alexandre*, also depicts travel in the East, primarily into Asia Minor, the Fertile Crescent, and Persia, but also into North Africa.[4] While the poem traces the life and many conquests of the Macedonian hero, a favorite subject of Western European authors of the period, the familiar theme of travel in the form of pilgrimage also surfaces in the poem. Teresa M. Rossi argues that the Castilian poet transforms the scene of Alexander's visit to the Temple of Amon into a reflection of thirteenth-century pilgrimage, even though the narrative takes place in pre-Christian Egypt.[5] Relating the importance of the scene to this part of the poem, the author states that "esta anécdota de devoción religiosa corona la campaña militar egipcia, la punta más occidental de la conquista mediterránea" (this anecdote of religious devotion crowns the Egyptian military campaign, the westernmost point of the Mediterranenan conquest).[6] Although much of the Iberian literature of the Middle Ages that includes travel in the Levant, and in particular in Egypt, has some connection with pilgrimage, not all representations of travel in these lands are itineraries or pilgrimage guides to the Holy Land, as we have seen in the case of the *Libro de Alexandre*.

In order to gain a more complete view of the role of eastern and specifically Egyptian travel in the medieval Iberian imaginary, one must take into account a broad variety of texts. Manuscript K-III-4 of the Royal Library of San Lorenzo de El Escorial provides such variety as it includes three thirteenth-century poems representing three distinct genres and verse forms, but all containing eastern journeys including Egypt. The first of the three poems, the *Libro de Apolonio*, is the romance tale of the journeys and misadventures of a young king throughout the Eastern Mediterranean. The second poem, the *Vida de madona Santa María Egipciaca*, is a version of the popular hagiography of the converted harlot St. Mary of Egypt. The third and final of these three is the *Libre dels treys reys d'Orient*, which tells a story composed of three biblical moments, but whose central story is a more developed narrative of an incident occurring during the Holy Family's flight from Bethlehem to Egypt. These three poems, written separately in the first half of the thirteenth century, all contain depictions of travel in Egypt, which provide us with a point of departure from which to examine eastern journeys in the medieval Iberian imaginary of this period.

The first of the poems included in the Escorial Manuscript K-III-4 is the *Libro de Apolonio*, a mid-thirteenth-century version of the "best-selling" medieval nautical

---

4 This work is recognized as the first poem of the *cuaderna vía* stanzaic style in Castilian.

5 The temple, also known as the Oracle of Amon, is located at the Siwa Oasis in modern-day Egypt near the western border with Libya. Siwa oasis is a remote location in the Libyan Desert (which stretches from the Nile westward into eastern Libya and also covers northern Sudan).

6 Teresa M. Rossi, "Alejandro Magno, el primer romero de las letras españolas: Entre vulgarización e invención," in *El Girador, I–II: Studi di lett. iberiche e ibero-americane offerti a Giuseppe Bellini* (Rome: Bulzoni, 1993), 861–66, at 862.

romance, the legend of King Apollonius of Tyre.[7] Although several analogues of the tale exist in Latin and the various European vernaculars, the earliest known Iberian version is of interest to scholars for its numerous peculiarities. This version is widely recognized as the most Christianized account of the legend, even though the action takes place in a pre-Christian milieu; the Iberian author infuses his reworking of the tale with many aspects of a thirteenth-century ethos, creating "vivos cuadros de costumbres del siglo XIII" (lively popular vignettes of the thirteenth century).[8] Elsewhere I have emphasized the expanded roles that the two principal female characters play in this version, and the bibliography on differences between this version and its sources and analogues is extensive.[9] The thirteenth-century *Libro de Apolonio* follows the basic narrative outline of the other versions of the legend, but with significant differences that make it a unique poetic creation.

The basic outline of the Apollonius legend begins with the young protagonist leaving his kingdom of Tyre to find an eligible wife. His quest brings him to the neighbouring realm of Antioch where he attempts to answer a riddle in order to win the hand of the princess, but the evil king Antioco deceives the young protagonist so that he may keep his daughter for his own incestuous use.[10] When Apolonio answers the riddle successfully and reveals the king's incest with his daughter, the young protagonist is forced by the evil king's murderous rage to flee into exile. After a series of misadventures, Apolonio loses all of his worldly possessions and arrives naked and alone on the shores of Pentapolis.[11] There he eventually wins a place at court of the good King Architrastres and the love of his daughter Luciana. Apolonio and the princess Luciana marry, and when she is in the advanced stages of pregnancy, the news arrives that the evil King Antioco is dead. Through a series of misadventures on their return journey to Apolonio's homeland of Tyre, the protagonist, his wife Luciana, and their newborn daughter Tarsiana are separated. The rest of the narrative follows the separate stories of the three characters until they are happily reunited near the end of the poem.

---

7 Although the title of this work within the manuscript appears as *Libre de Appollonio*, the standard spelling *Libro de Apolonio* has become so entrenched in the criticism over the past 150 years that I have decided to use this title when referring to the work.

8 Pedro L. Barcia, *El mester de clerecía* (Buenos Aires: Centro Editor de América Latina, 1967), 38.

9 Such scholarship includes the following: my articles "Luciana's Story: Text, Travel, and Interpretation in the *Libro de Apolonio*," *Hispanic Review* 79 (2011): 1–15, and "'De pan y de tresoro': Sacrament in the *Libro de Apolonio*," *La corónica* 40 (2012): 93–120; Pablo Ancos's "Vocalidad y textualidad en el *Libro de Apolonio*," *Troianalexandrina: Anuario sobre literatura medieval de materia clásica* 3 (2003): 41–76; and Alan Deyermond's "Emoción y ética en el *Libro de Apolonio*," *Vox Romanica* 48 (1989): 153–64.

10 For this summary of the legend I have used the Castilian versions of the names of the characters. This is significant because the names of the characters vary widely, and Apolonio's wife, who is named Luciana in the *Libro de Apolonio*, goes unnamed in many of the other medieval versions.

11 This is most likely Pentapolis (Cyrene/Cyrenaea), located near Marj/Barca in Libya just northeast of Benghazi.

Egypt appears in the *Libro de Apolonio* a little more than half way through the 656-stanza poem. When Apolonio and his pregnant wife Luciana are on their triumphant return journey to Tyre, the newly married queen goes into a difficult childbirth. The baby is born healthy, but it appears that Luciana herself dies in the labour. Apolonio and his crew construct a watertight coffin for his supposedly deceased wife. They send Luciana's coffin out onto the sea with rich clothing, precious coins, and a handwritten letter in hopes that someone will recover the body and provide the young queen a proper burial. Physicians in Ephesus recover the coffin and find Luciana to be alive (unbeknown to Apolonio), and they promptly install her as the abbess of a convent in the city. Because Apolonio believes that his misfortunes are due to some fault on his own part, he decides to undertake an expiatory journey to Egypt.

Apolonio first goes to the land of Tarsus that he had visited earlier in the narrative in order to leave his newborn daughter in the care of the governor and his wife. Apolonio tells the couple that until he is able to marry his daughter to a suitable husband, he will refrain from cutting his hair or nails, and that, "quiero en Egipto en tan amiente estar" (I want to remain in Egypt in the meantime).[12] The narrative at this time leaves Apolonio to wander in Egypt and focuses on the story of his child Tarsiana. The young girl is raised as a daughter to the governor of Tarsus, and her true identity is kept a secret from her. It is not until Tarsiana's nursemaid Licórides is on her deathbed that the young girl learns of her true identity. At this time, the dying nursemaid confesses to the young girl that

> El rey Apolonio, un noble cavallero,
> señor era de Tiro, un reçio cabdalero;
> ese fue vuestro padre, agora es palmero,
> por tierras de Egipto anda como romero.[13]

> [The King Apollonious, a noble knight, was the lord of Tyre, a principal and upright man, he was your father, he is now a palm bearer, through the lands of Egypt he walks as a pilgrim.]

Egypt is a sanctioned place for the expiation of guilt, and therefore an excuse for Apolonio's long absence from his daughter. And although this is the last explicit mention of Egypt in the poem, the importance of the locale should not be overlooked.

The references to Egypt in the *Libro de Apolonio* are brief but significant when compared to the other locales mentioned as destinations in the poem. In terms of any discussion of the geography of the narrative, it is important to make note of the imaginary character of the geographical and cultural landscape that the poem presents. While the place names used in the *Libro de Apolonio* are ones that refer to real locations in the Eastern Mediterranean, there is nothing in the poem that describes their individual locations or their cultural specificities. When Apolonio and the other characters travel

---

12 *Libro de Apolonio* in Carina Zubillaga, *Poesía narrativa clerical en su contexto manuscrito: Estudio y edición del Ms. Esc. K-III-4* (Buenos Aires: Dunken, 2014), 347d. The translations of the poems into English are my own.

13 *Libro de Apolonio*, 360.

from one city to another in the poem, the poet does not provide any indication of distance or direction between these points of axis. The poet also avoids adding any observations that would differentiate the various locations in the poem; if the peoples of these lands speak different languages, have distinguishing traditions or ways of dressing, or engage in different religious or ritual traditions, the poet provides no such indication. The poet presents these places as homogenous locales with unspecified locations.

The theme of travel is a constant in the poem, but of the locations mentioned in the poem (Tyre, Tarsus, Pentapolis, Ephesus, Egypt, and Mytilene), Egypt is perhaps the only locale that would have been broadly recognizable to a thirteenth-century Iberian audience.[14] This, of course, is due to the prominent place that Egypt plays in familiar biblical narratives.[15] While the most highly educated readers/listeners of the original Iberian audiences may have had some frame of reference for the other mentioned places in the Eastern Mediterranean, the broader audience may have recognized only Egypt. This fact, along with Egypt's narrative role as a space for purification and expiation of guilt, highlights the importance of this location in the narrative despite its scant appearance in the poem.

The second thirteenth-century poem found in the manuscript K-III-4, the *Vida de madona Santa María Egipciaqua* (alternatively known as the *Vida de Santa María Egipciaca*), also has a connection to travel in the Eastern Mediterranean, and from Egypt in particular.[16] This hagiography, like the *Libro de Apolonio*, tells a story widely known throughout Europe in the Middle Ages, as many versions in Latin and various medieval European vernaculars are extant. Not only was this specific saint's life a popular one throughout the Middle Ages, but this category of saint, the converted harlot, was one of the most admired saintly types in medieval times (other examples of the type include Thaïs (the former courtesan), Mary (the niece of Abraham), Pelagia of Antioch, and of

---

14 France is also mentioned twice in the poem (548, 583), but not as a place that the characters visit; rather, it is used as a symbol of a kingdom that is very wealthy.

15 Several other locales of the *Libro de Apolonio* are also referenced in the Bible, but none with the frequency or intensity of Egypt. Tyre is mentioned in both the Hebrew Bible and the New Testament, and perhaps its most vivid appearance is in the prophecy of its destruction in the *Book of Ezekiel*. Antioch is mentioned a number of times in the *Acts of the Apostles*. References to Tarsus are exclusively in connection to the Apostle Paul who was born there. The city called Pentapolis in the *Libro de Apolonio* is believed to be the one located in the province of Cyrene, Libya (northeast of Benghazi). Cyrene is mentioned in the deuterocanonical book of *Second Maccabees*, as well as in the *Gospel of Mark* where it is referenced as the homeland of the man named Simon who carried Christ's cross. None of these cities appear as the focus of familiar biblical narratives in the way that Egypt does in both the Hebrew Bible (as the place of the enslavement of the people of Israel) and the New Testament (as the location of the Holy Family's escape from Herod's murderous rage).

16 While the title *Vida de Santa María Egipçiaca* has been the most widely used in the history of academic inquiry into the thirteenth-century poem, more recent criticism has begun to use the title that appears in the manuscript, *Vida de madona Santa María Egipçiaqua*. This is due, in part, to avoid confusion with other versions of the legend, such as the fourteenth-century version that also uses the title *Vida de Santa María Egipçiaca*.

course, Mary Magdalene). Two principal stemmata of Mary of Egypt's legend exist, and the thirteenth-century Iberian version pertains to the Western one, which focuses on the story of the harlot/wandering female hermit saint instead of the life of her male confessor. The role of Egypt is apparent from the work's title, as the protagonist is of Egyptian origin, and according to tradition, she travelled both in Egypt and the Holy Land in the fourth century CE. This version of the poem tells the story of the saint's life from childhood to death, and although the organization of the poem is often described as bipartite, the segment of the poem that describes the saint's pre-conversion life of sin is certainly shorter than that of her subsequent life of holiness.

The poem begins with a prologue that highlights the importance of repentance, and then goes on to introduce the reader to the saint herself:

> Esta de qui quiero fablar
> María la oí nombrar.
> El su nombre es en escripto,
> porque nasçió en Egipto.[17]

> [This woman of whom I wish to speak, I heard her being called Maria, her name is in writing, and she was born in Egypt.]

Although the exact location of her upbringing in Egypt is not specified, the reader is informed that María is so given over to sin that she abandons her parents in her youth (at age 12) to go to another realm:

> En Alexandria fue María,
> aquí demanda alverguería;
> allá va prender ostal
> con las malas en la cal.[18]

> [She travelled to Alexandria and looks for lodging, she ends up in the streets among the bad women.]

In her time in Alexandria, she becomes the most acclaimed prostitute of the city, and the poet communicates that the men of the city are constantly killing each other over her attention and favours. Approximately 280 verses (nearly 20 percent of the entire narrative) are devoted to María's early life in her unidentified hometown in Egypt and her time in Alexandria, a period that comes to an end with her encounter with a ship full of pilgrims bound for the Holy Land. María's interest in joining the voyage to Jerusalem is more professional than devotional, and she exaggerates her "forlorn" condition when she tells the pilgrims that

> En tierras de Egipto fuy nada
> e aquí fuy muy desaconsejada.

---

17 *Vida de madona Santa María Egipciaqua* in Carina Zubillaga, *Poesía narrativa clerical en su contexto manuscrito: Estudio y edición del Ms. Esc. K-III-4* (Buenos Aires: Dunken, 2014), 79–82.

18 *Vida de madona Santa María Egipciaqua*, 147–50.

Non he amigo nin pariente,
vo mal e feblemientre.[19]

[In the lands of Egypt I was born and here I was badly advised, I have neither relatives nor friends, things are going badly and feebly for me.]

María declares her Egyptian origins just before leaving her native land for the remainder of her life and the poetic narrative.

The next portion of the poem tells of María's journey to the Holy Land, her conversion experience in Jerusalem, and her entrance into a life of solitary and nomadic devotion in the desert eastward across the River Jordan. She spends the next forty-seven years of her life wandering in the wilderness in penitence and suffering until she encounters another wanderer, a monk named Gozimás from a nearby monastery whose tradition is to send its brothers into the desert each year for a time of ambulatory penitence and contemplation. The pair meet again after a year, and on the occasion of the third year, Gozimás finds María deceased in the desert. At this time a lion comes down from the mountain in order to aid the elderly monk in the burial of the saintly Egyptian.

The place of Egypt in the narrative is very different in the *Vida de madona Santa María Egipciaqua* than what we have seen it to be in the *Libro de Apolonio*, even though journeys in the Levant play an important role in both narratives. Both protagonists travel for secular as well as spiritual reasons: Apolonio travels to flee his persecutors, but also journeys to Egypt to expiate his guilt; María leaves Egypt to go to the Holy Land in order to continue with her sinful trade, but ends up wandering in the desert in penitential devotion. Although Egypt is a destination for Apolonio and a point of departure for María, this location, distant from the Iberian kingdoms of the poems' composition, plays a significant role in both narratives. Both travel in the Eastern Mediterranean and Egypt are significant themes in the first two poems of the manuscript.

The third and final narrative of Manuscript K-III-4 of the Escorial Library is a poem that has been known to critics by three titles: *Libre dels tres reys d'Orient*, the *Libro de los tres reyes de Oriente*, and the *Libro de la infancia y muerte de Jesús*. This brief poem, to which I will refer using title found in the manuscript itself, the *Libre dels tres reys d'Orient*, is composed of three scenes of the life of Christ based on canonical and apocryphal material.[20]

The first of the three narrative moments of the poem deals with the visit of the Three Kings to the newly born Christ child. The narrative tells of the Magi's interactions with Herod, their adoration of the infant Jesus, and their return to their homelands without relating the location of the newborn child to the authorities. The "Slaughter of the Innocents" ordered by Herod is also related in the poem, and it is at this point that Egypt enters the account familiar from Gospel narratives.

---

19 *Vida de madona Santa María Egipciaqua*, 339–42.

20 Perhaps the reason why no scholarly consensus has arisen in reference to the title is because of the small amount of scholarship that has been produced about the poem. Given the lack of standardization, I have chosen the title most authentic to the manuscript: *Libre dels tres reys d'Orient*.

In order to save the Christ child from the slaughter, the poem tells of the mystical orders given to Mary's husband:

> Josep jazia adormido,
> el ángel fue a él venido
> Dixo: "Lieva, varón, e ve tu vía
> "fuye con el Niño e con María;
> "vete para Egipto
> "que así lo manda el escripto."[21]

[As Joseph slept the angel came and said to him: "Rise, man, be on your way, flee with the Child and Mary, go to Egypt as it is commanded in the Scriptures."]

Travel has been a motif from the beginning of the narrative with the journey of the Magi, and now the Holy Family begins its journey to Egypt, which is the focus of the second narrative moment of the poem.

The matter of Holy Family's escape to Egypt receives scant treatment in the canonical Gospel narratives, but this particular journey is a favourite subject in the apocryphal gospels as well as in related literature and art. Margaret Chaplin, in one of the few articles specifically on this short poem, focuses on the scene of the thieves and places it in the context of other medieval apocryphal narratives about the Holy Family's flight to Egypt. Patricia Grau-Dieckmann has placed the "Flight to Egypt" narratives into a larger context of medieval graphic arts. José Fradejas Lebrero has found some similarities between this narrative and one in the *Evangelio árabe de la infancia*, but to date no direct corollary has been discovered. In the case of this final narrative, therefore, we are faced with material that is both rare and understudied.

The thirteenth-century author of the *Libre dels tres reys d'Orient* begins the second narrative nuclei of poem in a way that invokes many aspects of travel. The audience is told that Mary, Joseph, and their newborn son

> Madrugaron grant mañana,
> solos pasan por la montaña.
> Encontraron dos peyones,
> grandes e fuertes ladrones,
> que robavan los caminos
> e degollavan los pelegrinos.[22]

[They rise at dawn, alone they go through the mountain passes, they met on the road two mean and strong thieves who robbed pilgrims and then slit their throats.]

The danger of the journey is immediately communicated through the inhospitable terrain and the encounter with criminals. The reference to pilgrims also brings the scene into relation with the type of religiously motivated travel most recognizable to medieval a audience.

---

21 *Libre dels tres reys d'Orient*, in Carina Zubillaga, *Poesía narrativa clerical en su contexto manuscrito: Estudio y edición del Ms. Esc. K-III-4* (Buenos Aires: Dunken, 2014), 84–89.

22 *Libre dels tres reys d'Orient*, 96–101.

The two the more wicked thief criminals contemplate dividing the spoils from their pilgrim captives, and the suggests cutting the Christ child in half and each taking his own part in order to have an equal division of the booty. The good thief recommends putting off the distribution of the spoils until morning, and offers his house as lodging for the travelling family. During the stay, the good thief's infant son is cured of his leprosy when the Virgin Mary washes the child in the bathwater previously used to bathe the infant Jesus. In thanks for the miracle, the good thief "[e]scurriólos fasta en Egipto, / así lo dize el escripto" (and he sneaked them into Egypt, as it is written).[23] The scene of the encounter with the robbers on the road to Egypt, the longest of the three narrative moments of the poem, concludes with the poet telling his audience that the sons of both robbers follow their fathers' paths into a life of thievery.

The last and briefest narrative moment of the poem culminates with the Crucifixion. The sons of the two highway robbers are portrayed by the poet as being the thieves crucified on either side of Christ. The son of the good robber, the one who was cleansed of his leprosy on the road to Egypt, is portrayed as the thief who recognizes the divinity of Christ at the Crucifixion and joins Christ in paradise, while the other thief mocks the crucified Christ and is condemned to hell.

Egypt is portrayed as a place of safety in the *Libre dels tres reys d'Orient*, which is a different role than that found either in the *Libro de Apolonio* or the *Vida de madona Santa María Egipciaqua*. Travel is depicted in all three poems of Manuscript K-III-4 as being dangerous, but also as promising the possibility of rewards, and Egypt is variously portrayed as a place of repentance, of sin, or of succour. All three poems rely on the audience's prior knowledge of biblical narratives in order to locate Egypt within a vague imaginary of the Eastern Mediterranean, but the poem that does this most explicitly is the *Libre dels tres reys d'Orient*.

The elapsed period between the composition of the three poems discussed here and their subsequent compilation provides an opportunity for the examination of the evolving meanings of Egypt and Levantine travel for a Christian Iberian audience. The concern for the remainder of this article is the codicological context of the poems, as well as the political and societal changes that occurred between the time of their thirteenth-century composition and their fourteenth-century copying and binding.

There is a current scholarly consensus that manuscript K-III-4 dates from the second half of the fourteenth century and that the copyist was of Aragonese/Catalan extraction based on the handwriting and certain linguistic characteristics,[24] but consensus has not been reached on the original use of the manuscript due to its numerous irregularities. The manuscript contains one multicoloured illumination and elaborated initial capitals in red, which may lead to the conclusion that it was meant to be a presentation copy, but

---

23 *Libre dels tres reys d'Orient*, 206–7.

24 C. Carroll Marden notes, after detailed examination, that the simplest explanation for the linguistic rarities in the manuscript is that "the present manuscript was copied by a scribe familiar with both Catalan and Aragonese or with a dialect on the border between those two linguistic territories" (*Libro de Apolonio: An Old Spanish Poem* (Baltimore: Johns Hopkins University Press, 1917), 29).

this seems to be contradicted by the fact that the folios are of paper (*papel ceutí*) rather than vellum and that the rubrication is haphazard in places. Despite the irregularities of the manuscript, it does appear certain that at least a century had passed between the composition of the last of the poems and their combination into the late fourteenth-century Manuscript K-III-4.

Interpretations of the combination of the *Libro de Apolonio*, the *Vida de madona Santa María Egipciaqua*, and the *Libre dels tres reys d'Orient* into a single manuscript could occasion two related categories of results. One possible type of codicological investigation could aim to locate possible rationale or intentionality for the unique combination of these three poems, but because we know virtually nothing about the compiler/scribe or the location of manuscript's production, we must rely on the content of the manuscript alone to reveal this information. A related approach could focus on the reception of the poems in relation to one another, especially in light of the historical and social context in which the three poems were united. Because modern researchers are privy to at least some of the historical and social changes between the first half of the thirteenth century and the second half of the fourteenth, as well as to the extant literary production of that intervening time, an interpretation based on the production of the manuscript and the reception of the poems is hypothetical in nature, but represents a potentially fruitful line of inquiry.

The compilation of the three poems into a single manuscript potentially affects the way they are received, as their arrangement into a single codex creates a web of connections not present when they are considered individually. While the majority of the criticism has examined the poems individually and outside of their codicological context, a few critics have studied the three poems' relationship to one another. Authors of articles about the poems, as well as editors of critical editions of the individual works, often make brief mention of the other poems in the manuscript, but scholars have not generally engaged in systematic studies of the three poems' commonalities. Alan Deyermond, in an article on the *Apolonio*, for example, mentions only in passing that

> la acción de todas las obras se desarrolla en el este del Mediterráneo y sus regiones costeras e incluye una estancia bastante larga en Egipto; los protagonistas viajan para escaparse (en dos casos para escaparse de la muerte que les amenaza), enfrentándose con graves peligros (tempestad, naufragio, salteadores o piratas); el tema central es el conflicto entre la virtud y el vicio.[25]

> [The action in all these works takes place in the eastern Mediterranean and its coastal regions and it includes a very lengthy stay in Egypt; the protagonists travel to escape (in two cases to escape from death), facing great perils (storm, shipwreck, robbers and pirates); the central theme is the conflict between virtue and vice.]

Carina Zubillaga has more recently carried out two studies across the poems of the manuscript: "La impronta de la muerte en el contexto codicológico del Ms. Esc. K-III-4" and

---

25 Deyermond, "Emoción y ética," 153.

"Vestimentas compartidas y otros cuidados: las formas de la generosidad en el Ms. K-III-4." The most extensive recent study of the codex as a unit is Andrew Beresford's "The *Vida de Santa María Egipciaca* and the Question of Manuscript Unity." Despite the title of Beresford's article, the author examines all three poems of the manuscript, as well as the short prose piece on the last folio of the manuscript often referred to as the *Vida y passion de Cristo, Nuestro Señor*. Beresford's extensive bibliography contained in the article's footnotes makes his treatment a point of departure for any modern examination of the manuscript, and I agree with Beresford in his contention that many factors "suggest that the compiler's methodology was one that was founded in a careful process of selection and design."[26] If the process of compilation appears deliberate, but we lack access to details about the specific context of the manuscript's assembly, then the *effect* of the interrelation of the poems in a broad Iberian context is the most productive avenue of codicological investigation.[27]

Although none of the poems is a travel log nor primarily about Egypt, all of them deal with travels in the Eastern Mediterranean and their protagonists spend extended periods in Egypt, as Deyermond has noted above, and these themes are amplified when the poems are considered in relation to one another. Travel's meaning is not univocal in the manuscript, but in all three poems travel represents both danger and potentiality. In Apolonio's case, travel begins as something undertaken out of necessity and changes into a means of acquiring prestige and an expanded dominion. María's journeys, in the beginning of her story, are undertaken for lustful motives, but her spiritual wanderings eventually increase her spiritual status to such a degree that she becomes a worker of miracles who is recognized as a saint. Even the Holy Family's journey, which begins as a hastily undertaken escape, ends with the miraculous curing, both physically and spiritually, of a person who would have otherwise been a lost cause. When considering the manuscript in its entirety, Egypt also expands from being merely a place of pilgrimage in the *Libro de Apolonio*, a place of departure in the *Vida de madona Santa María Egipciaqua*, and a place of refuge in the *Libre del tres reys d'Orient*, to a location with expanded importance in the historical context in which the codex was compiled.

The relevance of Iberia's easterly gaze would increase over the course of the thirteenth and first half of the fourteenth centuries due to the significant political and social developments in the Peninsula, North Africa, and the Levant. The Christian kingdoms' centuries-long struggle with the Muslim political power in the south of the Peninsula

---

26 Andrew M. Beresford, "The *Vida de Santa María Egipciaca* and the Question of Manuscript Unity," in *Text & Manuscript in Medieval Spain: Papers from the King's College Colloquium*, ed. David Hook (London: King's College Hispanic Series, 2000), 79–102, at 83.

27 The contention that the poems were carefully selected for inclusion in the manuscript, rather than being the product of randomness, opens up a potentially fruitful line of inquiry. There are many points of comparison among three poems that remain unexplored. Physical transformation, for example, is an issue in all three poems: Apolonio transforms into a "wildman" when he undergoes his pilgrimage in Egypt; María transforms from an acclaimed beauty to a shrivelled and nearly genderless being; the son of the good robber from a state of illness to wellness when he is cured of his leprosy.

would come to a climax in 1212 with the combined Christian military's decisive defeat of Muslim armies in the famous battle of Las Navas de Tolosa. This triumph would turn the tide in favour of the northern kingdoms and have profound effects on the two largest powers of the Peninsula, the kingdom of Castile and the newly united crown of Aragon.

In Castile, the victory at Las Navas de Tolosa was part of a campaign of expansion that would intensify during the subsequent reign of Fernando III (1217–1252) and would lead at least in part to an increased confidence in external politics and a flowering of cultural production under the reign of his son Alfonso X (1252–1284). Alfonso saw himself in a position to take an active role in political affairs outside of the Peninsula, signing treaties with England against France and making imperial claims. Although Alfonso obtained the required electoral votes to win the title of Holy Roman Emperor, he was finally persuaded by Pope Gregory X to renounce the claim. The reign of Alfonso X was more successful in the realm of culture, as the immense scholarly production of his travelling court won him the byname "the Wise". The court poets, scholars, and translators produced a wide variety of works, but it is particularly noteworthy that they translated a vast number of texts from Hebrew and Arabic into Castilian and wrote works of world history situating Castile into a broader political, intellectual, and historical framework.

In the east of the Peninsula, the consolidation of the crown of Aragon occurred through the dynastic union of the kingdom of Aragon with the county of Barcelona in the second half of the twelfth century. Both halves of the union had expansionist aims, and although the combined crown would eventually lose its holdings north of the Pyrenees in costal France, it would expand over the generations into newly conquered Valencia, the Balearic Islands, and eventually into the Italian Peninsula and beyond. Peter II of Aragon (I of Barcelona) held the crown at the dawn of the thirteenth century and participated in the Battle of Las Navas de Tolosa. He died shortly afterward in 1213, leaving his realm to his son James I, known as "the Conquerer".

While the Christian kingdoms of Iberia were negotiating their relationship with Muslims within the Peninsula during the High Middle Ages, many of the other Christian kingdoms of Europe had been engaged with Islamic forces in the Levant and North Africa through the crusades, principally in the twelfth and thirteenth centuries. It is not the case that Iberian nobles lacked the desire that many of their co-religionists outside of the Peninsula had to take up the cross and go to the Holy Land, but rather they were implored not to do so by various popes of twelfth century; the reason for this was the need for focused attention to the struggle against Islam closer to home.

> During the first half of the twelfth century western Christians came to recognise [sic] the Iberian conflicts as equivalent to the campaigns in the Holy Land, reimaging them as *bone fide* crusades, but among the Spanish, at least initially, this did not lead to a decline in the significance of Jerusalem; rather it fostered an attempt to bring the peninsular crusade into the orbit of the one in the East.[28]

---

28 Patrick J. O'Banion, "What has Iberia to do with Jerusalem? Crusade and the Spanish Route to the Holy Land in the Twelfth Century," *Journal Of Medieval History* 34 (2008): 383–95, at 385.

Throughout this period, the crusades to the Holy Land were not ignored in Spain, but rather postponed. There was even hope for uniting the more direct route to the Levant and one that would traverse Spain and North Africa: "Such a route would pass through the peninsula itself and unite two of the great crusading arenas into a single Mediterranean-wide struggle against Islam."[29]

From the very beginning, the issues of crusade and economics were intertwined for European Christendom, and in the thirteenth century, even though the military cause was going badly, the economic connection remained. This affected not only the Levant, but also Egypt and the rest of the African Mediterranean coast:

> Crusading led to the growth of merchant shipping, and when the military tide turned with the loss of the Christian principalities in the Levant, both traders and Crusaders looked for new points of contact in Egypt and North Africa. In 1248 King Louis IX of France led a disastrous crusade against Egypt, and in 1270 he returned to lay siege to Tunis, where he died of a fever.[30]

While the Christian kingdoms of Spain had largely avoided becoming involved in the crusades in the Holy Land, they had not abstained from economic dealings with North Africa. Now, as the thirteenth century continued, the time was ripe for the Iberian political, economic, and military aims to intersect across the Mediterranean.

Both Castile and the crown of Aragon had relations with North Africa in the thirteenth century, some based on trade on others based on tendencies toward conquest and crusade. T. N. Bisson, in *The Medieval Crown of Aragon*, explains that on Aragon's behalf, James I "entered into negotiations with the hafsid caliph of Tunis soon after the conquest of Majorca [in the early 1230s], authorized mercantile colonies and mercenary forces to operate in Tunis, and collect tribute. There were similar initiatives in Ceuta, Tlemcen, even in Egypt."[31] The Castilian kings also saw the importance of Africa for the economic, military, and spiritual wellbeing of their own kingdom. According to Joseph O'Callaghan in the tome *The Gibraltar Crusade: Castile and the Battle for the Strait*, North African conquests were part of a larger program that included not only the lands directly across the Strait, but also African shores farther to the east. "Alfonso X also made diplomatic overtures to Egypt. Since the early thirteenth century, crusading strategists considered Egypt the key to control of the Holy Land."[32] Alfonso maintained diplomatic contact with Egypt throughout the early decades of his reign. The *Royal Chronicle* tells of envoys from Egypt arriving at Seville, probably in 1260, with exotic gifts to mark the solemn anniversary of the death of Fernando III.[33] A decade later, "Alfonso X and Baybars [Sultan of Egypt, also known as Abu l-Futuh] concluded a commercial treaty" and O'Callaghan

---

29 O'Banion, "What has Iberia to do with Jerusalem?," 384.

30 Roland A. Oliver and Anthony Atmore, *Medieval Africa, 1250–1800* (Cambridge: Cambridge University Press, 2001), 35.

31 Thomas Bisson, *Medieval Crown of Aragon: A Short History* (Oxford: Clarendon Press, 1986), 70.

32 Joseph O'Callaghan, *The Gibraltar Crusade: Castile and the Battle for the Strait* (Philadelphia: University of Pennsylvania Press, 2011), 19.

33 O'Callaghan, *The Gibraltar Crusade*, 20–21.

takes this as one indication that "maritime contacts between the merchants of Seville and the Egyptians may have occurred more frequently than documentation attests."[34]

While making diplomatic and trade agreements, conquest could not have been far from either Iberian monarch's mind, but agreement about the African endeavour was not always easy between Alfonso X of Castile and James I of Aragon:

> Meeting at Agreda in March 1260, the two kings, aside from resolving smoldering resentments, discussed the African Crusade. Commenting that Alfonso X intended to move "against the Saracens for the exaltation of the Catholic faith," Jaime I [James I] declared that "this should be preached in our realm" and permitted his vassals to aid him against the Saracens. The only caveat was that no harm should be inflicted on the Hafsid sultan of Tunis, with whom Jaime I enjoyed friendly relations.[35]

Despite the early agreement, the monarchs took separate paths to crusade. While Alfonso concentrated on the Straits of Gibraltar in order to open up the rest of African coast, James I decided to take a more direct approach to the *Tierra Santa*:

> He proposed a crusade (by which he meant an expedition to the Holy Land) to Pope Clement IV, only to be told that he was morally unfit for such a cause. Even so, in 1267 James was inspired by an invitation from the Mongol Khan–and perhaps also by the urgings of his unendowed bastards Fernando Sánchez and Pedro Fernandez—to mobilize a major crusade that set sail for the East two years later. James seems to have hoped thereby to allay the pope's suspicions and to cap his own life's work. Once under way, however, he lost his nerve in a storm and put ashore, with most of his fleet, at Aigues-Mortes; only the ships of the Infants reached Acre, but with too few men to accomplish anything.[36]

Even though neither monarch reached his goal, both set the stage for the continued presence of the Christian realms of Iberia in the lands of North Africa.

The situation of active involvement in Africa would continue for generations, especially for Aragon. Pedro III would maintain a fleet in Tunisia as his father had done, but Mediterranean involvement would intensify under James II (1291–1327). "In North Africa James promoted military and commercial interests, notably in Tunisia, but also, during the Castilian war, in Morocco, and even as far east as Egypt. In 1293 a treaty negotiated with the sultan Khalil rendered the count-king virtually the protector of Christians in the post-crusade Levant."[37] James II's influence was also felt in North Africa because of his patronage of Ramon Llull (also known as Lull or Lully; ca. 1232–1315), whose ideas about and actions regarding the region are well documented. Llull, a Majorcan, had begun his career as a poet and courtier before experiencing a conversion and becoming

34 O'Callaghan, *The Gibraltar Crusade*, 21.

35 O'Callaghan, *The Gibraltar Crusade*, 22.

36 Bisson, *Medieval Crown of Aragon*, 70.

37 Bisson, *Medieval Crown of Aragon*, 95.

a follower of Francis of Assisi. As a Franciscan tertiary, he followed in the footsteps of the poor man of Assisi, who had himself gone on a mission to the Egyptians and had met the Sultan Malik al-Kamil at Damietta in September 1219. Llull likewise became interested in dialogue with and conversion of people of other religions, and Llull promoted language schools for just that purpose throughout the Mediterranean. He visited North Africa several times, especially Tunis, where he would eventually inspire rioting that would lead to his death. By the beginning of the fourteenth century, the Iberian kingdoms were well ensconced in North African and Levantine relations.

The interactions of the Iberian kingdoms with North Africa and Egypt, as well as their interest in the Holy Land, do not remain solely on the level of the historical record, but also extend into the realm of literary production. Between the first half of the thirteenth century when the three poems of Escorial K-III-4 were composed and the last half of the fourteenth when they were copied and compiled into a single manuscript, there was much literary production that included the themes of Levantine crusades and interactions with North Africa and Egypt. While crusader ballads were a popular genre throughout Europe, the form did not come to the Iberian Peninsula until relatively late, and only one example survives. The crusader poem, *Ay Iherusalem*, a poem about the loss of Christian kingdom of Jerusalem in 1244, was written several decades later around 1274. Straddling the divide between chronicle and chivalric romance, the *Gran conquista de Ultramar* first appeared in 1290s. This Castilian chronicle was based on William of Tyre's Latin account of the crusades and came to the Peninsula through an intermediate French text. The different manuscript traditions attribute the chronicle alternately to the patronage of Alfonso X and Sancho IV, and the text was certainly amplified in subsequent renditions. To these texts can be added some of the writings of Ramon Llull, including especially his *Liber de fine* (1305) and *Liber de acquisitione Terrae Sanctae* (1309) in which he advocates for preaching as part of the campaign against the Muslims.[38] The scant evidence indicates that while literature specifically dedicated to the crusades is not absent from the Peninsula, it does not arrive there until the last quarter of the thirteenth century.

The topics of crusades or Iberia's connections with North Africa and the Levant do surface in other literature from the period as a tangential theme or as a small piece of a larger whole in a variety of genres. I do not intend to offer a full catalogue of such references here but rather provide a few prominent examples from canonical texts to give an indication of the treatment of these topics.[39]

---

[38] Preaching was only part of the program; military force was also to be used. In the *Liber de acquisitione Terrae Sanctae*, for example, Llull "proposed that while a great crusade moved from Constantinople into Syria and Egypt, in the West the Christians would undertake the conquest of Granada and the Moroccan port of Ceuta. By means of this pincers movement he hoped that Islam could be crushed" (O'Callaghan, *The Gibraltar Crusade*, 126).

[39] Other examples of texts that could be plumbed for references to or indications of interest in the themes of North Africa, Egypt, and the Levant would be contemporary hagiography, and from the early fourteenth century, the *Libro de buen amor*.

One particularly fertile compendium from the Iberian Peninsula for references to various aspects medieval society is the *Cantigas de Santa Maria*, compiled at the court of Alfonso X of Castile, most likely between the middle of the thirteenth century and the monarch's death in 1284. There are four extant manuscripts of the collection, each containing different quantities of canticles or songs, but the number of them altogether (including various prologues) equals 429. This collection provides many portrayals of North Africa, Egypt, and the Eastern Mediterranean in a generation subsequent to that of the composition of the poems contained in Manuscript K-III-4.

This vast collection of Marian canticles contains five narratives that deal specifically with pilgrimage to the Holy Land (numbers 5, 155, 287, 383, and 401),[40] and of these, crusade to the Holy Land appears in two (5 and 401).[41] Two additional canticles (46 and 165) have to do with crusade but do not involve pilgrimage, and in these cantigas the Muslim protagonists face the Virgin's intervention in military matters, and in one of the cases, the protagonist is converted to Christianity. Africa is mentioned generically in five canticles of the collection (95, 265, 325, 366, and 385), and in the last of these, Puerto Santa María, a newly conquered port city in the south of Spain, near Cadiz, is mentioned as an ideal place from which to launch attacks against the Muslims in Spain and Africa. Abu Yusuf Yaqub ibn Abd Al-Haqq (known as Aboyuçaf), who was the Marinid ruler or Sultan of Morocco 1258–1286, is a main character in four cantigas (169, 181, 215, and 323). He is the antagonist in the famous cantiga 181 in which the Muslim king of Marrakesh uses a banner with the Virgin's image on it to defeat the sultan in battle. Egypt is specifically mentioned in four cantigas (14, 165, 403, and 422). In three of these, Egypt appears in biblical references: 14 and 403 mention the flight of the Holy Family to Egypt, and 422 contains a reference to Egypt in the context of the Final Judgement. A more direct reference to contemporary medieval Egypt is cantiga 165.[42] In this narrative, Baibars I, Sultan

---

40 Cantiga 5 is the familiar tale of chaste empress, who is accused of infidelity while her husband is away in the Holy Land; in cantiga 155 a hermit suggests that a thief from Alexandria go on pilgrimage to Jerusalem as penance for his sins; in cantiga 287, Holy Land pilgrimage is undertaken by the protagonist couple in penitence for the husband's murderous tendencies; the action of cantiga 383 occurs principally on a Holy Land pilgrimage, and therefore the theme is very developed; cantiga 401 is a petition from Alfonso for divine assistance in fighting Moors in Holy Land and in Spain.

41 There are several references to the Holy Land, most often referred to as *"Ultramar,"* as well as to Jerusalem that do not have to do with pilgrimage or crusade. Cantiga 1 references the three kings as being of *"Ultramar,"* and could be considered to be on a "pilgrimage" as they make their devotional journey to visit the Christ child. Cantigas 34 and 261 mention spices of *Ultramar.* In cantiga 337, a man who wants to go on a Holy Land pilgrimage, but cannot, goes there in a vision. Cantiga 187 takes place at a monastery in Jerusalem. In cantiga 314 a man asks to be taken to Jerusalem when he falls ill, but does not actually go there; in cantiga 337 pilgrimage is merely suggested or desired. Cantiga 419 references Jerusalem specifically in relation to the life of the Virgin Mary. Along these lines, without mentioning "Ultramar" or "Jerusalem" specifically, cantiga 424 is entirely about the adoration of the three kings. The text mentions that they had travelled through many lands before arriving in Bethlehem, including Tarsus, which is a city that plays a pivotal role in the *Libro de Apolonio.*

42 There are three additional references to the medieval city of Alexandria in *cantigas* 65, 145, and 155. Number 65 has to do with an excommunicate who ends up going to Rome, but is denied

of Egypt from 1260 to 1277 (also known as Bondoudar), attacks the Christian-held city of Tartus (Antartus or Tortosa) in Syria. When Bondoudar discovers that the Virgin is protecting the city, this Sultan of Egypt invokes the Qur'anic Mary, and then desists from attacking the stronghold. The *Cantigas de Santa Maria* provides many indications of Iberia's evolving interest in North Africa and the Eastern Mediterranean.

We have seen the appearance of famous historical figures associated with Egypt and North Africa more generally in the *Cantigas de Santa María*, but perhaps no figure captured the Western imagination to the extent that did Salah ad-Din Yusuf ibn Ayyub, better known in the West as Saladin. This first sultan of Egypt and Syria founded the Ayyubid dynasty and captured the attention of the West through his military leadership against the crusaders in the Holy Land during the closing decades of the twelfth century. Saladin frequently appears in European literary production in the subsequent centuries, and it is perhaps surprising that many of these portrayals were neutral or even positive, despite the historical Saladin's antagonistic role in military campaigns against the Western kingdoms. Margaret Jubb has analyzed such representations and found that the "bulk of critical Western commentary on Saladin focusses [sic] on his early years, on his rise to power first in Egypt and then in Syria."[43] One finds such a portrayal in Don Juan Manuel's *Libro del Conde Lucanor* or the *Libro de Patronio*. As Jubb has noted, many Western tales of Saladin focus on the Sultan's travels (real or invented), and this is the case in "Exemplo L" of Juan Manuel's collection of moralizing tales. In the course of the *exemplum*, the initially flawed Saladin makes moral progress through his journey to Spain and his answering of a riddle. In "Exemplo XXV" of the same collection, the theme of travel, this time from west to east, is again present, and the depiction of Saladin that surfaces is one of wisdom and generosity.[44] These two tales from the *Libro del Conde Lucanor* serve to foment the legend of the Egyptian sultan rather than to present a retelling of the events of the crusades, as had been the case in Saladin's appearance in the late thirteenth-century Iberian *Gran conquista de Ultramar*. The depictions that we find in this literature, from crusader ballads, to chronicles, to exemplary literature, are varied in tone, theme, and purpose, but they come together to form a larger picture of the developing role of Iberian connections (at least imagined ones) to the East.

---

readmittance into the church, and later goes to Alexandria where he find a madman who helps him with his case. Number 145 is about John (known as the "Merciful" or "Almsgiver"), the patriarch of Alexandria. He was a seventh-century figure known for his works of charity. Number 155 is about a thieving knight in Alexandria who is ordered to fill a vessel with water in penitence. With the help of the Virgin he fills it with tears.

43 Margaret A. Jubb, *The Legend of Saladin in Western Literature and Historiography* (Lewiston: Edwin Mellen Press, 2000), 5.

44 For an opposing view, see Ana Adams's "Ser es fazer: El saber y la masculinidad de Saladín en *El Conde Lucanor,*" *Corónica: A Journal Of Medieval Hispanic Languages, Literatures, And Cultures* 40 (2012): 145–68. In it the author analyzes Don Juan Manuel's treatment of Saladin by placing these two *exempla* in a broader context of the portrayals of Muslims in the collection and approaches the text through the lens of masculinity. Adams concludes that the portrayal of Saladin is not as positive as many critics have concluded.

Much had occurred in literature and history, as we have seen, between the time that the *Libro de Apolonio*, the *Vida de madona Santa María Egipciaqua*, and the *Libre dels tres reys d'Orient* were composed at the beginning of the thirteenth century, and the time that they were copied and combined into a single manuscript in the second half of the fourteenth. Iberia was a different place in this new period and so was the broader Mediterranean; more importantly, perhaps, the horizons of the Iberian imagination were broader. But how could these changes have affected the perception, on the part of the compiler or the audience, of the combined poems in Escorial K-III-4?

Perhaps one of the most basic differences between the perception of the texts in the two periods involves the transformation of imaginary landscapes into more concrete ones. This is more evidently the case with the *Libro de Apolonio* than the other two poems, as the narrative occupies a more expansive geography. Elizabeth Archibald, in her volume on the Latin *Historia Apollonii Regis Tyri*, which was the source text for the *Libro de Apolonio*, had already postulated this affect in the reception of the Latin narrative in an even earlier period. She contends that the plot "may also have acquired a new interest in the age of the Crusades, when biblical cities like Tyre became familiar names in European politics."[45] The interest that Archibald was imagining with such a comment may have been a northern European one in which the Levant would have already been a more tangible place from the twelfth century onward. In an Iberian context, how much more would this be the case from the late thirteenth century onward due to the circumstance already described? How much would this be augmented when the vernacular Apollonius narrative is combined with two other poems that underline the biblical and hagiographic importance of the same region?

Jerusalem to the upper Levant would have been increasingly familiar for in the Iberian imagination by the time that the manuscript K-III-4 was compiled, but even more familiar would have been locations in North Africa. Egypt plays a new and more significant role in the case of the Iberian texts because of the new perspectives possible for the peninsular kingdoms in relation to North Africa, especially once the military situation within Iberia had been secured after the battle of Las Navas de Tolosa.[46] Archibald notes that in many other vernacular versions of the Apollonius legend, the protagonist's long

---

45 Elizabeth Archibald, *Apollonius of Tyre: Medieval and Renaissance Themes and Variations; Including the Text of the 'Historia Apollonii Regis Tyri' with an English Translation* (Cambridge: Brewer, 1991), 47. Many of the places described in the Apollonius legend had crusading significance. Antioch would have been familiar from crusade lore as it experienced two major sieges during the period of the crusades: the first in 1097–98 when the crusaders took the city, and the second in 1268 when it was lost to Baibars. The famous siege of Tyre in 1187, during which the Christian-held city was besieged by Saladin, was a rallying point for Christian crusaders in the Third Crusade as the defeat of Saladin put a halt to his series of victories.

46 This would also be the case for the other major African locale mentioned in the *Libro de Apolonio*: Pentapolis (Cyrene/Cyrenaea) would have been located at present day Marj/Barca in Libya just northeast of Benghazi. This city is even farther west along the northern coast of Africa, about halfway between Alexandria and Tunis, and we have already seen the importance of Tunis in the Iberian imaginary, especially in terms of trade and diplomacy with Aragon.

stay in Egypt is either replaced with actions in other locales, abbreviated, or is eliminated altogether.[47] Such is the case in the late fourteenth-century English version of the Apollonius legend included in John Gower's *Confessio Amantis*, in whose English historical context Egypt would have ceased to play an important role in politics or military matters. Egypt's importance in the *Libro de Apolonio* is amplified by both recent Iberian history, and by the combination of the Apollonius legend with two other texts, the *Vida de madona Santa María Egipciaqua* and the *Libre dels tres reys d'Orient*, in which there is a literal connection between Egypt and the Holy Land.

Beyond the place names and the geographical locations treated in the poems, the events of the narratives contained in the manuscript could have had certain resonance in the minds of the compiler or audience of Escorial K-III-4. The manuscript's portrayal of numerous storms at sea that sweep Apolonio off course and make dangerous María's passage to Jerusalem could recall James II of Aragon being thwarted from his planned crusade to the Holy Land when the previously mentioned storm set him ashore in southern France instead of the Holy Land in 1269. In the *Libre dels tres reys d'Orient*, the Wise Men coming from faraway lands to Bethlehem could have been identified with the crusading kings of Europe arriving in the Holy Land. In a similar way, the Magi and the Holy Family fleeing from the machinations of Herod could have been seen as representations of the crusaders being expelled from the Holy Land by the likes of Baibars and Saladin. In the case of the *Vida de madona Santa María Egipciaqua*, the fact that María arrives to the Holy Land on a ship full of pilgrims is significant as the crusaders identified themselves as armed pilgrims. The armed figures, who most critics identify as angels (although they are never explicitly identified in the poem), that prohibit María's entry into the Holy Sepulchre could likewise be seen as a reflection of the militarization of the places in the Levant that were sacred to Christians. Many other connections could be drawn between Iberia's interest in North Africa and the Levant and the content of these narratives, but these examples begin to paint a picture of new readings/receptions possible when the poems are considered in conjunction with one another in a context in which crusader and Mediterranean trade zeal had more deeply infiltrated the Iberian Peninsula.

Alan Deyermond briefly mentioned the common elements of Levantine journeys and long stays in Egypt in the three poems of Escorial K-III-4 in an article in 1989, and I have shown here that these similarities could be more than a fortunate coincidence. I would not argue that the narratives of Escorial K-III-4 are poems about crusade or conquest; rather, given the context of the Iberian kingdoms' increased interest in these topics from the second half of the thirteenth century onward, these issues are significant and worth exploring. Although the place of Egypt and Levantine journeys in the individual poems would have been less significant in the context of their separate composition in the first half of the thirteenth century, we have seen that these aspects are amplified in their later reception by the three poems' subsequent codicological combination and by the new realities of fourteenth-century Iberia and its relationship to North Africa, Egypt, and the Holy Land.

---

47 Archibald, *Apollonius of Tyre*, 68.

Chapter 5

THE PETRIFICATION OF ROSTAM: THOMAS HERBERT'S RE-VISION OF PERSIA IN *A RELATION OF SOME YEARES TRAVAILE*

NEDDA MEHDIZADEH

ABSTRACT

In his travel account of his journey to Safavid Persia in 1626, *A Relation of Some Yeares Travaile*, Thomas Herbert includes a summary of a heartbreaking episode from Abolqasem Ferdowsi's medieval epic poem, *Shahnameh*. This poetic meditation on the legends and histories of Iran was circulated orally by way of the performances of poetic orators called *naqqals* in the early modern period, a tradition meant to engender unity within an empire fragmented by conquest. Not only did these performances act as cultural reminders for natives but they also served as sources of entertainment for locals and travellers alike, particularly within the vibrant, metropolitan Safavid capital of Isfahan. It is likely during his visit to this capital city that Herbert would have encountered stories about the *Shahnameh*'s most beloved, most valiant, and most famous warrior, Rostam. But of all the stories about his life—both his successes and his heartbreaks—Herbert only retells the story of his death. Mehdizadeh's essay explores the reasons for this inclusion, arguing that Herbert seeks to disempower a national symbol of resilience and strength by turning Rostam—a metonymy of Iran—into a fossil. But even as he attempts to contain this symbol of nationhood into something dead and unmoving, Herbert discovers the figure's power to move him.

Keywords: Persia, Iran, Safavid, Shah Abbas I, England, English East India Company, *Shahnameh*, Abolqasem Ferdowsi, Rostam, naqqal, Naqsh-e Rostam, Naqsh-e Jahan, Thomas Herbert, *A Relation of Some Yeares Travaile*, Achaemenid, Alexander the Great, Isfahan, Persepolis

> The crocodile, the lion, the elephant
> Are one with the mosquito and the ant
> Within the grip of Death: no beast or man
> Lives longer than his life's allotted span.

—Shahnameh[1]

---

[1] Abolqasem Ferdowsi, *Shahnameh: The Persian Book of Kings*, trans. Dick Davis (New York: Penguin, 2006), 427.

FOLLOWING A GREAT feast hosted by the king of Kabol, the mighty warrior Rostam is invited to hunt within the ruler's expansive domains. He is unaware, however, that this invitation is part of a plot concocted by his host and his half-brother, Shaghad, to lure him into a forest prepared with freshly dug pits strategically filled with spears and pikes. With the final moments of his life upon him, Rostam enthusiastically accepts the invitation and offers a final reflection about the inevitability of death. He tells us that in death all living things are equal, as "no beast or man / Lives longer than his life's allotted span." His words are equally poignant and painful for the reader who already knows what awaits this most beloved figure of Abolqasem Ferdowsi's medieval epic poem, *Shahnameh, The Persian Book of Kings*.[2] Rostam has inadvertently enfolded himself within his rumination on the indiscriminate finality of life, and as he embarks upon the hunt, he does so without knowing that he has become the prey.

The final, heartbreaking moments of Rostam's life epitomize the narrative's exploration of the cycle of kingship, the value of honour and fidelity, and the preservation of culture.[3] Over the course of 40,000–60,000 rhyming couplets,[4] Ferdowsi weaves together the fragments of history and legend that circulated among Iranians orally for centuries into a timeless tapestry meant to preserve cultural narrative.[5] His mission to do so was

---

2 The earliest extant *Shahnameh* is dated 1217, though it is most likely that the text was composed and produced earlier than this date. For more information, see Sheila R. Canby, *The "Shahnama" of Shah Tahmasp* (New York: Metropolitan Museum of Art, 2011), 11–12.

3 In this article, I will be utilizing both "Persia" and "Iran" to represent different understandings of the geographical space that is the subject of this project. Deriving from *Pars*, the name of a region in south-western Iran bordering the Persian Gulf and the site of the ancient Persian capital, "Persia" was a Greek misattribution that replaced one part of Iran for the entire country—a misattribution that would linger for centuries to come. "Iran," on the other hand, is derived from the Old Persian *ariyanam* (*ariya*, "noble, lordly"), and is the name that has always been used to refer to the country by native Iranians (*Irooni*). Greek historians would later refer to it as *Persis*, which would, over time, become Persia. It was not until 1934 that Reza Shah Pahlavi instituted a decree asking all foreign nations to refer to his country by its appropriate assignation, Iran. I will refer to the county and its people as "Iran" and "Iranians" in this essay when discussing Iranian history and literature. However, I will use "Persia" and "Persians" when referring to early modern sources in order to maintain fidelity to the manner in which these English writers envisioned and understood the country.

4 As Dick Davis discusses, the poem "is some 50,000 lines long, and they are very long lines at that, each approximately equivalent in length to two lines of standard English iambic pentameter verse." For more information about the structure of the *Shahnameh*, see Dick Davis, *Epic and Sedition* (Fayetteville: University of Arkansas Press, 1992), xv. For more information about the scope and effects of the *Shahnameh*, see Canby, *The "Shahnama" of Shah Tahmasp*, 11–17.

5 Begun by the poet Daqiqi and completed by Ferdowsi following Daqiqi's death, the *Shahnameh* preserves an ancient past that was in danger of being lost. Ferdowsi's tome preserves what scholars agree are various mythical and historical narratives native to ancient Iran. Despite this agreement, there is still obscurity surrounding which sources the poet turned to in order to set the stories to a cohesive, written document. While it remains unclear how Ferdowsi brought these fragments together, it is generally agreed that his objective to create a written document had to do with ownership over the national epic. For more information, see Kumiko Yamamoto, *The Oral Background of Persian Epics: Storytelling and Poetry* (Leiden: Brill, 2003), 1–20.

largely motivated by witnessing the effects of the Arab invasion in the seventh century; the country's conquerors had attempted to erase Iranian language, religion, and tradition as well as replace Iranian history and mythology with their own written version of the stories of the *Shahnameh* in order to serve their imperialist agendas. Ferdowsi responded to these moves by setting the oral histories of Iran into poetry, but doing so in a way that would honour those ancient traditions. Taking his readers to a time that predates Iran's introduction to Islam—from its prehistoric beginnings to the end of the Sasanian dynasty—Ferdowsi writes the *Shahnameh* predominantly utilizing "pure" Persian as opposed to the Arabized version that had begun taking shape in Iran and developing a lyrical, poetic style that mimicked its deep, oral traditions of storytelling.[6]

Ferdowsi's preservation of historical and mythical tradition in Iranian culture would prove to have a lasting effect for centuries to come. Indeed, the *Shahnameh* is far-reaching and considered one of the most important works of literature ever produced by an Iranian writer. Azar Nafisi, author of *Reading Lolita in Tehran*, quite aptly describes the relationship between politics and poetry, culture and literature, and nationhood and legacy within Iranian culture in her foreword to Dick Davis's translation of Ferdowsi's poem. She narrates an anecdote describing the lessons she learned about her heritage from her father—himself an author who published a version of the *Shahnameh* geared toward a youthful audience. Nafisi remembers her father teaching her and her brother about the importance of the classic work, saying:

> My father always insisted that Persians basically did not have a home, except in their literature, especially their poetry. This country, our country, he would say, has been attacked and invaded numerous times, and each time, when Persians had lost their sense of their own history, culture and language, they found their poets as the true guardians of their true home [...] my father would say, We have no other home but this, pointing to the invisible book, this, he would repeat is our home, always, for you and your brother, and your children and your children's children.[7]

As Nafisi describes, given the epic's production during a moment of cultural uncertainty, the *Shahnameh* has become a cultural treasure acting as a compass that points Iranians back toward the foundation of their true values. Through its discussion of themes such as kingship, inheritance, and most importantly honour and love of country, the poem takes readers through intertwining episodes that demonstrate a continuity of its guiding themes and the inevitability of connection between these themes to future generations. As a result, pivotal moments in Iran's history are often understood and shaped through this national epic.

The narrative fragments that make up the *Shahnameh* helped piece Iran together following one of the most devastating conquests of the country led by Timur I—or Tamburlaine the Great—who reigned from 1370 to 1495. Already weakened by Mongol

---

6 Canby, *The "Shahnama" of Shah Tahmasp*, 11.

7 Azar Nafisi, foreword to *Shahnameh, The Persian Book of Kings*, by Abolqasem Ferdowsi, trans. Dick Davis (New York: Penguin, 2006), ix.

invasions from 1256 to 1260, Iran was "unable to offer united opposition against Timur's invasions. The brutality of Timur in Iran was legendary, evidenced by, for example, the erection of a gruesome pyramid from the skulls of 70,000 inhabitants of Isfahan who dared to resist him."[8] The effects of this devastating invasion was long lasting, and it would take approximately 120 years after these events that the first Safavid shah, Shah Ismail I, would be "face[d] with the task of 'reconquering' his own country."[9] In order to do so, the new emperor enforced a common faith in Shi'i Islam as a way to unify Persians and separate them from their non-Muslim and Sunni neighbours.[10] He was largely successful in these efforts, beginning with reclaiming the contested region of Tabriz in northern Persia. His predecessors, however, were largely unsuccessful in maintaining those lands won, illuminating the timeless lessons about the importance of good leadership and honourable kingship so apparent in the *Shahnameh*.

It would be 100 years after Shah Ismail I's rule before Persia would again see tremendous progress and reunification under his great-grandson and the fifth king of the Safavid dynasty, Shah Abbas I. In 1598–1599, this young ruler was able to recover some territories in the northeast by defeating the Uzbeks—a major victory for the Persians. He was also responsible for establishing a burgeoning national economy that blossomed with the move of the Persian capital from Qazvin to Isfahan which welcomed travellers and traders from all over the world.[11] Not only was this rebuilding of Persia through trade and diplomacy significant in itself, but it also breathed new life into an image of Persia as a revered culture situated within a long classical, biblical, and historical tradition—a tradition well known by Persians and Europeans alike, and reinforced with a renewed commitment to arts and culture.[12]

The roadmap that offered directives for Safavid rule to reclaim lands, rebuild kingdoms, and rediscover a place within a global exchange in many ways came directly from the pages of the *Shahnameh*. As Safavid shahs attempted to piece their country back together, they each turned to the *Shahnameh* for guidance. It was not long before the beginning of his reign, for example, that Shah Ismail I ordered the creation of an elaborate illuminated manuscript in the early sixteenth century that was later to be completed

---

8 For more information about Mongol and Timurid invasions, see Kaveh Farrokh, *Iran at War: 1500–1988* (Oxford: Osprey, 2011), 9.

9 Rudolph P. Matthee, *The Politics of Trade in Safavid Iran: Silk for Silver, 1600–1730* (Cambridge: Cambridge University Press, 1999), 74.

10 For information on the structural and ideological differences between Shi'i and Sunni Islam, see Chibli Mallat, *Introduction to Middle Eastern Law* (Oxford: Oxford University Press, 2007).

11 For information on the history of the Safavid dynasty, see Andrew J. Newman, *Safavid Iran: Rebirth of a Persian Empire* (New York: I. B. Tauris, 2006), 13–24.

12 Persia's place in Judeo-Christian history is generally favorable. For example, Cyrus the Great is famous for having freed the Jews during the Babylonian Exile. Herbert himself visits the ancient site of Persepolis during his 1626 journey to Persia, and imagines it still stands in its all its splendour even as "Age and Warres" during his have reduced the palace to rubble. And in Christopher Marlowe's *Tamburlaine*, the pinnacle of the title character's victory is parading through Persepolis: "Your majesty shall shortly have your wish / And ride in triumph through Persepolis" (2.5.48–49).

under the rule of his son, Shah Tahmasp I.[13] With 258 illustrations, 759 folios, and gilded leather binding, this manuscript depicts detailed and ornate images representing scenes from the epic poem, honouring the tradition of the *Shahnameh* for courtly practices of the Safavid dynasty.

Even Shah Abbas I continued the tradition by instituting a more performative version of the *Shahnameh*. Under his reign, and following the move of the capital from Qazvin to Isfahan, the emperor encouraged the recitation of episodes from the *Shahnameh* by storytellers known as *naqqals*.[14] These performances often occurred in coffee houses, which "brought together individuals from different social backgrounds and professions, from kings and nobles, through poets and artists, to merchants and craftsmen who worked in bazaars."[15] These community spaces became important social centres not just for natives but also Iran's foreign guests—a place for drinking, smoking, socializing, and enjoying such performances. The *naqqals* would recount well-known stories by memory using expressive tones and elongated vowel sounds that connected each line in one continuous utterance—a specific manner of poetic reading that still exists today. These *naqqals* reinvigorated the tradition of oral storytelling, making poetry like Ferdowsi's accessible to a wider audience.

Within their poetic arsenal, the *naqqals* would often recount stories about the most famous, and arguably most beloved, character of the *Shahnameh*: Rostam. Their performances often transported audiences to the famous *haftkhan*, or the seven trials Rostam was entrusted to overcome, the relentlessness with which he defends Iranian kings, and even the heart-wrenching moment Rostam kills his son in a battle before realizing who his opponent truly is. For all of his successes and heartbreaks, readers of the *Shahnameh* see the story of Rostam as the story of Iran itself. He is "the epitome of magnanimity, manliness, heroism, and loyalty to the Persian throne," states translator and scholar Dick Davis, whose introduction to *Rostam: Tales of Love and War from the Shahnameh*, explains that "[t]here is something anarchic about [Rostam] [...] Much of the glamour of Rostam's legend lies in the tension between this fierce independence, which places him outside of authority, and his seemingly inexhaustible (until it is in fact exhausted) service to the Persian monarchy and the country it controls."[16]

Rostam is characterized by the qualities of most heroic figures—on the one hand, deep loyalty and strength guide his actions, but on the other he must resist what is expected in order to fulfill his duties as hero. Indeed, not only does Rostam sit "outside

---

13 The *Shahnameh* of Shah Tahmasp I was produced in stages by multiple artists beginning in 1522 and largely completed in 1537, with two more paintings included in 1540 (Canby, *The "Shahnama" of Shah Tahmasp*, 14).

14 While Shah Ismail I utilized *naqqals* to promote Shi'i Islam, Shah Abbas I utilized these performers for the recitation of poetry in coffee houses. For more information about the history of *naqqals*, see Yamamoto, *The Oral Background of Persian Epics*, 20.

15 Yamamoto, *The Oral Background of Persian Epics*, 21.

16 Abolqasem Ferdowsi, *Rostam: Tales of Love and War from the Shahnameh*, trans. Dick Davis (New York: Penguin, 2009), ix–xi.

of authority," he seemingly sits outside of a rigid sense of Iranianness—as the son of Rudabeh, the princess of Kabul and Zal, an impressive Iranian warrior raised by a mythical bird, he is the embodiment of the multicultural milieu that has shaped the country itself. Every move he makes, every decision he weighs is always done for the betterment of Iran, and as a result becomes a national hero for those within the *Shahnameh* as well as those who read the *Shahnameh*. To hear Rostam's story is to hear Iran's story of triumph over adversity, of nationhood in the face of complex histories, of resilience in the face of danger. His story persists as a story of the continuation of honour even after the deceit that leads to his death.

Shaghad's betrayal of Rostam is particularly troubling for English traveller Sir Thomas Herbert who, with the help of his translators, most likely encountered the *Shahnameh* during his journey into Persia in 1626. The embassy to Persia—an embassy sanctioned by King James I and the English East India Company—was meant as a diplomatic and fact-finding mission, and Herbert joined this embassy as a gentleman attendant to English ambassador Sir Dodemore Cotton.[17] Despite the expedition's intention, Herbert's travelogue, *A Relation of Some Yeares Travaile*, exposes a deeper interest in Persia's ancient past than in its rather lively present. While Herbert follows generic travel writing tropes that include the topography and customs of the destination, his travel narrative focuses much more attention on the empire's ancient and classical history. He is unlike contemporary travel writers who tend to draw more attention to interesting ceremonies, troublesome rulers, or exotic objects. Instead, his travel narrative combines first-hand observation with an intimate knowledge of classical writers that paints an image of Persia with competing temporalities: one of its antique, fallen past under the Achaemenid dynasty and the other of its thriving, cosmopolitan present under Safavid rule. This temporal exchange is one that he returns to consistently within his narrative, whether visiting ancient, historical sites or vibrant, cosmopolitan city centres.

Herbert's curiosity about a multi-temporal Persia even exists within a vibrant, metropolitan city like the Safavid capital of Isfahan. Though he briefly mentions the multiculturality of the city by noting the presence of "English, Dutch, Portugals, Arabians, Turkes, Iewes, Armenians, Muscouians, and Indians," he is more interested in the architectural details of the buildings within the *maydan*, or city square.[18] Interestingly, this discussion is reminiscent of his account of the ancient ruins of Persepolis, a place that also seems void of life and where he likewise offers details about the structure's measurements and materials. While I offer a more comprehensive discussion of these sections of Herbert's travelogue in the third section of this essay, what is important to note from the outset is Herbert's fascination with what is immovable. Despite being surrounded by fellow travellers, locals, and even timeless stories that are perpetually re-circulated by the fluidity of poetic expression through the city's *naqqals*, Herbert insists on petrifying Persia into a lifeless, inanimate object.

---

17 For more information about the embassy to Persia, see D. W. Davies, *Elizabethans Errant: The Strange Fortunes of Sir Thomas Sherley and His Three Sons* (Ithaca: Cornell University Press, 1967).

18 Thomas Herbert, *A Relation of Some Yeares Travaile* (London, 1634), M3v.

Much of *A Relation of Some Yeares Travaile* depends on biblical and classical foundations, a clear expression of Herbert's interest and knowledge of Persia's past. This is an empire whose time had ended centuries ago—at least, this theory is what Herbert had learned through his studies of classical texts like Xenophon's *Cyropedia* and Herodotus' *Histories*—two Greek-language texts that had become popular in England with nearly contemporary English-language translations—and the biblical stories about the transfer of empire from the Book of Daniel. With this understanding engrained in his mind prior to his journey, Herbert might have become confused by the life and vibrancy he actually witnessed when arriving in Persia in 1626, and his travelogue becomes an exercise to make sense of what he had encountered. Indeed, his fascination with the complexity of his experience is one he continues to write and re-write through a series of extensive revisions of this travelogue over the course of a fifty-year period.

Though Herbert calls upon faded memories and his knowledge of classical materials in order to further develop his popular narrative for a loyal readership, it is important to note that his section on "Isfahan" is almost forgotten in his revision process. This section experiences no change structurally and modest expansions narratively, and Isfahan's general architectural layout remains the main focus of the section rather than the people he presumably meets. In this section readers also discover his account of Rostam—both his retelling of Rostam's death as well as a description of a tomb named in his honour. Because of Herbert's tendency to construct an imagined, multi-temporal Persia throughout his travel narrative, and because he likely encountered stories of the *Shahnameh* while in Isfahan, his inclusion of Rostam in this section is unsurprising. What is puzzling, however, is how uninterested he is in the warrior's life.

It is my contention that Herbert seeks to turn Rostam—as a metonymy of Iran— into a fossil in an effort to disempower a national symbol of resilience and strength. By setting Rostam's story—specifically the story of his death—to writing, Herbert attempts to contain the fluidity of the poetic performances of the *naqqals*, the fluidity that keeps Rostam's story alive and in circulation. Their narratives about Rostam and other figures from Ferdowsi's national epic breathed new life into a burgeoning imperial capital, and the circulation of these stories reinvigorated unity and direction for the Safavids. As a result, Herbert attempts to supersede this constant movement through an act of writing (and compulsive acts of revision). The reason, I argue, for Herbert's rhetorical petrification is to counteract the vibrancy he encountered within Persia, to reduce it back into the fallen, dead past that does not seem to want to stay dead. In this essay, I put Herbert's text into direct conversation with Ferdowsi's poem; by centring Rostam and his story, I demonstrate that Herbert's reduction of this figure attempts to obscure his intentions. Through this discussion we will see that travel literature offers more complex understandings of encounter that move unexpectedly and untidily across boundaries of space and time, destabilizing a pervasive presumption of travel as unidirectional, beginning in Europe and ending in Eastern empires like Safavid Persia, Ottoman Turkey, or Mughal India. Even as Herbert tries to contain and petrify symbols of nationhood, honour, and greatness like Rostam through his writing and revision process, he resurrects the Persia he tries to contain with each revision of his text.

The Wonder of a Nation

> This is the song of Rostam, who's been given
> Few days of happiness by Fate or heaven.
> He fights in every war, in every land;
> His bed's a hillside, or the desert sand.
> Demons and dragons are his daily prey,
> Devils and deserts block his weary way.
> Fate sees to it that perfumed flowers, and wine,
> And pleasant vistas, are but rarely mine—
> I'm always grappling with an enemy,
> Some ghoul or leopard's always fighting me.[19]

Rostam enters the *Shahnameh* through a description of his birth. Coming into the world as the warrior he would become, his mother's long and arduous labour astounds those who stood in attendance: "all who saw this mammoth baby gazed / In wonder at him, murmuring and amazed."[20] From the start, Ferdowsi sets Rostam apart from all others. His greatness in size as an infant is prophetic, marking him for greatness in spirit and strength as an adult. This figure would fulfill his promise as a champion of Iran, having the opportunity to prove himself at a young age. With the many invasions Iran would face—invasions Azar Nafisi's father warns her about when she is a child—Rostam appears at the right time. A hero who represents strength and honour, however, must have a trusted companion, and Rostam finds one in a saffron-coloured foal named Raksh who exhibits the same stamina and power as his new owner. As the only horse who can withstand his weight and might, Raksh becomes not only Rostam's true and steady companion for the duration of his life, but his mirror image as well.

During the early years of Rostam's life, Iran's leadership fluctuates between good, honourable rulers to bad, ineffective ones to good and honourable ones again in a recurring cycle true to the transition of power. When a new king, Kai Kavus, assumes the throne, Rostam assumes responsibility to support him for the protection of Iran.[21] This king, however, would prove to bring havoc to the country. His arrogant desires lead him to plans for conquering a mystical land in Mazandaran, the country ruled by sorcerer kings (*divs*). The expedition is unsuccessful, and Kai Kavus is captured. Rostam—to free his sovereign in order to protect Iran from outside invaders—sets out on a journey known as the *haftkhan* (or, seven trials). From slaying dragons to defeating demons to freeing captured kings, Rostam fulfills every trial that tests his strength, his honour, and his leadership, and it is through these events that Rostam solidifies his reputation as the greatest, most formidable warrior of Iran.

Before Rostam can complete his final trial, he must liberate the imprisoned Kai Kavus by defeating the most potent *div*, the King of Mazandaran; this *div*, however, fearful of

---

19 Ferdowsi, *Shahnameh*, 156.

20 Ferdowsi, *Shahnameh*, 105.

21 *Kai* means "king" in Persian.

a battle with a famous warrior, attempts to escape using sorcery to transform into a "mountainous crag"[22] at the sight of his unconquerable adversary. The Iranian people refuse to permit this cowardly disappearance, and try to manipulate the rock in order to expel the sorcerer king, failing with every attempt. Rostam, however, experiences no difficulty:

> Then Rostam opened his arms, and without testing its weight, lifted the rock, while the army looked on in wonder. He walked with the craggy mass, while a crowd of men followed him, calling down blessings on him, and scattering gold coins and jewels over him. He carried it to the space in front of the king's pavilion, where he flung it down and placed it at the Persians' disposal.[23]

Literally unmatched, Rostam is able to do what no other warrior can. He easily manoeuvres the massive, magical rock from its place, demonstrating his unprecedented strength and ability. His connection to Iran—a power that transcends physicality—gives him the ability to carry the weight of Iran on his shoulders, and to dismantle threats against it. His bravery and his otherworldly strength elicits love and respect from his companions as they watch the act with the same "wonder" inspired by his birth and "follow" him as they shower him with blessings, coins, and jewels.

It is perhaps because of this deep love for Rostam that the hearts of all his followers break upon learning that he inadvertently kills his own son, Sohrab. While in Samangan for a subsequent battle, he meets the beautiful Tahmineh, the king of Samangan's daughter. After they spend the night together, Rostam leaves her with a special trinket: a clasp that, if Tahmineh bears a daughter, must be woven in the child's hair, and if a son, placed around his arm. Nine months later, Tahmineh gives birth to a son, Sohrab, and when he turns ten years of age, she reveals his father's identity. Elated that he descends from a long line of strong warriors—his father the most prominent among them—Sohrab vows to fight all of Rostam's enemies in order to place him on the throne which he believes is his father's rightful place. Though his mother warns against such aspirations, Sohrab's lineage becomes common knowledge through his own triumphs, giving their enemies the leverage they need to enact the worst fate between this father and son.

The news travels, and finds its way to Afrasyab—an enemy king who for decades had been vying for the Persian throne and is one of Rostam's greatest adversaries. Hoping to take advantage of a weak reign by Kai Kavus—a king who had led his people and Iran toward troubling times—Afrasyab plans an attack. Having learned of Sohrab's identity, Afrasyab sends word to the young fighter encouraging his skills and offering support for his military ambitions. Sohrab—whose plans to place his father onto the throne of Iran included one day besting Afrasyab but not before bringing down the impotent Kai Kavus—takes the opportunity, wondering if he will meet his father during the war. With Rostam's clasp tucked away beneath his armour, Sohrab encounters his father, never knowing with whom he is battling. As they fight, Sohrab emulates Rostam in both

---

22 Ferdowsi, *Shahnameh*, 170.
23 Ferdowsi, *Shahnameh*, 171.

strength and strategy. But even after the arduous combat, Rostam successfully delivers the fatal blow, plunging a dagger into his son's chest. Sohrab, who had devoted his life to reuniting with his father, reveals his identity:

> I brought this on myself, this is from me,
> And Fate has merely handed you the key
> To my brief life: not you but heaven's vault—
> Which raised me and then killed me— is at fault.
> Love for my father led me here to die [...]
> One from this noble band will take this sign
> To Rostam's hands, and tell him it was mine,
> And say I sought him always, far and wide,
> And that, at last, in seeking him, I died.[24]

Sohrab still does not know his killer is his father, but Rostam finally learns the painful truth: the young warrior who had almost bested him in their battle is indeed his son. Making the moment even more painful is the knowledge that Sohrab's entire life has been devoted to emulating, locating, and honouring his father only to die as his identity is revealed. He threatens his killer, indicating that "this sign"—the clasp—will alert Rostam to his son's fate, inspiring wrath within the famous hero who will undoubtedly avenge his child. Sohrab's words are not entirely misdirected; realization dawns on Rostam, devastating him. "When Rostam heard the warrior's words, his head whirled and the earth turned dark before his eyes, and when he came back to himself, he roared in an agony of anguish."[25] The emotional turmoil he faces breaks Rostam down at the news. He honours his son's last wish: to bid Kai Kavus "[h]ave no rancor in [his] heart against" the warriors he fought alongside him.[26]

In some ways, Sohrab's story must end because of his ambitions to ensure that his father sit on the throne to rule Iran. What we know of Rostam's character, however, is that he is meant to serve Iran through other means. His role is meant to restore order, rather than to represent it. This responsibility is one his character both achieves throughout his lifetime as well as inspires in others long after he dies. Not only does he do so within the *Shahnameh*, but as we have seen with the developments within the Safavid dynasty, he inspires such order for kingdoms to come. As a figure who acts as a metonymy for Iran itself, any other connections—filial or otherwise—have no place in the narrative. His true connection is his connection to Iran, and it is he who must restore order in times of trouble, dooming his character to heartbreak.

While it is true that Rostam is loved so deeply by characters from the *Shahnameh* as well as its readers, he is a complicated and flawed character; though he devotes his life to using his formidable strength to protect Iran from unrest, invasion, and bad leadership, his path is not always honourable. As Dick Davis has discussed in his book *Epic and*

---

24 Ferdowsi, *Shahnameh*, 209.

25 Ferdowsi, *Shahnameh*, 210.

26 Ferdowsi, *Shahnameh*, 213.

Sedition, even Ferdowsi betrays his frustration with his beloved hero in moments when Rostam exercises poor judgement. Rostam's failing as a father, Davis argues, "lies partly in his generally excessive temperament (which resulted in the boy's conception, and to which Ferdowsi refers during the course of the combat [with Sohrab])" and that this temperament can indeed be "seen as precipitating the tragedy."[27] But as Davis reminds us, when compared to other moments of filicide in the text, Rostam's killing of Sohrab is the only instance where the father does not know he is killing his son. This realization makes Rostam human in the eyes of the readers (and other characters) rather than contemptible. Though flawed, Rostam's heartbreak resonates timelessly, and conjures sympathy within the *Shahnameh*'s readers.

When the reader finally reaches the moment Rostam enters the plot against his life, we do so after we have witnessed his "wonder[ous]" birth and his "wonder[ous]" life, with all of its complicated devotion to honour. But, as Rostam's prophetic words about death reveal, no matter one's size or greatness, "no beast or man / Lives longer than his life's allotted span." While readers know that this hero—like all others—will reach his death eventually, it is painful to see it occur not on the battlefield against a worthy adversary but at the hands of deceitful enemies who trick him and take advantage of his compromised position.

Trapped with Raksh beneath the earth in the treacherous pits, Rostam watches as Shaghad taunts him from above. But he uses his gift for strategy to fight this last battle. He tells his traitorous brother to string his bow with two arrows for him in the event a lion comes to attack; Shaghad who is "filled with joy at the thought of his brother's death," fulfills his request.[28] Shaghad's joy, however, turns to fear immediately when he realizes that the tables have turned:

> Rostam picked up the bow, and notched an arrow to the string. His brother was filled with fear at the sight of the arrow, and to shield himself he went behind a huge, ancient plane tree, the trunk of which was hollow, although it still bore leaves. Rostam watched him go, and then, summoning his last strength, he drew back the bowstring and released the arrow. The shaft pierced the tree and his brother [...] Shahghad cried out with the pain of his wound, but Rostam soon put him out of his misery.[29]

Though Rostam's death is heart-wrenching—in its brutality and its deceit—readers witness his last fight with relief. His enemies hoped to contain his greatness, to put an end to the life he lived; while they succeeded in bringing him to his last breath, they were unable to quench the life of his legacy. His greatness would only extend beyond Ferdowsi's rhyming couplets, and enter a world of immortality that would touch not only Iranians but readers from every corner of the world across time.

---

27 Davis, *Epic and Sedition*, 107.

28 Ferdowsi, *Shahnameh*, 429.

29 Ferdowsi, *Shahnameh*, 429.

Re-vision of Time

> All things are the more, most things the better for Addition. In honour and
> wealth no fault is found with encrease; full meales & full pleasures too; brim-
> full have no guard upon them. The fuller the better: If the husbandry bestowed
> upon this Book hath improv'd the soile, since you view'd it last, the Lyme was
> yours and charge of bringing; the spreading only belongs to mee as your day
> labourer.[30]

Due to the ephemeral nature of oral transmission, it is impossible to know the exact
series of stories from the *Shahnameh* Herbert would have encountered while in Isfahan.
But with no extant translations of the *Shahnameh* in any European language at the time,
it is likely that the English traveller would have encountered these narratives within
the public, social spaces of Isfahan, and the story he is most likely to have encountered
would have been from the most popular series: those about Rostam, especially the
battle between him and his son, Sohrab. Given that Iranian culture was often defined by
its orality—a tradition Iranians still hold onto today—the *naqqals* were in many ways
the gatekeepers of history and literature, and became an important medium through
which locals and travellers would have gained access to the complex poetic material
of Ferdowsi's medieval poem. Through these orations, Herbert learns about Rostam,
revealing his acknowledgement of the figure as beloved and his intolerance for Rostam's
manner of death:

> In his time this Champion *Rustan* liued and was of great account with his
> Master, whose loue a while protected him from domestique Aduersaries, other-
> whiles his owne valour was his safeguard. By which two he enioyed great digni-
> ties and reports, till old age ouertook him, which kild him not, but his traiterous
> brother *Shawgad*, out of no other cause then pale Enuie, sought his destruc-
> tion, and effected it; by digging pits, couered with boughes, which seeming
> harmelesse, gaue him miserable ruine, into one of which as he was in chase;
> he fell, and calling out for helpe, his deuillish brother affoorded it; with death-
> bringing-darts, basely destroying a valiant Champion, and one who most of all
> others, gaue glory to him and his owne Family, who notwithstanding ere hee
> died with two arrowes shot out of the pit, slue his trayterous brother and his
> father in Law.[31]

The opening of this passage highlights Rostam's character. Herbert explains that "this
Champion" lived under the protection of his "Master"—presumably, the rulers he
served—as well as "his owne valour." His account of Rostam, here, complements the most
well-known stories of the figure outlined in the second section of this essay. But even
as he acknowledges Rostam's characterization as a beloved and valorous "Champion,"
Herbert's retelling of his life and successes is reduced to one labyrinthine sentence. The

---

30 Thomas Herbert, *A Relation of Some Yeares Travels* (London, 1638), B1r.

31 Herbert, *A Relation of Some Yeares Travaile* (1634), M4v–N1r.

focus of the passage quickly turns to Rostam's death, suggesting to his readers that the importance of this story lies in the warrior's final moments.

This message becomes even more evident with each subsequent edition of Herbert's travelogue. Spanning a fifty-year period and culminating in a total of three additional volumes published in 1638, 1664, and 1677, *A Relation of Some Yeares Travaile* undergoes extensive revisions each time Herbert revisits his travels. In most cases, these revisions rely on faded memories and expanded discussions of the classical and biblical material he had only touched upon in previous iterations of his work. These expansions make the moments where Herbert chooses *not* to revise even more important, and peculiarly, his discussion of Rostam's life and death remains largely the same across editions. Given his predilection for classical and ancient Persian accounts, one might expect an expanded discussion of a story situated deeply within Iran's historical and mythical past, not least because the composition of it would permit Herbert an extended stay within a different time and place—a tendency his narrative exposes about him. Rather, Herbert, attempts to contain Rostam's story deliberately, seemingly crystallizing his narrative into an immovable sediment set within a bygone era.

Herbert discusses his motivation for expanding his original travel text in the first place by offering a note to his readers in the 1638 publication of *Some Yeares Travels*.[32] Excerpted in the epigraph to this section, he explains that "[a]ll things are the more, most things the better for Addition." The logic behind his approach is that the very notion of "addition" or increasing something—really, anything—is to improve it. In matters of wealth and honour, in consumption (such as with food or pleasure), "brim-full have no guard upon them." And he credits the encouragement of this perspective to his avid readers, those who made the new editions a possibility by virtue of their desire for more. "If the husbandry bestowed upon this Book hath improv'd the soile, since you view'd it last, the Lyme was yours and charge of bringing; the spreading only belongs to mee as your day labourer." The readers, Herbert explains, are also responsible for the growth and care of the book, and it is because of their insatiable appetites that he is able to visit Persia again and again—not through additional expeditions but through his writing.

The acts of revision Herbert undergoes allow him to maintain Persia as an object of desire; he keeps Persia on the horizon through a rhetorical return. According to the *Oxford English Dictionary* (*OED*), "revise" comes from the Latin root *revīsere* "to pay another visit (to), to go back and see, to go and see again, to revisit, to take another look at" (*OED*, "revise," v.). His revision of the text, then, translates into a re-vision of Persia that manifests differently within each version of his narrative, resulting in a new, imagined encounter between England and Persia every time the next edition is published. Herbert speaks to this process in an unusual interjection delivered in Latin within the author's note in the 1638 edition: "Turpe mihi abire domo, vacuum[.] redire est" (It is shameful to me to leave home and return empty(handed)).[33] Herbert bestows *Some Yeares Travels*

---

32 The initial title of the 1634 publication of Herbert's travelogue, *A Relation of Some Yeares Travaile*, undergoes a slight change to *Some Yeares Travels* in the subsequent editions.

33 Herbert, *A Relation of Some Yeares Travels* (1638), B1r.

as a "souvenir"—a tangible memory and an idea—in an act of translation situated within his Latin invocation. Herbert revises his work in much the same way a translator might make a text legible and accessible to a wider audience; his readership expands as he attempts to make Persian culture—and, with the Rostam narrative, literature—legible and accessible to readers who would otherwise never encounter Ferdowsi's poem.

Herbert's interest in providing access for a reader to a hitherto unexplored area of Iranian history and literature has its limits, however. While he seems taken with the story about Rostam's death, he has no significant interest in revisiting it. The absence of meaningful revision for this excerpt—and for the section on "Isfahan" where it appears—becomes even more apparent when compared to other areas of the travelogue that do see significant changes, such as his description of his encounter with the ruins of Persepolis. When Herbert encounters the ruins of the ancient palace, he is immediately transported to ancient Persia even as he sifts through the stones that remain. His section meticulously details the materials and measurements of the remaining structure, but he devotes an equal amount of time to discussing the effect that his contact with Persia's past has on him. And with each subsequent edition, Herbert's account of this encounter becomes fuller, more vivid, more classically situated, and in some cases his expression becomes more effusive.

Persepolis, for Herbert, is far from an inert, ancient site; while its ruins stand frozen within the moment of its destruction, it remains a formidable presence in the present. Herbert finds himself caught between two temporalities from the outset, and begins the section on "Persepolis" with the moment of conquest when Alexander the Great "more easily gaue a Period to this glorious Citie, by one blaze, at the whoorish councell of the *Athenian Thais*, so that, through his riot and her villany, this Imperiall Citie felt the flames of Warre, which *Alexander* afterwards deplored with teares, but helpless."[34] In a passage characteristic of Herbert's narrative style, we see that his language echoes the multitemporality characteristic of the site:

> [...] the wals are rarely engrauen with Images of huge stature, and haue beene illustrated with Gold, which in some places is visible, the stones in many parts so well polisht, that they equall for brightnesse a steele mirrour: this Chamber has its wals of best lustre. But Age and Warres, two great consumers of rare monuments, has turned topsie-turuie, this, as many other things, and left nought but wals to testifie the greatnesse of that glory and triumph it has enioyed.[35]

The Persia Herbert shows us is one he imagines before its destruction: the engraved walls have not yet eroded, their images have not yet the absence of their illustrious gold, and the marble of which the palace is made has not yet lost its lustre. Persepolis is a site that, though historically devastated by Alexander's conquest, refuses to yield to its destruction. In fact, even Alexander, according to Herbert, "deplored" his act "with teares, but helpless."

---

34 Herbert, *A Relation of Some Yeares Travaile* (1634), H4v.

35 Herbert, *A Relation of Some Yeares Travaile* (1634), I2r.

Herbert imagines this moment as though it is unfolding before him, a moment he is brought to by the power of an encounter with Persia's past. That this passage reads in the present tense further underscores Herbert's insistence on remembering a moment in history as though he is present during its time of greatness. In fact, he literally remembers himself as he describes seeing his reflection in the marble that makes up the palace: "composed of hard Marble (no strange thing, all the mountaine being the best black Marble in the World, in many of which polisht stones I could see my face).["36] Or, as he describes in more detail in 1638, "[t]he walls are very eminent in this chamber, of black shining Marble, in many places so bright and jetty, as we could easily view our reflex, no steel mirror comparing with it."[37] Herbert cannot help but see himself within this revered time even as he invokes the conjunction "but" to remind himself and his readers that "Age and Warres, two great consumers of rare monuments, has turned topsie-turuie, this, as many other things," rhetorically rerouting us safely back to the rubble representative of what the great empire has now become.

Not only does his narrative grow in this section with deeper accounts of dead Persian kings and ancient Persian customs, he even includes an etching of Persepolis with an expanded, birds-eye view created by Wenceslas Hollar in 1663, a contrast to William Marshall's three-quarter-page engraving of the crumbling pillars based on Herbert's sketches found in the 1634 and 1638 editions.[38] Hollar's depiction literally fills the gaps of the ruins by putting some of the structure back together again, just as Herbert attempts to do with his own writing. Fulfilling his goal to improve his account—"the better for Addition"—as he promises in his note to his readers, Herbert indulges in his own desire to inhabit a different, more glorious time so long as he can rhetorically manoeuvre back out of it.

Herbert's desire for time travel and intimacy with ancient Persia in his account of Persepolis contrasts with his unwillingness to rhetorically revisit Rostam's narrative in the "Isfahan" section. When Herbert confronts the ruins of its past, he sees ancient Persia as a fallen site that he can resurrect through his writing; Isfahan, on the other hand, represents the very notion that Persia is in fact not dead and gone, that it has not yielded to its destruction centuries ago. This revival under the Safavids, therefore, seems to discomfort Herbert, and so we see him use his writing to renegotiate what he encounters. His description of Isfahan and the impressive *maydan*—or Isfahan's vast city square flanked by the king's palace, a mosque, and other structures—is reminiscent of his discussion of the ruins of Persepolis. He offers detailed descriptions of the structures, the materials used to create them, and measurements to offer the reader a sense of their grandness. But because the cosmopolitan city gives Herbert no opportunity to anchor these descriptions to a fallen past, he turns to a digression about a legendary warrior betrayed and killed by his half-brother.

---

36 Herbert, *A Relation of Some Yeares Travaile* (1634), I1r.

37 Herbert, *A Relation of Some Yeares Travels* (1638), V1v.

38 For more information see John Carswell, "A Young Man Abroad: Sir Thomas Herbert's Travels to Persia in 1626 A.D.," in *The Sultan's Turret: Studies in Persian and Turkish Culture*, ed. Carole Hillenbrand (Boston: Brill, 1999), 19–41.

Embedded in his survey of Isfahan's architecture is his discussion of Rostam's death—as we have seen. Herbert seems uncomfortable with Shaghad's betrayal, referring to him as Rostam's "deuillish brother," accusing him of "pale Enuie," and charging him with "destroying a valiant Champion"; his tone here mirrors the same regret he expresses at the thought of Alexander destroying Persepolis. But even as he reveals this regret, we also see the same relief he experienced while in Persepolis with the reminders of the empire's fall. Like he does with the ancient site, Herbert hunts for monuments on which he can fixate within "Isfahan" as a way to anchor it to its past, and finds one honouring Rostam himself. In this section, Herbert describes seeing a monument "[a] little further, vpon a high imperious mountaine is *Rustans* Tombe, more eminent for height and perspicuitie, then beautie or admiration, his Image is cut very artificially vpon a blacke shining marble mountaine neere *Persae-polis*, called *Nogdi-rustan*."[39] The site Herbert presumably refers to in this passage is known as Naqsh-e Rostam, or "the image of Rostam," an ancient burial site for four Achaemenid kings located near Persepolis (just outside the city of Shiraz), roughly 250 miles (over 400 km) away from Isfahan, where Herbert claims he can see it just "[a] little further, vpon a high imperious mountaine."

Approximately 2 miles (4 km) away from Persepolis is a mountain called Hussain Kuh, upon which engravings of mythological heroes are carved and the remains of Darius the Great, Xerxes, Ardashir I, and Darius II reside. While these remains were initially attributed to Jamshid and Kianid Kings, "since these stonemasonries show the victory of Iranian heroes over the enemies, such sculptures were attributed to Rostam-e Zal and called this place as Naqsh-e Rostam."[40] It was later discovered, however, that they in fact belonged to the four kings of the Achaemenid period, while the etchings were created in the Sasanid period (224–651 CE). These tombs, therefore, were not erected in memory of Rostam nor is "his Image [...] cut very artificially vpon a black shining marble mountaine"; rather, Rostam—because of his legacy—was etched into the tombs in order to suggest the greatness of Iran's Achaemenid rulers. Herbert's reference to this site makes his relationship to the figure of Rostam even more puzzling. While it is possible he was just misinformed about Naqsh-e Rostam, or even misunderstood what he had been told, this confusion does not explain the implication that the site is visible from Isfahan, just one paragraph away from his account of Rostam's death.

Interestingly, however, it is this discussion about Rostam's so-called monument that exhibits the most meaningful revision in the section on "Isfahan." In the 1638 edition, Herbert's tone shifts as he seems disappointed with Isfahan's dearth of monuments. He explains

> Monuments should come now to our description: but I found few to feed my eyes upon. *Rustans* Tomb must be one (two miles from *Spahawn*) behind

---

39 Herbert, *A Relation of Some Yeares Travaile* (1634), M4v.

40 A. Shapur Shahbazi, *The Authoritative Guide to Naqsh-e Rostam* (Tehran: Safiran, 1393/2014), 12. Zal is Rostam's father; Rostam-e Zal is a manner of addressing Rostam as the son of Zal.

the Garden wee last spoke of [...] To see it, wee foot it to the very top of an Imperious Mount, where is only a hollow Cave, whether cut by Art or Nature scarce discernable.[41]

In 1664, Herbert adds to this description stating that it is "[a] Tomb scarce to be discerned by reason of its ruine."[42] Not only does Herbert geographically relocate Naqsh-e Rostam in his description drawing it closer to Isfahan—not to mention incorrectly name this monument as the figure's final resting place—but he also underscores the "ruine" associated with this tomb, further aligning it with other structures or monuments that have "turned topsie-turvie" over time. Rather than expanding these revisions "the better for Addition," Herbert delivers misinformation about the tomb in order to fulfill his project to cement Rostam's identity to a dead and immovable past. His narrative does not account for the life and vibrancy of Rostam, and by virtue of this petrification, isolates the life and vibrancy of Isfahan.

Through his writing and revision of his Persian travels, Herbert attempts to renegotiate the temporal boundaries of the Safavid Empire. By reminding himself and his readers of Persia's fallen, ancient past, he contains the constant revival of an empire that refuses to remain dead. But even as Herbert attempts to manipulate time to control the nonlinear movements of Persia's histories, he does not succeed in assuming the authority he seeks. What Herbert neglects to account for is the unwieldy way time moves, and the surprising ways it moves him. Much like the ephemerality of the oral tradition of storytelling, time moves unexpectedly and refuses to be pinned down. Though Herbert tries to contain Persia—to freeze its progress and to deter its insistence on turning the *Shahnameh* into a roadmap for success—he fails. As a result of Herbert's attempt to petrify symbols of nationhood, honour, and greatness like Rostam through his revision process, he continually resurrects Persia's glorious past within its thriving present. Indeed, Persia continues to work on him, challenging his desires and sense of self, revealing how it is more alive and vibrant than he ever expected.

---

41 Herbert, *A Relation of Some Yeares Travels* (London, 1638), X4r.

42 Herbert, *A Relation of Some Yeares Travels* (London, 1664), Z3v.

Chapter 6

BETWEEN WORD AND IMAGE: REPRESENTATIONS OF SHI'ITE RITUALS IN THE SAFAVID EMPIRE FROM EARLY MODERN EUROPEAN TRAVEL ACCOUNTS

ELIO BRANCAFORTE

ABSTRACT

This essay will present close readings from several early modern European travel accounts that describe Shi'ite religious practices in the Safavid Empire and that integrate images into the written narrative. The depictions, in order to be properly understood, need to be considered in conjunction with the author's text—otherwise valuable information about the subject matter risks becoming lost, which also increases the possibility for the misinterpretation of the portrayal. These images in the works of Pietro Della Valle, Adam Olearius, and Jean de Thévenot help transmit a particular world view for the European readers who encountered this foreign subject matter for the first time; the appeal to the visual component is meant to help the viewer "see" the practices of Islamic culture via a copperplate engraving. These inquisitive European travellers, who seek to call attention to the remarkable religious customs that they observe, all emphasize that they have produced eyewitness accounts ... a fact that the images are meant to support. Using both text and image, these authors present their representations of contemporary Muslim societies and thus contribute to the European understanding of the "other," in this case by participating in the transfer of knowledge about religious customs and values that they observed while journeying through the Safavid Empire.

Keywords: Safavid, word and image, Shi'ite, travel literature

AT THE BEGINNING of the seventeenth century, the Safavid Shah 'Abbas I (1571–1629)[1] actively encouraged foreign travel to Iran, and created a hospitable situation for trade and diplomatic exchange. Europeans from a number of Catholic and Protestant

---

[1] On this important Safavid ruler, see David Blow, *Shah Abbas: The Ruthless King Who Became an Iranian Legend* (London: I. B. Tauris, 2009); and Sheila R. Canby, *Shah 'Abbas: The Remaking of Iran* (London: British Museum Press, 2009). For historical background on the Safavids see Andrew Newman, *Safavid Iran: Rebirth of an Empire* (London: I. B. Tauris, 2006).

lands were attracted by "his outward looking agenda [...] centered on a new resplendent capital, Isfahan. This coincided with and was partly responsible for, an active European interest in Iran as a land of religious, commercial, and strategic opportunity."[2] Some came as missionaries hoping to establish residency in Isfahan; many others came as merchants wishing to take advantage of the silk or jewel trade; still others arrived as ambassadors trying to convince the Safavids to attack the Ottomans. There were also curious travellers who wanted to learn more about Persia on their way further east. What all those European travellers had in common was their interest in describing the land, its peoples, customs, history, along with details of the flora and fauna.[3] These early modern voyagers, most of whom arrived from areas of religious strife, and had witnessed numerous wars on the European continent during the sixteenth and seventeenth centuries, saw the split between Sunnis and Shi'ites as paralleling the Protestant/Catholic divide. Religious difference in Iran was therefore a prime concern, and most European travel accounts devote a number of pages to pointing out how the natives worshipped, in what ways their rites were different from their Sunni neighbours, and what similarities existed between Shi'ite and Christian beliefs. A large number of publications about "the Turk" and the Ottoman state, along with important visual material, had been published throughout Europe during the sixteenth century, but Safavid Iran was relatively unknown to the late sixteenth-century and seventeenth-century European reader. This helps explain the interest in the new works about Persian customs, the people, and the form of religion practised there: Shi'sm.

The following essay will present close readings from several early modern European travel accounts that describe Shi'ite religious practices in the Safavid Empire and that integrate images into the written narrative. The depictions, in order to be properly understood, need to be considered in conjunction with the author's text—otherwise valuable information about the subject matter risks becoming lost, which also increases the possibility for the misinterpretation of the portrayal. These images help transmit a particular world view for the European readers who encountered this foreign subject matter for the first time, and the appeal to the visual component is meant to help the viewer "see" the practices of Islamic culture via a copperplate engraving. These inquisitive European travellers, who seek to call attention to the remarkable religious customs that they observe, all emphasize that they have produced eyewitness accounts ... a fact that the images are meant to support. In their attempt to acquire and present new information about Shi'ism, these early modern authors follow a trend in travel literature that can be noted since the late Middle Ages: "This attention to the narration of observed

---

2 Rudi Matthee, "The Safavids under Western Eyes: Seventeenth-Century European Travelers to Iran," *Journal of Early Modern History* 13 (2009): 138. See also his valuable "Safavid Iran through the Eyes of European Travelers," in Elio Brancaforte and Sonja Brentjes, *From Rhubarb to Rubies: European Travels to Safavid Iran (1550–1700)*, *The Lands of the Sophi: Iran in Early Modern European Maps (1550–1700)*, *Harvard Library Bulletin* 23 (2012): 10–24.

3 For examples of the kinds of objects these travellers took back with them to Europe see the exhibition catalogue by Brancaforte and Brentjes, *From Rhubarb to Rubies*.

experience, with special attention to human subjects, can in a general sense be seen as the ultimate relocation of the paradigm of travel from the ideal of pilgrimage to those of empirical curiosity and practical science."[4] Using both text and image, these authors present their representations of contemporary Muslim societies and thus contribute to the European understanding of the "other," in this case by participating in the transfer of knowledge about religious customs and values that they observed while journeying through the Safavid Empire.

Some travellers took notes along the way, or wrote letters back home about their journeys; others had professional artists in their retinue who recorded what they saw in sketches. These notes and sketches could then serve as the basis of a published travel account in their home country that combined, for example, a traveller's written descriptions of a city with an engraved cityscape that represented in pictorial form what the author tried to express in words. On the other hand, notes or sketches could be "adapted" by a publisher to fit the expectations of a reading public, sections of a narrative could be changed or censored by an author, a publisher, an ecclesiastic official, images could be altered, and the resulting work would be far removed from the "reality" of what the traveller had actually witnessed. Sonja Brentjes, in a compelling study that examines the process by which information produced by certain travellers or mapmakers about Safavid Iran made its way into print in early modern Europe, notes that:

> More often than not, arguably factual elements are complex constructions no less than are discussions of events, evaluations of customs, or reports on the sciences. Many elements of the verbal, cartographic, and pictorial representation of Safavid Iran in early modern Catholic or Protestan sources are of a literary character [...] they are seldom true or objective in the sense that they directly and reliably reflect the Iranian conditions at stake in a particular representation.[5]

In other words, one must take care when studying representations—verbal or pictorial—of Safavid Iran. They usually do not depict "reality" in the modern sense of the term, and the information presented was often recycled from previous accounts or invented entirely by someone who had never actually visited the country.

***

The subject of religion was of great interest not only to early modern visitors to Iran but also to the publishers of their travel accounts, since they knew that the topic could help sell books. For example, in the work by Thomas Herbert, *A Relation of Some Yeares Travaile* (London: William Stansby and Jacob Bloome, 1634), that chronicles the author's travels

---

4 Jaś Elsner and Joan-Pau Rubiés, Introduction to *Voyages and Visions: Towards a Cultural History of Travel* (London: Reaktion Books, 1999), 31.

5 See Sonja Brentjes, "Immediacy, Mediation, and Media in Early Modern Catholic and Protestant Representations of Safavid Iran," *Journal of Early Modern History* 13 (2009): 175.

to "the Territories of the *Persian* Monarchie: and some parts of the Orientall *Indies, and Iles adiacent*" the title page (see Figure 6.1) announces that the book will speak "Of their Religion, Language, Habit, Discent, Ceremonies, and other matters *concerning them.*" The accompanying frontispiece portrays on the left an "Abdall or Priest" (namely a dervish) pointing toward the heavens, while a threatening Qizilbash with a raised scimitar stands on the right; below these two dominating figures we find two smaller scenes of religious worship, with people wearing turbans kneeling and praying to a strange demon (left) and to a cow (right). Herbert's observations concerning religious practices were later used by other writers such as John Ogilby (1600–1676)[6] and Thomas Hyde (1636–1703).[7]

A careful observer such as the German doctor Engelbert Kaempfer comments on the role of dervishes in Safavid society, discusses madrasas and mosques, and gives a detailed description of Shah Sulaiman I's ceremonial departure in 1684 from Isfahan for the Festival of Sacrifice (Eid-e Qurban) outside the city (that is accompanied by an engraving depicting the scene).[8] Several other travellers write—with varying degrees of accuracy—about the differences between Sunnis and Shi'ites, and about 'Ashura rites such as Jan Janszoon Struys,[9] the French travellers Jean-Baptiste Tavernier[10] and Jean Chardin,[11] the Dutch painter Cornelis de

---

6 John Ogilby, *Asia. The First Part: Being an Accurate Description of Persia, and the Several Provinces Thereof: The Vast Empire of the Great Mogol, and Other Parts of India, and Their Several Kingdoms and Regions: With the Denominations and Descriptions of the Cities, Towns, and Places of Remark Therein Contain'd: The Various Customs, Habits, Religion, and Languages of the Inhabitants: Their Political Governments, and Way of Commerce: Also the Plants and Animals Peculiar to Each Country* (London: Printed by the author at his house in White-friers, 1673).

7 Thomas Hyde, *Historia Religionis Veterum Persarum, Eorumque Magorum [...] Zoroastris Vita, Ejusque Et Aliorum Vaticinia De Messiah È Persarum Aliorumque Monumentis Eruuntur [...] Atque Magorum Liber Sad-Der (Zoroastris Praecepta Seu Religionis Canones Continens) È Persico Traductus Exhibetur. Dantur Veterum Persarum Scripturae & Linquae [...] Specimina* (Oxford: Sheldonian Theatre, 1700).

8 See Engelbert Kaempfer, *Amoenitatum Exoticarum Politico-Physico-Medicarum Fasciculi: V. Quibus Continentur Variae Relationes, Observationes & Descriptiones Rerum Persicarum & Ulterioris Asiae, Multâ Attentione in Peregrinationibus Per Universum Orientem* (Lemgo: Typis & impensis H.W. Meyeri, 1712). The engraving of the procession is located between pages 210–11.

9 See Jan Janszoon Struys, *The Perillous and Most Unhappy Voyages of John Struys: Through Italy, Greece, Lifeland, Muscovia, Tartary, Media, Persia, East-India, Japan, and Other Places in Europe, Africa and Asia [...]*, trans. John Morrison (London: printed for Samuel Smith at the Princes Arms in S. Pauls Church-yard, 1683), especially 263–66 for a description of 'Ashura in Shamakhy.

10 Jean-Baptiste Tavernier, *Les Six Voyages De Jean Baptiste Tavernier, Ecuyer Baron D'aubonne, Qu'il a Fait En Turquie, En Perse, Et Aux Indes* (Paris: G. Clouzier, 1676). In volume 1, chapter 7 he discusses the "religion of the Persians, the great feast of Hocen & Hussein, and that of the camel" (423–30).

11 Jean Chardin, *Voyages de Monsieur le Chevalier Chardin en Perse et autres lieux de l'Orient* (Amsterdam: Jean Louis de Lorme, 1711). In volume 2 the author includes a description of the Persian religion (311–454), along with his own thoughts about the Persian religion (448–49). In the

**Figure 6.1. Frontispiece for Thomas Herbert, *A Relation of Some Yeares Travaile*
(London: William Stansby and Jacob Bloome, 1634). Call number: Typ 605.34.450.
Houghton Library, Harvard University.**

Bruyn,[12] and the Capuchin friar Raphaël du Mans, author of *Estat de la Perse* (1660), who lived in Isfahan for almost half a century and who provided information for a number of European travellers to Iran.[13]

We shall turn now to the travel accounts of three European visitors who went to Iran during the seventeenth century, namely Pietro Della Valle, Adam Olearius and Jean de Thévenot. Specifically, I will focus on some of their observations regarding religion. These travellers write about the differences between Sunnis and Shi'ites, describe religious practices of the Iranians, and comment on Shi'i rites that they observed. I will pay special attention to what they write about the commemorations for the deaths of 'Ali and his second son, Husayn (the rites for the latter are known as 'Ashura). After presenting the narrative descriptions of these rites I will examine those engravings in the three travel accounts that illustrate these specific Shi'ite rituals and consider what information from the written account was included in the image.

Shi'i Muslims consider 'Ashura as their most important religious event, the day on which they commemorate the martyrdom of Husayn, one of the Prophet's grandsons, who was killed near Karbala in 680 CE.[14] Husayn was the leader of a small group of the Prophet Muhammad's descendants and their families that was defeated by an Umayyad army of some 4,000 men. Shi'ites hold commemorative events in honour of the martyred Imam at which elegies are recited and the events leading up to Husayn's death are recounted. Participants seek to symbolically recreate the tragedy and engage in the martyr's act of self-sacrifice by shedding blood (e.g. cutting themselves with knives), beating themselves with chains, crying, and experiencing hunger and thirst in remembrance of the sufferings experienced by Husayn and his family.[15]

***

---

third volume Chardin explains the differences between Sunnis and "Chia" (163–72), comments on the feast of the camel (164–65) and briefly mentions the martyrdom of 'Ali (211).

12 Cornelis de Bruyn, *Voyages De Corneille Le Brun Par La Moscovie, En Perse, Et Aux Indes Orientales. Ouvrage Enrichi De Plus De 320 Tailles Douces […] Et Quelques Remarques Contre Mrs. Chardin & Kempfer. Avec Une Lettre Écrite À L'auteur, Sur Ce Sujet* (Amsterdam: Freres Wetstein, 1718). In volume 1 de Bruyn writes about Beyram (188), the commemoration of 'Ali's death (190), Abraham (193), the rites in honor of Hussein (217–22), and Persian customs with regard to births, marriages, death, and burial (222–26).

13 Raphaël du Mans, *Estat De La Perse En 1660*, ed. Charles Schefer (Paris: Ernest Leroux, 1890), with an account of 'Ashura (53–56). See also Francis Richard, *Raphaël Du Mans, Missionnaire en Perse au Xviie Siècle* (Paris: Société d'histoire de l'Orient, 1995).

14 See Kamran S. Aghaie, "'āshūrā' (Shī'ism)," in *Encyclopaedia of Islam, Third Edition*, Brill Online, 2013, http://referenceworks.brillonline.com.ezp-prod1.hul.harvard.edu/entries/encyclopaedia-of-islam-3/ashura-shiism-COM_23855.

15 For a useful overview of which European travellers witnessed the 'Ashura ceremonies in Safavid Iran, see Jean Calmard, "Shi'i Rituals and Power II. The Consolidation of Safavid Shi'ism: Folklore and Popular Religion," in *Safavid Persia: The History and Politics of an Islamic Society*, ed. Charles Melville (London: I. B. Tauris, 1996), 139–90.

Pietro Della Valle (1586–1652)

Born into a wealthy aristocratic Roman family, Pietro Della Valle became one of the most important travellers of the seventeenth century.[16] As a result of a failed love affair, the young Della Valle went to Naples from 1609 to 1614 where he encountered scholars interested in Oriental literature, history, science, and philosophy, including a certain Mario Schipano. Della Valle ended up travelling throughout the Middle East, Turkey, Persia, and India from 1614 to 1626, and sending Schipano a series of letters that he hoped the medical professor would publish for him.

Calling himself "the pilgrim," Della Valle travelled to Istanbul, Cairo, Damascus, and other Ottoman cities, accompanied by servants and a painter. He started learning Turkish and wrote about Sunni rites; in Egypt he purchased two mummies (now in Dresden). With the assistance of Jewish merchants and teachers he was able to buy several Arabic and Turkish dictionaries, grammars, and treatises on medicine. Finding himself in Aleppo in 1616, instead of returning to Italy he decided to travel to Iran with a caravan on its way to Baghdad. The reason for this spontaneous decision was to offer his services to Shah 'Abbas I, who had a reputation for tolerance toward Christians. He hoped he could sway the shah to launch a "crusade" against the Ottomans and convert to Catholicism. On the way to Iran, Della Valle met and fell in love with the daughter of a well-off Assyrian family (who were Nestorian Christians) named Sitti Ma'ani.[17] They were married soon after, and travelled together to Isfahan at the beginning of 1617. Sitti Ma'ani was a remarkable young woman, who knew Armenian, Arabic, Persian, and Georgian; she opened many doors for Della Valle, and helped him obtain information about the Safavid court and society.

Della Valle was able to meet Shah 'Abbas in February 1618 at his court in Farahabad on the Caspian Sea and meet members of the court there. Together with his wife, he followed the shah's army to Qazvin and Ardabil, hoping for a war with the Ottomans. Della Valle learned Persian and bought a number of manuscripts on various subjects during his stay in Isfahan from December 1618 to October 1621. The couple decided to travel to India, but because of the Persian and English blockade of the Portuguese on Hormuz they had to wait for a ship on the coast, at Minab. Sitti Ma'ani, who was pregnant, caught a fever, miscarried, and died in 1621. Della Valle was distraught, and almost died from the same fever. Eventually he was able to embalm her body in camphor and take her back to Italy via India, hidden in his luggage. Back in Rome, in 1626, in a great public ceremony with poetry and music, Sitti Ma'ani was buried in the Della Valle family

---

16 For basic background on Della Valle see Joan-Pau Rubiés, "Della Valle, Pietro (1586–1652)," in *Literature of Travel and Exploration: An Encyclopedia*, ed. J. Speake (New York: Fitzroy Dearborn, 2003), 326–28; entry 50 of Brancaforte and Brentjes, *From Rhubarb to Rubies*, 92–94; and John Gurney, "Della Valle, Pietro," in *Encyclopaedia Iranica Online*, www.iranicaonline.org/articles/della-valle. On Della Valle's "self-fashioning" see Nathalie Hester, *Literature and Identity in Italian Baroque Travel Writing* (Aldershot: Ashgate, 2008), esp. 51–93.

17 See Cristelle Baskins, "Lost in Translation: Portraits of Sitti Maani Gioerida Della Valle in Baroque Rome," *Early Modern Women: An Interdisciplinary Journal* 7 (2012): 241–60.

chapel in Santa Maria in Aracoeli. Della Valle ended up marrying his adopted Georgian daughter, named Mariuccia, and having fourteen children. He spent the next twenty-six years reworking his diary notes and letters to produce a published version of his travels that were published between 1650 and 1663. He also wrote a Latin geography of Safavid Iran,[18] a Turkish grammar, a description of 'Abbas I (Rome, 1628), along with other works.

Della Valle includes a great deal of information concerning religious practices that he encountered during his voyages. He writes about the differences between Sunni and Shi'ite religious practices, on 'Ashura, and the camel sacrifice in Isfahan. In order to illustrate some of these various rites and festivals, the 1666 Dutch edition of his travels (*De volkome beschryving der voortreffelijcke reizen* [...],[19] translated by J. H. Glazemaker), includes a number of engravings by an anonymous artist. A later German edition of the work, *Petri della Valle* [...] *Reiss-Beschreibung in unterschiedliche Theile der Welt* [...] (Geneva, 1674),[20] contains engravings by the Swiss artist Johann Jakob Thurneysen[21] that were copied from the Dutch edition.

Thurneysen's frontispiece (see Figure 6.2) in the German edition is completely new: it portrays the Ottoman sultan and the Persian shah—mirroring the Sunni/Shi'ite divide; and a small cartouche (below the putto holding the title of the work) that displays opposing war camps emphasizes the conflict between the two potentates.[22] Engravings

---

18 Sonja Brentjes and Volkmar Schüller, "Pietro Della Valle's Latin Geography of Safavid Iran (1624–1628): Introduction," *Journal of Early Modern History* 10 (2006): 169–219.

19 Pietro Della Valle, *De volkome beschryving der voortreffelijcke reizen van de doorluchtige reisiger Pietro Della Valle: in veel voorname gewesten des werrelts, sedert het jaer 1615 tot in 't jaar 1626 gedaan / uit zijn schriften, aan Mario Schipiano geschreven, door J. H. Glazemaker vert.* [...]; *met XXV konstige kopere platen en een reg. verçiert* (t'Amsterdam: voor Jan Rieuwertsz Boekverkoper, 1666).

20 Pietro Della Valle, *Petri della Valle, Eines vornehmen Römischen Patritii, Reiss-Beschreibung in unterschiedliche Theile der Welt/ Nemlich In Türckey/ Egypten/ Palestina/ Persien/ Ost-Indien/ und andere weit entlegene Landschafften/ Samt Einer ausführlichen Erzehlung aller Denck- und Merckwürdigster Sachen so darinnen zu finden und anzutreffen; Nebenst den Sitten/ und Gebräuchen dieser Nationen und anderen Dingen/ dergleichen zuvor niemals von anderen angemercket und beschrieben worden* (Genff: In Verlegung Johann-Herman Widerholds, 1674).

21 On the Swiss graphic artist and copper engraver Johann Jakob Thurneysen the Elder (also known under the name "Thourneysen, Thourneyser," etc.), who lived 1636–1718, see the *Allgemeines Künstlerlexikon Online*, s.v. "Thurneysen, Johann Jakob;" *Oxford Art Online*, s.v. "Thurneysen [Thourneysser], Johann Jakob, I;" and Tapan Bhattacharya, "Thurneysen, Johann Jakob," in *Historisches Lexikon der Schweiz*, www.hls-dhs-dss.ch/textes/d/D19161.php.

22 The publisher includes a helpful explanation of the frontispiece in the form of a short poem:

Erklärung des Kupffer=Tituls.
Es meynt der Groß=Türck zwar / er hab nicht seines gleichen
In diesem gantzen Rund / und müß ihm alles weichen;
    Weil er den Orient / und Constantinus=Statt
    Durch seiner Waffen Stärck siegreich bezwungen hat.
Doch hält sich der Monarch in Persen nicht viel minder/
Weil er die Reuterey viel besser und geschwinder

Figure 6.2. Frontispiece by J. J. Thurneysen for Pietro Della Valle, *Reiss-Beschreibung in unterschiedliche Theile der Welt ...* (Genff: In Verlegung Johann-Herman Widerholds, 1674). Call number: Spec. Coll. MCZ F832. From the collections of the Ernst Mayr Library, Museum of Comparative Zoology, Harvard University.

in the Dutch and German editions illustrate some of the more grisly elements relating to religious ceremonies: (a) how Shah 'Abbas received a special present for Noruz—the new year's celebration—namely the heads of 600 Turks on pikes. The author refers to Strabo in the text and notes that this kind of gift had a long tradition in Persia; (b) the forced circumcision of an old Armenian priest is vividly displayed along with the knife about to cut the foreskin; and (c) a description of the camel sacrifice at the little Bayram (which Della Valle terms the Muslim Easter) in Isfahan. The text recounts how the participants vie with each other to tear out a piece of its fur for good luck, and then once the "poor animal" has been killed, they fight to grab a piece of its meat to take back to their city quarter, where it is salted and preserved for good luck—the head is given to the Shah, however.[23]

In his "Letter 4. from Farahabad the first days of May and from Qazvin, 25 July 1618," Della Valle provides a description of the mourning rituals of 'Ashura, which he observed in Isfahan in January 1618, on the tenth day of the lunar month of Muharram. Della Valle begins his account of 'Ashura in Isfhan by providing some background about Husayn and his death, and notes that: "This Hussein is regarded to the point of folly by all the Mohammedans as a great saint; but by the Persians of the Shia belief also as the legitimate Imam and supreme head of their sect (from whom the kinds of Persia today claim descent)."[24] He goes on to describe various lamentation rites: many people wear black, and nobody bathes or shaves their head or beard. "Many poor people, too, are in the habit of burying themselves in busy streets up to the neck and even part of their heads,

---

Ins Felde bringen kan / und ist so wol bestellt /
Daß er dem Türcken=Reich die Segen=Wage hält.
Explanation of the Copper Plate.
The Grand Turk, to be sure, thinks that there is no one equal to him
In the entire globe and that everyone has to cede to him;
Because he has conquered the Orient and the City of Constantine
Through the strength of his weapons.
However the monarch in Persia holds his own,
Because he can take his cavalry better and faster
To the battle field, and he is so well-appointed
That he can balance the scales against the Turkish empire.

23 For an interesting and thorough study of this topic, see Babak Rahimi's work *Theater State and the Formation of Early Modern Public Sphere in Iran: Studies on Safavid Muharram Rituals, 1590–1641* (Leiden: Brill, 2012), along with his earlier article on "The Rebound Theater State: The Politics of the Safavid Camel Sacrifice Rituals, 1598–1695 C.E.," *Iranian Studies* 37 (2004): 451–78.

24 Pietro Della Valle, *The Pilgrim: The Travels of Pietro Della Valle*, trans. George Bull (London: Hutchinson, 1990), 142. In this section I provide Bull's English translation, but his version of events is abridged. The original reads: "[...] il quale Hussein, tenuto scioccamente da tutti i Mahomettani per gran Santo, ma da' Persiani, di credenza Sciaiti, per legitimo Imàm ancora, e supremo Capo della loro setta, da cui i Rè di Persia di hoggi si vantano di discendere," Pietro Della Valle, *Viaggi Di Pietro Della Valle Il Pellegrino, Descritti da lui medesimo in Lettere familiari All'erudito suo Amico Mario Schipano, La Persia-Parte Prima* (Rome: A spese di Biagio Deversin, 1658), 138–39.

in earthenware jars, wide all around from the feet and narrow to fit the head at the top."[25] These jars are buried in the ground with a person remaining inside for the entire day, while someone else asks alms of passersby. In order to express grief for the death of Husayn, other people paint themselves black from head to toe, resembling devils, and run through the streets naked—except for the private parts that are covered by a small black cloth. Others colour themselves red to symbolize blood and the martyr's violent death. They walk together, "beating time with castanets of bone or wood,"[26] singing sorrowful dirges.

Others perform in public like acrobats and receive alms. Every day around noon a mullah, wearing a green turban (an unusual colour, seen normally in Turkey) recounts the deeds and the death of Husayn from a raised seat in the square. His audience of men and women stand or sit on the ground or on benches around him while "from time to time he shows some painted figures illustrating what he is recounting" and tries "to move the onlookers to tears."[27] These preachings elicit moans from the listeners, especially the women, who beat their breasts and reply " '*Vah Hussein! Sciah Hussein!*' meaning 'Ah Hussein! King Hussein!' "[28]

On the tenth day of Muharram one can see: processions in all the streets of Isfahan, where people carry very long poles with flags; a camel carrying a coffin with three or four children inside, who represent the children of the martyr who were taken in captivity; a coffin covered in black velvet with a turban resting on it, along with a sword; a number of arms as trophies that are carried above the heads of certain men who dance and twirl around. One also finds men from neighbouring areas with large sticks, who are ready to fight with the men from other processions, not only for the sake of precedence, but also to represent the battle in which Hussein was killed. They also say that whoever dies during 'Ashura enters straightaway into Paradise.

The rites for the death of Hussein are the same as those for 'Ali, the only difference is that the former are more solemn, and more people take part in the processions. There is also more desire to fight with sticks—and many men return home with broken heads. They also say that during the following night, they burn statues of Omar and of other heads of the opposite sect that had Husayn killed, and publicly execrate them. "But this I did not see, so I omit it."[29]

---

25 Della Valle, *Pilgrim*, 143; "Vsano, molti poueri, di sotterrarsi per le strade frequentate, mettendosi sotto terra infin'alla gola, e con parte anco della testa, dentro a certi vasi di terra cotta fatti a posta, larghi da piedi intorno, e con la bocca stretta a misura del capo," Della Valle, *Viaggi*, 139.

26 Della Valle, *Pilgrim*, 143; "[...] sbattendo certi legnetti, ouero ossi, che hanno in mano," Della Valle, *Viaggi*, 139.

27 Della Valle, *Pilgrim*, 143–44; "[...] & alle volte mostra alcune figure dipinte di quel che racconta; & in somma per tutte le vie procura di muouer più che può i circostanti al pianto," Della Valle, *Viaggi*, 140.

28 Della Valle, *Pilgrim*, 144; "*Vah, Hußein! Sciah Hussein!* che significano Ah, Hussein! Rè Hussein!," Della Valle, *Viaggi*, 140.

29 "[...] ma questo, io non l'hò veduto, e però ne fò passaggio," Della Valle, *Viaggi*, 142; with thanks to Renzo Bragantini (Rome) for assistance with the translation.

The Italian editions of Della Valle's published account do not contain engravings that illustrate scenes from his journey, so I will refer to the German edition of the account. If we consider J. Thurneysen's engraving[30] that accompanies the description of 'Ashura (see Figure 6.3) we can see the following: six dark figures (three bearded men, three women) wearing loincloths and holding small sticks dance in the foreground, while in the lower left a head emerges from the ground while another figure seems to place a pot over the head. To the right a figure lying on the ground looks at a pot resting on the earth. The lower middleground has two standing men on the left; a woman with her head covered by a cloth sits on the ground while a bearded man reaches out to her; behind him two women gaze off in the distance. Above them on a raised platform in the centre sits a turbaned man who seems to be smiling slightly; three other turbaned men, two on the left, one on the right, gesture to people below the platform on the left and to others kneeling and standing on the platform to the right (consisting of a kneeling woman holding her hand to her breast; and bearded men some of whom have no head coverings, two of whom wear turbans). The scene is framed by a number of buildings that look vaguely "Southern European," with an arch in the background on the right.

What is perhaps most incongruous in this "composite" image concerns the fact that half-nude women are portrayed front and centre, in the foreground. Women would not have gone through the streets of Isfahan during 'Ashura painted black, with only a black cloth covering their nether regions. The artist, who obviously did not know very much about Iran, has chosen to depict a scene that could be situated in Italy (going by the architecture and the tile roof of the house). The large male figure dancing in the right foreground, in particular, seems to be derived from classical statuary, with a very well-developed, muscular, upper torso. The seated woman in the left middleground could be a Madonna facing a bearded Joseph; the bearded man below the windows of the apse-like structure on the right resembles a bearded Franciscan monk. Thurneysen has selected a number of elements from Della Valle's narrative—the mullah recounting the death of Husayn, the penitents who are buried in the earth, or who are coloured black, the women who look pathetically into the distance as they hear about the martyr and his family ... and the turbans provide a touch of exoticism to the proceedings. However, overall the engraving is not an accurate portrayal of 'Ashura in Isfahan.

Adam Olearius (1599–1671)

Adam Olearius is known as the author of a seventeenth-century travel account that chronicled the voyage of a German embassy to Isfahan from 1635 to 1639.[31] At the mid-point of the Thirty Years' War, Duke Frederick III, ruler of the small Northern German duchy of Holstein-Gottorf, decided that he would try to convince Shah Safi of Persia

---

30 Thurneysen's engraving is located in Part 2 of Della Valle's *Reiss-Beschreibung*, between pp. 132–33.

31 The biographical information about Olearius is quoted from entry 30 of Brancaforte/Brentjes, *From Rhubarb to Rubies*, 71–72. See also Dieter Lohmeier, "Nachwort," in *Vermehrte Newe Beschreibung der Muscowitischen und Persischen Reyse*, ed. Dieter Lohmeier (Tübingen: Niemeyer,

Figure 6.3. Depiction of 'Ashura ceremonies by J. J. Thurneysen in Pietro Della Valle, *Reiss-Beschreibung in unterschiedliche Theile der Welt ...* (Genff: In Verlegung Johann-Herman Widerholds, 1674). Call number: Spec. Coll. MCZ F832. From the collections of the Ernst Mayr Library, Museum of Comparative Zoology, Harvard University.

to export his country's silk via the Volga, through Muscovy and the Baltic regions, to Gottorf; from there it would be sold throughout Northern Europe. In 1635, after coming to an agreement with Tsar Mikhail Fyodorovich Romanov (1596–1645; founder of the Romanov dynasty), Duke Frederick decided to send an embassy to the shah's capital in Isfahan, which included the poet Paul Fleming (1609–1640) and nearly one hundred support personnel. Adam Olearius, the son of a tailor and a graduate of the University of Leipzig, was chosen to chronicle the mission as its official secretary.

After a long and hazardous journey in which the embassy had to contend with attacks by Cossacks and Dagestani Tatars, as well as shipwrecks on the North Sea and the Caspian, the travellers returned to Germany in 1639. Soon afterwards, a Persian delegation sent by Shah Safi arrived in Gottorf. It had been sent to Holstein in order to discuss details of the proposed agreement, express the shah's friendship to the duke, and invite further contact. As it turned out, the few bales of silk that the emissaries presented to Duke Frederick as a present from the shah were the only pieces of the precious material that Gottorf would ever obtain from the mission.

Olearius's monumental account of the journey, *Offt Begehrte Beschreibung der Newen Orientalischen Reise* (Schleßwig, 1647) and the considerably expanded second edition, *Vermehrte Newe Beschreibung der Muscowitischen und Persischen Reyse* (Schleßwig, 1656), are truly encyclopedic works that cover topics corresponding to our modern-day disciplines of ethnography, geography, biology, zoology, linguistics, and history.

Until his death in 1671, Olearius kept extremely busy at Gottorf preparing the different editions of the travel account, editing works of other travellers, working on a (never published) Persian-Turkish-Arabic dictionary, and co-translating the Persian poet Sa'di's *Gulistan* into German. He was appointed court librarian by Duke Frederick and given the task of cataloguing and expanding the ducal collection. Olearius's interest in the sciences led him to build an astrolabe, a microscope, a telescope, and his crowning achievement, a giant globe, which was later presented to Peter the Great. All these achievements earned Olearius the sobriquet "the Holstein Pliny."

Olearius provides a great deal of information about religious practices in Iran in his travel account of 1647,[32] from explaining the differences between Shi'ites and

---

1971), *1–*80; and Elio Brancaforte, *Visions of Persia: Mapping the Travels of Adam Olearius* (Cambridge, MA: Harvard University Press, 2003).

32 Adam Olearius, *Offt begehrte Beschreibung Der Newen Orientalischen Reise / So durch Gelegenheit einer Holsteinischen Legation an den König in Persien geschehen. Worinnen Derer Orter und Länder/ durch welche die Reise gangen/ als fürnemblich Rußland/ Tartarien vnd Persien/ sampt ihrer Einwohner Natur/ Leben vnd Wesen fleissig beschrieben/ vnd mit vielen Kupfferstücken/ so nach dem Leben gestellet/ gezieret. Item Ein Schreiben des WolEdeln etc. Johan Albrecht Von Mandelslo/ worinnen dessen OstIndianische Reise über den* Oceanum *enthalten. Zusampt eines kurtzen Berichts von jetzigem Zustand des eussersten* Orientalischen *KönigReiches Tzina* ... (Schleßwig: Bey Jacob zur Glocken, 1647).

I will also refer to the first English translation: Adam Olearius, *The Voyages & Travels Of The Ambassadors From The Duke of Holstein, to the Great Duke of Muscovy, and the King of Persia, And other adjacent Countries. With several Publick Transactions reaching neer the Present Times; In*

Sunnis,[33] to describing the burial practices of the "Kebber" (a Zoroastrian sect) with an accompanying engraving of their cemetery in Isfahan.[34] An engraving in the second edition of the account from 1656 depicts the Shi'ite burial procession of a Persian nobleman in Shamakhi (who died after drinking too much Aquavit with the German ambassadors); the accompanying text carefully explains in twelve distinct sections who the different members of the procession were, along with their functions.[35] The author also notes how Persians use a prayer stone, which is made of greyish earth and comes from "Netzeff und Kufa," (Najaf and Kufa) where Hossein's blood was spilled and where he lies buried with 'Ali.[36] The stone is octagonal, and Olearius notes that it is approximately the same size as the one depicted on the page. The stone contains the names of their twelve saints along with that of Fatima; they put it on the ground and touch their foreheads to it while praying.

Olearius was present on February 7, 1637—the 22nd of Ramadan—in Shamakhi at the commemoration of Imam 'Ali's death (that he terms "Aschur.")[37] He notes that the "Ceremonies and Devotions were performed in a House built for that purpose"[38] outside the city. The accompanying engraving (see Figure 6.4) (by Christian Rothgiesser?)[39]

Seven Books. Illustrated with diverse accurate Mapps and Figures. By Adam Olearius, Secretary of the Embassy. Rendred into English, by John Davies, of Kidwelly (London: Printed for Thomas Dring, and John Starkey, 1662).

33 Olearius, *Offt begehrte*, 465; Olearius, *Voyages and Travels*, 371.

34 Olearius, *Offt begehrte*, 429; Olearius, *Voyages and Travels*, 302 (without an illustration).

35 Adam Olearius, *Vermehrte Newe Beschreibung Der Muscowitischen vnd Persischen Reyse: So durch gelegenheit einer Holsteinischen Gesandschafft an den Russischen Zaar vnd König in Persien geschehen ...* (Schleßwig: Johann Holwein, 1656), 686–88.

36 Olearius, *Vermehrte*, 681 (although the page is misprinted, and has "691"). Husayn was killed near Karbala, where he is buried, whereas 'Ali is buried in Najaf. The English translation, *The Voyages and Travels* of 1662, which has very few illustrations, indicates that the stone is "somewhat above 3 inches Diameter" and that the earth derives from "*Metzef* and *Kufa*" thus distorting "Najaf" further; see Olearius, *Voyages and Travels*, 375.

37 I should note that there are substantial differences between the English and the German versions. The most striking is the personal tone of the German original, where the author uses the first person plural to describe what "we" did (for example, how the Chan invited the foreign guests to join him and view the spectacle); on the other hand, the English version retains the third person throughout.

38 Olearius, *Voyages and Travels*, 217; "[...] sonderlichen *Ceremonien* und *devotion* gehalten worden / und zwar neben einem vor der Stadt darzu erbauetem Hause," Olearius, *Offt begehrte*, 302.

39 Christian Rothgießer (d. 1659) produced a large number of engravings for Olearius and worked with him closely to illustrate his publications. On the artists at the court of Schleswig-Gottorf see Heinz Spielmann and Jan Drees, *Gottorf im Glanz des Barock: Kunst und Kultur am schleswiger Hof 1544–1713. Kataloge der Ausstellung zum 50-Jährigen Bestehen des schleswig-holsteinischen Landesmuseums auf Schloss Gottorf und zum 400. Geburtstag Herzog Friedrichs III* (Schleswig: Schleswig-Holsteinisches Landesmuseum, 1997); and Holger Borzikowsky, *Von Allerhand Figuren und Abbildungen: Kupferstecher des 17. Jahrhunderts im Umkreis des Gottorfer Hofes* (Husum: Husum Druck- und Verlagsgesellschaft, 1981).

Figure 6.4. Depiction of the commemoration of 'Ali's death in Shamakhi by Christian Rothgießer (?) in Adam Olearius, *Offt begehrte Beschreibung Der Newen Orientalischen Reise* (Schleßwig: Bey Jacob zur Glocken, 1647). Call number: A: 263.1 Hist. 2°. Herzog August Bibliothek Wolfenbüttel.

shows that special house, built of dark wood, at the centre of the image, with the walled city in the background. The house is raised up toward the back at an unnatural angle—most likely in order to show the gallery on the right side of the house where the notables were seated so that they could view the "*Chatib*, that is, their Prelate, clad in a blew

Garment, which is the Mourning-Colour of that Country."[40] Seated under a large awning on a chair that was 8 feet high (at the extreme right of the engraving), the orator read and sang for over two hours from the "*Machtelnama*," a book that recounted the life of 'Ali. The "Priests" standing around him would sometimes finish singing some of the verses, and at the end of every passage one from among them would cry out: "*Luanet Chudai ber kuschendi Aaly bad*, that is, *God's Curse be on him who kill'd Haly:* whereto the whole Assembly answer'd, *bisch bad kem bad*, that is, *rather more than lesse*."[41] The audience is moved to tears when it hears that 'Ali foresaw his death and could have avoided it; they "weep and sob most biterly"[42] when his death is described and the effect it had on his children. After the *Chatib* finishes his recitation, he receives a silk coat from the *Chan*. This is followed by a procession with three camels carrying coffins covered in black cloth (representing "*Haly*, and his two Sons, *Hassan* and *Hossein*."[43]) Next came two chests covered in blue cloth that contained 'Ali's written works, and then two superb horses with "several Bows, Arrows, Turbants, and Flaggs"[44] attached to the saddle. Subsequently a man carrying a long pole at the top of which was "a kind of Tower or Steeple, in which there were thrust four Cimitars, but they were cover'd with so many Ribbons, and other Toyes, that they could hardly be perceived."[45] Finally, a number of men carrying boxes (containing the Qur'an) on their heads, dancing to sorrowful music, passed by. "On the other side" many young boys holding sticks clapped each other on the shoulder and shouted "*Heder, Heder*, which is the name of *Haly, Hassan, Hossein*,"[46] and then they all returned to the city. This ceremony for 'Ali is celebrated throughout Persia with great sadness; there is no day of remembrance for Muhammad, however.

The engraving contains these various parts of the ceremony, as though they were all happening simultaneously: a camel carrying a coffin is in the foreground at the bottom left,

---

40 Olearius, *Voyages and Travels*, 217; "[...] der *Chathib* oder Hoherpriester in einem blawen Traurkleide; Dann was bey uns in der Trauerzeit die Schwartze / das ist bey ihnen die blawe Farbe," Olearius, *Offt begehrte*, 302. Willem Floor also makes reference to this engraving in his discussion of *takiyeh* in *The History of Theater in Iran* (Washington, DC: Mage, 2005), 135–37. On "ta'zia," the Shi'ite passion play, see also Peter Chelkowski, "Ta'zia," in *Encyclopaedia Iranica Online*, www.iranicaonline.org/articles/tazia.

41 Olearius, *Voyages and Travels*, 217; "*Laanet Chudai ber kuschendi Aaly bad*! Der sey vor Gott verflucht / welcher *Aaly* umbbracht. Darauff antwortet die gantze Gemeine: *bisch bad, kem bad*. Das geschehe lieber mehr als minder," Olearius, *Offt begehrte*, 302.

42 Olearius, *Voyages and Travels*, 217; "Fiengen die Perser alle an zuweinen," Olearius, *Offt begehrte*, 302.

43 Olearius, *Voyages and Travels*, 217; "[...] so *Aaly* und dessen zweyen Sohnen *Hassans* und *Hosseins* Sarge," Olearius, *Offt begehrte*, 302.

44 Olearius, *Voyages and Travels*, 217; "[...] auf welchen Bogen / Pfeile und kostliche Hauptbunde lagen / viel Siegesfahnen," Olearius, *Offt begehrte*, 304.

45 Olearius, *Voyages and Travels*, 217; "[...] einen kleinen runden Thurm / den sie *Nachal* nanten / auff welchem 4. Sebel gestecket / die man unter den auffgeheffteten Zieraht kaum sehen kunte," Olearius, *Offt begehrte*, 304.

46 Olearius, *Voyages and Travels*, 217; "[...] *Heider, Heider* (diß ist *Aalij* Name) *Hassan, Hossein*," Olearius, *Offt begehrte*, 304.

while one of the splendid horses carrying arms is at the bottom right, as the men with the boxes on their heads dance between the animals, in the centre. The boys shouting "*Heder*" are in the left middle ground, above the camel's head, and next to their group stands the man holding the long pole with the four swords. The image gives the impression of a somewhat chaotic scene with a great throng of participants—but it can be decoded with the help of the text. One should also note the presence of the two German visitors, standing at the bottom left edge of the awning, and distinguishable by their European clothes and hats: the European figure on the left is a nobleman, whereas the other figure next to him could be Olearius. This emphasizes the eyewitness value of the work, to which the author refers throughout his travel narrative.

The 'Ashura ceremonies that Olearius witnessed in Ardabil began on May 14, 1637. The author notes the seventy-two arrows that pierced Husayn and the extreme thirst that he suffered in the desert. During the time of 'Ashura Persians "live very soberly,"[47] they do not use razors, and drink water instead of wine. Children carry large banners that have snakes made of "Pastboard winding to and fro, much like *Mercury's* Caduceus" at the end.[48] After sunset, men gather in tents illuminated by torches, they also have long poles with oranges stuck on the end, they cry out "*ja Hossein* ... with such violence, that it chang'd the colour of their countenances."[49] On the tenth day there is an oration in the courtyard of the shrine to Shah Sefi with the same ceremonies as the ones performed for 'Ali in Shamakhi. Even though Olearius did not witness it, he tells of a special banner that

> shakes of it self, as often as they pronounce the name of *Hossein*, during the Sermon [...] and that when the Priest makes a recital of the particular of his death, how he was wounded with seventy two Arrows, and how he fell down from his horse [...] that, the staff breaking, it falls to the ground.[50]

That evening, the German ambassadors were invited to the *Chan's* palace, where they sat on chairs that had been specially prepared for them (instead of sitting on the ground with their hosts). Paper lanterns were attached to the walls, there were also wax candles and paper lanterns in great number; porcelain vessels filled "with Suger'd and Perfum'd waters"[51] were set before them. Representatives of the five main quarters of Ardabil sang "a Serenade" for the Governour, verses in honour of 'Ali and Husayn, for two hours ...

---

47 Olearius, *Voyages and Travels*, 235; "leben messig," Olearius, *Offt begehrte*, 327.

48 Olearius, *Voyages and Travels*, 235; "[...] mit gegen einander gekerten Schlangen gezieret / *Eschder* genant," Olearius, *Offt begehrte*, 327.

49 Olearius, *Voyages and Travels*, 235; the German edition has "rieffen und schreyen [...] auch so hefftig / daß sie gantz braun wurden" (that they turned completely brown), Olearius, *Offt begehrte*, 327.

50 Olearius, *Voyages and Travels*, 235; "[...] sol / wenn Hosseins Name in selbiger *Parentation* gedacht wird / sich starck bewegen / wo aber die Word verlesen werden: das Er mit 72. Wunden beschädigt vom Pferde gefallen / soll sie so sehr schwancken / daß sie oben am Holtz gantz abbricht un[d] herunter fält," Olearius, *Offt begehrte*, 328.

51 Olearius, *Voyages and Travels*, 235; "[...] von süssen und wolriechenden Wassern," Olearius, *Offt begehrte*, 328.

but the author notes "they may be rather said to cry out and roar, than to sing."[52] At the same time, seven almost naked youths, painted black and resembling devils, were dancing. They were poor boys, called "*Tzatzaku*," and they knocked small stones against each other and sometimes against their chests to convey their grief for Husayn's death. When these ceremonies had ended, the *Chan* regaled his guests with a fireworks display, "which most of the *Persians* took very ill at his hands, and thought it not over religiously done of him, to give such Divertisements to the *Christians* during the time of their *Aschur*, which ought to represent onely things conducing to sadnesse and affliction."[53] Nonetheless, the Germans enjoyed the display, and Olearius notes the various kinds of fireworks and ingenious inventions, such as: a little castle that was set on fire; a kind called *Derbende*, in the form of a "Saucidge" and "Squibs and little Serpents, which falling among the people, set their Cotton Garments on fire."[54] The delegates returned to their quarters after midnight and went to bed hungry since they had expected supper at the palace. Just before sunrise there was another procession in honour of Husayn's burial. When the sun rose a large number of men gathered in the courtyard of Shaf Sefi's shrine and cut themselves with sharp knives ("Lanzetten")—there was so much blood that an ox could have been slaughtered there. Youths cut themselves above the elbow, made the blood spurt out, and then ran through the city in order to atone for their sins.

An unsigned engraving (see Figure 6.5), perhaps by the artist Franz Allen, depicts the nocturnal celebration in the courtyard of the *Chan*'s palace in Ardabil. The silhouettes of turbaned Persians can be seen in the foreground, and the German guests are seated on chairs along the wall on the right. Paper lanterns hang on the wall at the back, and various fireworks are going off all at once, most spectacularly from the "castle" firework. Since they are painted black, it is hard to distinguish the seven youths dancing to the right of the Persian holding the long pole with the light at the end. This engraving was only included in the first edition of 1647, it was not reproduced in later editions of the travel account—perhaps due to the poor quality of the image.

Jean de Thévenot (1633–1667)

Born in Paris in 1633 and independently wealthy, Jean de Thévenot also had the good fortune of having an uncle, Melchisédech Thévenot,[55] who compiled travel accounts from various countries and helped to inspire a passion for travel in his nephew. In 1652, the young

---

52 Olearius, *Voyages and Travels*, 236; "[...] sungen / oder rieffen viel mehr / was sie auß Leibes Krefften vermochten," Olearius, *Offt begehrte*, 329.

53 Olearius, *Voyages and Travels*, 236; "[...] zwar nicht ohne mißfallen etlicher Perser / welche vermeinten / daß an so hohem Traurfeste solche Feurwercke / die nur in Lust und Freudentagen üblich / sich nicht wol ziemeten," Olearius, *Offt begehrte*, 330.

54 Olearius, *Voyages and Travels*, 236; "[...] nach art der kleinen Schwermer / tumultuirete unter den Völckern herumb / nicht ohne schaden dero Kleider / welche / weil sie von *Catun*, leicht Feur fingen," Olearius, *Offt begehrte*, 330.

55 On Melchisédech Thévenot see chapter 2 of Nicholas Dew, *Orientalism in Louis XIV's France* (Oxford: Oxford University Press, 2009).

Figure 6.5. Depiction of 'Ashura in Ardabil by Franz Allen (?) in Adam Olearius, *Offt begehrte Beschreibung Der Newen Orientalischen Reise* (Schleßwig: Bey Jacob zur Glocken, 1647). Call number: 3000–4733. Universitätsbibliothek Braunschweig.

Thévenot travelled for three years through England, the Netherlands, German lands, and Italy. In Rome he met the French scholar Barthélemy d'Herbelot, and the two men decided to embark on a trip to the Ottoman Empire together.

> It is important to note that, inspired by the example of his uncle Melchisédech, he also intended from the outset of his explorations to keep meticulous records of his observations for later publication. Jean remained true to this resolution during the remaining 12 years of his life, valiantly maintaining his notes en route up until two weeks before his death.[56]

D'Herbelot was unable to go on the journey due to family affairs, so Thévenot decided to travel on his own. He learned Turkish and Arabic during this first trip to the Ottoman Empire, and also visited Anatolia, Egypt, Tunis and what were considered to be the ruins of Carthage before returning to Paris after an absence of seven years.[57] He left

---

56 Michael Brennan, "Thévenot, Jean de, (1633–1667)," in *Literature of Travel and Exploration: An Encyclopedia*, ed. J. Speake (New York: Fitzroy Dearborn, 2003), 1174.

57 See also the introduction by Stéphane Yerasimos of Jean de Thévenot, *Voyage Du Levant*, ed. Stéphane Yerasimos (Paris: F. Maspero, 1980), 5–27.

Paris in 1663 for Egypt, travelling to Alexandria, Damascus, Aleppo, Mosul, and Baghdad to Safavid Iran, where he learned Persian and spent five months in Isfahan before visiting Shiraz and the ruins of Persepolis. In November 1665 he sailed on an English ship to India, where he visited different regions over the span of thirteen months and collected plants for a herbarium.[58] After trying to recuperate for two months from cholera, he sailed for Bandar 'Abbas. In Shiraz Thévenot accidentally shot himself with his own pistol. After another period of convalescence in Isfahan he tried to return to Europe overland via Tabriz, but caught a fever and died in a small village on November 28, 1667. The first part of Thévenot's travel account—*Relation d'un voyage fait au Levant*—appeared in 1664–1665, and the other two parts were published posthumously by his friend the Sieur de Luisandre and François Pétis de La Croix. His journeys were translated into Dutch (1681–1682), English (1687), and German (1693), and reprinted several times in French and English.[59]

"The Religion of the *Persians* is in substance the same with that of the *Turks*, though, nevertheless, no Nations in the World hate one another so much upon the account of Religion as those two do: they look upon one another as Hereticks; not without appearance of reason." (1687).[60] This observation serves to introduce Thévenot's chapter on the "Religion of the Persians" (De la Religion des Persans), in which he mentions some of the differences between "*Schiai*"[61] and Sunnis. The Persians "celebrate their little *Bairam* or Easter of Sacrifices, in the same manner as the *Turks*"[62] by sacrificing sheep, sometimes an ox, but in Isfahan there is a special camel sacrifice. The

---

58 For this journey see the introduction by Francoise de Valence to Jean de Thévenot, *Les Voyages Aux Indes Orientales: Contenans Une Description Exacte De L'indostan, Des Nouveaux Mogols, Et Des Autres Peuples Et Païs Des Indes Orientales, Avec Leurs Moeurs Et Maximes, Religions, Fêtes, Temples, Pagodes, Cimetiéres, Commerce, Et Autres Choses Remarquables* (Paris: Honoré Champion, 2008), 7–23.

59 For the following section I will refer to this English edition of his travels: Jean de Thévenot, *The Travels of Monsieur De Thevenot into the Levant. In Three Parts. Viz. Into I. Turkey. II. Persia. III. The East-Indies*, trans. Archibald Lovell (London: Printed by Henry Clark for John Taylor, at the Ship in St. Paul's Church-Yard, 1687); as well as to the following French edition: *Voyages De Mr. De Thevenot, Tant en Europe qu'en Asie & en Afrique Divisez en trois Parties, qui comprenent cinq volumes ...* (Paris: Chez Charles Angot, 1689).

60 The citation in the original reads: "La Religion des Persans est en substance la même que celle des Turcs, quoique pourtant il n'y ait guere de Nations, qui se haïssent davantage entre'elles pour le sujet de la Religion que font celles-ci. Ils se regardent les uns & les autres comme heretiques; non sans apparence de raison...," 374.

61 This corresponds to part 2, chapter 13, of the English Thévenot, *Travels*, 106–110; and to chapter 13 of Thévenot, *Suite*, 374–387. The chapter that follows continues with the topic of religion and is titled: "Of Jews, Guebres, Banians, *and* Armenians" ("Des Juifs, Guebres, Banjan, & Armeniens"). Thévenot, *Travels*, 107; the French edition uses the term "Schiaïs," Thévenot, *Suite*, 376.

62 Thévenot, *Travels*, 107; "Ils celebrent le petit Baïram ou Pâque des victimes, de même que les Turcs," Thévenot, *Suite*, 377–78.

shah, or sometimes the governor of the town, dispatches the animal with a lance thrust, and some participants are always killed as they attempt to obtain a valued piece of the camel's meat.[63] Persians and Turks pray differently, and the former also

> lay down a little gray stone before them, which they always carry about, and every time they prostrate themselves on the ground, lay their Forehead on that stone, which is made of the Earth of *Kerbela*, the place where *Hussein*, the second Son of *Aly*, was killed by the men of *Yezid*; his tomb is there still.[64]

Thévenot goes on to describe the history and death of Husayn, the ceremonies surrounding 'Ashura, and mentions the feast of "*Serten*," which takes place forty days after 'Ashura. *Serten* signifies "*Head Body*" and "(say they)" it commemorates the day when Husayn's head joined itself to his body forty days after his death.[65] The chapter concludes with a mention of the rites performed in observance of 'Ali's death ("celebrated much after the same manner as that of *Hussein* his Son, but it lasts only a day");[66] a history of 'Ali's death; and the listing of other Persian festivals.

In the 1689 French edition of Thévenot's travels, which contains a few engravings by the Dutch artist Johannes van den Aveele,[67] there are two images in the first volume relating to religion from the author's stay in Istanbul: the first, from the chapter "Of the *Bairam*, the Turks *Easter*," depicts the festivities associated with the day, showing a man on a swing in the foreground, and a kind of simple ferris wheel in the background;[68] the second image relates to the funeral rites of the Turks, and shows how they do not sew up the burial shroud so that the dead person can kneel in front of the Angels more easily, when he is to be examined by them.[69]

Thévenot prefaces his description of the 'Ashura ceremonies that he witnessed in Shiraz in July 1665 with an account of Husayn's death at Karbala. "Having suffered Hunger and Thirst [...] he [...] marched couragiously towards [his Enemies] [...] charged into the thickest

---

63 Thévenot, *Travels*, 107–8; Thévenot, *Suite*, 378–79.

64 Thévenot, *Travels*, 108; "[...] mettent à bas devant eux une petite pierre grise, qu'ils portent toûjours, & toutes les fois qu'ils se prosternent en terre, ils appliquent le front sur cette pierre, qui est faite de la terre de Kerbela, qui est le lieu ou Hussein second fils d'Aly fût tüé par les gens de Yezid; son tombeau y est encore [...]," Thévenot, *Suite*, 380.

65 Thévenot, *Travels*, 109; "[...] Serten, c'est-à-dire, tête corps [...] disent-ils," Thévenot, *Suite*, 385.

66 Thévenot, *Travels*, 109; "[...] celebrée presque de même que celle d'Hussein son fils, mais ce n'est que durant un jour," Thévenot, *Suite*, 385.

67 On this Dutch graphic artist and copper engraver, who lived 1655–1727, see the *Allgemeines Künstlerlexikon Online*, s.v. "Aveele, Johannes van den"; *Oxford Art Online*, s.v. "Aveele, Johannes van den."

68 The engraving is found in Thévenot, *Voyages de Mr. De Thevenot*, vol. 1, pt. 1, chap. 35, between 140–41; see also Thévenot, *Travels*, pt. 1, bk. 1, chap. 35, 45–46.

69 The engraving is found in Thévenot, *Voyages de Mr. De Thevenot*, vol. 1, pt. 1, chap. 43, between pp. 178–79; see also Thévenot, *Travels*, pt. 1, bk. 1, chap. 43, "Of the way of Mourning for the Dead among the Turks, their manner of Burying, and of their Burying-places," 57–58.

of them with extraordinary vigour,"[70] before being defeated. His wives and children were taken prisoner "to *Yezid*, who treated them honourably, seeming to be grieved at the death of *Hussein*."[71] The author notes the fact that during the ten-day commemoration period the Persians dress in black, some of them wear black turbans, they refrain from shaving "nor commit any debauch."[72] "The inferiour sort of people signalize their Zeal by a thousand foolish pranks":[73] some of them bury themselves in the earth with only their head sticking out (which is covered with a pot filled with soil); others ("those Fools")[74] mix soot with oil and smear it all over their naked bodies (a black cloth covers their private parts); others take Armenian bole (a red earthy clay), dissolve it in oil and stain themselves blood red. The most "sincere" penitents cut themselves, "in the Head too, so that the blood comes running down on all sides."[75] With naked sabres in their hands and yelling "*Ya Hussein*" (Oh, Husayn) at the top of their lungs, they strike two stones together, producing a "wretched Musick"[76] as they run through the streets of the city. A mullah recounts the particulars of Husayn's death at night in a public square, causing the audience members to break into tears; such sermons are also held during the day, which is when "many persons of Quality"[77] attend. In Isfahan, on the tenth and last day, the shah must be present at the ceremonies dressed in mourning.

In Shiraz Thévenot describes the processions that passed by the governor's house, carrying banners, "the Rabble naked and besmeared in the manner I mentioned before."[78] Many children on horseback followed, symbolizing the children of Husayn who had been taken prisoner. Horses draped in black with arms attached to the saddle passed by next, then men carrying coffins covered with black velvet with a turban on each one. They all continued out of the city gate to finish the commemoration at the Mosque of Khatun (named after one of 'Ali's daughters) for a final sermon that was followed with food (mainly rice and a soup made with wheat) being given as alms to the poor.

The engraving[79] (see Figure 6.6) by Johannes van den Aveele (who actually signed his work: "*Joh: v: den Aveele inv. et fecit*") combines some of the most striking features of

---

70 Thévenot, *Travels*, 108; "[...] mais après avoir encore souffert la faim & la soif [...] il alla donc à eux courageusement, il donna dans leur gros avec une vigueur extraordinaire," Thévenot, *Suite*, 381–82.

71 Thévenot, *Travels*, 109; "[...] à Yezid, qui les traita honorablement, témoignant même du déplaisir de la mort de Hussein," Thévenot, *Suite*, 382.

72 Thévenot, *Travels*, 109; "[...] ne font aucune débauche," Thévenot, *Suite*, 382.

73 Thévenot, *Travels*, 109; "Le menu Peuple signale son zele par mille folies," Thévenot, *Suite*, 382.

74 Thévenot, *Travels*, 109; the term used is "ces fous," Thévenot, *Suite*, 383.

75 Thévenot, *Travels*, 109; "[...] même à la tête, en sorte que le sang coule de tous côtez," Thévenot, *Suite*, 383.

76 Thévenot, *Travels*, 109; "[...] une miserable musique," Thévenot, *Suite*, 383.

77 Thévenot, *Travels*, 109; "[...] plusieurs personnes de qualité," Thévenot, *Suite*, 384.

78 Thévenot, *Travels*, 109; "[...] toute cette canaille nuë & barboüillée de la maniére que j'ai dit," Thévenot, *Suite*, 384.

79 The engraving is located in Thévenot, *Suite*, vol. 2, chap. 13, between pp. 382–83. See also Brancaforte and Brentjes, *From Rhubarb to Rubies*, entry 60, 105–6.

Figure 6.6. Depiction of 'Ashura in Shiraz by Johannes van den Aveele in Jean de Thévenot, *Suite du Voyage de Mr. de Thevenot Au Levant ...* (Paris: Chez Charles Angot, 1689). Call number: M: Gv 125:4. Herzog August Bibliothek Wolfenbüttel.

Thévenot's account as though they were all occurring simultaneously—as was also the case with Rothgiesser's image accompanying the commemoration of 'Ali's death outside the gates of Shamakhi. The picture can be divided into three main sections. (1) First, in the foreground, the viewer is given a "closeup," so to speak, of some of the most dramatic elements of the ceremony. Three stages of the burial of penitents is displayed: at the bottom left, a man who is praying prepares to descend into the hole that his companion is digging for him, while the earthen pot that will cover his head rests in the bottom left-hand corner of the image. To the right, still in the foreground, a man places a pot over a penitent's head, and slightly to their left one can see a pot resting on the ground, which represents the final stage of this ritual. The pot at the centre is being showered with blood that pours from a self-inflicted head wound by two half-naked penitents who are at the centre foreground of the engraving. To their right we see two other men who seek forgiveness for their sins by knocking together stone blocks and creating "music" for the proceedings. (2) In the right middleground on a high dais a mullah has stood up from his chair and recounts the events leading to Husayn's death. Two figures kneel to the right of the chair, a throng of turbaned men crowd around the dais to hear the sermon, while other figures listen from windows above, to the right of the mullah. (3) A procession from the background is about to join up with another procession that enters the large square from a crenellated tower. The latter procession includes, from the back, two coffins, horses carrying weapons, and children on horseback that pass in front of the governor's house. It snakes its way from right to left until it reaches the middleground from where it continues from left to right. The architecture is a hodgepodge of classical columns that frame the image on the extreme left- and right-hand sides; it has elements of medieval European castle construction; and includes vaguely "Oriental" structures, such as the minarets in the background (one of which has an Ottoman-style crescent moon attached at the top). The drapings on the governor's house, above the mullah's dais, and at the top right of the engraving give the image a theatrical feel: 'Ashura is on display for the European viewer.[80] Although van Aveele invented a great number of components in the image and did not know what Shiraz (or any Safavid Iranian city) actually looked like, one can say that he was able to provide a comprehensible tableau of 'Ashura from the narrative that was available to him as source material.

Conclusion

Early modern travellers to the Middle East, the Ottoman Empire, and the Safavid Empire were instrumental in collecting knowledge about these areas in their accounts, and they also brought back texts on history, religion, geography, science, and literature to Europe for further study. The sixteenth and seventeenth centuries see the first chairs in Arabic, Persian, and Hebrew established at European universities along with the publications of fundamental grammars in "Oriental" languages, such as Guillaume Postel's *Grammatica Arabica* (Paris, 1538) and Lodewijk de Dieu's *Rudimenta Linguae Persicae* (Leyden, 1639). Spurred initially by an interest in early Christianity and classical antiquity and then by the Ottoman threat to Christendom, European scholars sought to learn about the customs and rituals in these far-off lands. To varying degrees, early modern European travellers to Safavid Iran were sensitive to the concept of religious difference, and several sought to give detailed information about Shi'ism in their accounts for their readers. Whether Protestant or Catholic, they had an innate sense of superiority vis-à-vis Islam. Nonetheless, whether out of duty, or out of scholarly interest, they sought to shed light on the strange rituals they observed and provide explanations about the various activities that were to be found at commemorative festivals such as 'Ashura. Publishers were also interested in promoting the topic of religion when it came to selling books and would also highlight the fact that their accounts included new information about Shi'ite rites and rituals. Title pages or visual elements of books—such as frontispieces or engravings accompanying the narrative—would often include familiar tropes designed to elicit the attention of a potential consumer ... such as a dervish mutilating himself, or a turbaned Ottoman soldier standing with upraised sword in front of a mosque, ready to threaten Christian Europe. One can also think of works such as *Catharina von Georgien* (1657) by

---

80 Babak Rahimi provides an analysis of this same engraving in *Theater State*, 1–6, and makes a reference to the idea of the Orientalist stage of Edward Said.

the German dramatist Andreas Gryphius that describe the tribulations of the Georgian queen who preferred to die as a Christian martyr rather than marry Shah 'Abbas I.

Publishers would hire artists in order to enhance the selling potential of a work: "Travel accounts that contained little or no illustration in their first edition were often reprinted with sumptuous frontispieces, engravings, and maps in the next edition."[81] This was the case for the Dutch and German publishers of Della Valle's travel account, as well as for the French edition of Thévenot's narrative that have been considered here. The Swiss artist/engraver of the German edition, and the Dutch artist/engraver of the French edition point to the international character of the publishing trade—but they also help substantiate the claim that many representations of Safavid Iran were created by artists who had never travelled to the country themselves. The engravings in Olearius's account may be considered the most "authentic," since they were produced by an engraver working under the traveller's supervision, presumably using sketches drawn in situ, and during the voyager's lifetime in contrast with the engravings in the Della Valle and Thévenot editions, that were produced decades after the travellers had died. In short, the visual representations of Safavid Iran in travel accounts must be examined individually and carefully, in order to determine to what degree they are constructed from an artist's imagination and/or from previous images, and how much they represent the "reality" of what they are supposed to depict.

---

81 Brancaforte and Brentjes, *From Rhubarb to Rubies*, 6.

Chapter 7

VISIONS AND TRANSITIONS OF A PILGRIMAGE OF CURIOSITY: PIETRO DELLA VALLE'S TRAVEL TO ISTANBUL (1614–1615)

SEZIM SEZER DARNAULT

AYGÜL AĞIR

ABSTRACT

This chapter examines Pietro Della Valle's travel narratives related to his visit to Istanbul (1614–1615) during his voyage to the Ottoman Empire, Persia, and India. It focuses on the Ottoman capital; its architecture, including mosques, mausoleums, palaces, and kiosks related to the sultans and dignitaries that Della Valle covered extensively in his travel accounts; as well as other "curiosities." Della Valle's self-fashioning through his pilgrimage of curiosity reveals the identity and the milieu of this Roman nobleman who styled himself as *il pellegrino* (the pilgrim). His travel to Turkey in the early seventeenth century coincided with the reign of Sultan Ahmed I, a time when Europe and the Ottoman Empire were redefining their relationship. Published in the 1650's, Della Valle's *Viaggi*, describing his travels, was widely disseminated throughout Europe. The essay analyzes how Della Valle connected the European/Italian and Ottoman worlds through myriad boundary crossings as a cultural mediator, translator, and transmitter during a time of transition from the Renaissance to the Baroque age. The chapter's conclusion suggests that Della Valle's travel accounts not only communicated the Ottoman World to European audiences of his time but also played a significant role in shaping European perception of the Ottoman Empire in the eighteenth century, before the introduction of Orientalism.

Keywords: Pietro Della Valle, travel, curiosity, Istanbul, cultural transitions

In memory of Semra Germaner (1944–2015)

DURING HIS TRAVELS extending from the Ottoman Empire to Persia and India, aristocrat and traveller Pietro Della Valle (1586–1652) spent more than a year, from

August 15, 1614 to September 25, 1615, in Istanbul.[1] Della Valle's detailed letters recounting his travels began to be published during the second half of the seventeenth century and were disseminated in Europe rapidly. Della Valle's *Viaggi*,[2] relating his travels in the Ottoman Empire, Persia, and India was printed in Italian in Rome in 1650–1663 with the note *"con licenza de' Superiori"* (permitted to be published). This book was later translated to French (1661–1663), Dutch (1664–1665), and German (1674). *Viaggi*'s sections covering Della Valle's travels to India and accounts related to his return to Italy were translated to English (1664). In later years, *Viaggi*, which had been widely circulated through Europe, became a source of inspiration to travellers as well as one of the best-known and most influential literary works of the seventeenth century.[3] Goethe indicated that Della Valle was one of the writers who introduced him to the East and was a primary source in the structuring of his work *West-östlische Divan*.[4]

Unlike his predecessors, Della Valle was neither a missionary nor a tradesman; as he pointed out, he was a pilgrim and his journey was "decidedly a pilgrimage of curiosity."[5] His observations as a self-fashioned nobleman are enlightening about his identity and taste. His travels in Turkey coincide with the period of Ahmed I (r. 1603–1617), a time when Europe and the Ottoman Empire were redefining their relationship. Della Valle's *La Turchia*, the first volume of his travel accounts, emerged in 1650. Although considerable research has been devoted to Della Valle and his travels, rather less attention has been paid to his visit to Istanbul. This essay investigates Della Valle's perceptions

---

Acknowledgements

This work sprang from the National Endowment for the Humanities (NEH) Summer Seminar "Re-mapping the Renaissance: Exchange between Early Modern Islam and Europe," which was held at the University of Maryland, College Park from June 13 to July 2, 2010. As a participant, the first author acknowledges with gratitude the grant of the National Endowment for the Humanities and the directors of the seminar Adele Seff and Judith E. Tucker for providing the opportunity to be a part of this enlightening workshop. We would like to thank our editor, Montserrat Piera, for her hard work, dedication, and continued support as she put this volume together. Particularly, we are indebted to Professor Semra Germaner (1944–2015) from Mimar Sinan Fine Arts University in Istanbul, Turkey for introducing Pietro Della Valle to us; this essay is dedicated to her memory.

I Ettore Rossi, "Pietro Della Valle Orientalista Romano (1586–1652)," *Oriente Moderno* 33 (1953), 51.

2 Pietro Della Valle, *Viaggi di Pietro della Valle il Pellegrino, descritti da lui medesimo in lettere familiari all'erudito su amico Mario Schipano. Divisi in tre parti cioè: La Turchia, La Persia e l'India colla vita e ritratto dell'autore* (Brighton: G. Gancia, 1843); For the first edition of the book see Pietro Della Valle, *Viaggi di Pietro della Valle il pellegrino: con minuto ragguaglio di tutte le cose notabili osseruate in essi: discritti da lui medesimo in 54. lettere familiari ...; mandate in Napoli all'erudito ... Mario Schipano: diuisi in tre parti, cioè la Turchia, la Persia, e l'India ...* (Rome: Appresso Vitale Mascarde, 1650–1663).

3 Donald F. Lach and Edwin J. Van Kley, *A Century of Advance: Trade, Missions, Literature* (Chicago: University of Chicago Press, 1993), 380.

4 Johann Wolfgang von Goethe, *Notes and Essays for a Better Understanding of the West-East Divan*, trans. Martin Bidney and Peter Anton von Arnim (New York: State University of New York Press, 2010).

5 Joan-Pau Rubiés, "Della Valle, Pietro (1586–1652)" in *Literature of Travel and Exploration: An Encyclopedia. vol. 1, A to F*, ed. Jennifer Speake (New York: Fitzroy Dearborn, 2003), 326.

and interpretations of Istanbul's visual culture "between two worlds"—European and Ottoman—in the early modern period. We focus on his view of the Ottoman capital, its architecture, including mosques, mausoleums, palaces and kiosks related to the sultans and dignitaries that Della Valle covered extensively in his travel accounts, as well as other "curiosities." In so doing, we aim to reveal how he connected the European/ Italian and Ottoman worlds through myriad boundary crossings as a cultural mediator, translator, and transmitter during a time of transition from the Renaissance to the Baroque age.[6]

A Self-Fashioned Man: Pietro Della Valle's Life and Travels

Pietro Della Valle was born in Rome on April 11, 1586.[7] There were two cardinals from the Della Valle family, one of the noble families of Rome, during the terms of Pope Honorius II and Pope Leo X. The family gave its name to a street in Rome and a church (Sant' Andrea Della Valle) built in the 1590s. Della Valle, who received a Catholic education, was interested in music and literature and was thoroughly acquainted with the history and culture of the antique world. He was also a member of the *Accademia degli Umoristi*, one of the leading culture academies of Rome and Naples.[8] Della Valle might have encountered Oriental manuscripts in Naples.[9]

The expedition to Barbary that Della Valle undertook with the Spanish fleet in 1611 aroused his interest in the East. In pursuit of this interest, Della Valle decided on a pilgrimage to the Holy Land. The suggestion of his close friend Mario Schipano,[10] an academician from Naples, to make this trip influenced his decision. Della Valle and Schipano agreed to correspond and exchange information during his travels. Della

---

6 See Brinda Charry and Gitanjali Shahani, eds., *Emissaries in Early Modern Literature and Culture: Mediation, Transmission, Traffic, 1550–1700* (Burlington: Ashgate, 2009).

7 For Della Valle's life and travels see Giovanni Pietro Bellori, *Vita di Pietro della Valle il Pellegrino* (Rome, 1662); Ignazio Ciampi, *Della vita e Delle Opere di Pietro della Valle il Pellegrino: Monografia Illustrata con Nuovi Documenti* (Rome: Barbèra, 1880); Luigi Bianconi, *Viaggio in Levante di Pietro della Valle* (Florence: Sansoni, 1942); Chiara Cardini, *La Porta d'Oriente: Lettere di Pietro della Valle: Istanbul 1614* (Rome: Città Nuova, 2001); George Bull, *The Pilgrim. The Travels of Pietro della Valle* (London: Hutchinson, 1989); J. D. Gurney, "Pietro della Valle: The Limits of Perception," *Bulletin of the School of Oriental and African Studies, University of London* 49 (1986): 103–16; Severina Parodi, *Cose e Parole nei Viaggi di Pietro Della Valle* (Florence: Presso L'Accademia Della Crusca, 1987); J. H. Whitfield, *Pietro Della Valle* (Birmingham, 1992); Ettore Rossi, "Pietro Della Valle Orientalista Romano," 49–64.

8 Michele Maylander, *Storia delle Accademie d'Italia*, vol. 5 (Bologna: Cappelli, 1930), 369–81.

9 See *La Conoscenza del Mondo Islamico a Napoli (XV-XIX secolo) / The Islamic World Through Neapolitan Eyes (Sixteenth-Nineteenth Centuries)*, ed. Luca Berardi (Naples: Università di Napoli, 2015).

10 Even though he sometimes uses friendly language, the fact that he addresses him as "your highness" (V. S.) shows his deep respect for Schipano, who seems to have directed Della Valle's letters with his questions.

Valle planned to describe the events, customs, people, and places, and Schipano was to organize the letters in a historical narration. Guided by his curiosity and considering the Orient "a valuable subject of learning,"[11] Della Valle's travel was a part of his self-fashioning.[12]

Della Valle's travel started in Venice in 1614 and extended to the Ottoman Empire, Persia, and India. During his trip to the Ottoman Empire between the years 1614 and 1617, Della Valle visited Istanbul, Alexandria, Cairo, the Sinai Peninsula, Gaza, Jerusalem, Damascus, and Baghdad. He met Sitti Maani Gioerida in Baghdad and married her in 1616 after which they continued the journey together. Pietro and Maani proceeded to Persia in 1617 and witnessed the Safavid campaign against the Ottomans in northern Persia. In his letters, Della Valle described Lar, Isfahan, Persepolis, and Shiraz in great detail. Upon his wife's death, on December 30, 1621,[13] during their visit to Persia, Della Valle had her body embalmed using the techniques he had learned in Egypt, and he carried it with him for almost five and a half years until she was buried in his family sepulchre in Rome with a grandiose funeral ceremony on March 27, 1627.[14]

After his travels to Western India in 1623–1624, he set out for Muscat and Basra. On his return trip, he travelled to Alexandria and then set sail for Italy, arriving on February 5, 1626. Della Valle continued his studies and, with his particular interest in music and literature, set up a "cabinet of curiosities" in his palace.[15] He died in 1652 and, like his wife Sitti Maani Gioerida, was buried in the family sepulchre in the Santa Maria in Ara Coeli Church in Rome.

The information and descriptions in the letters Della Valle wrote during his twelve years of travel to the Ottoman, Safavid, and Mongol Empires are one of the major sources regarding the early seventeenth century characteristics of the places that he visited. Della Valle's pilgrimage, as Rubiés writes, "was a quest for a positive and universal human quality behind cultural and religious differences."[16] As a "cosmopolitan humanist traveler"[17] and on-scene witness, Della Valle's travel accounts narrating Istanbul reflect multifold transitions across both time and geography.

---

11 Michael Harrigan, *Veiled Encounters: Representing the Orient in 17th-century French Travel Literature* (Amsterdam: Rodopi, 2008), 11.

12 Robert John Weston Evans and Alexander Marr, *Curiosity and Wonder from the Renaissance to the Enlightenment* (Burlington: Ashgate, 2006).

13 Rossi, "Pietro Della Valle Orientalista Romano," 52.

14 See the memorandum book which contains poems in Arabic, Armenian, French, Greek, Italian, Latin, Persian, Spanish, and Turkish: *Funerale della Signora Sitti Maani Gioerida della Valle celebrato in Roma l'Anno 1627 descritto dal Signor Girolamo Rocchi* (Rome, 1627).

15 Joseph Connors, "Borromini, Hagia Sopha and S. Vitale," in *Architectural Studies in memory of Richard Krautheimer*, ed. Cecil Striker (Mainz: Von Zabern, 1996), 44–45.

16 Joan-Pau Rubiés, *Travel and Ethnology in the Renaissance: South India through European Eyes, 1250–1625* (Cambridge: Cambridge University Press, 2002), 366.

17 Rubiés, *Travel and Ethnology in the Renaissance*, 397.

The Road to Istanbul: Troy and the Shared Tradition of Pilgrimage

After going from Naples to Rome, Pietro Della Valle went to Venice on June 8, 1614 to set out from Malamocco on an old galleon named *Gran Delfino*. Once the ship left the Italian peninsula behind, Della Valle begins to quote from Virgil's *Aeneid*. Thus, in a sense, he makes Virgil's work his guide on this journey and he refers to the lines "*Unde iter Italiam cursusque brevissimus undis*" (and the shortest course by sea to Italy) from the *Aeneid* for the Ceraunian Mountains (Albania) that are the travellers' first station.[18] Della Valle calls the East "*Aurora*," following Virgil.[19] This location, also referred to as the Otranto Strait, is the shortest passage to the east. The reference reminds the reader of the Ottoman campaign to Otranto in 1480–1481, known in Europe as the Ottoman invasion of Italy.[20] Correspondingly, when describing Europe's interest in the Turcs, Yérasimos identifies the first period as starting with the conquest of Constantinople and extending to the death of Mehmed II, with some highlights such as the conquest of Negroponte and the capture of Otranto. He identifies the second period as "beginning in the reign of Süleyman the Magnificient and ending with the Ottoman–Venice Treaty (1573) following the Battle of Lepanto."[21] By citing geography on his road to Istanbul, Della Valle is also referring to history, as can also be seen in the following lines.

As the voyage proceeded, the ship passed close to the ruins of antique Buthrotum, present-day Epirus south of Albania. After staying four days in Corfu, Della Valle headed for Zakynthos Island. He states that on the way he saw the Echinades islands where a sea battle took place earlier, most probably referring to the Battle of Actium or/and the Battle of Lepanto in 1571. At his next stop, after Zakynthos and on the way to Chios, he notes "Negropont" that witnessed the Ottoman–Venetian battle of 1463–1479. Following his stay in Chios, Della Valle proceeded to Tenedos on August 3, 1614. He went by boat from Tenedos to Troy, a venue he had read a lot about, with his servants, Tommaso and Lorenzo, and a priest named Andrea. They were joined by a Franciscan monk from Istanbul. Although Della Valle believed he was seeing the ruins of Antique Troy, he had in fact encountered ruins of the Roman period.[22] After viewing the ruins and flora of the area, Della Valle and his companions returned to Tenedos, where they spent the night.[23]

Moreover, intending to present the historical geography of his destinations, Della Valle collates quotations from mythology, works of writers of antiquity[24] as well as those of his contemporaries, and his personal experience. For instance, it is obvious that Della Valle employed Filippo Ferrari's *Epitome geographicum: in quattour libros divisus* published

---

18 Virgil, *Aeneid*, III:293.

19 Rossi, "Pietro Della Valle Orientalista Romano," 59.

20 For the Ottoman occupation of Otranto see Norman Housley, *Crusading and the Ottoman Threat, 1453–1505* (Oxford: Oxford University Press, 2012).

21 Stéphane Yérasimos, *Hommes et Idées dans L'Espace Ottoman* (Istanbul: Éditions Isis, 1997), 49.

22 Rossi, "Pietro Della Valle Orientalista Romano," 51.

23 Della Valle, *Viaggi*, 3–5, 9, 16.

24 These included Procopius and Solinus as well.

in 1605; a copy of this book with Della Valle's own notes is preserved at Biblioteca Estense in Modena.[25] Pierre Bélon's *Les observations de plusieurs singularitez et choses mémorables trouvées en Grèce, Asie, Judée, Égypte, Arabie et autres pays estranges*, published in 1553, is also one of the major sources that he consulted.[26] He referred to Bélon for existing information as well as a way of highlighting his own new, and contradictory, information. For instance, in Troy, quoting Virgil as well as the writings of Pierre Bélon, Della Valle indicates the existence of structures that Bélon did not record.[27] He writes of taking a stone from these "precious ruins," ascending to the highest point, and drawing a sketch—to be coloured later—of the area, including Mount Ida. By reporting that the numerous column bases he saw at the seaside in Troy were not smaller than those of the *Rotonda* [Pantheon] in Rome, Della Valle connects the two cities to each other.

Troy holds an important place in his first letter describing his journey to Istanbul. One reason that Della Valle gave such wide coverage to Troy is no doubt the many meanings attributed to the city for centuries, such as the legend of Troy. One of the first of these attributes is the belief that the ancestry of the Romans goes back to Troy. In this context, Della Valle describes Troy with a quote from Virgil: *"et gentis cunabula nostrae"* (the cradle of our races).[28] Another aspect of the importance of Troy is its embodiment of the notions of East/West as well as the concepts of "empire" and "dominion."[29] Ousterhout points out that following the inclusion of Asia Minor in the Roman Empire, Troy came to be considered the "mother city" of Rome and that "pilgrimage" to Troy became an ideological obligation for Roman emperors.[30] Maintaining this antique tradition, after the conquest of Istanbul the Ottoman Sultan Mehmed II visited the city[31] previously visited by the Roman emperors Julius Caesar, Hadrian, and Caracalla.[32] Della Valle, who went to see the city just before his arrival in Istanbul, considered Troy the first important stop of his pilgrimage. Before reaching the Ottoman capital, he once again reminds readers of the key concepts of the Trojan legend. However, Della Valle presents the ancient traits of these settlements in mythology rather than describing their use by the Ottomans. Noting that the Dardanelles divide Europe from Asia, he draws a parallel with

---

25 Salvante, *Il Pellegrino in Oriente*, 290.

26 Pierre Bélon, *Les observations de plusieurs singularitez et choses mémorables trouvées en Grèce, Asie, Judée, Égypte, Arabie et autres pays estranges* (Paris: G. Corrozet, 1553). Pierre Bélon's book is noteworthy about displaying the botanical diversity at the Ottoman Lands to Europe. See also Luigi Zangheri, "Il Giardino Ottomano, L'Italia e la Cultura Europea," in *Incontri di Civilta nel Mediterraneo. L'Impero Ottoman e L'Italia del Rinascimento, Storia, Arte e Architettura*, ed. Alireza Naser Eslami (Florence: Leo S. Olschki Editore, 2014), 91.

27 Della Valle, *Viaggi*, 11–12, 15.

28 Virgil, *Aeneid*, III:105.

29 Robert Ousterhout, "The East, the West, and the Appropriation of the Past in Early Ottoman Architecture" *Gesta* 43 (2004), 165.

30 Ousterhout, "The East, the West, and the Appropriation," 165.

31 Kritovoulos, *Kritovulos Tarihi 1451–1467*, trans. Ani Çokona (Istanbul: Heyamola Yayınları, 2012), 537.

32 Ousterhout, "The East, the West, and the Appropriation," 165.

the Strait of Messina. In his narrative, geographical citations such as Messina, Otranto, and Negroponte tacitly become historical zones of connection. As a "cosmopolitan humanist traveller,"[33] when describing structures and geography, Della Valle generally draws parallels with Italy and accentuates the resemblances rather than the differences between Italy and the Ottoman Empire.

The "On-Scene" Witness: Topography of the Ottoman Capital and Urban Projects

Della Valle departed from Gallipoli on a small boat and reached Istanbul on August 15, 1614. The letters written by Della Valle, who came to Istanbul at the age of twenty-eight, show that he was a very curious, exceptionally attentive person who had a facility for languages and could easily establish contacts with people. Della Valle lived in Pera in a house that was connected to the French embassy where Achille de Harlay de Sancy, a linguist and ambassador interested in the Orient, was in mission (1611–1620).[34] Della Valle usually sent his letters to Naples with a Dominican priest.[35] The ten letters penned from Istanbul give detailed descriptions of locations, people, life, and events of the Ottoman capital. As an on-scene witness, he observed this period in an accurate and detailed manner; thus his letters are of a documentary character.

His letter dated October 25, 1614 is from Istanbul. He must have thought that Schipano, to whom the letter is addressed, wanted him first to describe the works of Antiquity in the city, as he begins his own observations with the comment that, having studied the earlier works on this subject, Petrus Gyllius has provided lots of information and that he (Della Valle) would be unable to say anything more. Gyllius's *De Bosphoro Thracio libri* III and *De topographia Constantinopoleos et de illius Antiquitatibus libri IV* dated 1561, describing Istanbul's antiquities, was one of Della Valle's main sources.[36] In his letters, Della Valle indicates that he aims to follow the path of Gyllius who had visited Istanbul fifty years earlier. In contrast to Gyllius, however, Della Valle was interested in Ottoman Istanbul as well as its antiquities.

Hester, in her study on Baroque travel writing, argues that *Viaggi* presents a "performative (and theatrical) force" that "moves along several interconnected lines."[37] Through his narration, it is often seen that Della Valle acts as a performer and spectator. For instance, Della Valle writes that he has counted more than seven hills in Istanbul

---

33 Rubiés, *Travel and Ethnology in the Renaissance*, 397.

34 For Harlay and Della Valle see Emanuel Constantin Antoche, "Un Ambassadeur Français à la Porte Ottomane: Achille de Harlay, Baron de Sancy et de la Mole (1611–1619)," in *Istoria ca datorie. Omagiu Academicianului Ioan Aurel Pop*, ed. Ioan Bolovan and Ovidiu Ghitta (Cluj-Napoca: Academia Romana, Centrul de Studii Transilvane, 2015), 747–60.

35 Della Valle, *Viaggi*, 91. Della Valle's residence may have been a private unit within the French embassy.

36 Procopius was also one of the Della Valle's sources; Procopio Cesariense, *De Gli Edifici di Giustiniano imperatore*, trans. Benedetto Egio (Venice, 1547); Della Valle, *Viaggi*, 33.

37 Hester, *Literature and Identity*, 59.

and, looking from a distance, has seen dense housing areas as if there were no gardens in the city. He describes Istanbul as "a figure, like from the theater, very agreeable."[38] When he writes that the tiles of the houses and the lead-covered mosques in combination with the cypress trees create an exquisite view, he enables his reader almost to visualize this "extraordinary" panorama. "Looking from the outside," he notes, "there can be no city more beautiful."[39] Thinking that the comparison would please the people of Naples and especially Schipano, Della Valle adds the description "the most beautiful city of the world, just like Naples."[40]

In his description of the scenery in the dense city fabric, he particularly emphasizes Divanyolu—which caught his attention—connecting the Ottoman Palace directly to Europe through Edirne Kapı (Charisius Gate). In other words, Della Valle draws attention to Divanyolu's strategic and, symbolically more important, theatrical functions. According to Hester, *Viaggi* is related to the "Italian culture of spectacle from the theater in Naples [...] to the extravagant Catholic ceremonies, such as holiday processions [...] that were staple in Rome at that time."[41] Della Valle writes that Divanyolu is wider, compared to other streets, and that it is the only straight road in the city, calling it the "long road." In fact, the Ottomans renamed the old Roman road *Mese* as Divanyolu, based on the imperial processions passing through it. The road was also the main connector of the street network between the south and the north of the city.[42]

Referring to it as *"canale"* (canal), Della Valle describes the Bosphorus in detail. His account of the Sultan's resting area on the European bank of the Bosphorus also provides clues about the city's topography at the beginning of the seventeenth century. The place which he depicts as a "small bay" is most likely Dolmabahçe (filled garden), converted into a square (*meydan*) by filling the sea during this period. Dolmabahçe was one of the major large-scale projects during the reign of Ahmed I. The traveller puzzled over how the square was formed. He explains that large anchors were placed in the bay and then topped with soil from nearby hills. The filled space was protected against stormy weather with levees made from large boulders. The square that he refers to as *piazza* was in fact the private gardens of the sultan (*Hasbahçe*). Della Valle recounts that plays were staged here.[43] The narration stresses the theatrical character of this urban space; his portrayals of Sultan Ahmed I watching the plays from his hall, which he calls *balconi* (balcony), provide visions of Dolmabahçe at the beginning of

---

38 Della Valle, *Viaggi*, 21.

39 Della Valle, *Viaggi*, 22.

40 Della Valle, *Viaggi*, 40.

41 Hester, *Literature and Identity*, 58.

42 See Maurice Cerasi, *The Istanbul Divanyolu: A Case Study in Ottoman Urbanity and Architecture*, with the collaboration of Emiliano Bugatti and Sabrina D'Agostino (Würzburg: Ergon Verlag in Kommission, 2004); Albrecht Berger, "Streets and Public Spaces in Constantinople," *Dumbarton Oaks Papers*, 54 (2000): 161–72; Doğan Kuban, *Istanbul, An Urban History: Byzantion, Constantinopolis, Istanbul* (Istanbul: Economic and Social History Foundation of Turkey, 1996), 271 fig. 144.

43 Della Valle, *Viaggi*, 46.

the seventeenth century.[44] *Balconi* might be the observation *loggia*, perhaps the outer sofa of the Sultan's kiosk. His decriptions give valuable information on the architectural characteristics of the earliest sultan kiosk/palace at Dolmabahçe. Other sources of the period correspond with his writings about this area. For instance, the map of Istanbul of Seyyid Nuh designed during the seventeenth century verifies the description of Della Valle (Figures 7.1–7.2).[45]

Williams notes that "Renaissance pilgrims rarely write in the first person singular, about things which they have done on their own."[46] Thus, Della Valle's underlining of his eyewitnessing singles him out from Renaissance travellers. Although Rubiés notes that "it would be exaggerating to suggest that Valle's style was directly inspired by Caravaggio's naturalism," Della Valle must certainly have been familiar with discussions of Caravaggio's work.[47] Both Caravaggio and Della Valle lived at Rome (as well as Naples) in the early 1600s and their biographies were written by their contemporary Giovanni Pietro Bellori (1613–1696). In his paintings,[48] Caravaggio places himself as an on-scene witness as Della Valle likewise communicates his own experience to the viewer. Through his narrative, Della Valle performs both as spectator and on-scene actor.[49] Witnessing the construction of the Sultan Ahmed Mosque while he was in Istanbul, he writes "this new [one] that today's Sultan is building, that I re-saw this morning."[50] Built in the Hippodrome area in 1609–1617, Sultan Ahmed Mosque was the focal point of numerous disputes. The major concern was there not being enough of a congregation in this area that was surrounded by palaces and close to Hagia Sophia (Figure 7.3).[51] Moreover, some

---

44 "é venuto capriccio al Gran Signore di riempir tutto quel seno del mare"; Della Valle, *Viaggi*, 46.

45 See Fig. 7.1, Aygül Ağır, "Seyyid Nuh's Map of Venice (seventeenth century)," *Portolana. Studia Mediterranea*, no. 3 (2007): 315–25; see also Eremya Çelebi Kömürcüyan, *İstanbul Tarihi: XVII. Asırda İstanbul*, ed. Hrand D. Andreasyan and Kevork Pamukciyan (Istanbul: Eren, 1988), 252.

46 Wes Williams, " 'A Mirrour of Mis-haps, a Mappe of Miserie': Dangers, Strangers, and Friends in Renaissance Pilgrimage," in *The "Book" of Travels: Genre, Ethnology, and Pilgrimage, 1250–1700*, ed. Palmira Johnson Brummett (Leiden: Brill, 2009), 216.

47 Rubiés, *Travel and Ethnology in the Renaissance*, 387 and n81.

48 Such as *Martyrdom of St Matthew* (1599) and *The Raising of Lazarus* (ca. 1609)

49 For Della Valle as actor, see Hester, *Literature and Identity*, 61. For performing travel see Sabine Ashulting, Lucia Muller, and Ralf Hertel, eds. *Early Modern Encounters with the Islamic East: Performing Cultures*, Transculturalisms, 1400–1700 series (Farnham: Ashgate, 2012).

50 'Questa nuova che si fabbrica del Grand Signore d'oggi alla quale pur questa mattina, ho dato una rivista,' Della Valle, *Viaggi*, 149; for Sultan Ahmed Mosque see Zeynep Nayır, *Osmanlı Mimarlığında Sultan Ahmet Külliyesi ve Sonrası (1609–1690)* ([Istanbul]: İTÜ Mimarlık Fakültesi Baskı Atölyesi, 1975); See also Halil İbrahim Düzenli, "Mimar Mehmed Ağa ve Dünyasi: Risâle-i Mi'mâriyye Üzerinden 16. ve 17. Yüzyıl Osmanlı Zihniyet Osmanlı Zihniyet Kalıplarını ve Mimarlığını Anlamlandırma Denemesi / Mehmed Agha the Architect and his World: A Study on 16th–17th Centuries Ottoman Mental Structures and Architecture in the Context of Risale-i Mi'Mariyye" (PhD dissertation, Karadeniz Technical University, 2008).

51 Gülru Necipoğlu, *The Age of Sinan. Architectural Culture in the Ottoman Empire* (Princeton: Princeton University Press, 2005), 514–15.

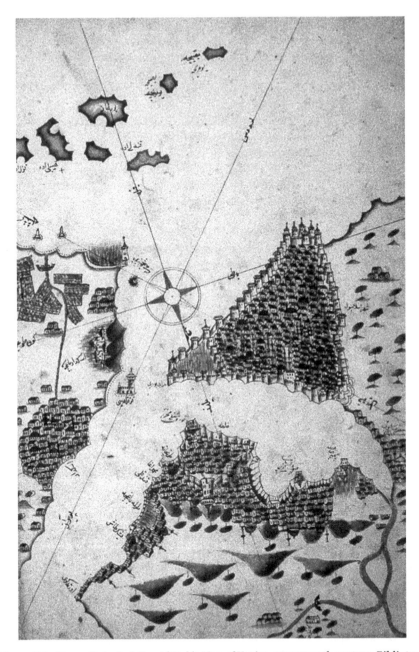

Figure 7.1. View of Istanbul, Seyyid Nuh's Map of Venice, seventeenth century. Biblioteca Universitaria di Bologna, MS 3609, c. 10v (© Alma Mater Studiorum Università di Bologna-Biblioteca Universitaria di Bologna, reproduction or duplication is not allowed).

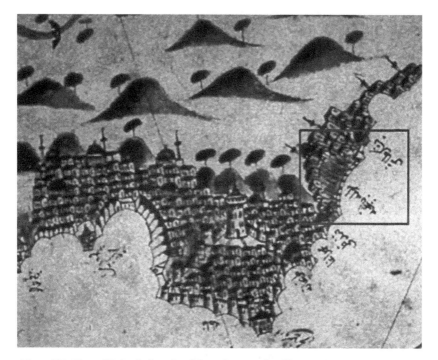

Figure 7.2. View of Dolmabahçe, detail from the Seyyid Nuh's Map of Venice, seventeenth century. Biblioteca Universitaria di Bologna, MS 3609, c. 10v (© *Alma Mater Studiorum Università di Bologna-Biblioteca Universitaria di Bologna*, reproduction or duplication is not allowed).

Byzantine remains and two palaces by Architect Sinan were demolished to obtain the necessary space for the building.[52] Another criticism was that, unlike other imperial mosques, the expenditure made for the Sultan Ahmet Mosque was not met by war spoils. According to the prominent Ottoman intellectual, Gelibolulu Mustafa Âli, this situation was described as sultans' spending the means of the treasury for "superfluous" construction projects.[53] The Venetian *bailo* (ambassador) Contarini also notes that a great amount of money was spent for the "*superbissima*" mosque.[54] Correspondingly, stating that the commissioner of the Sultan Ahmed Mosque is "not intelligent," Della Valle claims that those who conduct the construction are robbing (*gli rubino*) the sultan, the workers are ignorant, and more than is necessary is being spent on machinery and equipment.[55] Della Valle's detailed descriptions about the construction process of the buildings displays his particular interest in and knowledge about the architecture. According

---

52 Orhan Ş. Gökyay, "Risale-i Mimariyye. -Mimar Mehmet Ağa- Eserleri," in *İsmail Hakkı Uzunçarşılı'ya Armağan* (Ankara: Türk Tarih Kurumu, 1976), 158–63.

53 Necipoğlu, *The Age of Sinan*, 514–15.

54 Necipoğlu, *The Age of Sinan*, 514–15.

55 Della Valle, *Viaggi*, 149.

Figure 7.3. View of the Sultan Ahmed Mosque and Hagia Sophia facing each other.
Photo: Şükrü Sönmezer.

to the traveller, the most significant feature of this mosque is the fact that it faces the Hippodrome.[56] He also remarks that although the construction is proceeding slowly, when completed it will be beautiful with its white marble workmanship.[57] As witnessed by Della Valle, Necipoğlu states that "the decision to confront the ancient monument with a stunning mosque in the 'modern' Ottoman style involved a grand urban gesture, the remodelling of the Hippodrome."[58]

No doubt the Topkapı Palace, which only the fortunate were allowed to enter, was of particular interest to travellers and foreign delegations. Della Valle probably also shows special interest in the Topkapı Palace because he thinks Schipano would be very interested (Figures 7.4–7.5). He begins by observing the palace through the window of his house, which belongs to the French embassy. From his window he can "see" the grounds of the palace with its large gardens and the uninterrupted wall with towers that surrounds it.[59] Della Valle finds the stables and the imperial kitchens within the local

---

56 Della Valle, *Viaggi*, 149.

57 Della Valle, *Viaggi*, 149; for further discussion on the construction of the Sultan Ahmed Mosque see *Risale-i Mimariyye: An Early Seventeenth-century Ottoman Treatise on Architecture. Facsimile with Translation and Notes*, ed. Howard Crane (Leiden: Brill, 1987), 64–69.

58 Necipoğlu, *The Age of Sinan*, 517.

59 Della Valle, *Viaggi*, 36.

Figure 7.4. View of the Topkapı Palace. Photo: Ahmet Hamdi Bülbül.

palaces better located than those in palaces in Italy. The reason that he writes first about the stables and the kitchens must be their visibility from the outside. The panorama of Istanbul made by the earlier visitor/painter Melchior Loricks can also give an idea of how Della Valle perceived the Topkapı Palace.[60]

Having observed the Palace with great curiosity, he describes it in detail like a drawing. This "narration of eye witnessing" has been identified as "on the spot por-traiture."[61] His accounts also contain insights about the protocol of the Topkapı Palace.[62] During Della Valle's stay in Istanbul, the Venetian *bailo* was Cristoforo Valier (1612–1615).[63] Della Valle was highly impressed by the audience of Valier and his

---

60 See "Constantinople Prospect" (folded plate in portfolio) in Erik Fischer, *Melchior Lorck* (Copenhagen: Royal Library, Vandkunsten, 2009).

61 Palmira Brummett, "Introduction: Genre, Witness, And Time In The 'Book' of Travels," in *The 'Book' of Travels: Genre, Ethnology, and Pilgrimage, 1250–1700*, ed. Palmira Johnson Brummett (Leiden: Brill, 2009), 34; Muzaffar Alam and Sanjay Subrahmanyam, *Indo-Persian Travels in the Age of Discoveries, 1400–1800* (Cambridge: Cambridge University Press, 2007), 43.

62 See Gülru Necipoğlu, *Architecture, Ceremonial, and Power: The Topkapı Palace in the Fifteenth and Sixteenth Centuries* (Cambridge, MA: MIT Press, 1991).

63 Cristoforo Valier (1565–1618) died on his return to Venice. See Eric Dursteler, "The Bailo in Constantinople: Crisis and Career in Venice's Early Modern Diplomatic Corps," *Mediterranean Historical Review* 16, (2001): 17, 30; see also Serap Mumcu, "Venedik Baylosu'nun Defterleri / The Venetian Baylo's Registers (1589–1684)," *Hilâl. Studi Turchi e Ottomani* 4 (2014), 116–17; Maria Pia Pedani Fabris, *Elenco Degli Inviati Diplomatici Veneziani Presso i Sovrani Ottomani* (Venice: n.p., 2002), 32–33. It is also obvious that Della Valle was familiar with the Venetian *bailo*'s reports, since he mentions Ottaviano Bon (1604–07), Venetian representative in Istanbul.

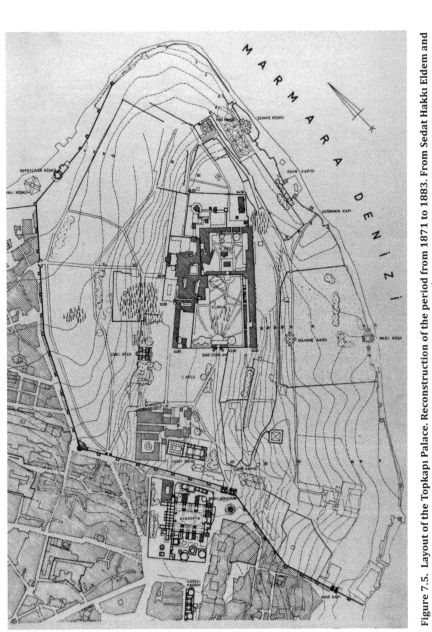

Figure 7.5. Layout of the Topkapı Palace. Reconstruction of the period from 1871 to 1883. From Sedat Hakkı Eldem and Feridun Akozan, Topkapı Sarayı. Bir Mimari Araştırma (İstanbul: Millî Eğitim Basımevi, 1982).

Figure 7.6. The Topkapı Palace, First Gate (Bâb-ı Hümâyûn). Photo: Ahmet Hamdi Bülbül.

retinue. The procession began by passing the First Gate of the Palace (*Bâb-ı Hümayûn*) (Fig 7.6); Della Valle compares the first court of the palace with the market place of Naples (*la piazza del mercato*) to allow his audience to visualize its size. The crowd extended to the portico that was perceived as an *anticamera* (*revak*) by the traveller. He describes the procession in great detail in order to visualize it for Schipano. The traveller notes that he read Sansovino's *Dell'historia universale dell'origine et imperio de'Turchi* which is considered one of the earliest volumes to arouse the interest of Europeans in Turks.[64]

Della Valle also witnessed the Sultan's observing, from Alay Kiosk (Procession Kiosk) located on the outer wall of the palace, the Ottoman army setting out for the Safavid campaign.[65] Della Valle then follows the passage of the Ottoman troops to the Asian side where they would be stationed. He finds the arrangement of the Ottoman tents similar to the organization of the Sultan's palace. The well-ornamented tents of the grand vizier

---

64 Francesco Sansovino, *Historia Vniversale dell'origine et imperio de'Turchi. Raccolta, & in diverfi luoghi di nuovo ampliata, da M. Francefco Sanfovino; Nella quale fi contengono le leggi, gli offici, i coftumi, & la militia di quella natione; con tutte le cofe fatte da loro per terra, & per mare. Con le vite particolari de Principi Othomani; cominciando dal primo fondator di quell'Imperio, fino al prefente Amorath. 1582. Con le figvre in disegno de gli habiti, & dell'armature de foldati d'effo gran Turco* (Vinegia, 1582).

65 Della Valle, *Viaggi*, 133.

Öküz ("the Ox") Kara Mehmed Pasha (1614–1616)[66] have been organized like the rooms of an Ottoman palace and, by using *çuha* fabrics, some types of court were formed at the centre of the groups of tents.[67] In a similar way, this detailed textual description of groups of tents can often be seen in the illustrations of Torquato Tasso's (1544–1595) *Gerusalemme Liberata* published in 1590. One can say that Della Valle incorporated Tasso's visual information into his text. As Hester also points out, Della Valle's account "incorporates elements of Italian literary texts and genres most notably Petrachian lyrical poetics, the epic (especially those of Aristo and Tasso)."[68]

Della Valle provides valuable information about the *konaks* (palatial mansions) of the viziers. During his stay at Istanbul he witnessed the execution of the grand vizier Nasuh Pasha (1611–1614). While writing about the grand vizier, Della Valle gives clues about his palace. His mansion at the seashore had a stable with many magnificent horses.[69] Nasuh Pasha's palace, with its stables that could accomodate several horses, probably occupied a large area in the city.[70] While accompanying the Venetian *bailo* (Valier), he also had the chance to visit the *konak* of the new grand vizier Öküz ("the Ox") Mehmed Pasha. Della Valle reports that, like the Topkapı Palace, the building serves as the residence as well as the office for the viziers. By comparing the architectural organization of Mehmed Pasha's *konak* with that of Topkapı Palace, he in a way investigates the palatial typology. His information that, like Topkapı Palace, the *konak* has a *appartamenti delle donne* (space for women) and there is a gatekeeper at each gate reveals additional significant clues about the typology.[71] He describes the *konak* in great detail, noting its several gates and interconnected courts. The stairs located in the last court lead to the rectangular private audience hall where the Pasha receives his official visitors.[72] By reporting that he was struck by the length of the timber used in this room, supplied from the Black Sea region, Della Valle provides significant architectural details of the period's building techniques and materials. The open hall that he mentions might be the *sofà* of the *konak*. He reports that a series of *sofàs* surround the three sides of the room. His descriptions give important information about the interiors of the vizier *konaks* which

---

66 Mustafa Naima, *Târih-i Na'îmâ: (Ravzatü'l-Hüseyn fî hulâsati ahbâri'l-hâfikayn)*, ed. Mehmet İpşirli (Ankara: Türk Tarih Kurumu, 2007), 2:416–17.

67 Della Valle, *Viaggi*, 123.

68 Hester, *Literature and Identity*, 52.

69 Della Valle, *Viaggi*, 52; Horses were particularly important in the Ottoman Empire. It was not permitted to export Arabian horses except as gifts. For instance, the sultan had given to the Venetial *bailo* Cristioforo Valier a horse along with some precious textiles, which shows that the Venetian *bailo* had established a good relationship with the Sultan. See Maria Pia Pedani Fabris, *Venezia Porta d'Oriente* (Bologna: Il Mulino, 2013), 107.

70 Della Valle, *Viaggi*, 53. For further discussion on waterfront palaces see Tülay Artan, "The Kadırga Palace: An Architectural Reconstruction" *Muqarnas*, 10, Essays in Honor of Oleg Grabar (1993): 201–11.

71 Della Valle, *Viaggi*, 63–65.

72 See Necipoğlu, *The Age of Sinan*, 40–41, especially see illus. 13 for the comparison with the Sokollu Mehmed Pasha's Palace (ca. 1570s).

did not survive: "sitting on the *sofàs* covered with carpets and the walls of the room are covered with *maioliche* (tiles) mainly in blue." As commonly seen in large *konaks*, the building does not face the street; the walls surrounding its gardens open to the street by some windows. This account of the *konak* conveys to readers that high garden walls are a main characteristic of Ottoman residential architecture.

Della Valle writes that large gardens or orchards are set in Üsküdar and along the villages of the Bosphorus, with spacious residences, owned by Ottoman dignitaries, lining the seashore.[73] These mansions with seascapes possesed landscapes composed of alleys, pools, fountains, cypress trees, and diverse flowers.[74] He describes the Ottoman garden kiosks, employing the word *"pyramid"* when explaining their form.[75] He is interested in the garden kiosks because of their distinctive character as open to the landscape, having shutters but no doors or windows, and interiors furnished by *sofàs*. His depiction of the houses, facing the Bosphorus and having gardens in their backyard, are reminiscent of the Ottoman waterfront palaces and kiosks that would be built widely starting the eighteenth century.[76] Moreover, the theatrical character of the waterfront residences (*yalıs*) must have been well perceived by Della Valle.[77]

The Go-Between: Translating Ottoman Architecture

In his second letter, dated October 15, 1614, Della Valle describes Hagia Sophia and the mosques of Istanbul in great detail. Speaking of the flawless beauty of mosques, the traveller explains that four or five mosques commissioned by various sultans are of great interest.[78] This treatment indicates that Della Valle perceived accurately the representational role and visibility of sultanic mosques within the city. In this part of the account, the comparison between the Istanbul mosques and San Pietro in Rome is noteworthy. Della Valle employs the term *tempio* (temple) instead of *moschea/moscheta* (mosque).[79] Equally important, saying that mosques are in the form of *tempio*, Della Valle refers to architecture of antiquity and uses the words *quadro e tondeggi* (quadrangular and round) to indicate to

---

73 Della Valle, *Viaggi*, 22–27; see also Gönül Aslanoğlu Evyapan, *Old Turkish Gardens. Old Istanbul Gardens in Particular* (Ankara: METU, 1999).

74 Della Valle, *Viaggi*, 30; See Maurice Cerasi, "Open Space, Water and Trees in Ottoman Urban Culture in the XVIIIth–XIXth Centuries," *AARP Environmental Design* 2 (1985): 36–49.

75 For Ottoman garden kiosks see Sedat Hakkı Eldem, *Türk Bahçeleri* (İstanbul: Kültür Bakanlığı, 1976), 291; Nurhan Atasoy, *Hasbahçe. A Garden for the Sultan: Gardens and Flowers in the Ottoman Culture* (İstanbul: Aygaz, 2002), 28.

76 Della Valle, *Viaggi*, 22, 29; See Shirine Hamadeh, *The City's Pleasures: Istanbul in the Eighteenth Century* (Seattle: University of Washington Press, 2007).

77 See Tülay Artan, "Architecture as a Theatre of Life: Profile of the Eighteenth Century Bosphorus" (PhD dissertation, Massachusetts Institute of Technology, 1989).

78 Della Valle, *Viaggi*, 23. The mosques in question are the Fatih, Eyüp, Bayezid, Şehzade and Süleymaniye sultanic mosques.

79 Sansovino also employs the word *templum/tempio* for the 'mosque'. Sansovino, *Historia Vniiversale*, 45.

their design.[80] This usage obviously recalls the quadrature of the circle, one of the fundamental geometrical issues of antiquity as well as Renaissance architects. Klaiber states that "libraries such as Sant'Andrea della Valle [...] possessed several of the standard architectural books in various editions, including those of Palladio, Serlio, Vitrivius (including Barbaro's edition), Alberti and Labacco."[81] Della Valle may have been familiar with the works of the Renaissance architect and theoretician Sebastiano Serlio (1475–1554) and may have consulted *Il terzo libro* (...) *nel qual si figurano, e descrivono le antiquita di Roma, e le altre che sono in Italia, e fuori d'Italia* during his journeys.[82] Serlio's seven books on architecture had been compiled in one extended volume, with the addition of an index by Gian Domenico Scamozzi and his son Vincenzo Scamozzi; the volume was published in 1584.

Della Valle also must have also read the works of Vincenzo Scamozzi, who was one of the influential architects and theoreticians of Italy in the early seventeenth century. In his *L'Idea dell'Architettura Universale* (*The Idea of Universal Architecture*) published in 1615, Vincenzo emphasized the universality of antique architecture and its application to contemporary designs. In this context, Della Valle draws attention to the similarity between the Istanbul mosques and Michelangelo's San Pietro design with its domed central plan scheme, and he presents the concepts of antiquity and universal architecture. A compelling example of the influence of the San Pietro in Rome on Della Valle is his project to design a "New Rome" in 1619 for the Christian community of Isfahan. In this new city, the church and the piazza that he proposed to build would employ San Pietro and Michelangelo's Piazza del Campidoglio, in small scale, as exact models.[83]

The Renaissance period revived antiquity both in the Ottoman Empire and Europe, and Hagia Sophia became one of the prototypes for new buildings. Della Valle remarks that, similarly, Turks employed Hagia Sophia, which they encountered when they came to Istanbul, as a model for their mosques.[84] In addition to comparing the major buildings of the Ottoman Empire and Italy during his period in the former, Della Valle also includes influential structures of antiquity. For instance, according to Della Valle, Hagia Sophia is

---

80 Della Valle, *Viaggi*, 23.

81 Susan Klaiber, "Architecture and Mathematics in Early Modern Religious Orders," in *Geometrical Objects: Architecture and the Mathematical Sciences 1400–1800*, ed. Anthony Gerbino (Cham: Springer, 2014), 104.

82 Margaret Daly Davies (ed.) *Pietro della Valle's research and documentation in the Levant, Part I: Della Valle's exploration of the ruins of Persepolis in 1621 excerpts from: Pietro della Valle: Viaggi di Pietro della Valle il Pellegrino. Con minuto ragguaglio di tutte le cose notabili osservate in essi* (Rome, 1650-63), including: "Giovan Pietro Bellori: Vita di Pietro Della Valle il Pellegrino," in *Viaggi di Pietro della Valle il Pellegrino*, 2nd ed., vol. 1 (Rome, 1662) (Fontes 66) (Heidelberg: Universitätsbibliothek der Universität Heidelberg, 2012), http://archiv.ub.uni-heidelberg.de/artdok/volltexte/2012/1868 accessed November 2014.

83 Rossi, "Pietro Della Valle Orientalista Romano," 61.

84 Hubertus Günter, "Doğuda ve Batıda Antikitenin Yeniden Doğuşu," in *Mimar Sinan'ı Anma Etkinlikleri 2010: Sinan ve Çağı* (Kayseri: Mimarlar Odası Kayseri Şubesi, 2011), 221–36; for further information, see Necipoğlu, *The Age of Sinan*, 82–103; Doğan Kuban, *Ottoman Architecture*, trans. Adair Mill (Woodbridge: Antique Collectors' Club, 2010), 458–67.

not as large as old San Pietro (fourth century) and it is its dome rather than its longitudinal basilical plan that is noteworthy.[85]

Viaggi takes the reader on a journey of perception and comparison, crossing boundaries of places, times, and people. Discussing the use of Hagia Sophia in the Ottoman period, Della Valle notes that the Sultan preferred Hagia Sophia for worship due to its proximity to the Topkapı Palace, and he maintained a special entrance to the building as well as a private place where he prayed. He indicates that the Turks valued and appropriated this influential building of antiquity. Della Valle had a clear perception of the close relation between the Ottoman Palace and Hagia Sophia.[86]

When describing the exterior spaces, Della Valle dwells upon the innovation brought to architecture by the Turks. Remarking that the domes were covered with lead, he also points out that niches, ledges, and other similar elements were used to make windows and spans more pleasing to the eye.[87] Repeating that Turks imitated Hagia Sophia in the mosques built in Istanbul both in the past and recently, Della Valle adds that they organize the central dome and other domes according to their taste.[88] Della Valle pointed to large courtyards surrounded by porticos with lead-covered domes built in front of mosques and the *şadırvans* (fountains) in these courtyards as another innovation. Continuing to list other elements that are distinctive to him in the exterior, Della Valle uses the terms *campanile* in the form of *candeliere* to describe the minaret, but he does not fail to point out that there is a crescent rather than a cross at the finial.[89] More importantly, Della Valle thought that if he made drawings of these mosques that looked particularly attractive with all their *ornamenti* and took them to Italy, the architects there would want to imitate these buildings.[90] In this context, Joseph Connors reveals that in his design of Sant' Ivo alla Sapienza (1642) in Rome, Francesco Borromini probably made use of the information provided by Della Valle.[91] Della Valle must have been particularly familiar with Borromini as the dome of his family church, Sant'Andrea Della Valle, was designed by leading Baroque architects Francesco Borromini and Carlo Maderno in the early 1620s.[92] Moreover, the dome of Sant'Andrea Della Valle, as explained by Huemer, is considered "as the first to be remodeled on" Michelangelo's design for San Pietro, a building that Della Valle (re)visits through the *Viaggi*.[93]

---

85 Della Valle, *Viaggi*, 23.

86 See Çiğdem Kafescioğlu, *Constantinopolis/Istanbul: Cultural Encounter, Imperial Vision, and the Construction of the Ottoman Capital* (University Park: Penn State University Press, 2009), 150.

87 Della Valle, *Viaggi*, 25.

88 Della Valle, *Viaggi*, 25.

89 Della Valle, *Viaggi*, 25.

90 Della Valle, *Viaggi*, 26.

91 Connors, "Borromini, Hagia Sophia and S. Vitale," 44–45.

92 Sant'Andrea Della Valle had been mentioned in *Viaggi*; see *Viaggi*, xv; Howard Hibbard, "The Early History of Sant'Andrea Della Valle," *The Art Bulletin* 43 (1961): 289–318.

93 Frances Huemer, "Borromini and Michelangelo, III: The Dome of Sant'Andrea Della Valle," *Notes in the History of Art* 20 (2001): 23–29.

Della Valle, in his letter dated September 4, 1615, aims to investigate the tradition in Istanbul of central plan with dome from its beginning until the "modern" period. He visits Hagia Sophia and the Istanbul mosques one more time before leaving the city. His exposition resumes with the dome of Hagia Sophia and carries on to the construction of the Sultan Ahmed Mosque. It is important to realize that his interpretation encompasses multifold transition zones. As Hester points out, "[h]e moves on different stages along both a horizontal and vertical axis: between east and west and also in descending into tombs or climbing towers, mountains, and pyramids."[94] For instance, he notes that he climbed to the dome of Hagia Sophia which is something he did not do in San Pietro in his native city of Rome. Observing that the building is not like Bélon's description, Della Valle uses the statement, "[o]ur Rotonda [Pantheon] is a hundred times better." According to Della Valle, Hagia Sophia is a *mastina* (massive) building, its dome is noteworthy although not big enough, and the building cannot be compared to the Rotonda (Pantheon). Following his comparison of these two buildings, the traveller visited the mausoleum of Süleyman the Magnificent. The mosque of Sultan Süleyman (Figures 7.6–7.9) built by Architect Sinan is one of the major buildings that obviously lured the traveller by its characteristics. Della Valle wrote that the most beautiful mosque was the *Solimania* mosque of Sultan Süleyman, that mosques were given the name of the person who had them built, and that, if commissioned by a sultan, the particular sultan would also be buried there.[95]

In his accounts of the mausoleums in Istanbul, Della Valle points out that beginning with Mehmed II, mausoleums were built for the sultans who commissioned mosques and were located in the mosque complex rather than within the mosque itself. He remarks that the mausoleums of sultans who did not commission a mosque in Istanbul were located within the site of the Hagia Sophia.[96] The latter mausoleums are those of Selim II (1566–1574), Murad III (1574–1595), and Mehmed III (1595–1603). The traveller informs the reader that some mausoleums had *rotonda* (circular) plan schemes, while others had *quadrata* (quadrangular) plans, almost in *tempietti* (small temples) form.[97] It is interesting to note that Della Valle, referring to the mausoleums, uses the term *tempietto*, which was employed by Renaissance architects, particularly Bramante and Palladio, for their central planned small-sized chapels. He highlights that even the most magnificent of these mausoleums, referring to the mausoleum of Selim II (1576–1577), was not more impressive than the chapel of Pope Sixtus V (r. 1585–1590).[98]

Sultan Selim II had this mosque built in his name in Edirne. However, the mausoleum of Selim II, designed by the well-known sixteenth-century Ottoman architect Sinan, is located within the site of Hagia Sophia (Figure 7.10). Della Valle writes that Selim

---

94 Hester, *Literature and Identity*, 59.

95 Della Valle, *Viaggi*, 26.

96 Della Valle, *Viaggi*, 38.

97 Della Valle, *Viaggi*, 38.

98 Pope Sixtus V's given name was Felice Peretti. See J. N. D. Kelly, "Sixtus V," in *The Oxford Dictionary of Popes* (Oxford: Oxford University Press, 1986), 271–73.

Figure 7.7. Süleymaniye Mosque, seen from the Golden Horn. Photo: Tarkan Okçuoğlu.

II added two minarets to Hagia Sophia along with some extensive work.[99] These two minarets, constructed following Selim II's Ottoman defeat in Lepanto, perhaps symbolize "the triumph of Islam," the (re)conquest of Hagia Sophia, and its Islamization. The mausoleum of Selim II has a dome-covered octagonal plan in a quadrangular form. Its characteristics such as the exedras used to enlarge the central area, a two-layer dome, and marble revetments are similar to those of late Roman period structures.[100] Particularly with its tiles, the richly decorated mausoleum of Selim II resembled "the garden of paradise" as is indicated by its inscription.[101] Della Valle draws attention to the rich decorative program of the interior and conveys to his readers the visual richness created by the multicoloured view displayed by the elegant *maioliche, lavora a lettere* (calligraphy) and other [Ottoman] *arabeschi* decorations and plain white sections on the

---

99 Della Valle, *Viaggi*, 38.

100 Çiğdem Kafesçioglu, "The Visual Arts," in *The Ottman Empire as a World Power 1453–1603*, ed. Suraiya N. Faroqhi and Kate Fleet (New York: Cambridge University Press, 2013), 2:522; Apdullah Kuran, *Sinan: the Grand Old Master of Ottoman Architecture* Washington, DC: Ada Press, 1987), 87–89; Apdullah Kuran, "Mimar Sinan'ın Türbeleri," in *Mimarbaşı Koca Sinan Yaşadığı Çağ ve Eserleri*, ed. Sadi Bayram (İstanbul: İstanbul Vakıflar Genel Müdürlüğü, 1988), 223–38.

101 Hakkı Önkal, *Osmanlı Hanedan Türbeleri* (Ankara: Kültür Bakanlığı, 1992), 164–70.

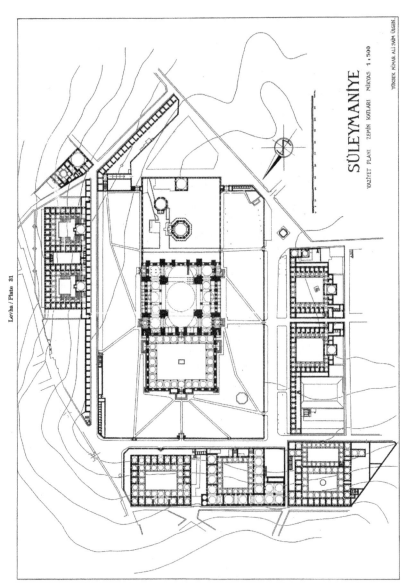

SÜLEYMANİYE

VAZİYET PLANI ZEMİN KATLARI MİKYAS 1 : 500

YÜKSEK MİMAR ALİ SAİM ÜLGEN.

Figure 7.8. Plan of the Süleymaniye complex. From Ali Saim Ülgen, Mimar Sinan Yapıları (Ankara: Türk Tarih Kurumu, 1989).

İST SÜLEYMANİYE CAMİİ RÖLÖVESİ M.1/200

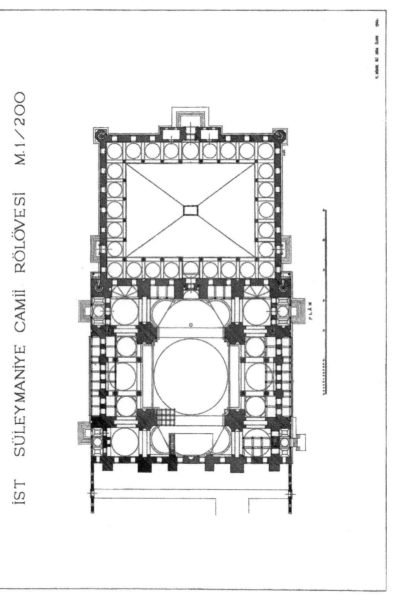

PLAN

T. NİMAN ALİ SAİM ÜLGEN 1943.

Figure 7.9. Plan of the Süleymaniye Mosque. From Ali Saim Ülgen, Mimar Sinan Yapıları (Ankara: Türk Tarih Kurumu, 1989).

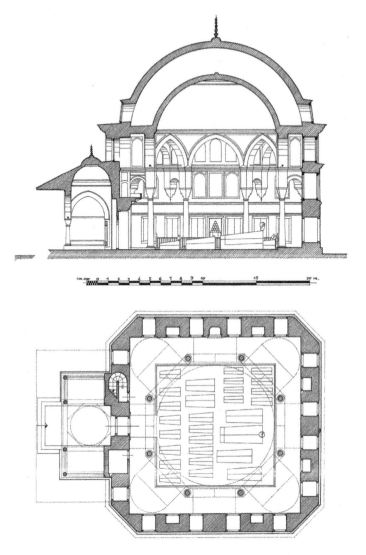

Figure 7.10. Plan and section of the the Mausoleum of Sultan Selim II. From Ali Saim Ülgen, Mimar Sinan Yapıları (Ankara: Türk Tarih Kurumu, 1989).

walls, as well as the carpets and the sarcophagi covered in silk and gold-threaded fabrics with the turban-shaped head pieces.[102]

At about the same time Pope Sixtus V as the major protagonist of the Counter-Reformation, had an important role in the shaping of Rome. For instance, one of the

---

102 Della Valle, *Viaggi*, 38.

most influential projects of the period was the completion of the dome of San Pietro. Furthermore, the obelisks brought from Egypt by Roman emperors were erected in the city to create focal points to which the boulevards extending the churches would lead. In this way, as Ostrow indicates, a pagan/antique monument was turned to a symbol of the "triumph of Christianity" with the erection of an obelisk at San Pietro Square.[103] In the Sistine Chapel that Pope Sixtus V had built for himself in the S. Maria Maggiore Church completed in 1589, a central plan with a dome resting on eight columns—similar to the mausoleum of Selim II—was used. The interior of this magnificent chapel built by Domenico Fontana (1543–1607), a celebrated architect of the period, was sumptuously adorned with frescos and sculptures.[104]

Through comparing the architecture of the mausoleum of Selim II and the chapel of Pope Sixtus V, Della Valle is also comparing these two well-known and influential contemporaneous protagonists. As Della Valle mentions at the beginning of his narration, Selim II was defeated by the pope in the magnificence of the buildings.[105] In a sense, the comparison reminds the audience of the encounter of Selim II with the pope and the forces of the Holy League at the Battle of Lepanto in 1571.[106]

Back to Italy: Collecting and Transmitting

Pietro Della Valle's letters, illustrating Istanbul four hundred years ago, are valuable sources for urban studies, and architectural history, as well as in many other areas. The long-standing interest in his letters can be explained by his rational view as a Roman intellectual formed within the Renaissance tradition at the onset of the Baroque age. Through his "pilgrimage of curiosity" he explored the city, art and architecture, administrative/social organization, and daily life. His writings not only recorded the Ottoman capital but also communicated the Ottoman world to the European world.

During his travels, Della Valle found numerous similarities between Italy and the Ottoman Empire in terms of topography, cities, monuments, spaces, and processions. Like many other travellers who visited Istanbul, he compared Istanbul and Rome, evaluated Istanbul's mosques through the domed central plan tradition, and questioned the universality of the architecture of antiquity. He was also interested in buildings that reflected the Eastern tradition, such as the Ottoman palaces and kiosks. Although he investigated the Ottoman monumental architecture in detail, the traveller did not cite the names of any of the major architects such as Sinan (d. 1588) and Sedefkar Mehmet Agha (d. 1622).

---

103 Steven Ostrow, "The Counter Reformation and the End of the Century," in *Rome (Artistic Centers of the Italian Renaissance)*, ed. M. Hall (Cambridge: Cambridge University Press, 2005), 282.

104 Steven F. Ostrow, *Art and Spirituality in Counter-Reformation Rome: The Sistine and Pauline Chapels in S. Maria Maggiore* (New York: Cambridge University Press, 1996).

105 Pius V was the pope at the time of the Battle of Lepanto.

106 In addition to the papal forces, The "Holy League" was composed of Venetian, Genoese and Spanish fleets.

One of the essential images that Della Valle aimed to communicate to his Italian readers was the panorama of Istanbul. The poem titled *Ninfa Galata* (Nymphe of Galata), which he wrote for a girl from "Constantinopolis", appears as a quintessential example of a poetic panorama;[107]

> Amorous, sweet wind
> That ripples over the salty waves
> Between the Western shores
> Blow and travel to the Orient,
> Reach, I beg you, that shore
> Where the plane trees provide shade,
> Where in the middle of the mosques
> A lofty tower hovers over the roofs,
> Where I find the Grand Seraglio
> And the great temple of Sophia
> At the foot of a lovely hill
> Where I already left my soul behind ...

Similarly, he writes about the drawings of the city made by other painters as well as his own. Before leaving Istanbul, he describes a panoramic view of Istanbul displaying its towers, mosques, dungeons, and streets with trees; he desires to commission a Flemish painter to record the scene, believing it would arouse a considerable interest in Italy.[108] Additionally, he reports that he drew a sketch of the Topkapı Palace but he will be making a second, more accurate, one to bring back to Italy.[109] He writes that he will order the same for his house in Rome, for the *sofà* that he saw while visiting the palace of the grand vizier.[110] In general, the travel accounts serve also as a source of information for those of his audience practising architecture, and the traveller takes "an active role in appropiating Turkish culture back home."[111] For instance, in the late sixteenth century, Italian architect Palladio applied Ottoman architecture as a source of inspiration. Howard's study shows how prints, books, and costume books as well as Venetian *bailo* Barbaro's reports may have penetrated Palladio's imagination and been influential in the design of the church of Redentore in Venice (1577–1592).[112] Similarly, Della Valle aimed to bring back images from some paintings of the imperial mosques for the architects in Italy to emulate. As

---

107 'Amoroso venticello, / Che tra i lidi d'Occidente,/ Increspando le onde salse, / Spiri e corri in Oriente,/ Giungi, prego, a quella riva / Dove i platani fanno ombra, / Dove in mezzo alle meschite / Alta torre i tetti adombra, / Dove incontro al gran Serraglio / E al gran tempio di Sofia / Nella falda d'un bel colle / Lasciai già l'anima mia,' Rossi, "Pietro Della Valle Orientalista Romano," 55. Special thanks to Elio Brancaforte for the translation from Italian to English.

108 Della Valle, *Viaggi*, 143.

109 Della Valle, *Viaggi*, 107.

110 Della Valle, *Viaggi*, 80.

111 Nebahat Avcıoğlu, *Turquerie and the Politics of Representation, 1728–1876* (Farnham: Ashgate, 2011), 24.

112 Deborah Howard, "Venice between East and West: Marc'Antonio Barbaro and Palladio's Church of the Redentore," *Journal of the Society of Architectural Historians* 62 (2003), 306–25.

pointed out previously, Connors argues that in his design of Sant' Ivo alla Sapienza (1642) in Rome, Francesco Borromini used the information provided by Della Valle.[113]

Della Valle reports taking many drawings and objects back to Italy. These were sources and objects of knowledge such as books, drawings, and antique medals as well as commodities such as drugs, plants, and textiles that were typically seen in the "cabinet of curiosities" of the period. He had great interest in antique objects, and according to him each antique object is worthy of collection. As stated earlier, he writes of taking a stone from the ruins of Troy to bring back to Italy. After reporting that he purchased over thirty antique silver and gold medals, he adds that, even if he does not have enough knowledge on this matter, he will leave the choosing to his friends in Italy who are specialists.[114] Subsequently, in the eighteenth century, the number of Europeans travelling to the Ottoman Empire to collect antique coins, medals, and inscriptions would greatly increase and royal collections would begin to form.[115] In his letter dated September 4, 1615, Della Valle describes in detail the linguistic books that he purchased in Istanbul.[116] Book printing and collecting, which became prevalent during the Renaissance, represent the "triumph of the book," as described by Jardine.[117] During this period, both Europe and the Ottoman Empire had a growing interest in books, and kings, the nobility, and tradesmen started to collect them. For instance, the first (Ottoman) Turkish language book entered the collections of the French king in 1668–1669.[118] Moreover, although the first dragoman school had been established in 1557 in Istanbul,[119] European interest in learning the languages of the east proliferated at the end of the seventeenth century, and France sent young students to the Ottoman Empire in 1669 to gain the education of dragoman.[120] In the same way, Della Valle wanted to communicate directly with the Ottomans and their culture. He writes of (Ottoman) Turkish, Arabic, and Persian language lessons that he took during his stay in Istanbul.[121] Beside the books, Della Valle planned to take some official Ottoman documents with him on his return to Italy. He

---

113 Connors, "Borromini, Hagia Sophia and S. Vitale," 44–45.

114 Della Valle, *Viaggi*, 148.

115 Fatma Müge Göçek, *East Encounters West: France and the Ottoman Empire in the Eighteenth Century* (Cary: Oxford University Press, 1987), 98.

116 Della Valle, *Viaggi*, 147.

117 Lisa Jardine, *Worldly Goods: A New History of the Renaissance* (New York: Norton, 1996), 133–80.

118 Annie Berthier, "Turc," in *Manuscrits, xylographes, estampages: les collections orientales du Département des manuscrits: guide*, ed. Annie Berthier (Paris: Bibliothèque Nationale de France, 2000), 54–56.

119 The school was housed at the Venetian Embassy in Istanbul. See Nevin and Raniero Speelman-Özkan, "I dragomanni / Dragomanlar," in *Il Palazzo di Venezia a Istanbul e i suoi Antichi Abitanti Istanbul'daki Venedik Sarayı ve Eski Yaşayanları*, ed. Maria Pia Pedani, Hilâl. Studi Turchi e Ottomani 3 (Venezia: Edizioni Ca'Foscari, 2013), 57 .

120 See Frédéric Hitzel, *Enfants de Langue et Drogmans* (Istanbul: Yapı Kredi Yayınları, 1995).

121 Della Valle, *Viaggi*, 133. Nevin Özkan, "Pietro Della Valle, Osmanlı Topraklarında Bir İtalyan Gezgin (Roma 1586–1652) Pietro Della Valle—Onyedinci Yüzyıla Ait Bir Notdefterinin İncelenmesi," *Ankara Üniversitesi Dil ve Tarih-Coğrafya Fakültesi Dergisi* 46 (2006): 1–16.

writes that his Ottoman teacher's father, David—who worked at the Palace for Murad III—left behind some state documents upon his death.[122] Della Valle was willing to take these very *curiossime* (curious) documents, including those signed by an Ottoman prince and his correspondences with the Christian princes.

The traveller describes the costumes and headgear that he encountered in the Ottoman Empire. He notes that among the many places that he had visited before, he had never seen women and men dressed more beautifully than the Turks and Greeks.[123] Della Valle desired to illustrate his writings about Ottoman daily life and especially Ottoman costumes. He planned to commission an album to display the costumes of the men and women from diverse religions and nationalities living in Istanbul.[124] According to him, these drawings, made by Turks, even if not perfect, would help the Italian audience to gain some acquaintance with Ottoman styles and prove that the Turks *veduto con gusto* ("have been seen with some taste").[125] He also writes about the oil portraits of the Ottomans made by a Flemish painter that he met at the residence of the French ambassador Achille de Harlay de Sancy.[126] Previously traveller artists such as Nicolas de Nicolay (1517–1583) had produced costume books for European audiences. However, Della Valle desired to have paintings that reflect scenes from Ottoman daily life. More importantly, his writings suggest that his aim is paintings with some theatrical "*mise-en-scènes*" (staging) of daily life. For instance, in a painting that he planned to commission, three women would be sitting and having a conversation while drinking their coffee *alla turca* style.[127] Such compositions would later be widely realized by the European painters with the *Turquerie* style.[128] Carle van Loo's *Sultan's Wife Drinking Coffee* and Jean Baptiste Vanmour's *Women Drinking Coffee* are similar to the scenes that he planned to commission. The publication of the *Viaggi* in 1662–1664 in France raises the idea that perhaps the travel accounts were among the influential sources of the *Turquerie*. It is also noteworthy that painters such Jean Vanmour (1671–1737), referred to as *Peintres du Bosphore* by Auguste Boppe,

---

122 David must have been David Passi, an influential person serving at the Ottoman palace during the reign of Murad III.

123 Della Valle, *Viaggi*, 72, 81.

124 Della Valle, *Viaggi*, 120. The illustrations that Della Valle envisioned to publish as the fourth volume of *Viaggi* never appeared. In the the third volume, the editor Biagio Deversin noted that the fourth volume would not be published. Although some simple sketches and plans have been included in the previous volumes, the remaining illustrations probably may have been lost. See Cardini, *La Porta d'Oriente*, 111–12 n113.

125 Della Valle, *Viaggi*, 43.

126 Della Valle, *Viaggi*, 143.

127 Della Valle, *Viaggi*, 144.

128 For *Turquerie* see Auguste Boppe, *Les Peintres du Bosphore* (Paris: ACR, 1989); Hélène Desmet-Grégoire, *Le Divan Magique: L'Orient Turc en France au XVIIIe siècle* (Paris: Sycomore, 1980); *Topkapı à Versailles: Trésors de la Cour Ottomane*, exhibition catalogue, Musée National des Châteaux de Versailles et de Trianon, 4 mai–15 août 1999 ([Paris]: Association Française d'Action Artistique: Editions de la Réunion des Musées Nationaux, ca. 1999); see also Günsel Renda, "The Ottoman Empire and Europe: Cultural Encounters," in *Cultural Contacts in Building a Universal Civilisation: Islamic Contributions*, ed. Ekmeleddin Ihsanoğlu (Istanbul: IRCICA, 2005), 277–303.

were part of the retinue of the European ambassadors. Similarly, Della Valle, who resided in a house within the French embassy and was in close contact with the ambassador, can be seen as an example of the link between art and diplomacy.

The visual excitement created by the textiles[129] and preciosities of the Ottoman Empire are the main characteristics of the works of the *Peintres du Bosphore*. Similarly, Della Valle talks very often about the diversity and exquisiteness of the precious gems such as pearls, rubies, and diamonds that he saw in Istanbul. He describes his audience in front of Sultan Ahmed I who was sitting behind a small table decorated with precious gems; Della Valle indicates that he could not take his eyes away from the diamonds on the Sultan's fingers and the feathers on his headgear.[130] Elsewhere the traveller mentions a sword that he had seen in a jewellery store and which was ordered by the grand vizier for the sultan. Despite the rough and disorganized workmanship, Della Valle notes that he was impressed by the generous use of gold, rubies, and diamonds.[131] He describes with great fascination Ottoman velvets, silks, damasks, textiles, and carpets, with their diverse colours and textures and sumptuous detail. He also desires to take with him on his return some textiles that he has purchased and received as gifts, and believes that they will delight the ladies in Rome.[132] Besides their visual characteristics, Della Valle also examined their commercial value and collected detailed information about the commodities that he encountered in the Ottoman Empire. For instance, Della Valle is also one of the first travellers to write about coffee and coffeehouses;[133] besides its medical effects, he indicates the commercial value of coffee by describing it as a "good source of revenue for the Sultan because of its tax." He indicates that he will take some coffee with him on his return to Italy.[134]

Undoubtedly, through his travel accounts, Della Valle functioned as a cultural mediator for the flow of the culture, knowledge, and commodities of the Ottoman Empire to Europe.[135] Through his complete book published in the 1660s in France, Holland, and Germany, his influence went beyond the borders of Italy and spread widely throughout Europe. Yet, Rubiés indicates that: "it is clear that Della Valle's self-fashioning as a curious and cosmopolitan pilgrim was socially re-fashioned, and found a niche in the intellectual gallery of Baroque Europe."[136] Although he followed the footsteps of his precedessors, his accounts display a genuine manifold repertory rather than conventional visions

---

129 Ottoman textiles were highly admired and sought after in Europe. See Suraiya Faroqhi, "Ottoman Textiles in European Markets," in *The Renaissance and the Ottoman World*, ed. Anna Contadini and Claire Norton (Burlington: Ashgate, 2013), 231–44; Suraiya Faroqui, *A Cultural History of the Ottomans. The Imperial Elite and its Artefacts* (London: I. B. Tauris, 2016), 166–72.

130 Della Valle, *Viaggi*, 106.

131 Della Valle, *Viaggi*, 34.

132 Della Valle, *Viaggi*, 44.

133 Fernand Braudel, *The Structures of Everyday Life: The Limits of the Possible* (Berkeley: University of California Press, 1992), 256.

134 Della Valle, *Viaggi*, 75–76.

135 See Nurhan Atasoy and Lale Uluç, *Impressions of Ottoman Culture in Europe: 1453–1699* (Istanbul: Turkish Cultural Foundation, Armağan, 2012).

136 Joan-Pau Rubiés, *Travel and Ethnology in the Renaissance*, 386.

for the richly illustrated narratives of his successors—such as Jean-Baptiste Tavernier (1605–1689), Guillaume-Joseph Grelot (ca. 1630–ca 1680), Jean de Thévenot (1633–1667), and Jean Chardin (1643–1712). As one of the most influential travellers of the early seventeenth century, Della Valle, along with his travel accounts, is arguably one of the bridges in shaping the European perception of the Ottoman Empire that occurred in the eighteenth century, before Orientalism.

Part III

To the East and Back:
Exchanging Objects, Ideas, and Texts

Chapter 8

GIFT-GIVING IN THE CARPINI EXPEDITION TO MONGOLIA (1246–1248 CE)[1]

ADRIANO DUQUE

ABSTRACT

In his article, Adriano Duque examines the dynamics of gift-giving during the Carpini expedition to Mongolia in 1246. Drawing from current theory by Derrida and Mauss, the article analyzes the personal and political expectations generated by gifts and how they allowed Christian friars and Mongolian rulers to articulate relations of reciprocity and power.

Keywords: Mongolia, Carpini, travel, maps, gifts

ON APRIL 16, 1246 Pope Innocent IV sent three Franciscan friars (Lawrence of Portugal, John of Plan Carpini, and Benedict the Pole) on an expedition to Mongolia. While it is plausible that Lawrence of Portugal did not complete the trip, Carpini and Benedict completed the journey with alleged the purpose of converting the Tartars to Christianity and to ask them to cease all attacks against Christians.[2] Along the way, the friars encountered a series of local chieftains who inquired about their mission. In order to be granted access, the friars had to deliver a number of gifts that served as tolls. However, when they arrived at the Mongol camp, they refused to present any gifts to the great khan. This objection caused a significant delay in their mission. After witnessing the coronation of Güyük (1246–1248) as the third great khan of the Mongol Empire, they were admitted into the court, where they received a dispatch from the great khan to the pope.

---

1 An earlier version of this paper was presented at the Mongolia Society Annual Meeting in March 2014. I am indebted to Agnes Moncy and several members of the Mongolia Society for their input in writing this essay. All mistakes remain my own.

2 "Regi et populo Tartarorum viam agnoscere veritatis," *Monumenta Germaniae Historica. Epistolae saeculi XIII* (Berlin, 1887): 2:75.

Gift-giving occurred in Christian and Mongol societies, but its significance depended on the economic and symbolic value that each culture placed on the gift.[3] For Christians and Mongols alike, gift-giving was used to circulate goods and to promote ties and bonding among individuals. Gift-giving was articulated in the different stages that required varying degrees of involvement from the giver and from the receiver: giving, receiving and reciprocating. In this sense, gift-giving was not a one-way action. Moreover, it invariably placed the receiver in a situation of indebtedness and obligated him to acknowledge a social difference that could not be resolved until the gift was returned or reciprocated. The meaning of the term "gift" is further clarified by the use that Benedict and Carpini make of the word *munera* instead of *donum*. In a recent article on amatory love in the works of Plautus, Netta Zagagi defines *munus* as a "specific kind of donum" characterized by a sense of obligation. A denial of *munus* could be seen as a breach of contract, inasmuch as it disregarded the obligation which the receiver had of corresponding the donor.[4] The word *donum*, on the other hand, entailed notions of generosity and liberality and excludes the need of remuneration.[5] The term *munus* excluded any idea of reciprocity, and acknowledged instead a sense of acknowledgement.[6] Unlike *donum*, *munus* marked "the gift that one gives, not the gift that one receives" and indicated the contractual obligation between two parties.[7]

From this point of view, it is possible to say that gift-giving in the Carpini expedition involved a "ritual practice through which the current value of a relationship may be communicated and maintained."[8] When Christian friars delivered their gifts to the Mongol rulers, they were in fact attempting to create a social bond which Mongol rulers invariably interpreted as a demonstration of fealty.[9] Taking on this idea, the following pages will examine how the expeditionaries to Mongolia used gifts not only as a means of negotiating their passage across territories but also as a way of negotiating their own presence vis-à-vis Mongol society. After considering the idea of the gift as a diplomatic tool, the article will go on to examine the Mongol perception of gift-giving. Finally, it will focus on the knowledge that the Christian ambassadors had of the practice of gift-giving among Mongols and how they used it to their own benefit.

Gift-giving in the Carpini expedition is predicated on the dynamics of contractual exchange that took place in the Middle Ages. According to Marcel Mauss, acts of

---

3 Marcel Mauss, *The Gift: Forms and Functions Of Exchange In Archaic Societies*, trans. Ian Cunnison (New York: Norton, 1967).

4 Netta Zaggagi, "Amatory Gifts and Payments: A Note on Munus, Donum, Data in Plautus," *Glotta* 65 (1987): 130.

5 Zaggagi, "Amatory Gifts and Payments," 131.

6 Florin Curta, "Merovingian and Carolingian Gift-Giving," *Speculum* 81 (1006): 678.

7 Roberto Esposito, *Bios: Biopolitics and Philosophy (Posthumanities)* (Minneapolis: University of Minnesota Press, 2008), x.

8 Helmuth Berking, *Sociology of Giving* (London: Sage, 1999), 5.

9 See Jacques Godbout, *The World of the Gift*, trans. Donald Winkler (Montreal: McGill University Press, 1998), 20.

gift-giving in the Middle Ages were mediated by a "necessary generosity" between magnates and kings, dependants and protectors, retainers or lords. Far from being interpreted as a ritual, reciprocal gift-giving is seen as "the main form of expression of relations between peers based on mutual trust."[10] The gift, however, was not a stable entity, but reconfigured the relation between givers and receivers, opening the door for a model of monetary exchange.[11] The arbitrariness of Carpini to either give or refuse to give certain gifts when prompted has an interesting correlation in the expedition of William of Rubruck in 1253. On that occasion William of Rubruck refused to give a gift to the great khan, causing great distress among Mongols. In his analysis of this episode, A. J. Watson has explained that William was in fact avoiding the obligations of gift-giving, but also avoiding a declaration of fealty.[12] By offering no gifts, William of Rubruck would in fact be offering a true gift of self, a gift that demanded nothing in return, and that excluded an action of self-interest.[13]

Gift-Giving in Diplomatic Exchange

Relations between Christians and Mongols in the Carpini expedition are expressed mainly through acts of gift-giving in contexts of diplomatic exchange. According to Adam of Salimbene, by September 1247 the friars were back in Cologne, where they led vast gatherings to tell their stories and to show the presents which the great khan had given to the pope. These gifts included a wooden cup with numerous nodes representing the faces of a woman, and a *capella* (possibly a dalmatic or chasuble for celebrating mass). He compared them to the wonder caused by a walnut tree in Apulia where the face of Christ had already appeared and which was inextricably linked to Frederick II:

> Iste ostendit michi et aliis fratribus unam cuppam ligneam, quam portabat, ut daret domno pape; in qua cuppa erat in fundo cuiusdam pulcherrime regine ymago, ut vidi oculis meis, non artificialiter seu opere pictorio ibi depicta, sed ex virtute constellationis ibi impressa. Et si in centum partes secta fuisset, semper impressionem illius ymaginis habuisset. Et ne hoc alicui ad credendum impossibile videatur exemplo alio possumus demonstrare et fidem astruere. Nam imperator Fridericus in Apulia donavit quandam ecclesiam fratribus Minoribus, que erat antiquissima et destructa et ab omnibus derelicta; et in loco ubi altare fuit prius inmense magnitudinis creverat arbor nucis, que secta in qualibet asside domini nostri Iesu Christi crucifixi habebat ymaginem. Et si cencies secata fuisset, totiens crucifixi ymaginem habuisset. Quod, quamvis

---

10 Florin Curta, "Merovingian and Carolingian Gift-Giving," 675.

11 J. A. Galloway, "One Market or Many? London and the Grain Trade of England," in *Trade, Urban Hinterlands and Market Integration c. 1300–1600*, ed. J. A. Galloway (London: Centre for Metropolitan History, 2000), 23–42.

12 A. J. Watson, "Mongol Inhospitality, or How to Do More with Less? Gift-Giving in William of Rubruck's *Itinerarium*," *Journal of Medieval History* 37 (2011): 90–101.

13 John Milbank, "The Ethics of Self-sacrifice," *First-Things* 91 (1999): 33–38.

ex miraculo hoc demonstraverit Deus, eo quod in illo loco nata sit nucis arbor, in quo agni inmaculati passio representatur in hostia salutari et sacrificio reverendo, tamen ex virtute constellationis tales impressiones posse fieri aliqui assevérant. Item idem frater Iohannes dixit nobis, quod pulcherrimam capellam portabat ad donandum domno pape. Et appellabat capellam, ut nobis exposuit, omnia pontificalia paramenta, que ad missam celebrandam diebus sollemnibus necessario requiruntur.[14]

[He showed me and the friars a wooden cup that we had brought as a present for the pope, in the bottom of which I saw with my own eyes the image of a beautiful queen not painted but formed or made in any artificial way, but "by the influence of stars." And if you cut it a hundred times, it would still keep the same image. And so that no one may fall in disbelief, I can give you another example, and maintain credibility. For Emperor Frederick had given to the Brothers Minor in Apulia a very old church, all ruined and deserted; and in the space where the altar had been, there had grown up a nut-tree of incredible size. Cut lengthwise, each section presented the face of Christ, and if you had cut it a hundred times, a hundred times would the image have appeared. Which even God demonstrated with a miracle but which the tree having grown in that place where was wont to be renewed the Passion of the spotless Lamb in the saving host and venerable sacrifice. Yet there are some of the firm opinion that it may have been caused by the influence of a constellation. In addition, Father John told us that he was carrying a beautiful cape as a present to the pope. As he told us, they call cape any papal robe required to celebrate mass on solemn days.][15]

Neither Carpini nor Benedict mention these gifts. The meaning of the friars' visit to Cologne is further complicated by the fact that a few weeks later, on October 3, the people of the German city would celebrate the declaration of William II of Holland as king of Germany, in detriment of Frederick II who had been excommunicated on Palm Sunday, 1239. Either reflecting or forging a coincidence, Adam of Salimbene saw the arrival of the friars as an opportunity to make his case against the emperor and described the wonder of the Mongolians gifts as a mockery of Frederick's lack of piety and common sense.

Comparing the marvel of the gifts to the prodigies that had appeared in a church reconstructed by Frederick II in Apulia, Adam of Salimbene attributed them to an *opus stellarum*, an act of sorcery. This declaration played well with the reputation that Frederick II had of being highly superstitious.[16] The lack of evidence as to these prodigies seems to support this point. Having hinted at Frederick's ability to distinguish magic from reality, Adam of Salimbene was quick to stress the importance of Mongol gifts as

---

14 Adam de Salimbene, *Cronica fratris Salimbene de Adam ordinis Minorum. Monumenta Germaniae Historia. Scriptores (in Folio)*, ed. Oswad Holder-Egger, vol. 32 (Hannover, 1913), 206.

15 All translations in this essay are my own.

16 Giovanni Crocione, *Le tradizioni popolari nella letteratura italiana* (Florence: Olschki, 1970), 111. The term *opus stellarum* was widely attributed to Ptolemy. Roger Bacon later included it in his works: "anima sapiens adjuvabit opus stellarum, quemadmodum seminator fortitudines naturales, unde et nociva potet repellere, et utilia promovera" (a wise soul will help the work of the start, just

vital elements of diplomacy and a living proof of the papal expedition to Mongolia. Drawing this on scriptural authority, Adam of Salimbene explained the meaning of these presents as indications of Mongolian acquiescence, and used two biblical passages from the Book of Proverbs to explain that the gifts were a diplomatic present (Donum hominis dilatat viam ejus / et ante principes spacium ei facit [A gift opens the way / and ushers the giver into the presence of the great])[17] and a sign of submission (Multi colunt personam potentis / et amici sunt dona tribuentis [Many seek the favour of a generous man, / and everyone is a friend to a man who tributes]).[18]

Gift-Giving from a Mongol Perspective

A look into papal records reveals that even though the wooden cup may have been an exceptional piece, silk capes were not an uncommon gift to Christian friars during their expeditions to Mongolia. A look into the inventory of the papal treasure made by Boniface VIII in 1295 reveals among other objects a *panno tartarico* or dalmatic in light green (1540), and a wooden cup with a silver rim, reminiscent of the Mongolian burlwood tea bowls (1619).[19] Authors like Thomas Allsen and Lauren Arnold have identified the *panno tartarico* with the *nasij*, a silk cloth to which golden ornaments are added, usually on the weft. The *nasij* was so desired by the Mongols for wearing and gift-giving that they enslaved whole villages of Muslim weavers of the cloth. [20]

The presence of numerous samples of *panno tartarico* in royal treasures and inventories around Europe suggests that the *panno tartarico* was undoubtedly a diplomatic gift.[21] The meaning of this gift can be inferred from a passage in Benedict the Pole's *Relatio*. According to Benedict, the friars saw over five thousand men who paid homage

---

as one who sows facilitates the forces of nature, and this allows him to reject harmful things and to promote useful ones) (Roger Bacon, *Opus maius ad Clementem IV, Pontificem Romanum*, (London, 1733), 247.

17 Prov. 18:16. All biblical texts in this essay are taken from the *Bibliba Vulgata Clementina*, ed. Michael Tweedale (2005).

18 Prov. 19:6.

19 Arch. Seg. Vat. Indice 4, fol. 50. Cf. Émile Molinier. "Inventaire du trésor du Saint-Siège sous Boniface VIII (1295)," *Bibliothèque de l'école des chartes* 49 (1888), 226–37. Marco Antonio Boldetti lists a dozen dalmatics that Pope Boniface VIII donated to the church of Anagnina. Marco Antonio Boldetti, *Osservazioni sopra i cimiteri de'santi martiri ed antichi christiani di Roma* (Rome, 1720), 306.

20 Lauren Arnold, *Princely Gifts and Papal Treasures: The Franciscan Mission to China and its Influence on the Art of the West, 1250–1350* (San Francisco: Desiderata Press Art ,1999), 36; Thomas T. Allsen, *Commodity and Exchange in the Mongol Empire: A Cultural History of Islamic Textiles* (Cambridge: Cambridge University Press, 1997), 3. The *capella* was possibly related to the Mongolian *deel*, a loose calf-length tunic made of one piece of material. It has long sleeves, and changes in colour and material from one group to the other. Paula L. W. Sabloff, *Modern Mongolia: Reclaiming Genghis Khan.* (Philadelphia: University of Pennsylvania Press, 2001), 76.

21 Allsen, *Commodity and Exchange*, 22. Cf. Susan Wise Bauer, *The History of the Medieval World: From the Conversion of Constantine to the First Crusade* (New York: Norton, 2010), 37.

to the great khan, clad in luxurious robes to attend the festivities: "inter quos dicti fratres numerabantur, induti et ipsi desuper tunicas suas baldakino, prout necessitas urgebat, quia nulli nuntiorum nisi adcurate vesti vultum regis electi et coronati licuit intueri" (those among which the friars were included, were dressed with an honour cloth over their robes, according to the demands of the situation. Because none of the ambassadors were allowed to see the face of the newly elected and crowned king unless they were properly dressed).[22]

To the Mongols, the acceptance of gifts implied a diplomatic acknowledgement on the part of the Europeans of their submission to Mongol rule.[23] In fact, the act of giving luxury presents responded not to an act of kindness, but to a necessity of a society basing its power not on territorial possession but on "the acquisition and retention of followers." According to Allsen, these gifts were necessities in their political culture:

> For the Mongolian rulers, as for many others, the creation of a following required a sustained system of what might be called conspicuous redistribution. And once started, such presentations, like the Roman bread and circuses, essentially expenditures on legitimacy and loyalty, could not be halted or even significantly reduced, and typically became a permanent and heavy drain on the treasury. Indeed, for the nomads at least, the imperial treasury was essentially a mechanism or the redistribution of luxuries, most especially cloth and clothing.[24]

The meaning of gift-giving in Mongolian society was further supported by the fact that Mongols used the same word to denote the ideas of "peace" and "subjection." According to Peter Jackson, Mongols embraced an ideology of universal subjection. Every ruler was *de iure* subject to the Mongols, and whoever opposed them was a rebel. "In fact," writes Jackson, "the Turkish word for 'peace' was also used to express subjection (il/el): there could be no peace with the Mongols in the absence of subjection."[25] Consequently, the meaning of the presents must be interpreted, at least from the point of view of the Mongols, as an act of sovereignty that was consistent with the tone of the letter that Great Khan Güyük sent to the pope. In this letter, Güyük demanded that the pope come to him and prove that his desire for peace (i.e. submission) was a genuine move. This in turn would comply with the divine support that had allowed the conquest of the Mongols:

> From the rising of the sun to its setting, all the lands have been made subject to me. Who could do this contrary to the command of God? Now you should say with a sincere heart: "I will submit and serve you / Thou thyself, at the head of all the Princes, come at once to serve and wait upon us! At that time I shall

---

22 Benedictus Polonus, "Relatio de itinere fratrum minorum at Tartaros," in *Relation des Mongols ou Tartares*, ed. M. D'Avezac (Paris, 1838), 381–82.

23 Arnold, *Princely Gifts and Papal Treasures*, 119.

24 Allsen, *Commodity and Exchange*, 104.

25 Peter Jackson, *The Mongols and the West, 1221–1410* (Harlow: Pearson, 2005), 46.

recognize your submission. If you do not observe God's command, and if you ignore my command, I shall know you as my enemy."[26]

The disparity of interpretations of the Mongol gifts points, on the other hand, to a problem of meaning. As the Salimbene rendition tells us, presents are not mere exchanges of gifts, but call for a categorical representation of social relations where the gift is merely a commodity capable of eliciting social forms of discourse. In his effort to interpret the meaning of Güyük's letters, Salimbene did not hesitate to associate him with the perceived weakness of Frederick II, and connect it with a number of popular traditions often dismissed as forms of popular superstition. Eliciting a correct interpretation of the gift would thus guard Christians against the perils of irrational fear and credulity.

The Purification of Gifts

Likewise, for Mongolians the gift was a vehicle for spiritual power and had the potential to destroy the person who received it. In order to cast away all evil, gifts had to go through a process of ritual purification involving the passing between two fires. Fire-worship is well attested in the thirteenth century.[27] There is little doubt that while for the Mongols the crossing of fire was intended to drive away any spirits occupying their guests, the Christian friars excluded such a perception.[28]

The exact meaning of this ritual remained unknown to Christian envoys, who nevertheless insisted on narrating it as a key element of their interaction with Mongol chieftains. Furthermore, the way in which the Carpini and Benedict narrative was written suggests that Benedict would provide a lengthy oral explanation on this passage. Both Carpini and Benedict consider purification as an act of superstition. Both authors locate the episode upon their encounter with Batu, at the beginning of their journey, just as they enter Mongol territory:

> Ministri itaque Bati, postulata ab eis receperunt munera, scilicet quadraginta pelles castorum et octoginta pelles taxonum; quse munera portata sunt inter duos ignes ab eis sacratos, et Fratres coacti sunt sequi munera, quia sic mos est apud Tartaros expiare nuncios et munera per ignem.[29]

> [And Bati's subordinates, having demanded gifts from them, that is forty beaver skins and eighty badger skins, they passed the gifts between two fires, and demanded that the Friars follow the presents, for this is a custom among Tartars, to purify ambassadors and presents through fire.]

---

26 Christopher Dawson, *The Mongol Mission: Narratives and Letters of the Franciscan Missionaries in Mongolia and China in the 13th and 14th Centuries* (London: Sheed Ward, 1980), 85.

27 Walter Heissig, *The Religions of Mongolia*, trans. Geoffrey Samuel (Berkeley: University of California Press, 1980), 69.

28 Michael Burgan, *Empire of the Mongols* (New York: Infobase, 2009), 88.

29 Benedictus, "Relatio de itinere fratrum minorum at Tartaros," 379.

In his explanation of this episode, Carpini presented the circulation of gifts between fires as part of the superstitions of the Mongols, comparable to their alleged veneration of the moon and their natural fear of fire:

> Solem etiam dicunt esse matrem luna, eo quod lumen a sole recipiat. Et vt breuiter dicam per ignem credunt omnia purificari. Vnde cum nuncii veniunt ad eos, vel principes, vel qualescunque persona, oportet ipsos et munera qua portant per duos ignes transire, vt purificentur. Item si cadit ignis de coelo super pecora, vel super homines, quod ibidem sape contingit, siue aliquid talium euenerit eis, per quod immundos seu infortunatos se reputant, oportet similiter per incantatores mundari. Et quasi omnem spem suam in talibus posuerunt.[30]

> [They say that their mother is the moon, receiving her light from the sun. And to abbreviate I will say that they believe that everything can be purified with fire. Hence when the ambassadors come to them, or even princes, or anybody, they make them cross between two fires, so that they get purified. Likewise, if fire comes from the sky on their cattle or on a man, something that happens quite often, they consider themselves soiled or unfortunate, and magicians must cleanse them. And so they rested all their beliefs in such things.]

Purification by fire was no simple matter, and it also required the involvement of the gift-giver. From what we can read in the Carpini and Rubruck accounts, the ritual of gift purification required the giver to also pass between fires, a religious ritual that Christian envoys invariably perceived as an offence. One of the clearest explanations comes from Philip IV of France's expedition to Arghun in 1289. In his response, Arghun expressed surprise over the delegates' refusal to kneel before him, as he was no Christian ruler, and he said that "if this was by the king's wish he had nothing to say, and that everything that pleased the king would please him also, but he desired that he send him envoys in the future who would salute him in the fashion customary at his Court, without crossing fire."[31]

Another to encounter a similar situation was William of Rubruck. Travelling a few years after Carpini (from 1253 to 1255), it was told how when Andrew of Longjumeau too arrived at a Mongol camp, he was asked to pass the gifts between two fires, as were his men. On that occasion, William was spared the ritual because he himself was carrying no gifts:

> Unde hoc fuit duplex causa quare oportuit fratrem Andream et socios eius ire inter ignes: tum quia portabant exennia, tum quia illa spectabant ad illum qui iam defunctus fuerat, scilicet Keuchan. A me nichil requisitum est de talibus quia nichil portavi.[32]

---

30 Carpini, Giovanni Plan, "Historia Mongalorum," in *Relation des Mongols ou Tartares*, ed. M. D'Avezac (Paris, 1838), 61.

31 Henry Howorth Hoyle, *History of the Mongols from the 9th to the 19th century*, vol. 3 (London, 1876), 352.

32 *William of Rubruck. Itinerarium. Relation des voyages de Guillaume de Rubruck, Bernard le Sage et Saewuld*, ed. Francisque Michel (Paris, 1839), 167.

[This was the reason why Friar Andrew and his companions had to pass trhough fires; they bore presents, and they were destined for one who was already dead, Keu Chan. Nothing of the sort was required of me, because I brought nothing.]

The Giver's Worth

William's explanation of the ritual purification act indicates to what extent the gift influenced the giver's worth and was perceived as a valid interlocutor. The act of gift-giving asserted the friar's status as an ambassador but demanded a proportionate value congruent with existing social standards. In this sense, the Franciscan friars were encouraged to use their social capital. The performative excellence of gift-giving became the procedural drive, key to the emergence of the friars as respected men among Mongols. The value of the gift hovered over the Franciscan friars as a constant reminder of their obligation as gift-bearing representatives of the Christian pope.

A major way in which the Franciscan friars were instructed to exhibit their worth was by producing lavish gifts for Mongol rulers. A look into the papal delegations to the Mongols reveals, in fact, that gift-giving was not an unusual feat, but caused frequent misunderstandings. According to the sources, we know that Pope Gregory X sent presents to Qublay around 1275 and that Pope Nicholas IV did the same around 1291. Likewise, Pope Benedict XII sent Giovanni de Marignolli with a horse to Emperor Shundi, a gesture that the Mongol perceived as a favourable omen, making an artist paint the animal at once.[33] We also know from Rubruck that Andrew of Longjumeu travelled in 1249 with expensive gifts and treasures from the pope. His gifts included a chapel tent, lined with scenes representing the Annunciation and other events of sacred history, "pour leur montrer et enseigner comment ils devaient croire" (to show and teach them how they should believe).[34] Longjumeau was sent back to Louis IX with the more customary letters of ultimatum demanding further tributes. After such a reception, Louis IX and Innocent IV were keen not to reinforce this impression with future envoys.[35]

While crossing territories involved toll-paying, upon their encounter with the Mongol rulers the Franciscan friars were encouraged to produce gifts congruent with their status and the importance of the ruler who had sent them. One of the clearest examples occurs upon Carpini's encounter with Corenza or Curoniza, a commander of troops among the Kalmuks, which Carpini describes as lord of all those Tartars camped in front of the people of the west.[36] Having arrived at his camp, the friars were first asked what they would produce in terms of presents. They replied that the pope was sending no presents, but they offered to give them some of the possessions they were bringing for their own personal use. They were then met with disbelief and stupor: if they came from such a great man, how was it that they produced such insignificant presents?

---

33 Arnold, *Princely Gifts and Papal Treasures*, 95

34 Jean de Joinville, *Histoire de Saint Louis*, ed. Natalis de Wailly (Paris, 1874), 133.

35 Jackson, *The Mongols and the West*, 30.

36 Henry Hoyle Howorth, *History of the Mongols: The So-Called Tartars of Russia and Central Asia*, vol. 2 (London, 1880), 69.

Tertia die pervenerunt at ducem unius exercitus qui prefecture erat octo milibus armatorum; cujus ministri postulantes et recipients munera ipsos at ducem suum Curoniza perduxerunt. Insuper multa munera tam a principibus quam ab illis majoribus et minoribus petuntur ab eis, et si non dantur vilipendunt eos, imo quasi pro nichilo habent eos; et si a magnis viris mittuntur, nolunt ab eis modicum munus habere, sed dicunt: a magno homine venitis, et tam modicum datis? Unde accipere dedignantur: et si nuncio bene volunt facere facta sua, oportet eos dare majora.[37]

[On the third day eight thousand of the armed ones came to the duke belonging to the army of one of the prefectures, whose legates after demanding and receiving presents led in front of the chief Curoniza. Moreover, they asked for presents from the principal ones but also from the rich and the poor, and if they did not produce them, they were despised, and they considered them to be of no importance. And if they encountered great forces, they would not accept a modest gift, saying: you come from a great man and you give so little? Whereas they refuse to accept: and if the legates want to carry on their mission, they must give them better presents.]

The stupor of the Mongolians of Curoniza underscores the idea that a gift was never voluntary, and that gifts were given and reciprocated in set ways. Marking the transition from an economy of gift exchange to a monetary system, gift-giving allowed the establishment of relations of mutual trust in which prestations were exchanged for gifts. For Georges Duby, the society of this system was founded on "an infinitely varied network for circulating the wealth and services occasioned by necessary generosity: gifts of dependents to their protectors, of kin folk to brides, of friends to party-givers, of magnates to kings, of kings to aristocrats of all of the rich to all of the poor."[38] Conversely, the gifts made to the rulers were not also an expression of their recognition, but also a guarantee of prosperity for their entire people.[39]

The ritual of gift-giving is again repeated when the friars arrive at the court of the new great khan. According to Carpini, the ceremony of coronation involved a complex ritual where the over four thousand subjects of the great khan produced a variety of gifts. The coronation of Güyük lasted four days and included a deliverance of gifts to all those whom the great khan sought to please. In keeping with its solemnity, Güyük's enthronement on was attended by a large number of foreign ambassadors: the grand duke of Moscow, Yaroslav II of Vladimir; the incumbents for the throne of Georgia; the brother of the king of Armenia, Sempad the Constable; the future seljuk sultan of Rum, Kilij Arslan IV; and ambassadors of the Abbasid caliphate and of the Delhi sultanate.[40]

---

37 Carpini, "Historia Mongalorum," 275.

38 Georges Duby, *Guerriers et paysans (VII–XIIe siècle): Premier essor de l'économie européenne* (Paris: Gallimard, 1973), 62.

39 Florin Curta, "Merovingian and Carolingian Gift-Giving," 374.

40 Jean-Paul Roux, *L'Asie centrale, histoire et civilization* (Paris: Fayard, 2007), 312.

The ritual of gift-giving played an important role in the ceremony and was perceived as part of a submission ritual. At a conceptual level, gift-giving reinforced the idea of ritual veneration and allowed attendees to Güyük's coronation to express the terms of their relation to the newly invested great khan. This is expressed by Carpini in no uncertain terms when he writes: "Cum autem pervenissemus ad ipsum, fecit longe a se nobis ponere stationes, et misit ad nos servos suos procuratores, qui quererent a nobis cum quo eidem inclinare vellemus, hoc est dicere, quemvis ei munera dare" (As soon as we reached him, he ordered us to place our tents far away from him, and he sent his commissioners so that we could tell them what was it that we wanted to bow with, that is, giving what presents).

Perhaps driven by this conviction, the friars refused to grant any gifts to the great khan. Citing his own words before Corenza, Carpini explains that he had no presents (*munera*) from the pope, as he himself had decided to send the friars. Following suit, he acknowledges that he produced some presents to their representative Eldegay, establishing a clear distinction between a possible tribute and the acknowledgement of a toll that would allow them to proceed with their mission:

> Cui respondimus ut prius Corenze dixeramus, scilicet quod dominus Papa non miserat munera, sed nos de hiis que habebamus, de gratia Dei et domini Pape pro expensis, ipsum, sicut possumus, volumus honorare. Datis muneribus et acceptis, interrogavit a nobis procurator ipsius, qui Eldegai appellatur, causam adventus nostri.[41]

> [To whom we responded what we had already said to Corenza, that the pope had not sent any presents, but that we would be happy to oblige with those that we had by the grace of God and at the expense of the pope. Having given and accepted the presents, the agent—whose name is Eldegai—asked us the reason for our journey.]

Refusing Gifts

Gift-refusal was rooted, as we have seen, in a careful distinction between toll and tribute. Unlike the tributes that the friars refused to pay, tolls were always made in species and involved the action of an intermediary with limited powers over his territory. This aspect is made clear upon their encounter at the camp of Batu, at which point they produced forty beaver skins and eighty badger skins. The fact that Batu is presented as a gate-keeper in the Volga justifies the payment of gifts and constitutes also a recognition of status. From there on, the friars will be assured free entrance to Güyük's camp.

Toll payment in the Carpini expedition constituted an acknowledgement of the power which will insure the favourable outcome of the mission. As they narrated their encounter with different chiefs, the Franciscan friars were careful to establish the relation that they bore with the great khan. Marking a principle of authority, these

---

41 Carpini, "Historia Mongalorum," 348.

genealogies allowed the friars to establish principles of legitimacy and to justify toll-paying to certain groups over others. This aspect gains special relevance in the proximity of Kiev. Having come across some men who pretended to be there on behalf of Corenza, the friars accused them of lying and of trying to acquire gifts which the friars were carrying along.

> Ipse enim miserat contra nos in Kioviam quosdam satellites suos, mendaciter qui nobis dicerenret ex parte Corenze quos essemus nuncio et quod veniremu, ad ipsum; et hoc ideo faciebat quamvis non esse verum, ut posset a nobis munera extorquere.[42]

> [Indeed it was him who sent against us some of his attendants, to lie to us and say that they were coming from Corenza and to ask whom we were representing and what we came for. And even this was not true. They did it so that they could extract gifts from us.]

The payment of tolls or the act of gift-giving constituted, as we have seen, a sign of recognition, but it clashed with the friars' refusal to produce any papal gifts.

In a recent article on gift-giving in Rubruck's *Itinerarium*, Anthony Watson has studied William of Rubruck's unsuccessful attempts to negotiate his way through the Mongol hierarchy with gifts of food. Using Rubruck's account of his journey, Watson analyses the utility of gifts of food across different cultural contexts and concludes that Rubruck ultimately gained status among the Mongols through his 'gift of self,' demonstrating how social standing can be negotiated through finding the appropriate cultural grammar for gift-giving.

The friar's refusal of gift-giving rested on the Christian doctrine of papal submission and the need to acknowledge earthly limitations of power. Refusal of gift-giving has a clear scriptural precedent in the book of Isaiah, where the acceptance of a gift engages the need of retribution: "Omnes diligunt munera, sequuntur retributions" (they all love bribes and chase after gifts).[43] Unlike an act of gift-giving, the refusal to grant a gift denied the recipient the right to dispose of the gift and the meaning associated with it. By refusing to give gifts to the Mongol ruler, the Franciscans acknowledged a lack of meaning in their mission and established themselves as the only valid interlocutors. They were henceforth the only ones who could explain the intentions of the pope.

For Jean Luc Marion, the refusal of the gift interrupts the normal succession of events and constitutes a primary way to find the pure gift.[44] If one of the agents refuses to reciprocate or accept the gift, the archaic cycle of gift-giving is broken. In this sense, the "gift of self" granted by the friars revealed an effort to gain social status among Mongols and was predicated as an attempt to obliterate the obligations of gift-giving.

---

42 Carpini, "Historia Mongalorum," 346.

43 Isaiah 1:23.

44 Jean Luc Marion, *Étant donné: Essai d'une phénoménologie de la donation* (Paris: Presses Universitaires de France, 1998), 74–78.

Conclusion

Reaching beyond the scope of this article, it would be important to position the friars' approach in the context of gift-giving in medieval Europe. The point is that the Franciscan friars seemingly were unable to produce a different perspective on gift-giving, one that might combine the rituals of vassalage coming from the gift-giver—as was customary in Western societies—with the Mongolian rituals of lordship signalled by the lavish expenditure of the great khan. As reflected in this essay, gift-giving in the Carpini expedition provides important insights into the development of Christian–Mongol relations in the mid-thirteenth century and a useful tool to channel social and diplomatic relations. Inasmuch as it evoked related social practices, gift-giving also expressed the need to grapple with cultural meaning and understanding. The meaning and use of gifts resided not in a unitary form of exchange, transaction, or tribute, but in a metaphorical process that exposed relations of dependency and fealty.

When the Franciscan friars refused to give gifts to the great khan, they brought gift-giving to the forefront and enabled their relationship with Mongol rulers to come under review. Negotiation within the ritual of gift-giving suggests finer nuances of meaning in Christian–Mongol relations that go beyond mere cultural differences. Gift-giving in the Carpini expedition helped portray the Franciscan friars as neither subjects nor dominating persons. As such, the Mongolian notions of gift-giving were increasingly challenged by more flexible, differentiating and contextualizing approaches conducted by the Franciscan friars that searched for new ways to contextualize the difficult and complex relationship between East and West. In that sense, the unacknowledged developments of gift-giving and the relative sacredness of this act may be taken to confirm the paradoxical features of gift-giving, and the puzzling ability of gifts to challenge existing relations.

Gift-Giving

	Carpini	**Benedictus**
Gift as sign of submission	• Mongol subjects give to image of the emperor (224) • Gifts as tribute (286) • The great khan receives presents (286) • Presents are to be given to the great khan (306) • The legitimate child of the great khan receives tributes (309) • Giving presents is like bowing (348) • The subjects give presents to the great khan (360)	• Gifts are tributes given by subjects to the great khan (381)

Gift as safe conduct	• Friars give presents to Mongols, who pass them between two fires (306)	• Ministers pass gifts between two fires (379)
	• The friars have to give presents if they want to continue their business (341)	
	• The friars cannot continue unless they produce gifts (342)	
Required gifts	• Mongols demand presents from everyone. A big person gives great gifts (274)	• Ministers demand gifts and receive them (379)
	• The great khan demands presents from his subjects (306)	
	• The friars are told they need to give presents (310)	
	• The friars are extorted (342)	
	• Corenza's men require gifts (379)	

Chapter 9

THE EAST–WEST TRAJECTORY OF SEPHARDIC SECTARIANISM: FROM IBN DAUD TO SPINOZA

GREGORY B. KAPLAN

ABSTRACT

This study centres on a form of Jewish sectarianism, or Karaism, which traces its roots to ancient currents of thought in the Middle East and which "travelled," or was intellectually transmitted, from east to west upon the establishment of Islamic hegemony in eighth-century Spain. The trajectory by which ideas that challenged rabbinic authority came to flourish in Islamic Spain as a result of the tolerant climate that facilitated their transmission is an object of focus, as is the reverberation of Karaism in the late medieval Jewish communities which came under Christian control during the Reconquest. Particular emphasis is placed on works that played key roles in documenting the transmission of Karaite doctrines to late medieval Spain, including Benjamin of Tudela's *Itinerary* and Abraham ibn Daud's *The Book of Tradition*, as well as on the dissemination of these doctrines during early modern times by *conversos*, descendants of forced converts from Judaism to Christianity. The "travel" of these doctrines from Spain to the places where *conversos* reunited in exile, in particular the community in seventeenth-century Amsterdam that included Baruch Spinoza, is ultimately understood to form a key component in shaping Spinoza's anti-Rabbinism in his *Theological-Political Treatise*.

Keywords: *conversos*, Karaism, Sadducees, Baruch Spinoza, Benjamin of Tudela

AS A CONSEQUENCE of the late medieval decimation of Iberian Jewry, sectarian ideas that received currency within Spain for centuries resurfaced in communities formed in the Sephardic diaspora. The seeds of this sectarianism were sown in the wake of the eighth-century Islamic conquest of Christian Iberia. During the following two hundred years, Muslim hegemony in Al-Andalus produced the political stability that fuelled economic prosperity and a flourishing culture in which exposure to Middle Eastern schools of thought encouraged Jewish defiance of traditional religious authority. The legacy of this cross-cultural contact created a lasting impact in Karaism, according to which Rabbinic Judaism lacked the antiquity, and thus the authority, of the Old Testament.

Rather than physical movement from one place to another, the present study focuses on the travel and spread of religious concepts. My point of departure is the arrival to Spain of Karaism and the ensuing rabbinic reaction that perceived it as a continuation of a sectarian threat that had persisted since biblical times. The dissemination of this notion, grounded in a conflation of Karaites with Sadducees, would contribute to the inception of the Sephardic diaspora and would resurface again within the intellectual climate of the European nations where exiled Jews and *conversos*, descendants of Jews who had been forcibly baptized, escaped from the Inquisition. From the incursion into Spain of Jewish sectarianism to seventeenth-century Amsterdam, where the most important community of Iberian Jews formed in exile, a link can be established between the medieval tendency to denounce Karaism in anachronistic terms and the redirection of this sentiment in the most thorough attempt to undermine the Oral and Mosaic traditions, the *Theological-Political Treatise* of Baruch Spinoza (1632–1677).[1]

In a supplementary note (Annotation 25) added in the years after the publication in 1670 of his *Theological-Political Treatise*, Spinoza, the most renowned and influential thinker to emanate from the Sephardic community of Amsterdam, makes his only reference to the "opinion" of "Rabbi Abraham ben David," the Arabic form of the Cordovan historian and philosopher Abraham ibn Daud (ca.1110–ca. 1180).[2] The source of Ibn Daud's "opinion" regarding the antiquity of the Jewish canon is Ibn Daud's *The Book of Tradition*, which was written in 1160–1161.[3] With his chronicle of Rabbinic Judaism, Ibn Daud produced the most important medieval work against Jewish sectarianism and an ardent defence of an uninterrupted rabbinic tradition since biblical times.

The Book of Tradition was written at a crucial historical juncture in the evolution of Spanish Jewry, when Karaism had spread to Iberia from the Middle East. The popularization of Karaism is observed by Benjamin of Tudela, whose *Itinerary* documents his travels through the Middle East between 1169 and 1171. Tudela records the presence of Karaites within Jewish communities that were in proximity to centres of Islamic culture, including those of Cyprus, in the Holy Land in Askelon, where around "200 Rabbanite Jews dwell [...] [and] also about forty Karaites," and in Damascus.[4] He also observes that Jews are not permitted to reside within Constantinople, although both Rabbinites and Karaites inhabit a ghettoized area:

> No Jews live in the city, for they have been placed behind an inlet of the sea. An arm of the sea of Marmora shuts them in on the one side, and they are unable to go out except by way of the sea, when they want to do business with the

---

[1] Benedict de Spinoza, *Theological-Political Treatise*, ed. Jonathan Israel, trans. Michael Silverthorne and Jonathan Israel (Cambridge: Cambridge University Press, 2007).

[2] Spinoza, *Theological-Political Treatise*, 269.

[3] Abraham ibn Daud, *The Book of Tradition*, intro. and trans. Gerson D. Cohen (Philadelphia: Jewish Publication Society of America, 1967).

[4] Benjamin of Tudela, *The Itinerary of Benjamin of Tudela*, trans. Nathan Adler (Malibu: Joseph Simon, 1987). Tudela's references to Karaites can be found on the following pages: Cyprus (75), Askelon (88–89), and Damascus (91).

inhabitants. In the Jewish quarter are about 2,000 Rabbinite Jews and about 500 Karaites, and a fence divides them.[5]

In the cosmopolitan centres of Constantinople and Damascus, as well as in remote corners of the Mediterranean such as Askelon, Karaism was nurtured by Islamic ideologies such the primacy lent to sacred writings (in conjunction with logical analogy) in determining spiritual law by Hanafites, followers of the eighth-century legal scholar Abu Nu'man Thabit Abu Hanifah.[6] The defiant character of Karaism has also been linked to contact with Islamic scholars in Babylonia who encouraged independent investigation of ambiguous passages in sacred texts.[7]

The east–west transmission of Karaism to all corners of the Mediterranean was completed with Islamic military conquests during the seventh and eighth centuries. As a result of the tolerant nature of Islamic hegemony in Al-Andalus, which achieved caliphal status in 929, ideologies arriving from the East informed cross-cultural dialogues in literary, scientific and religious spheres, including the evolution of Jewish sectarianism. At the zenith of the Cordovan caliphate, two of the most renowned intellectuals, Ibn Hazm (994–1064) and Samuel ibn Nagrela (993–ca. 1056), detected the fruits of this dialogue in Spain. According to the Muslim historian and theologian Ibn Hazm, Karaism had acquired a following among Jews on the frontier between an emergent Castile and a region that had been long held by Muslims:

> The Ananites are the adherents of Anan, descendant of David, of the tribe of Judah whom the Jews call Karaites and heretics. Their teaching forbids the transgression of the laws of the Torah and what is enjoined in the books of the prophets, peace be on them. However, the doctrines of the rabbis, whom they regard as falsifiers, they reject outright. This sect inhabits Iraq, Egypt, and Syria. Within Spain they live in Toledo and Talavera.[8]

Ibn Nagrela, a contemporary Jewish theologian, also noticed the foothold gained by Karaism on the border between Islamic lands and those controlled by Christians (the latter called Edom by Nagrela) and the division among Jews this movement created: "there was never any sectarian practice among them [...] except in a number of villages near the land of Edom. These people are reported to have secret sectarian leanings, but they deny this."[9]

Ibn Hazm and Ibn Nagrela identify the presence in Spain of a sect that took shape in eighth-century Babylonia, within the orbit of a rabbinic authoritative tradition whose

---

5 Benjamin of Tudela, *Itinerary*, 72.

6 On the influence of Islamic ideologies on Karaism, see Kaufmann Kohler, "Karaites and Karaism," *The Jewish Encyclopedia*, vol. 7 (New York: Ktav, 1906), 438–47, at 438–39.

7 Salo Wittmayer Baron, *A Social and Religious History of the Jews*, vol. 5, 2nd ed. (New York: Columbia University Press, 1957), 212–13.

8 The English translation of Ibn Hazm is by Gerson D. Cohen in his introduction to Abraham ibn Daud's *The Book of Tradition*, xlvi.

9 The English translation of Ibn Nagrela is by Gerson Cohen (Daud, *The Book of Tradition*, xlvii).

influence had been expanding since late antiquity. After the destruction of the Second Temple in 70 CE, Jewish spiritual authority was transferred from a centralized polity governed by Mosaic Law to centres where generation after generation of scholars interpreted the Old Testament as the Oral Law, which was reputed by Rabbinites to be contemporary to (and thus of the same authority) as the Law given to Moses. The allusions made by Ibn Hazm and Ibn Nagrela reveal a cross-cultural awareness of a revival of this polemic in the figure of Anan ben David (ca. 715–ca. 795), who gained a following among Babylonian anti-Rabbinites from various sects that became Karaism. As its growth was fuelled by contact with Muslim scholars and theologians working to develop doctrines that questioned orthodoxy, anti-Rabbinites "unite[d] under its aegis the chief opposition to the central controls administered by exilarchs and academies in the name of the Talmud."[10]

The opposition to rabbinic authority around which Karaism formed is evident in the earliest known account of Anan's activities by Natronay bar Hilay (ca. 795–ca. 865), the ninth-century *Gaon*, or chief sage, of the Babylonian Jewish academy in Sura. The account is found in the *Seder Rav 'Amram Gaon bar Sheshna*, which was the first Jewish prayer book and which was widely used throughout Europe.[11] According to Natronay's rabbinite assessment, Karaites are collectively categorized as "heretics, mockers, and despisers of the words of our Rabbis."[12] The attention paid by Natronay in *Seder Rav 'Amram Gaon bar Sheshna* and in response to denouncing Karaism reveals that the movement had concretized while acquiring more followers, as such renewing the process that had led to the formation of the Sadducees during the time of the Second Temple (516 BCE–70 CE). In some of the earliest observations on the Sadducees, the Romano-Jewish historian Flavius Josephus (37 CE–ca. 100 CE) notes in *The Antiquities of the Jews* that their origins are ancient.[13] Prior to that, in *The Jewish War*, he revealed that Sadducees were a discordant sect: "but Sadducees, even towards each other, show a more disagreeable spirit, and in their relations with men like themselves they are as harsh as they might be to foreigners."[14] While Josephus does not go into great detail, the anti-Rabbinism among those who came together under the rubric of Sadducees is evident in the few lines he devotes to them in *The Jewish War*: "The Sadducees, the second order, deny Fate altogether and hold that God is incapable of either committing sin or seeing it; they say

---

10 Baron, *A Social and Religious History of the Jews*, 230.

11 Rav Amram Gaon Bar Sheshna, *Seder Rav 'Amram Gaon bar Sheshna* (Jerusalem: Mekhon, 2013).

12 The English quotation from the *Seder Rav 'Amram Gaon bar Sheshna* is by Martin A. Cohen, "Anan ben David and Karaite Origins," *The Jewish Quarterly Review*, n.s., 68 (1978): 129–45 at 135. On Natronay, see Marina Rustow, "Karaites Real and Imagined: Three Cases of Jewish Heresy," *Past and Present* 197 (2007): 35–74, at 36–38.

13 Flavius Josephus, *The Antiquities of the Jews*, trans. William Whiston, bk. 18, chap. 1, para. 2: "The Jews had for a great while had three sects of philosophy peculiar to themselves; the sect of the Essens, and the sect of the Sadducees, and the third sort of opinions was that of those called Pharisees," www.gutenberg.org/files/2848/2848-h/2848-h.htm#link182HCH0001.

14 Flavius Josephus, *The Jewish War*, intro. and trans. G. A. Williamson (Harlow: Penguin, 1970), 130.

that men are free to choose between good and evil, and each individual must decide which he will follow."[15] In "act[ing] as they please," the discordant Sadducees are united in their rejection of rabbinic authority. As Josephus explains in *The Antiquities of the Jews*, Sadducees, in opposition to Pharisees, centred this rejection on the grounds that rabbinic traditions lacked historical documentation:

> The Pharisees have delivered to the people a great many observances by succession from their fathers, which are not written in the laws of Moses; and for that reason it is that the Sadducees reject them, and say that we are to esteem those observances to be obligatory which are in the written word, but are not to observe what are derived from the tradition of our forefathers.[16]

In the same manner that Sadducees channelled the anti-Rabbinism of diverse sects, this animus was later reactivated by Karaites through merging discordant groups in Babylonia.[17] Karaite preachers and scholars, including Benjamin Nahawandi (fl. ninth century) in Babylonia and Cid Abu'l-Taras (fl. eleventh century) in Castile, worked to popularize resistance to Rabbinic Judaism, which eventually met by opposition. Rather than engage in an intra-communal dialogue regarding Karaite doctrines, including ideas espoused by Nahawandi (who continued Anan's work of consolidating Karaism) that actually brought the sect closer to the Talmud, swift retribution from Christian authorities was sought.[18] Against a heresy that could not be extinguished, anti-Karaite persecution organized by the Spanish rabbinate and influential Jews at court was successful in securing royal decrees in 1178 and 1232 that prohibited Karaism.[19]

The anti-Rabbinism common to Sadducees and Karaites caused the two groups to be conflated as Rabbinites reacted to the core issue of the polemic, as Gerson Cohen explains: "Since Sadduceeism had been defined in Rabbinic literature as a system acknowledging the validity of only the written Torah, medieval Jews generally designated Karaites by 'sectarian' and 'Sadducee' almost interchangeably."[20] The tendency to confuse Sadducees and Karaites is a by-product of Ibn Daud's ignorance of contemporary Karaism in *The Book of Tradition*, in which he criticizes the views presented in only one Karaite text.[21] Ibn Daud's claim that Karaites "never did anything of benefit for Israel,

---

15 Josephus, *The Jewish War*, 130.

16 Flavius Josephus, *The Antiquities of the Jews*, bk. 13, chap. 10, para. 6.

17 On the difficulties associated with this process, see Baron, *A Social and Religious History of the Jews*, 230–32.

18 On the approximation of Nahawandi's ideas to Talmudic law, see Kohler, "Karaites and Karaism," 438–39.

19 On this period in anti-Karaite persecution, see Carlos Sáinz de la Maza, "Alfonso de Valladolic y los caraítas: sobre el aprovechamiento de los textos históricos en la literatura antijudía del siglo XIV," *El Olivo* 14 (1990): 15–32, at 19–21.

20 Daud, *The Book of Tradition*, xxxviii.

21 This text is an unidentified commentary on the Pentateuch by the eleventh century Karaite scholar Jeshua ben Judah, who is also known as Abu'l-Faraj (Daud, *The Book of Tradition*, 99–101).

nor produced a book demonstrating the cogency of the Torah or work of general knowledge or even a single poem, hymn or verse of consolation"[22] reflects, as Gerson Cohen explains, the fact that Ibn Daud was not familiar with the many Karaite texts that were available, and his insistence in the biblical origins of the Karaite sect indicates, as Gerson Cohen asserts, that "[t]o Ibn Daud they were all of a piece—heretics, Sadducees."[23]

Ibn Daud sacrifices historical accuracy to achieve his main goal of establishing the continuity of Rabbinic Judaism, and it may be said that he is motivated more by a desire to put a quick end to what he perceived as a long-standing threat than an attempt to engage in a polemic concerning particular Karaite doctrines. The popularity of Karaism is greatly diminished by Ibn Daud, who claims that the quasi-epic figure of Joseph ben Ferrizuel all but eliminated its presence in Castile, and that, after its resurgence, it was again suppressed. While these suppressions did occur, Ibn Daud's insistence in "the shear meagerness" of the number of Karaites appears to contradict Tudela's revelation that Karaism had extended westward to Iberia.[24] Moreover, Ibn Daud provides an anachronistic account of the birth of the Karaite movement in Spain immediately after situating the sect in ancient Israel:

> When the Jews used to celebrate the festival of Tabernacles on the Mount of Olives, they would encamp on the mountain in groups and greet each other warmly. The heretics would encamp before them like two little flocks of goats. Then the rabbis would take out a scroll of the Torah and pronounce a ban on the heretics right to their faces, while the latter remained silent like dumb dogs.

> Among those [heretics] living in the Holy Land there was *al-Sheikh* Abu'l-Faraj, may his bones be committed to hell. It happened that a certain fool from Castile, named Cid Abu'l-Taras, went over there and met the wicked *al-Sheikh* Abu'l-Faraj, who seduced him into heresy. Under the guidance of the latter, Abu'l-Taras composed a work animated by seduction and perversion, which he introduced into Castile and [by means of which] he led many astray. When Abu'l-Taras passed on to hell, he was survived by his accursed wife, whom [his adherents] used to address as *al-Mu allima* and on whom they relied for authoritative tradition. They would ask each other what *Mu allima*'s usage was, and they would follow suit. [This went on] until the rise to power of the Nasi R. Joseph b. Ferrizuel, surnamed Cidellus, who suppressed them even beyond their former lowly state. He drove them out of all the strongholds of Castile except for one, which he granted them, since he did not want to put them to death (inasmuch as capital punishment is not administered at the present time). However, after his death, the heretics erupted until the reign of King Don Alfonso son of Raimund, king of kings, the *Emperador*. In his reign there rose nesiim who pursued the ways of their fathers and suppressed the heretics [again].[25]

---

22 Daud, *The Book of Tradition*, 99–100.

23 Daud, *The Book of Tradition*, xlix–l.

24 Daud, *The Book of Tradition*, 92.

25 Daud, *The Book of Tradition*, 94–95.

In spite of his assertion, with respect to the number of Karaites in Spain, that "[i]ndeed, they are dwindling steadily," Ibn Daud describes an east-to-west transmission of Kariasm, the "heresy" he mentions, whose eleventh-century resurgence fuelled sectarianism in Spain, as detected by Ibn Hazm and Ibn Nagrela.[26]

For Ibn Daud the true problem was the continuity of a sectarian challenge to authority since the biblical period, which enlisted it as a threat with profound implications for the survival of Judaism. The magnitude of this threat is elucidated by Gerson Cohen:

> The tracing of the roots of medieval sectarianism to the schisms and heresies of the Second Temple had additional implications, particularly in the context in which the origin of heresy was narrated [...]. [T]he history of the Jews in the days of the Second Temple [...] constituted one long and progressive series of incidents leading to the destruction of the Temple [...]. Ibn Daud found this picture perfectly appropriate to his needs [...] he described the calamities that befell the Jews as consequences of the intemperate and irresponsible [...] defiance of the Rabbinic sages, and thus the calamities of Jewish history could all be traced to defiance of Rabbinic discipline.[27]

The divisive consequences of currents of thought that challenged spiritual hegemony would have been clearly evident to Ibn Daud, who was born a few decades after the fundamentalist Almoravid conquest of Al-Andalus, and who witnessed the twelfth-century rise of Almohad reformism.

In a manner that foreshadows the introduction to *Mishneh Torah* by his younger contemporary, Moses Maimonides (1138–1204), Ibn Daud presents an ambitious objective in his prologue, in which he expresses the same discontent as Maimonides with respect to widespread ignorance of the Oral Law:[28]

> The purpose of this Book of Tradition is to provide students with the evidence that all the teachings of our rabbis of blessed memory, namely, the sages of the Mishna and the Talmud, have been transmitted: each great sage and righteous man having received them from a great sage and righteous man, each head of an academy and his school having received them from the head of an academy and his school, as far back as the men of the Great Assembly, who received them from the prophets, of blessed memory all. Never did the sages of the Talmud, and certainly not the sages of the Mishna, teach anything, however trivial, of their own invention, except for the enactments which were made by universal agreement in order to make a hedge about the Torah.

> Now should anyone infected with heresy attempt to mislead you, saying: "It is because the rabbis differed on a number of issues that I doubt their words," you

---

26 Daud, *The Book of Tradition*, 99.

27 Daud, *The Book of Tradition*, xxxix.

28 Cf. (Moises) Maimonides, *Mishneh Torah*, ed. and trans. Moses Hyamson, vol. 1 (Jerusalem: Boys Town, 1965), 4b.

should retort bluntly and inform him that he is "a rebel against the decision of the court"; and that our rabbis of blessed memory never differed with respect to a commandment in principle, but only with respect to its details; for they had heard the principle from their teachers, but had not inquired as to its details, since they had not waited upon their masters sufficiently.[29]

Ibn Daud (like Maimonides) is openly disenchanted with contemporary Jewish spirituality, and this disenchantment is understood by taking into consideration Ibn Daud's depiction of anti-Jewish persecution after the arrival to Al-Andalus of Islamic fundamentalism:

The rebels against the Berber kingdom had crossed the sea to Spain, and after having wiped out every remnant of Jews from Tangiers to al-Mahdiya [...]. They tried to do the same thing in all of the cities of the Ishmaelite kingdom in Spain [...]. When the Jews had heard the report that the rebels were advancing upon them to drive them away from the Lord, God of Israel, those who feared the Lord's word fled for their lives [...]. Some were taken captive by the Christians, to whom they willingly indentured themselves on condition that they be rescued from Muslim territory. Others fled on foot, naked and barefoot.[30]

The "rebels against the Berber kingdom" were Almohad forces, who initiated a movement to convert the Jews to Islam. Anti-Jewish persecution after centuries of co-existence repeated events that had placed Iberian Jewry into peril prior to the arrival of Muslim forces, which conquered a Visigothic monarchy that had mandated the conversion of Jews to Christianity during the 600s.[31]

The consternation caused by the perceived role of Karaism in deteriorating Jewish spirituality by undermining its authoritative base, which could make Jews vulnerable to conversionist efforts, is evident in Ibn Daud's contention that Karaites are "rebel[lious]" and in Maimonides' claim that "[t]he wisdom of our wise men has disappeared," and both respond by defending the foundation of Rabbinic Judaism, which is the "Great Assembly" to which Ibn Daud refers above.[32] While for Sadducees and Karaites the inability to historically document the Great Assembly made the Rabbinic tradition baseless, for Rabbinites the belief that it took place served as a direct tie between the prophets of the Old Testament and the earliest Rabbinic scholars whose historical identities are known. During the period when this synod is traditionally thought to have existed, from the fifth century BCE until the third century CE, the Great Assembly was comprised of 120 individuals, including Ezra, the prophet who established it, and later sages such as Simeon the Righteous, and established many Jewish conventions and doctrines in addition to setting the Jewish biblical canon.

---

29 Daud, *The Book of Tradition*, 3.

30 Daud, *The Book of Tradition*, 97.

31 On Visigothic anti-Jewish persecution, see James Parkes, *The Conflict of the Church and the Synagogue* (London: Soncino, 1934), 345–70.

32 Daud, *The Book of Tradition*, 3; Maimonides, *Mishneh Torah*, 4b.

The crucial role of Ezra, a biblical figure who is thought to have organized the Great Assembly and served as its first high priest, is an essential point for both Maimonides and Ibn Daud.[33] Maimonides presents this concept in direct terms, as historical fact:

> Ezra and his court received it [the Oral Law] from Baruch and his court. The members of Ezra's court are called 'The Men of the Great Synagogue.' They were Haggai, Zechariah, Malachai, Daniel, Hanniah, Mishael and Azaria, Nehemiah, the son of Hachaliah, Modechai, Zerubel and many other sages, numbering altogether one hundred and twenty elders. The last of them was Simon the Just, who is included among the hundred and twenty. He received the Oral Law from all of them and was a high priest after Ezra.[34]

While Ibn Daud does not allude to the prophet Ezra directly among the early members of the Great Assembly, his inclusion in that body is implied in Ibn Daud's depiction of the birth of the Karaite threat during the second generation of the Great Assembly:

> Then the people were divided in two: half of the people followed Simeon the Righteous and his pupil Antigonus and their school in accordance with what they had received from Ezra and the prophets; and the [other] half followed Sanballat and his sons-in-law. They offered burnt-offerings and peace-offerings outside the house of the Lord and enacted statutes and ordinances as they devised out of their own heart. In this temple Manasseh son of Joshua son of Jehozadak served as priest, and Zadok, with his colleague Boethus, assumed leadership. This was the genesis of the heresy.[35]

Ezra's importance as a patriarch of Rabbinism is a concept that Ibn Daud and Maimonides emphasize for a common motive, namely, that of his role as perhaps the most important figure in the transmission and preservation of the Oral Law in the face of growing sectarianism.

The success of Ibn Daud in enlisting Karaites as heretics contributed to mounting anti-Judaism in Spain that ultimately lead to the forced conversion to Christianity of a sizeable part of Spanish Jewry and the expulsion of all remaining Jews in 1492. A direct connection can be postulated between Ibn Daud's conflation of Sadducees and Karaites and the perpetuation of this notion by Abner de Burgos (ca. 1270–ca. 1347), a Jewish theologian who converted to Christianity and became a renowned anti-Jewish polemicist whose most significant work was an anti-Jewish dialogue that was originally composed in Hebrew before being translated into Castilian in the fourteenth century as *Mostrador de justicia*.[36] Abner reveals early on that one of his principal motives for composing

33 For an assessment of the debate over this issue, see Reuven Chaim (Rudolph) Klein, "Was Ezra a High Priest?," *Jewish Bible Quarterly* 41 (2013): 181–86.

34 Maimonides, *Mishneh Torah*, 1b–2a.

35 Daud, *The Book of Tradition*, 17–18.

36 Abner of Burgos (Alfonso de Valladolid), *Mostrador de justicia*, ed. Walter Mettman, 2 vols. (Opladen: Westdeutscher, 1994–96).

Mostrador is to loosen the grip of Rabbinic authority: "los más de los judios creen en los dichos de ssus ssabios del Talmud, e muy pocos sson dellos que ossan yr contra aquellos sabios. Por ende enfforçarsse-a la nuestra rrazon contra ellos quando nos aduremos prueuas contra ellos de los sus grandes ssabios abtenticos e onrrados entrellos."[37] In his assessment of *Mostrador*, Ryan Szpiech observes that Abner's depiction of sectarianism touches on a broader historical context that enlists Rabbinic persecution of Karaites as part of a "strategy [...] to awaken in his reader a real sense of uncertainty and concern over the state of the Jewish community in Christian Castile and to present himself as one who can help unify and defend tradition."[38]

Szpiech's conception of Abner's view is more fully understood in the context of the traditional conflation of Sadducees and Karaites as anti-Rabbinites. Abner groups all anti-Rabbinites as heretics and points out that the expression of their beliefs is suppressed and that they are denied the truth by rabbinic oppression, which in turn in the source of his anti-Rabbinism:

> Como que diz que el ereje judio, el que despreçia en lo que tienen rresçebido los judios de ssus anteçessores [...] tal omne como éste non puede auer endereçamiento por ninguna rrazon quel rrazonassen los otros judios, despues que desdennan e ponen dubda en sus opiniones rresçebidas dellos e que niega[n] las opiniones entendidas, las que podrian endereçar e ssoltar ssus dubhas. E por esto sson fallados en los judios muchos omnes que niegan el ssu Talmud dellos.[39]

> [It is said that the heretical Jew rejects what they have received from their elders [...] such a man cannot be set straight by any reasoning that his fellow Jews offer him, because they refute and doubt any received opinions and they repudiate those learned opinions which could contribute to setting him in the right course and dissipate his doubts. And for this reason, one can find among the Jews many men who deny their own Talmud.]

Abner appears to inherit from Ibn Daud the tendency toward anachronistic accounts of historical anti-Rabbinism. Like Ibn Daud, Abner depicts Sadducees as a continuation of a biblical tradition and Sadducees, rather than Karaites, inhabit the Castilian towns of Carrión de los Condes and Burgos.[40]

Abner's anti-Rabbinite platform became an integral component of *Fortalitium fidei contra Judaeos*, which was completed in 1460 by the Franciscan monk Alonso de Espina,

---

37 "Most of the Jews believe in the sayings of their Talmud wise men and very few of them dare to go against those wise men. Therefore, our arguments to convert them will be strengthened when we are able to furnish proofs to go against the said wise men, so honored among them." Abner, *Mostrador de justicia*, 1:43.

38 Ryan Szpiech, *Conversion and Narrative: Reading and Religious Authority in Medieval Polemic* (Philadelphia: University of Pennsylvania Press, 2012), 159.

39 Abner, *Mostrador de justicia*, 2:419.

40 Abner, *Mostrador de justicia*, 2:422.

to whom, as Henry Lea posits, "may be ascribed a large share in hastening the development of organized [anti-Jewish and anti-*converso*] persecution in Spain."[41] *Fortalitium* was the first text to propose that the monarchy support popular anti-Judaism, which had been mounting since the late fourteenth century, by expelling from Spain all Jews who would not convert to Catholicism, and by establishing an inquisition in order to eradicate heresy among *conversos*, who descended from hundreds of thousands of Jews forcibly baptized during a period lasting from the outbreak in 1391 of violent pogroms throughout Spain to 1412–1416, when renewed anti-Judaism produced a second wave of conversions.[42] Perhaps the most distinguishing feature of *converso* history is that conversion did not produce harmony among neophytes and those whose ancestors had been Christians for centuries. Instead, a discriminatory socio-religious hierarchy developed between the former, known as *conversos* or New Christians, and the latter, an Old Christian population of some seven to nine million individuals who acquired a sense of spiritual superiority because they were free of Jewish stock. Much has been written on why this situation occurred. In addition to the fact that the number of conversions was unprecedented, the nature of the conversions themselves, which were conducted *en masse* and which were not accompanied by instruction in Christian practices, ensured that many became insincere neophytes and continued to practise Jewish rituals in secret, a phenomenon known as crypto-Judaism. At the same time, some *conversos*, such as Christian theologians such as Alonso de Cartagena (1384–1456), became what appear to be sincere Christians.

The knowledge that crypto-Judaism existed became a dominant social preoccupation in Spain, and the result was the creation of a lower order of Christians who were perceived as inferior, whether this perception was based in reality or on the mere awareness that Jewish rituals were being performed in private. Medieval anti-Judaism fuelled anti-*converso* sentiment and Lea's assessment of the influence of *Fortalitium* reveals one of many occasions on which Spanish clergymen, at times *conversos* themselves as in the case of Abner, took advantage of a popular animus in order to perpetuate anti-Jewish and anti-*converso* persecution. Espina continues this tradition by giving a clerical voice to popular anti-Jewish libels, during the course of which he names a lost treatise by Abner as a primary source, although it is apparent, as Sáinz de la Maza has ascertained, that Abner's *Mostrador* was also a significant influence on *Fortalitium*.[43] In particular, as

---

41 Alonso de Espina, *Fortalitium fidei contra Judaeos* (Lyon, 1511); Henry C. Lea, *A History of the Inquisition in Spain*, vol. 1 (New York: Macmillan, 1906), 148–49.

42 Although Benjamin Netanyahu (*The Marranos of Spain: From the Late Fourteenth to the Early Sixteenth Century* (New York: American Academy for Jewish Research, 1966), 235–45) and Norman Roth (*Conversos, Inquisition, and the Expulsion of the Jews from Spain* (Madison: University of Wisconsin Press, 1995), 332) speculate that the number of *conversos* was much higher, scholars accept more conservative estimates such as Antonio Domínguez Ortiz's theory that there were 225,000 *conversos* in Spain around the time of the expulsion of 1492 (*Los judeoconversos en la España moderna* (Madrid: Mapfre, 1992), 43).

43 This lost treatise is Abner's, *Libro de las batallas de Dios* (Sáinz de la Maza, "Alfonso de Valladolic y los caraítas," 30).

part of his invective against Jewish sectarianism Espina perpetuates the conflated notion of Sadducees and Karaites inherited from Abner, which in turn perpetuates the same notion employed earlier by Ibn Daud. For Espina, both Karaites and Sadducees are biblical sects, and Espina also evokes the Castilian Kabblist Moses de León (1250–1305) as his source for asserting that Sadducees can be found Burgos and Carrión de los Condes.[44] With respect to the impact of Espina's *Fortalitium*, while his objectives were not realized during his lifetime, as confessor to Enrique IV of Castile (r. 1454–1474) Espina was able to convince the king in 1461 to request a papal bull to authorize a Castilian inquisition, which foreshadowed the process by which anti-*converso* persecution became institutionalized when Pope Sixtus IV granted such a bull to Queen Isabel of Castile (r. 1474–1504) in 1478.

After the inception of the Inquisition in 1480 and the dispersion of Sephardic Jewry after the expulsion of 1492 from Spain, and five years later from Portugal where many Jews had fled, a Sephardic diaspora, including expelled Jews and fleeing ex-*conversos*, resulted in the creation of exiled communities throughout Europe and the Mediterranean. The most prosperous and the most intellectually important of these communities formed in the 1590s in Amsterdam, where ex-*conversos* emigrated in order to practise Judaism openly in Reformation Holland. The tolerant atmosphere, evidenced by legislation such as the doctrine of freedom of conscience that formed part of the Union of Utrecht of 1579 (thus bringing into existence a Dutch republic that lasted until 1795) attracted Spinoza's forebears, who may have come from northern Spain before arriving in the Netherlands from Portugal.[45] Whereas Jews and ex-*conversos* who returned to Judaism encountered restrictive legislation in seventeenth-century France and were forced to live in ghettos in Rome and Venice, Amsterdam's Sephardic Jews reached new levels of prosperity in the most important European commercial centre of the period (commonly referred to as the seventeenth-century Dutch Golden Age), and they supported a flourishing rabbinic culture in which Spinoza received his early intellectual formation.

Sephardic culture was disseminated with the Sephardic diaspora, and Spinoza had access to a wide range of Hebrew works that he might have read after receiving a thorough education in Hebrew at the Talmud Torah school in Amsterdam, where he was educated until at least the fourth grade (typically completed by the age of fourteen), by which time he would have studied the Old Testament as well as rabbinic commentaries.[46] Whether or not Spinoza was ever a student of Saul Levi Morteira (ca. 1596–1660), who was trained in Venice and became the chief rabbi and Talmudic authority (and teacher of Talmud at Talmud Torah) during over four decades to some 1,500 descendants of ex-*conversos*, Spinoza would have undoubtedly been exposed to the anti-Karaite rabbinic view in Morteira's weekly sermons in the synagogue. Some of Morteira's critical

---

44 Sáinz de la Maza, "Alfonso de Valladolic y los caraítas," 31.

45 For the most comprehensive biography of Spinoza, see Stephen Nadler, *Spinoza: A Life* (Cambridge: Cambridge University Press, 1999). The possibility that Spinoza's ancestors lived in Spain before migrating to Portugal is examined by Lewis Brown, *Blesséd Spinoza: A Biography of the Philosopher* (New York: Macmillan, 1932), 3–18.

46 On Spinoza's education at Talmud Torah, see Nadler, *Spinoza*, 61–65.

references to Karaites have been identified by Marc Saperstein, including one from a sermon delivered during the 1640s that may have contributed to Spinoza's pejorative depiction of them. According to Morteira:

> There are three categories of those who arise against the divine Torah at various times. The first are those who deny the divinity of the Torah. The second are those who accept the divinity of the Torah but who claim that their religion is superior to ours. The third are those who accept our religion but who deny one part of it. Now the first are the philosophers; the second are the new religions, such as the Christians and Ishmaelites. The third are such as the Karaites and Boethusians.[47]

In listing Karaites with Boethusians, a sect from late Antiquity "closely related to, if not a development of, the Sadduccees," Morteira perpetuates the medieval conflation of medieval and late ancient heresy, which he would have learned during his rabbinic training in Venice.[48] It is instructive to note that Morteira's conception of non-believers in "the divinity of the Torah"—which would naturally include acceptance of the doctrine that the Oral Law was received from God simultaneously to the Mosaic Law—situates philosophers on a plane with other enemies of the rabbinic tradition, at attitude that may have encouraged Spinoza to question spiritual authority on his own terms.

While Spinoza was living within Amsterdam's community of ex-*conversos* in the process of returning to Rabbinic Judaism, an opposing view of Karaites became popular among Christian intellectuals. Classic Sephardic texts became available to Sephardim and *conversos* in exile because of the surge in Jewish and Christian presses that published these texts to appeal to a wide readership that not only included those with Sephardic ancestries but also many Protestants (and some Catholics) who participated in the sixteenth-century European revival of Hebraism. Upon learning Latin and entering non-Jewish cultural spheres such as his meetings with Collegiants that begun during the 1650s, Spinoza would have learned of the interest in Karaism among Hebraists. As Richard Popkin explains, influential polemicists such as the Scottish Calvinist John Dury (1596–1680) considered Karaites to be "pure Jews" and equated them with Protestants in their fight for freedom from the oppression of Catholics (who are equated to Pharisees).[49] Within academic circles, with which he was also familiar, Spinoza was no doubt aware of the important place reserved for Karaism among Dutch

---

47 Marc Saperstein, *Exile in Amsterdam* (Cincinnati: Hebrew Union College Press, 2005), 213. The translation of Morteira's sermon into English is by Saperstein.

48 Leopold J. Greenberg, "Boethusians," *The Jewish Encyclopedia*, vol. 3 (New York: Ktav, 1906), 284–85, at 284.

49 Richard H. Popkin, "Les Caraites et l'Empancipation des Juifs," *Dix-Huitième Siècle* 13 (1981): 137–47; "The Lost Tribes, the Caraites and the English Millenarians," *Journal of Jewish Studies* 37 (1986): 213–27. As Daniel Lasker explains: "Since Karaites did not follow standard rabbinic Jewish practices, and eschewed the Talmud, which the Christians attached as blasphemous and heretical, they were seen as following a purer form of Judaism. For Protestants in particular, Karaism was considered a Protestant form of Judaism as compared to Phariseeism (Rabbanism),

Christian Hebraists such as Levinus Warner (ca. 1618–1665) and the German Hebraist Johannes Rittangel (1606–1652), who visited Karaite communities in Eastern Europe before spending time in Amsterdam during the early 1640s.[50]

Dury, Warner and Rittangel exemplified a positive perception of Karaites that contrasted with the medieval rabbinic view. Perhaps in reaction to the newfound reverence for Karaism among Christian Hebraists, Spinoza was inspired to criticize the medieval perception of Karaites by the vision he had acquired during his Hebrew formation as a continuation of the heresy of the Sadducees. While ignoring contemporary reevaluations of the sect, Spinoza reveals the influence of the traditional conflation of Sadducees and Karaites in his *Theological-Political Treatise*. During his discussion of the antiquity of the Old Testament in chapter 10 ("Where the remaining books of the Old Testament are examined in the same manner as the earlier ones"), Spinoza asserts that, with regard to the prophets: "these books were composed long after Judas Maccabeus restored worship in the Temple, and the reason why they were written was that spurious books of Daniel, Ezra and Esther were being published at that time by certain malcontents, who were doubtless of the sect of the Sadducees."[51] In chapter 12 ("On the true original text of the divine law, and why Holy Scripture is so called, and why it is called the word of God, and a demonstration that, in so far as it contains the word of God, it has come down to us uncorrupted"), Spinoza classifies Sadducees as "infants" for their dependence on written texts:

> To the early Jews, religion was handed down in writing as law, evidently because in those times they were looked on as if they were infants. Later, however, Moses (Deuteronomy 30.6) and Jeremiah (31.33) proclaimed to them that a time would come when God would inscribe his law in their hearts. It was therefore appropriate for the Jews alone, and especially for the Sadducees, in their time, to fight for the law written upon tablets, but it is not at all appropriate for those who have the law inscribed on their minds.[52]

The fact that Spinoza never mentions Karaites directly is misleading. His knowledge of Sadducees, whom he names on five occasions in his *Theological-Political Treatise*, is limited, and it is based on part on what was written about Karaites during the Middle Ages as in Ibn Daud's *The Book of Tradition*. The division Spinoza creates between Pharisees and Sadducees is drawn along the same lines that inspired rabbinic oppression of Karaism. This concept is clear in the aforementioned Annotation 25, in which Spinoza elaborates on his conclusion in chapter 10 that "no canon of sacred books ever existed before the time of the Maccabees":[53]

---

which they deemed to be Catholic" (Daniel J. Lasker, "Karaism and Christian Hebraism," *Renaissance Quarterly* 59 (2006): 1089–116, at 1096).

50 On Warner and the Dutch Christian Hebraist interest in Karaism, see Yosef Kaplan, " 'Karaites' in the Early Eighteenth Century," *An Alternative Path to Modernity* (Leiden: Brill, 2000), 234–79.

51 Spinoza, *Theological-Political Treatise*, 149–50.

52 Spinoza, *Theological-Political Treatise*, 163.

53 Spinoza, *Theological-Political Treatise*, 153.

The so-called "Great Synagogue" did not begin until the conquest of Asia by the Macedonians. The opinion of Maimonides, Rabbi Abraham ben David and others that the presidents of this council were Ezra, Daniel, Nehemiah, Haggai, Zechariah and so on, is a ridiculous fiction, and rests on no other foundation than Rabbinical tradition, which insists that the Persian empire lasted a mere thirty-four years. This is the only way they can argue that the decrees of this Great Synagogue or Synod which was composed solely of Pharisees were accepted by the prophets, who had received them from God himself and handed them on to posterity by word of mouth not in writing. The Pharisees [i.e., the rabbis] may persist in believing these things with their usual obstinacy; but experts, who know the reasons for councils and synods and who are also aware of the controversies between the Pharisees and the Sadducees will readily be able too infer the reasons why this Great Synagogue or Council was called. It is certain in any case that no prophet participated in this Council, and that the decrees of the Pharisees which they call traditions, received their authority from this Council.[54]

Here Spinoza reveals that Ibn Daud was an important source for the *Theological-Political Treatise* by enlisting specifically as "ridiculous fiction" the first two chapters of Ibn Daud's *The Book of Tradition*, in which Ezra, Daniel, Nehemiah, Haggai, and Zechariah are situated within a line of rabbinic authority whose legitimacy is uninterrupted since biblical times. Ibn Daud displays in his epilogue his confidence that he has demonstrated the antiquity of "the written Torah as well as the oral Torah"[55]—with "oral Torah" referring to what would later be called rabbinic Judaism—to the detriment of anti-Rabbinites (to whom Ibn Daud refers collectively as Sadducees):

Now that we have completed the history of tradition we will recount the history of the kings of Israel during the days of the Second Temple, in order to refute the Sadducees, who claim that all of the consolatory passages in the books of the prophets were fulfilled for Israel in the days of the Second Temple.[56]

Spinoza's source is, in fact, one in which the history of Karaism is fabricated to the benefit of Rabbinism, both of which Spinoza endeavours to undermine.

This exploration into the impact of medieval Sephardic culture on Spinoza prior to his excommunication in 1656 suggests that medieval Hebrew texts exerted a strong influence on the formation of his ideas. With regard to the reception of one of the longest-standing Jewish sectarian movements by Spinoza, which is repeatedly depicted in terms concretized by Ibn Daud, it may be concluded from Spinoza's comments that his interest in anti-Rabbinism contradicted a Christian Hebraist view that he undoubtedly knew well. For Spinoza, the long-standing tradition of heresy, whether Saduceeism or Karaism, is, like Phariseeism, exemplary of what he in essence perceives as the "ridiculous fiction" of both the Talmud and Mosaic Law.

---

54 Spinoza, *Theological-Political Treatise*, 269–70.

55 Daud, *The Book of Tradition*, 9.

56 Daud, *The Book of Tradition*, 103.

In a broader context, the present study illustrates that textual discourse evoking the travel of an idea, just as travel narratives, as Montserrat Pierra asserts in the Introduction to this volume, "provide us with a privileged *locus* of investigation of issues of multiculturalism". With respect to the present textual analysis, religious discord may be understood as springing from "multiculturalism," and the involvement of an Islamic dimension reveals what Piera identifies as "the pivotal role that a common maritime and mercantile *ethos* had in the forging of interactions between several supposedly inimical traditions". As I point out above, the toleration practised in Al-Andalus was the inspiration for cross-cultural dialogues, and the travel from east to west, or intellectual development, of the Jewish sectarianism fuelled by these dialogues is an illustration of what this collection of essays endeavours to demonstrate, that is, a "remapping" of the impact of pre-Renaissance east–west cross-cultural interaction.

Chapter 10

PIETY AND PIRACY: THE REPATRIATION OF THE ARM OF ST. FRANCIS XAVIER

MARIA DEL PILAR RYAN

ABSTRACT

A 1695 epigram described the threats that pirates posed to the fleet that was returning the arm of St. Francis Xavier to Europe from the Far East, via Goa, India. Through the epigram, we catch a glimpse of the functional agreements and practices between military men, merchants, and missionaries during the age of exploration. This essay examines the testimony about relics in counter-Reformation canonization proceedings, how sacred objects were protected from pirates in the Mediterranean Sea and Atlantic and Indian Oceans, the role the ship's chaplain played in this specific defensive mission, and whether the rhetoric about the threat of pirates paralleled the rhetoric about the danger of Protestants.

Keywords: Cross-cultural engagements, cultural translations, pirates, relics, canonization, missions, Saint Francis Xavier, Jesuits

IN 1695, AN Italian Jesuit published a book, *Tria Fortium David, Hoc Est Jesu Christi*. In it, Antonio Barone included an epigram describing the threats that pirates posed to the fleet that was returning the arm of St. Francis Xavier to Europe from Goa, India.[1] The voyage of the relic had occurred eight decades earlier, between 1617 and 1618, and neither the beautification documents of 1619 nor the canonization documents of 1622 emphasized the dangers of pirates when they discuss the translation of the saint's bones. The epigram itself is quite short: fourteen lines celebrating the sanctified victory of Francis Xavier's mortal remains over the barbarous threat of infidels during transit from the Indies.

As Peter Burke has argued, most "students of the saints have assumed that they are witnesses to the age in which they lived. For a historian of mentalities, however, they

---

1 Antonio Barone, S. J., *Trias Fortium David, Hoc Est Jesu Christi* (Naples, 1695). A copy of this book can be found at the Burns Library at Boston College, along with an impressive collection of Xaveriana. The full text of the epigram is at the end of this essay.

have to be treated as witnesses to the age in which they were canonised."[2] Through Barone's epigram, St. Francis Xavier also serves as a witness to the decades after his canonization, as the age of exploration was entering its third century. The epigram serves as yet another reminder of the divisive forces of war and religion, an idea that is not restricted to the seventeenth century.[3] Through this epigram, we catch a glimpse of the functional agreements and practices that developed between military men, merchants, and missionaries during the age. An examination of the journey of Xavier's body reveals how relics were imagined in a post-Trent mind, and how the rhetoric about the threat of pirates to Xavier's relics paralleled the rhetoric about the danger of Protestantism and Protestant states to Roman Christendom and Catholic states.

The life and death of Francis Xavier made him among the most notable counter-Reformation saints of the Roman church.[4] Xavier, from an aristocratic family that could trace its pedigree back to Carolingian times, was educated at Xavier Castle before going to university in Paris, where he met Ignatius Loyola and the other men who would form the Society of Jesus.[5] On April 7, 1541, his thirty-fifth birthday, Xavier set sail from Lisbon for India, having accepted the call to spread the Gospel message to all corners of the world. Thirteen months later, he arrived in Goa. He spent roughly a decade in India and the Far East, eventually being smuggled, with two companions, down the Cochin Chinese coast and north into the China Sea by a man named Avan, who was known as *o Ladrão*, the "Thief" or "Pirate."[6] Francis Xavier died on December 3, 1552 in Sancian, an island "literally [...] in sight of China."[7] Now referred to as Shangchuan Island, and not far from the mouth of the Pearl River, Xavier had been isolated there by traders who feared being caught breaking the Chinese laws against foreigners entering the Ming Empire. These laws had been enacted to curb the piracy that was rampant along the coast.[8]

Upon his death, Francis Xavier was placed in a coffin filled with lime, to ensure quick decomposition, and lowered into a grave on Sancian Island. Two and a half months later,

---

2 Peter Burke, "How to Be a Counter-Reformation Saint," in *Religion and Society in Early Modern Europe 1500–1800*, ed. Kaspar von Greyerz (London: Allen & Unwin, 1984), 48.

3 For a discussion of an oceanic *longue durée*, see Fernand Braudel, *The Mediterranean and the Mediterranean World in the Age of Philip II*, vol. 1, trans. Siân Reynolds (New York: Harper & Row, 1972).

4 In addition to Burke, "How to Be a Counter-Reformation Saint," see R. Po-chia Hsia, *The World of Catholic Renewal, 1540–1770* (Cambridge: Cambridge University Press, 1998), 122–37.

5 The Society of Jesus was approved as an order in 1540, but Xavier was not present in Rome at the time. Rita Haub, "Francis Xavier: An Introductory Life," *Archivum Historicum Societatis Iesu* 71 (2002): 223.

6 Jean Lacouture, *Jesuits: A Multibiography*, trans. Jeremy Leggatt, (Washington, DC: Counterpoint, 1995), 98.

7 William L. Hornsby, "A Visit to the Tomb of S. Francis Xavier at Sancian," *Woodstock Letters* 31 (1902): 402.

8 Liam Matthew Brockey, *Journey to the East: The Jesuit Mission to China, 1579–1724* (Cambridge, MA: Belknap, 2007), 28–29.

the grave was opened in preparation for the trip to Malacca, and "the body was as fresh as on the day of its burial."[9] Indeed, some Catholics of earlier generations heard hagiographic stories of a shovel hitting the body and causing blood to flow from it.[10] Xavier was buried again in Malacca a month later, but not in the presence of Jesuits. Without supervision, the body was removed from the coffin and laid in the grave, "which was filled with earth [and] rudely pressed down so that it bruised his face in several places."[11] In August 1553, five months later, Jesuits opened the grave and discovered the mistreatment of the body as they placed the "still uncorrupt," but newly bruised, body in a new coffin to begin its journey to Goa.[12] This journey began three and a half months after this latest disinterment, and went into port in Cochin two months after that. The body was viewed there by a Jesuit, and its incorruptibility was related in a message to Goa.[13] A month after that, on March 15, 1554, fifteen months after the saint's death in Sancian, the body of Francis Xavier arrived in Goa, travelled in a procession from the harbour to the College of St. Paul, and was exhibited for three days.[14]

The *Annales* School, among others, holds that religion and the economy have confronted each other from the very beginning of civilization, and that as they travelled the road together, "one of the partners—the economy—became more pressing, made more demands."[15] In the Mediterranean, the Red Sea, and the Indian Ocean, mercantile relationships were the avenues, and had priority, for the determination of intellectual or cultural exchanges. The seventeenth-century recorders of Xavier's journey would have disagreed, and emphatically stated that they "must not omit mentioning the after-fate of the vessel which brought the precious deposit from Malacca to Goa. As soon as the crew had disembarked and all the cargo landed, she opened and sunk, as if unwilling to be employed in any less glorious office."[16]

---

9 *Documenta Indica* III, 74–75, 654–67, cited in J. Humbert, "Transfer of the Body of the Body of St. Francis Xavier Before 1659," *Indian Ecclesiastical Studies* 5 (1966): 24. The city-state of Malacca is a former Portuguese colony in the south of modern Malaysia.

10 Humbert, "Transfer of the Body of St. Francis Xavier Before 1659," 24.

11 *Doc. Ind.* III, 122, 671–73, cited in Humbert, "Transfer of the Body of St. Francis Xavier Before 1659," 25. This bruising would have occurred three or four months after his death.

12 *Doc. Ind.* III, 76, 672–73, cited in Humbert, "Transfer of the Body of St. Francis Xavier Before 1659," 25.

13 *Doc. Ind.* III, 251, cited in Humbert, "Transfer of the Body of St. Francis Xavier Before 1659," 52.

14 The body was then placed on the epistle side of the high altar, until the church was demolished in 1560 for a rebuilding project. In the years after this, the coffin was kept in the Father Rector's room, in the room of the Master of Novices, on the altar of St. Thomas in the newly rebuilt church, and in the sacristy. *Doc. Ind.* III, 76–77, 176, cited in Humbert, "Transfer of the Body of St. Francis Xavier Before 1659," 26.

15 Fernand Braudel, *The Wheels of Commerce*, trans. Sian Reynolds (New York: Harper & Row, 1982), 559.

16 D. Bartoli and J. P. Maffei, *The Life of St. Francis Xavier, Apostle of the Indies and Japan*, ed. and trans. F. W. Faber (New York: P. O'Shea, 1889), 541. Italian Daniello Bartoli (1608–1685) entered

This record of Xavier's journey, originally published in 1653, reflects the hardening of lines in the counter-Reformation. In many ways, the writing of one sixteenth-century Jesuit who explained that an incorrupt body was a sign of a life untainted by corruption seems more modern than the biography a century later.[17] In this earlier document, written in 1555 by a member of Ignatius Loyola's inner circle, the elements of recognition and reception of the saints reflected a dynamic between Roman church and believer; this dynamic created avenues to reconcile faith and reason. In accepting the report that a sweet odour surrounding the body of a saint indicated that his or her life and work remain sanctified, a believer could actively acknowledge the legitimacy of the cult of saints. The later historiography created a more static relationship between church and believer, consistent with the counter-Reformation, but denying the believer earlier ways to reconcile faith and scientific advancements. Rather than the earlier invitation to consider how the physical and spiritual intersect in the sanctified body and life of a saint, the later writers challenge the reader to believe that a ship threw itself to the bottom of the sea after the saint left its care.

The Scientific Revolution and Enlightenment required modern minds to acknowledge that an incorrupt body did not always mean an intact one. The politics of canonization reflect these changes. The bodies or body parts of saints on display in Rome today, for instance, do not closely resemble people merely sleeping or limbs recently severed. While they may be in remarkable condition considering their age, it is difficult to argue that these relics remain scientifically incorrupt with the passage of time. The earlier statement from 1555 foreshadows the influential role the Society of Jesus would have in the Roman church during the Scientific Revolution. This statement from the earliest years of the religious order reconciles faith with the yet-unnamed biological and environmental sciences, stressing the sanctified incorruptibility of the life, as much as the body. Confessional wars shaped the efforts to canonize Xavier in the late sixteenth century, and confessional wars then shaped the historicizing of the canonization process.

The 1653 version of Xavier's journey remained the primary one for over two centuries. It is a version of dramatic detail. With regard to Xavier's body, the authors state that "it was juridically inspected from time to time by the doctors and prelates of Goa, who always found it, not only incorrupt, but flexible, and of its natural color."[18] On two occasions, someone "applied their finger to the wound in the shoulder caused by the rough usage when he was interred at Malacca, and both times the finger produced a flow of blood and water. Fresh blood likewise flowed from his neck and stained the brocade pillow which supported his head,—once when the body was pressed into a coffin somewhat too short" for the tall saint.[19]

---

the Society of Jesus in 1623, the year after the canonization of Ignatius Loyola and Francis Xavier. He, with Maffei, published the biography of Xavier in 1653. Bartoli served for decades as the official historiographer of the Society of Jesus.

17 Juan Polanco, secretary to Ignatius Loyola, to Miguel Torres, Rome, November 21, 1555, *Doc. Ind.* III, 303–4, cited in Maria Cristina Osswald, "The Iconography and Cult of Francis Xavier, 1552–1640," *Archivum Historicum Societatis Iesu* 71 (2002): 264.

18 Bartoli, Maffei, and Faber, *The Life of St. Francis Xavier*, 541.

19 Bartoli, Maffei, and Faber, *The Life of St. Francis Xavier*, 541. Punctuation is from the original.

"It is true," this seventeenth-century version continues, "the saint seems not to have been pleased at the amputation of his arm: at least, from thenceforward the body, though still uncorrupt, did not retain the same florid complexion, or look altogether so handsome, as before."[20] The amputation of Xavier's arm was on orders from the general of the Society of Jesus. At the end of the sixteenth century, Father Claudio Acquaviva sought to unify the Jesuits under interior and exterior models. It was a time of crisis in the order, especially between Spanish and Italian Jesuits, and the pope who had just died had allowed for, and even encouraged, this division, in order to assert the papacy's supremacy.[21] After this pope's death, a general congregation of the Society of Jesus was held in 1593–1594, and the initiative to canonize Ignatius Loyola and Francis Xavier was part of the plan for the order's repair.[22]

This canonization initiative for Loyola and Xavier reveals the fluid identities of the two men and of identity itself in the early modern age. Both saints were Spanish, but were not of Spain in their service to the church of Rome. Ignatius Loyola had left Spain for Rome under a cloud of suspicion from the Spanish Inquisition, and never returned to his homeland.[23] Francis Xavier had been sent to the Indies by the king of Portugal, and never returned to Europe. When the Portuguese king heard of Xavier's death in the Far East, he petitioned the pope directly for Xavier's canonization, bypassing the Society of Jesus, the order that Xavier co-founded.

By the early seventeenth century, Superior General Acquaviva's effort to re-unify the Society of Jesus through the canonization of Ignatius Loyola and Francis Xavier gained momentum, and the return of Xavier's relics to Rome was a part of this initiative. In 1607, some Jesuits petitioned General Acquaviva to authorize transfer of Xavier's head to Rome: "Repeated requests resulted in the separation of the right arm. That, apparently, satisfied them."[24] Therefore, in 1614, Rome sent a request to the Jesuits in Goa to send this relic;[25] on November 3, 1616, "by order of the Fr. General and in order to hasten the process of canonization, the right arm of Xavier's body was amputated, to be sent to Rome."[26]

---

20 Bartoli, Maffei, and Faber, *The Life of St. Francis Xavier*, 542.

21 See John W. Padberg, S. J., Martin D. O'Keefe, S. J., and John L. McCarthy, S. J., eds. and trans., *For Matters of Greater Moment: The First Thirty Jesuit General Congregations* (St. Louis: Institute of Jesuit Sources, 1994), 10–13. The first three superior generals of the Society of Jesus were Spanish, as were the members who had been in Ignatius Loyola's inner circle. Acquaviva, the fifth superior general, was Italian. The fourth superior general had been from an area of the Low Countries that is now in modern-day Belgium.

22 Humbert, "Transfer of the Body of St. Francis Xavier Before 1659," 26.

23 Maria del Pilar Ryan, *El Jesuita Secreto: San Francisco de Borja* (Valencia: Biblioteca Valenciana, 2008), 177–78.

24 Georg Schurhammer, "Ausztige aus den Briefen der Jesuitengenerale an die Obern in Indien (1549-163 *sic*)," *AHS/ 22* (1953), 161, cited in Osswald, "The Iconography and Cult of Francis Xavier," 265.

25 *Monumenta Xaveriana*, vol. 2, Monumenta Historica Societatis Iesu 144 (Madrid: Typis Gabrielis Lopez del Homo, 1912), Letter 16, November 25, 1614.

26 Humbert, "Transfer of the Body of St. Francis Xavier Before 1659," 26.

The importance of Xavier and the other first Jesuits to the order can be seen in a decree of the General Congregation of 1615–1616 that stated that "Relics of the saints entrusted to our houses and colleges are not to be given away by any of Ours. Whoever does otherwise is to be punished, in accord with the judgment of the superior general."[27] And relics of Francis Xavier were, indeed, entrusted to Jesuit houses and colleges. Xavier's body has been with the Goan Jesuits since 1554; his lower right arm is at the Gesù in Rome. His upper right arm was divided among the Jesuit colleges of Malacca, Macao, and Cochin in 1619; the extra bit of the elbow went to Macao. Father General Muzio Vitelleschi, who had been elected in this latest general congregation to succeed Acquaviva, had all of Xavier's internal organs removed from the corpse and distributed to Jesuit settlements worldwide; "smaller portions of the arm were sent to Meehl in Cologne; an ear went to Lisbon, half a toe, to his birthplace, pieces of breastbone, to Tokyo, and a tooth to Oporto."[28]

While the Society of Jesus expected obedience from its members regarding the relics of the saints, and threatened punishment, the laity invented ways to be piously disobedient. From the official historiography from the seventeenth century, we learn that the body of Francis Xavier had been displayed for veneration. The feet of the saint were uncovered, so that the faithful could kiss them as devotion prompted: "an old woman indiscreetly pious, anxious to have some relic of the saint, instead of kissing the foot, bit a piece off one of the toes; but she could not conceal her theft, for the flowing blood immediately betrayed her."[29] The narrator concluded about Francis Xavier, "Thus was our Lord pleased to honor a virginal body which had been so instrumental to his glory."[30]

The virginity of Francis Xavier was in contrast to the conversion story of Ignatius Loyola, in which a battlefield injury turned him from a life of debauchery. Among the symbols associated with Xavier is the lily, indicating purity and virginity. In the early modern era, the emergence of the individual, masculinity, and authority were all contested topics between Catholic and Protestant states and institutions. Members of the Society of Jesus, arguably the first modern religious order for men, were charged by

---

27 Congregation 7, November 5, 1615–January 26, 1616, Decree 28 (In MS, d.37). John W. Padberg, S. J., "The Third General Congregation: April 12–June 16, 1573," in *The Mercurian Project: Forming Jesuit Culture, 1573–1580*, ed. Thomas M. McCoog, S. J. (Rome: Institutum Historicum Societatis Iesu, 2004), 261.

28 Georg Schurhammer, *Gesammelte Studien*, IV, 345–48, cited in Osswald, "The Iconography and Cult of Francis Xavier," 263–64. While the rest of the list of relic destinations is from Schurhammer, the information about the elbow in Macao comes from Naresh Fernandes, "Tomb Raider," *Transition* 84 (2000): 4–19. Jeffrey Chipps Smith notes that "Queen Marie de' Medici, who resided in Cologne in 1642 during her exile from France, presented Francis Xavier's rosary and his arm bone" to the rector; *Sensuous Worship: Jesuits and the Art of the Early Catholic Reformation in Germany* (Princeton: Princeton University Press, 2002),182.

29 Bartoli, Maffei, and Faber, *The Life of St. Francis Xavier*, 541.

30 Bartoli, Maffei, and Faber, *The Life of St. Francis Xavier*, 541–42.

Ignatius to be "contemplatives in action."[31] It does not have a branch for women, and its emphasis on intellectual, moral and spiritual strength served as an answer to Protestant attacks concerning the masculinity and moral rectitude of the Roman church and its clergy.[32] As one scholar has observed about the Ignatian tradition of the examination of conscience, "Jesuit piety itself is decidedly aggressive; Ignatius did not call it spiritual exercise for nothing."[33]

The idea of the sea as a gendered area has attracted much recent scholarship, and women were most often seen as interlopers in these areas of "masculine security."[34] Francis Xavier, when alive, embarked on a voyage with merchants, other missionaries, and military men. Francis Xavier's role in this world of rough and intrepid men, bringing the word of God to a hostile audience, reconciled the oft-conflicted ideas of virginity and masculinity.[35] The expression of masculinity was amplified by the threat of pirates to his relics returning to Europe.

The mid-seventeenth-century narrative of Xavier's journey by the Jesuit historiographer is a tale of strength and show of force. After Xavier's right arm was severed, on November 3, 1616, it "was transferred the year following from India to Portugal, when,

---

31 Kevin F. Burke, S. J., and Eileen Burke-Sullivan, *The Ignatian Tradition*, Spirituality in History Series (Collegeville: Liturgical Press, 2009), 25. The phrase was first used in print by Jerónimo Nadal, commissary for Ignatius Loyola.

32 For a more detailed examination of masculinity in the early Jesuit order, see Jodi Bilinkoff, "*A Christian and a Gentleman:* Sanctity and Masculine Honor in Pedro de Ribadeneyra's *Life of Francis Borgia,*" in *Francisco de Borja y su Tiempo: Política, religión y cultura en la Edad Moderna,* ed. Enrique García Hernán and Maria del Pilar Ryan (Valencia: Albatros Ediciones—Institutum Historicum Societatis Iesu, 2011), 447–55.

33 Elizabeth Rhodes, "Join the Jesuits, See the World: Early Modern Women in Spain and the Society of Jesus," in *The Jesuits II: Cultures, Sciences, and the Arts, 1540–1773,* ed. John W. O'Malley, S. J., et al. (Toronto: University of Toronto Press, 2006), 35. The Spiritual Exercises are a compilation of guided meditations, prayers, and contemplative practices developed by Ignatius Loyola.

34 Charles Kindleberger, *Mariners and Markets* (Hemel Hempstead: Harvester Wheatsheaf, 1992), 61–62. Another, and more recent, work is John C. Appleby, *Women and English Piracy, 1540–1720: Partners and Victims of Crime* (Rochester: Boydell, 2013).

35 St. Francis Xavier was declared Patron of the Orient in 1748, and was declared Co-Patron of All Missions in 1927, with St. Therese of Lisieux (1873–1897). Therese had been canonized in 1925. After a trip to Rome with her father, she entered a French cloister at the age of fifteen and remained a cloistered nun until her death at age twenty-four. She was named a co-patron of missions because she prayed for priests on missions and became an "apostle to apostles" through her prayers and correspondence. For insight about the very different roles and role-modelling of these co-patrons, see the seminal work on post-feminist theology, see Grace Jantzen, *Power, Gender, and Christian Mysticism* (Cambridge: Cambridge University Press, 1995). For a recent study of St. Therese, see Thomas R. Nevin, *The Last Years of Saint Therese: Darkness and Doubt, 1895–1897* (New York: Oxford University Press, 2013). For a concise biography of St. Therese, known as the Little Flower, see Owen F. Cumming, *Prophets, Guardians, and Saints: Shapers of Modern Catholic History* (New York: Paulist Press, 2007).

had not God watched over it, Rome would not have *gained* what Goa had *lost*."[36] The relic had been accompanied to Europe by Father Sebastian Gonzales, the procurator of the Jesuit province. The priest and the relic were "in a small vessel, quite unfitted to contend in battle against the large ships of war usually met with on those seas: they found themselves pursued by a Dutch man-of-war,—a double enemy, on the score of religion as well as nationality."[37]

By the seventeenth century, the Red Sea, where the pirates threatened the relic, the Atlantic Ocean, the Indian Ocean and the Mediterranean had all become sites of exchange. But while the medieval Mediterranean was its own integrated system,[38] early modern waters were not. In the age of empire, the oceans were the means and representation of an emerging global network, "not because they were assumed to be empty, vast, and lawless, but because globally circulating processes were transforming them into a different kind of bounded legal space."[39] There were networks that operated independently of the state, and as with physical spaces, there were attempts to create monopolies on sacred spaces for both spiritual and political purposes. As a consequence, the relationships between military men, merchants, and missionaries were a balance of friction and familiarity.

The relationship between space and ecclesiology for the West has its roots in the Middle Ages. The Roman church came to identify itself in terms of physical space and to define itself in territorial and material, more than philosophical, terms.[40] The age of exploration and the confessional age were informed by these changes to the church's expression of identity; in turn, exploration and confessionalization informed changes to the church. And empires never exist in isolation. By nature, they create along their boundaries zones of contact between ethnic, religious, political, and cultural groups that, in turn, challenge the concepts of centre and periphery through various forms of encounter.

The form of encounter those on the vessel containing Xavier's relic feared was a violent one: "The Portuguese gave themselves up for lost: crowd what sail they would, there was no chance of outstripping their formidable adversary; still less had they to hope from an engagement, having neither soldiers nor ammunition."[41] But they had a holy weapon:

> All at once they remembered that they had the arm of St. Francis Xavier to defend them, and they entreated Father Gonzales to hold it up in sight of the

---

36 Bartoli, Maffei, and Faber, *The Life of St. Francis Xavier*, 542. Emphasis in the original.

37 Bartoli, Maffei, and Faber, *The Life of St. Francis Xavier*, 542. Punctuation is from the original.

38 See S. D. Goitein, "The Unity of the Mediterranean World in the 'Middle' Middle Ages," *Studia Islamica* 12 (1960): 29–42.

39 Lauren Benton, "Legal Spaces of Empire: Piracy and the Origins of Ocean Regionalism," *Comparative Studies in Society and History* 47 (2005): 724.

40 See Dominique Iogna-Prat, *La Maison Dieu. Une Histoire Monumentale de l'Église Au Moyen Age, v. 800–v. 1200* (Paris: Le Seuil, 2006).

41 Bartoli, Maffei, and Faber, *The Life of St. Francis Xavier*, 542.

enemy, whilst they on their knees would supplicate the saint to have pity—if not on them, who were unworthy of it—at least on so precious a portion of himself, and not permit it to fall into such impious hands. The Dutch were already so close upon them that they could hear their shouts of exultation in anticipation of an easy victory. Gonzales made his appearance, bearing the saint's arm. The crew instantly fell on their knees. The father advanced to the edge of the deck, directly facing the enemy, not invoking Xavier against them, but, crying aloud in his name, he threatened them, and forbade them to advance another yard. And assuredly it was the voice of God and of the saint, speaking through his mouth; for there stood the Dutch ship, with all her sails spread, yet as motionless as if she had been suddenly embedded in ice, the Portuguese brig in the mean time pursuing her passage to safety in Lisbon.[42]

In response, the "Dutchmen seemed stupefied, or as it were bewitched, as they witnessed the miraculous effects, the cause of which was totally unknown to them."[43] The rejection of relics as "magical trinkets" was held in common by the Protestant reform movements of the sixteenth century. As the Reformation continued, the sanctity of a saint's body was not the only contest about body. Protestants tried to create the body, especially Christ's, as transcendent, even in the sacrament of Communion. Protestants replaced the body with the Word; the altar with the pulpit. The debate about whether the events at the altar are bodily sacrifice had ramifications about the bodies of saints and about ideas of pilgrimage, both of which inform the narrative about the journey of Xavier's arm to Europe.[44]

The concept of holy people is not unique to Europe or Christianity. What does appear to be "uniquely Christian, though, is the idea that saints are not only extremely virtuous people, but also efficacious mediators with God on behalf of the living; more powerful dead than alive."[45] This, of course, was also an idea that came under fire in the Reformation, and one of the reasons that canonization processes came to a standstill during the middle decades of the sixteenth century. The voyages of commerce and missions, however, stimulated a re-framing of holiness: the "imputation of sainthood, like its converse, the imputation of heresy or witchcraft, should be seen as a process of interaction or 'negotiation' between centre and periphery, each with its own definition of the situation."[46]

And, as the confessional lines hardened, there were elements that were not going to be open for negotiation. Plague and heresy, for instance, "became connected as evils in need of eradication. In both cases, Xavier was considered an exemplary miracle worker. Thus Peter Paul Rubens's famous 'The Miracles of Saint Francis Xavier,' painted for the

---

42 Bartoli, Maffei, and Faber, *The Life of St. Francis Xavier*, 542–43.

43 Bartoli, Maffei, and Faber, *The Life of St. Francis Xavier*, 543.

44 For an analysis of the role of the body in sacrament, see Lee Palmer Wandel, *The Eucharist in the Reformation: Incarnation and Liturgy* (New York: Cambridge University Press, 2006).

45 Burke, "How to Be a Counter-Reformation Saint," 45.

46 Burke, "How to Be a Counter-Reformation Saint," 53.

Jesuit church in Antwerp, demonstrates the use of plague imagery as a metaphor for heresy."[47]

Protestants saw the use of the saints as a form of idolatry, and even the Roman church acknowledged faulty practice among the laity. One of the decrees of the Council of Trent declared, "Moreover, in the invocation of saints, the veneration of relics, and the sacred use of images, every superstition shall be removed."[48] Erasmus thought folly the practice of the veneration of saints: "So among the saints, those are most resorted to who are the most romantic and fabulous: as for instance, a poetic St. George, a St. Christopher, or a St. Barbara, shall be oftener prayed to than St. Peter, St. Paul, nay, perhaps than Christ himself."[49]

The European audience who were the consumers of the hagiography of Francis Xavier would have responded to Xavier's connection to the story of St. Christopher. The tall and strong Christopher carried pilgrims across a treacherous river, and one day carried the Christ child across. He became *Christoferens*, the bearer of Christ. Xavier carried the word of God over dangerous waters to those who had not yet received it, and protected those on the journey home.

The European audience were consumers of another image of his mission activity, an *Imago primi saeculi* of Xavier carrying an Indian, or at least a non-European, on his back. A half-century after the event allegedly occurred, Pedro Ribadeneira, a Jesuit and the first historiographer of the order, recorded a story told to him by Diego Laínez, one of the original founders of the Society of Jesus and successor to Ignatius Loyola as general of the order. Laínez said that, in 1537, "Xavier had awakened him during the night to relate the dream to him [in which Xavier] had an Indian or Ethiopian on his back, who had been so heavy that he was able to carry him only with great effort."[50] This story was recorded at a time that canonizations in the Roman church were restarting after the jarring effects of Protestant reform, and the story is an intentional display of masculinity, heroism, and service.

Although Francis Xavier carried the man in his dream over land, many of the miracles attributed to him during the canonization process, and before, involved water. As early as 1543, there was testimony to Xavier having brought back to life a child who had drowned in a well, which is one of the miracles seen in "The Miracles of Francis Xavier" by Peter Paul Rubens.[51] In 1546, in the Moluccas, in eastern modern Indonesia, Xavier allegedly lost a cross in a storm at sea and a crab delivered it to him once he was ashore. This is one of four miracles represented on the banner in St. Peter's during his canonization in 1622; a crab is often seen in Xavier's iconography. Another miracle attributed to

---

47 Paul Begheyn, "The Cult of Saint Francis Xavier in the Dutch Republic," *Archivum Historicum Societatis Jesu* 71 (2002): 311.

48 The Reverend J. Waterworth, trans., *The Canons and Decrees of the Sacred and Ecumenical Council of Trent* (London: C. Dolman, 1848), 235.

49 Desiderius Erasmus, Hans Holbein, illus., *In Praise of Folly: With Portrait, Life of Erasmus, and His Epistle* (Cambridge: Harvard University, 1922), 171.

50 Osswald, "The Iconography and Cult of Francis Xavier," 273.

51 Begheyn, "The Cult of Saint Francis Xavier in the Dutch Republic," 311.

the saint is that he converted seawater into fresh water for his shipmates while sailing from Malacca, in modern Malaysia, to China in 1552.

As the early modern world confronted how water was imagined as space, as opposed to how land was imagined as space, Francis Xavier emerged as a figure who transcended these challenges. The sailing ship is an important image associated with various episodes of his life, and figures prominently in his canonization documents. Many times "Xavier's prayers calmed storms at sea, preserved them from attacks of pirates, and generally steered the ship safely into port. Subsequent petitions [to him] for his intercession also brought miraculous salvation from emergencies at sea."[52] While early modern travellers were often suspect in issues of corruption, loyalty, and identity, Francis Xavier represented a transformative model, one whose physical passage through adversity, while alive and dead, represented a heroism and faith available through veneration to those who did not travel as well.

Francis Xavier's sainthood is a cultural indicator of early modern Europe. Like other heroes, in the argument of Peter Burke, "they reflect the values of the culture which sees them in a heroic light."[53] And heroism, and heroic sanctity, are fundamental characteristics of the post-Trent saints.[54] Even later in the seventeenth century, spiritual, political, and military heroism came together in the 1672 beatification documents of Pope Pius V and in his 1712 canonization documents. During the successful promulgation of Pope Pius V, the 1571 victory at the sea by the Catholic League over the Turks at Lepanto became an image in the Catholic consciousness, representing defeat of infidels, both Muslim and Protestant.

It was in this context that the short epigram about Francis Xavier and the pirates that opened this essay was written, as well as other testimonies about Xavier's mission. Of note are the testimonies by Fernão Mendes Pinto, the Portuguese explorer who became famous for his autobiography about his adventures in the Far East, and infamous for the outrageousness of his tales there.[55] Some of the passages of Fernão Mendes Pinto's *Perigrinations* "related to the heroic missionary, Padre Francisco, who was so much loved and esteemed by the adventurous merchants and soldiers who had the good fortune of coming near him."[56]

---

52 MHSI, Mon. Xavier., II, 707, cited in Osswald, "The Iconography and Cult of Francis Xavier," 270.

53 Burke, "How to Be a Counter-Reformation Saint," 45.

54 "Heroic" is first used to refer to exercises of virtues by Teresa of Avila, canonized with Ignatius Loyola and Francis Xavier in 1622; "heroic sanctity" is first used in the 1624 beatification documents of the third superior general of the Society of Jesus, Francis Borgia.

55 Fernão Mendes Pinto and Rebecca D. Catz, ed. and trans., *The Travels of Mendes Pinto* (Chicago: University of Chicago Press, 1989). In his twenty years of travels, Mendes Pinto was a soldier, merchant, diplomat, captive, and pirate. He was also a missionary, serving with Francis Xavier for a time as a Jesuit lay brother. He rejoined Xavier when Xavier left Japan, but returned to Portugal in 1554 with stories of the heroism and miracles of Xavier. Dissatisfied with the wealth and honour these stories brought him, Mendes Pinto abandoned the Society of Jesus in 1557.

56 Hornsby, "A Visit to the Tomb of S. Francis Xavier at Sancian," 405.

There were practical reasons for the Roman church and Catholic states to use the rhetoric of heroism in the late seventeenth century. In 1670, for example, the English government agreed to restrain its pirates in return for Spain's concession over England's conquest of Jamaica. This "crackdown in the Atlantic Ocean encouraged pirates to move into the Indian Ocean, where a large group planted itself on Madagascar and preyed on European shipping," including English vessels that they previously had been paid to leave alone.[57] Other European states during the seventeenth century's Golden Age of Pirates claimed that they could not control the actions of their subjects who happened to live outside of their own state's geographical boundaries or "beyond the line."[58] Being at sea meant having no clear space in the world, and the lines were blurred by cycles of inter-imperial war and peace. Moreover, mariners and would-be pirates had one eye always on return and the possibility, however remote, of being brought to trial for crimes on the high seas.[59]

The tensions in Europe, and those felt by Europeans outside Europe, were projected onto the widening world. In literature, especially, Protestants took interest in Christian lands like Ethiopia because these lands were never under the papal yoke. The Renaissance had stimulated a focus on the exotics of Africa and Asia; the Council of Trent strengthened these outward-looking trends, with its emphasis on missions. In action and rhetoric, the "politicization and militarization of oceanic space, as much as its globalization, distinguished European oceanic expansion from that of other seafaring peoples."[60] Pirates were both a reality and a manifestation of the tensions between the Protestants and Catholics, the Ethiopian and Roman churches, and Ethiopian Christianity and Jihadist Muslims.

The rhetoric about piracy retained these constant themes, even when the reality in time and space changed. Through the late medieval and early modern period, Europeans deplored "Mahometan tyranny" and conflated Islam and piracy as if they were one and the same, "the present terror of the world."[61] This "present terror" demonstrated the different needs for authenticity in this age; it is both captured from the past and created for the future. Antonio Barone wrote the epigram that opened this essay of the threats posed to the relic of St. Francis Xavier, and the heroic response from Naples, Barone's birthplace. The Jesuit Barone had never been to a general congregation of the Society of Jesus, and Naples was itself peripheral to the Jesuit metropolis in Rome. There was a close relationship between Jesuit efforts to evangelize and bring Christian civility to Naples and their missionary efforts in the New World and Asia.[62] Barone articulated the

---

57 Elizabeth Mancke, "Early Modern Expansion and the Politicization of Oceanic Space," *Geographical Review* 89, *Oceans Connect* (1999): 232.

58 Alan L. Karras, *Smuggling: Contraband and Corruption in World History*, Exploring World History (Lanham: Rowman & Littlefield, 2010), 24. See also Anthony Pagden, *Lords of All the World: Ideologies of Empire in Spain, Britain, and France c. 1500–c. 1800* (New Haven: Yale University Press, 1995).

59 Benton, "Legal Spaces of Empire: Piracy and the Origins of Ocean Regionalism," 707.

60 Mancke, "Early Modern Expansion and the Politicization of Oceanic Space," 226.

61 Adrian Tinniswood, *Pirates of Barbary: Corsairs, Conquests, and Captivity in the Seventeenth-Century Mediterranean* (New York: Riverhead, 2010), 99.

62 See Jennifer D. Selwyn, *A Paradise Inhabited by Devils: The Jesuits' Civilizing Mission in Early Modern Naples*, Catholic Christendom, 1300–1700 (Aldershot: Ashgate, 2004).

threats posed to the relic of St. Francis Xavier from a position, both geographically and confessionally, at the edge of waters politicized.

The Red Sea, where pirates threatened the relic of St. Francis Xavier, mimicked the early modern Mediterranean as an arena for patterns of interchange. There was extensive Ethiopian diaspora in the early modern Mediterranean. Muslims moved to Egypt for education or to Mecca, 70 kilometres inland from the Red Sea, for religious reasons. There were also pockets of Orthodox Ethiopian Christians in Jerusalem, Cairo, Cyprus, and Malta. There were small communities of Ethiopian scholars in Rome and Venice. This diaspora, as diasporas often do, hinged on pilgrimage, either religious or intellectual. In the sixteenth and early seventeenth centuries, the flow of writing was also one way. Few European missives were dispatched to the Red Sea, but there are many from Ethiopian Christians to their Mediterranean brethren, particularly addressing how to deal with Jesuit missionaries.[63]

In the early modern era the historical gaze shifts, sometimes expanding and sometimes narrowing. An element in this shift concerns the Catholic ideas of outsiders drawn into the Catholic Mediterranean from Africa as slaves, which competes with the Catholic ideas of missionaries who went to the New World or Asia, where the inhabitants remained. There is a liminality to pirates and Protestants that confronts narratives of slavery and redemption. Both privateers, their legitimacy created with letters of marque, and pirates were European outcasts who brought previously unknown seafaring expertise to the business of Barbary and Red Sea piracy. Piracy allowed these men to join a new and different social *milieu*, reneging their own culture and religion because they had been rejected by their own culture and religion.

In the mid-seventeenth century, there was an emergence of long-distance privateering and piracy to the Red Sea, in particular, from bases in the Caribbean and North America. These "ventures confirmed the breakdown of an attenuated Elizabethan pattern of enterprise, focused on Spain, which had influenced the activities of buccaneers from the 1650s to the 1680s. The intrusion of English predators [...] was part of a wider restructuring of privateering and piratical enterprise" at the end of the seventeenth century.[64] As a result of the pirate dispersal from the Caribbean, the emergence of Red Sea piracy was supported by promoters in North American ports, particularly New York, and was encouraged by the opportunities for profitable plunder in the region.[65]

The Red Sea was long, deep, and hazardous in many places for inexperienced navigators. The pirates displaced from the Caribbean and Atlantic had seafaring experience that gave them advantage in the Red Sea waters. The Red Sea supported the regular passage of pilgrims, trade in precious stones and materials, and ships laden with supplies of European money, including Spanish silver. These merchant ships were

---

63 See James De Lorenzi, "Red Sea Travelers in Mediterranean Lands: Ethiopian Scholars and Early Modern Orientalism, ca. 1500–1668," in *World-Building in the Early Modern Imagination*, ed. Allison Kavey (New York: Palgrave Macmillan, 2010), 173–200.

64 Appleby, *Women and English Piracy*, 32. For a globalized perspective, see Miles Ogborn, *Global Lives: Britain and the World, 1550–1800* (Cambridge: Cambridge University Press, 2008), 169–94.

65 Appleby, *Women and English Piracy*, 33.

normally large and well-manned, but often lacked effective ordnance. They were vulnerable to the small fleet of European pirates and privateers who "congregated at the Straits of Bab al-Mandab, a narrow exit and entry point, thus avoiding the dangers of coral reefs within the Sea itself."[66]

As concepts of space, boundaries, and identities were challenged, chaplains and missionaries urged men at sea to recognize what could best be described as a spiritual or moral genealogy. The epigram of the repatriation of Xavier's arm to Rome occurs in a historical moment when *patria* itself is challenged. The corruption of identity during oceanic travels is as big a threat to Christians as are pirates and mortal sin. A play about the life of the notorious pirate John Ward was one of the most popular of the early seventeenth century. The play's title, *A Christian Turned Turk*, reveals its plot, as well as larger questions about identity in the early modern world. What, in the age of European religious conflict, is a Christian? Of lesser importance, what is a Turk? In the play, Ward's "second-in-command Gismund answers to a request to identify the ship 'We are of the Sea', indicating that for him the pirate vessel represents an alternate political space, and that his allegiances are free from the claims of orthodox national identity."[67]

The popularity of the play challenges the audience, both contemporary and modern, to confront ideas of corruption, conversion, and renunciation. How does piracy corrupt someone enough to influence a man to convert to Islam? Does exposure to the English or to Protestants weaken a man enough to cause him to renounce the one true faith? The play portrays the Turk as a man who is strong on land but weak on the water; what are the dynamics of identity and dangers to it during travel?[68]

We return to the idea of the incorruptibility of the saint's body being about the incorruptibility of the man and his faith. In Fernão Mendes Pinto's work, Francis Xavier "is obliquely presented in the work as a warrior-priest who spurs men on to combat," and is often depicted with a sword.[69] This depiction also reflects the complementary roles of chaplain and ship's captain during the age, and the enormous burden of the missions placed on both. It was common in "sixteenth-century naval practice to devolve extraordinary responsibility upon the lone figure of the pilot; in the case of Spanish and Portuguese vessels, royal regulations gave the pilot sole charge over the ship's course."[70]

---

66 Appleby, *Women and English Piracy*, 33, citing K. N. Chaudhuri, *Trade and Civilisation in the Indian Ocean: An Economic History from the Rise of Islam to 1750* (Cambridge: Cambridge University Press, 1985), 129–31, 147–48, 156, 214; and John Ovington and Hugh George Rawlinson, eds., *A Voyage to Surat in the Year 1689* (London: Oxford University Press, 1929), 267–74.

67 Robert Daborne, *A Christian Turned Turk* (London, 1612), Scene 2, cited in Claire Jowett, *The Culture of Piracy, 1580–1630: English Literature and Seaborne Crime* (Farnham: Ashgate, 2010), 3.

68 For a strong analysis of identity in travel writing, see Julia Schleck, *Telling True Tales of Islamic Lands: Forms of Mediation in Early English Travel Writing*, Apple-Zimmerman Series in Early Modern Culture (Selinsgrove: Susquehanna University Press, 2011).

69 Fernão Mendes Pinto, *The Travels of Mendes Pinto*, ed. and trans. Rebecca D. Catz (Chicago: University of Chicago Press, 1989), 502.

70 Jonathan D. Spence, *The Memory Palace of Matteo Ricci* (New York: Viking Penguin, 1984), 69.

In the missionary world, similar responsibility was given to the chaplains on board ships. The priests would act as confessor to the captain and crew and try to convert any slaves that may have been loaded. Among the more traditional pastoral duties the Jesuits performed on board, they also celebrated feasts and other holy days: "On saints' days there would be full processions around the ships, with fathers dressed in vestments and boy acolytes holding candles, carrying relics and the host."[71] In fearful times, the chaplains would lead "the final prayerful pleas to God in front of the banners and holy relics unfurled on the upper desk before which all had knelt in prayer."[72]

In the case of Jesuit missionary Matteo Ricci, two French privateer vessels shadowed for a number of days the ship on which Ricci and other Jesuits had sailed out of Lisbon. When the privateers "sailed too close to the three large carracks of the India fleet, the carracks' captains ordered the guns run out, while the Jesuits, suffering grievously from seasickness, stood on deck, clasping their crucifixes and ready to exhort the crews into battle." The French sailed away.[73] Later, Ricci would acknowledge Xavier and "make of that faith his glory when he wrote in his *History of the Christian Expedition to the Kingdom of China* that he would never have tackled the project without crediting 'the man who first undertook it, and who by dying and leaving his remains there took possession, as it were, of this conquest.' "[74]

The Jesuits had more than otherworldly reasons for assuming these defensive postures. In the overlapping interests of military men, merchants, and missionaries, the

> loss of ships and cargo on the homeward run to Goa and Europe had important long-range effects on Jesuit finances, especially if the ships went down before reaching Portuguese-controlled Malacca, where they would have to pay massive transit dues, some of which would later reach the Jesuit missions in the form of payments remitted back to them by the crown.[75]

The interests of the Jesuits and the crown were linked.

These actions were not always in line with the Roman Church. At the Council of Trent, senior churchmen had urged penalties of suspension or even excommunication for those indulging in such trading (silk market, in this case).[76] But the missions needed to support themselves, and the arguments they used "verged on the specious: that it

---

71 *Documenta Indica*, ed. Joseph Wicki, S. J., *Monumenta missionum Societatis Jesu, Missiones Orientales*, vol. 2 (1577–1580) (Rome, 1970), 311, cited in Spence, *The Memory Palace of Matteo Ricci*, 77.

72 Bernado Gomes de Brito, *Tragic History of the Sea: 1559–1622*, ed. and trans. C. R. Boxer (Cambridge: Hakluyt Society, 1968), 68–72, cited in Spence, *The Memory Palace of Matteo Ricci*, 71.

73 *Doc. Ind.*, II, 306, 336, cited in Spence, *The Memory Palace of Matteo Ricci*, 68–69.

74 Matteo Ricci, *Histoire de l 'expeditione chretienne au royame de la Chine* (Paris: Desclee de Brouwer, 1978), cited in Lacouture and Leggatt, *Jesuits: A Multibiography*, 178.

75 Spence, *The Memory Palace of Matteo Ricci*, 178.

76 Spence, *The Memory Palace of Matteo Ricci*, 176.

could not be called trading if one did not literally *touch* the silk being shipped, or that one was not engaged in a business deal if one did not set foot in a Chinese market."[77]

The age of piracy, therefore, challenged order in a number of ways. Defining piracy and rules of the sea "became related to the question of legitimate sponsorship—indirectly important to understandings of sovereignty."[78] How significant is the separation of these colonies and missions from their metropoles? Where do the doctrine and practice diverge? For political, economic, and religious reasons, "the control of oceanic space had become not just a commercial question but part of the construction of power in the European state system."[79]

The short epigram that started this line of research and this essay asserts that the transitions and dislocations of experience occurred beyond the lifetime of Francis Xavier. In its overt declaration of heroism on the seas, there is something below the surface. It suggests that travel is the experience of distance and detachment, and that travellers observe their own time and place, as well as another's. In its reading and context, the epigram is a comment on the closing of the Middle Ages, a Roman church under siege, a post-Tridentine sanctity, and of life and death at sea, where multiple narratives and identities can exist.

The word "translation" gained widespread use in the thirteenth century to mean the transfer of the body or relics of a saint from one resting place to another, to carry it over land or sea. It is more widely understood now to turn an idea from one language to another. The function of a translation, whether of relic or word, is dependent on the experience and expectations of the target audience, who are influenced by the context and culture in which they find themselves.

In the early modern era, a time of political, intellectual, theological, and social upheaval, the translation of the relic of the arm of Francis Xavier was an act of creating order out of chaos. As Peter Brown has observed about the origins of the cult of saints and use of relics, "distances between groups and persons were overcome by gestures of grace and favor, and the dangerously long miles of the imperial communications system were overcome by a strenuously maintained ideology of unanimity and concord."[80] This was as true in the early modern world as in the late antiquity of Brown's scholarship.

In an age of confessional and imperial wars, translations—the movement of relics to people—lessened the need for pilgrimages, the movement of people to relics. In profound ways, if "relics could travel, then the distance between the believer and the place where the holy could be found ceased to be a fixed, physical distance."[81] Even within the

---

77 Spence, *The Memory Palace of Matteo Ricci*, 177.

78 Benton, "Legal Spaces of Empire: Piracy and the Origins of Ocean Regionalism," 704. See also Anne Perotin-Dumon, "The Pirate and the Emperor: Power and Law on the Seas, 1450–1850," in *The Political Economy of Merchant Empires*, ed. James D. Tracy (New York: Cambridge University Press, 1991), 196–227.

79 Mancke, "Early Modern Expansion and the Politicization of Oceanic Space," 233.

80 Peter Brown, *The Cult of the Saints: Its Rise and Function in Latin Christianity* (Chicago: University of Chicago Press, 1981), 89.

81 Brown, *The Cult of the Saints*, 89.

heroic language of the epigram, there is a utopian notion that rolls back the Reformation. The translation of the arm of the beloved, courageous, and pure Francis Xavier fulfilled the role of most relics: they "made plain, at a particular time and place, the immensity of God's mercy. They announced moments of amnesty. They brought a sense of deliverance and pardon into the present."[82] The incorruptible saint made the corrupt whole.

In early modern literature, translation was seen as something that could restore integrity to a narrative or identity where a hole was perceived. Translations can be used to examine how literary systems close or open, and whether there is a perception of self-sufficiency. Indeed, the efforts of both Francis Xavier and his immediate successors "to find a way into Guangdong Province in the second half of the sixteenth century foundered as a result of their inability to enter into a conversation with the local authorities."[83]

There were hundreds of miracles credited to Francis Xavier, and even his contemporaries wrote that many were exaggerations or inventions. A modern biographer even writes of the patron saint of missionaries that Xavier, "as usual, depended on the services of some native who had learned Portuguese. The fact that he is never known to have even attempted to hear the confession of any person in the East, except such as had a smattering of Portuguese or Spanish, is plainly indicative that he had no miraculous command of languages,"[84] which the hagiography had attributed to Xavier.

In the decade that he served as a missionary, Francis Xavier apparently was never able to perform sacramental duties in any language other than those he knew as a European aristocrat. The issues of piety and piracy that surround the repatriation of St. Francis Xavier's arm are part of a story of what was lost in translation in the early modern European efforts to conquer and save the world.

Appendix Barone's Epigram

Vel ad Indos Roma Xaverio vocanti praesto est contra Barbaros

Epigr. CLXIV

Ir ruerat, flammisque minax Badagus, armis:
Obvia nee fuerant, qui satis arma ferant.
Unus erat, sed inerme Caput, Saberus: in
Hostem At ruit: in certam nee pavet ire necem.
Christiadum sic urget Amor: quos ante sacrato
Fontis adhuc madidos tinxerat irnbre latex.
Hoc tulerit Lojola? Alio vel ab Orbe vocanti

---

82 Brown, *The Cult of the Saints*, 92.

83 Brockey, *Journey to the East*, 245. For a discussion of the language issues of the Jesuits in India, see Katharine Smith Diehl, "Review: Catholic Religious Orders in South Asia, 1500–1835," *The Journal of Asian Studies* 37 (1978): 699.

84 James Brodrick, *Saint Francis Xavier* (New York: Wicklow Press, 1952), 340.

Advolat, auxilio quo juvet ille suo.
Addit se lateri Comitem: radiisque corusco
Barbaricas subito disiicit ore manus.
Sat venisse, sat & vidissee hostemque videndo
Perculit. Haec oculis laurea quanta fuit!
Magna licet fuerit Jaus, quod sic vicit: ad Indos
At quod sic venit, gloria major erit.

Id. Epigr. CLXV

Te, Lojola, suo Tyberis dum clauderet alveo;
Alterius sensit Xavier Orbis opem.
Viventem nam multus adhuc te in vota vocabat:
Cui dexter facili Numine semper a des.
Fert cunctis Saberus opem; Lojola, sed ipsi
Qui sert Sabero, discite, quantus erat.

[Xavier was available to be called by Rome to the Indies, against the Barbarians. Epigram 164. The new Christians [of the Indies], before they were strengthened by weapons, encountered the menacing fire of the Badagus,[85] and failed before them. Although the leader was unarmed and had no saber, he rushed in against the enemy, able to fell them as surely as a murderous quake. Christian love is compelling: Before the font [of Baptism], one can be dipped and imbued with the sacred. Why did Loyola take this [step to call Xavier to the Indies]? From another world, God flies toward the call of need, to support one of his own. He accompanies his own from their side, hand and mouth flashing rays, suddenly scattering Barbarians. Enough came and enough saw the enemy unnerved. And this is how the presence of the Truth was acclaimed! What he won was more powerful than the Caste-Jaus. He came [and brought Christianity] to the Indies, all to the greater Glory to God!]

---

85 On June 16, 1544, Francis Xavier wrote about the Badagus, an indigenous tribe overrunning the Fishery Coast of India and raiding villages, causing newly-converted Christian communities to flee inland or out to rocks on the coast, where they were accosted by pirates and other raiders.

Chapter 11

THE OTHER WOMAN
THE GEOGRAPHY OF EXCLUSION IN
THE KNIGHT OF MALTA (1618)

AMBEREEN DADABHOY

ABSTRACT

This essay explores the imperial designs depicted in Fletcher, Field, and Massinger's *The Knight of Malta*, through the discourses of gender and race, arguing that the play locates its anxieties about traffic, travel, and trade in the Mediterranean in racialized female bodies. Moreover, by examining the play's treatment of its black, Muslim, female character, Abdella, we can see how whiteness becomes a means through which social, political, and cultural belonging can be articulated.

Keywords: Gender, Travel, Race, Religion, Malta, Islam, Ottoman Empire

THE MEDITERRANEAN SEA connects the continents of Europe, Asia, and Africa, and as such it binds and cleaves distinct lands, peoples, cultures, and religions. In fact, as a geography that facilitated traffic and exchange, in goods, ideas, and people, the Mediterranean was perhaps the most important contact zone in the early modern period. Its fluid and often shifting borders circumscribed religious and imperial geographies, from Christian to Islamic, and Hapsburg to Ottoman. This fickle sea could make or mar the fortunes of all who ventured into its waters. Indeed, the many tales of Mediterranean piracy, captivity, and slavery that circulated in the early modern period expose the profits and dangers of life in this geography.[1]

Moreover, narratives of border crossing and conversion reveal similar allures and fears associated with the Mediterranean, the freedoms and dangers it offered. Like all such zones that simultaneously intermingle and demarcate ideas and identities, the Mediterranean functions in English imaginative literature of the early modern period as

---

1 See for example, Daniel Vitkus and Nabil Matar's collection of early modern travel narratives, *Piracy, Slavery, and Redemption: Barbary Captivity Narratives from Early Modern England* (New York: Columbia University Press, 2001), and Claire Jowett's edited volume *Pirates? The Politics of Plunder, 1550–1650* (Basingstoke: Palgrave Macmillan, 2006).

a site of interest and anxiety. Even though it was geographically distant from England, the middle sea, situated as it was, seemingly at the centre of the world, certainly at the centre of valuable trade routes, offered English travellers and writers a location through which they could negotiate various forms of cultural, religious, and racial differences. Such projects facilitated England's nascent imperial and growing mercantile ambitions, and created an imaginative geography on which to plot not only their anxieties about being latecomers to the markets of the Mediterranean but also imagined triumphs through which they could overcome those same deficits.

Looking at the representation of the Mediterranean in imaginative literature exposes the anxieties that it engenders because of the kinds of encounters that it facilitates. The Mediterranean contact zone puts pressure on identity. How can travellers, voyagers, and citizens of this geography preserve their identities in the face of the cultural exchanges that are inherent to borderlands? Moreover, the occupations of the Mediterranean— trade, traffic, and warfare—create opportunities for identity flux and change. This essay conceives of the theme of travel and movement in the Mediterranean in broad, expansive, and elastic ways.

The geographic position of Malta, an island that occupies a contested region in the eastern Mediterranean, elicits much anxiety in *The Knight of Malta* (1618) because the identities of its inhabitants expose the dangers of inter-religious and inter-racial contact, an obvious result of travel and the movement—voluntary and forced—of bodies in this locale.[2] The movement in bodies central, a central feature of travel, facilitates exchange in ideas and cultural understanding and even reciprocity, but such movement also necessitates the construction of stronger, less permeable and porous borders around identity and

---

2 Previous work on critical work on *The Knight of Malta* has focused on the religious and cultural threat of the Ottoman Empire or on the various meanings associated with "turning Turk." Sandra Clark has examined the "trials and ordeals of continence" and their correspondence to female chastity. Grounding her inquiry in feminist and gender criticism, Clark finds that the discourse of female chastity masks patriarchal anxiety regarding control of women's bodies and sexualities. Sandra Clark, *The Plays of Beaumont and Fletcher: Sexual Themes and Dramatic Representation* (New York: Harvester Wheatsheaf, 1994), 25. Bindu Malieckal employs a post-colonial methodology in her critique by underscoring the role of race as the play's primary discursive strategy of cultural and ideological difference. She argues that the play's insistence on the difference inherent in blackness and Islam excludes the character of the Moorish woman from any possibility of goodness, faith, and redemption, constructing "the Islamic Other" as utterly beyond the pale of civilized, Christian society. Malieckal, " 'Hell's Perfect Character' ": The Black Woman as Islamic Other in Fletcher's *The Knight of Malta*," *Essays in Arts and Sciences* 28 (1999): 54. Using religion, particularly the nexus of Protestant and Catholic Christianity and Islam, as her primary hermeneutic, Jane Hwang Degenhardt examines the figure of the Knight as redeemed in the drama through a rehabilitation of his expressly Catholic vow of chastity. Degenhardt claims that by "recuperating the Order as an exemplary body of genteel, chaste, and honorable Christian men," *The Knight of Malta* presents an "an embodied masculine ideal," which models an appropriate method for cultural and imperial triumph. Jane Hwang Degenhardt, *Islamic Conversion and Christian Resistance on the Early Modern Stage* (Edinburgh: Edinburgh University Press, 2010), 153. Other selected studies on early modern

culture. The representation of the Mediterranean in English texts exposes the processes of constructing identity along racial and religious lines.

In many ways, *The Knight of Malta* investigates the situation after we have ceased travelling and asks what happens when we have opened our borders to the foreign influence. How can we maintain our culture in the face of both internal and external difference? *The Knight of Malta* animates and problematizes the threat of "turning Turk"—with its accompanied schematic of religious affiliation and betrayal—through the modalities of gender and race. Employing the generic architecture of Romance, the play imbricates categories of difference, such as gender, race, and religion in its construction of nation and community. In this chapter, I contend that *The Knight of Malta* offers an innovative optics through which questions of encounter and traffic—a capacious mode of envisioning travel—with Muslim regimes can be framed and answered. By tracing the circulation of women in the play, I uncover the affective and symbolic roles they occupy in addition to the suspicion they engender.[3] Finally, I claim that the dramatization of the national and imperial triumph of Malta (and Christendom) over the Ottoman Empire (and Islam) is achieved through the simultaneous absorption and exclusion of radical difference. Thus, a critical reconsideration of *The Knight of Malta* subtended by the geometry of religion, race, and gender reveals the scope and limits of imperial projects in and beyond the early modern eastern Mediterranean.

Exploring the intertextual links between *The Knight of Malta* and other late sixteenth- and early seventeenth-century Mediterranean plays topically engaged with Moors and Turks highlights the interest of English dramatists in that locale and the audience's cultural fascination with multiple forms of difference. Between 1579 and 1642 nearly fifty English plays featured characters that were religiously or racially different from their English audiences, out of which at least a dozen dramatized Muslim–Christian encounter, exchange, and desire and almost all featured a Mediterranean setting.[4] From Robert Greene's *The Battle of Alcazar* (1591) to Philip Massinger's *The Renegado* (1630), a small fraction in the field of English drama incorporating such *topoi* includes Thomas Dekker's *The Fair Maid of the West* (1597), William Shakespeare's *Othello* (1604), and

---

English drama and the Mediterranean include Daniel Vitkus's *Turning Turk: English Theater and the Multicultural Mediterranean 1570–1630* (New York: Palgrave Macmillan, 2008); Jonathan Burton's *Traffic and Turning: Islam and English Drama 1579–1624* (Cranbury: Associated University Presses, 2005); Benedict Robinson's *Islam and Early Modern English Literature: The Politics of Romance from Spenser to Milton* (New York: Palgrave Macmillan, 2007); and Bernadette Andrea's *Women and Islam in Early Modern English Literature* (New York: Cambridge University Press, 2007).

3 The feminist and material methodology I employ here is indebted to Jean Howard and her article on *The Fair Maid of the West*, "An English Lass amid the Moors: Gender, Race, Sexuality and Nationality in Heywood's 'The Fair Maid of the West'," in *Women, "Race," and Writing in the Early Modem Period*, ed. Margo Hendricks and Patricia Parker (London: Routledge, 1994). My focus here is on the production of gendered whiteness and blackness within a particularly Mediterranean context, whereas Howard's argument relies on the legibility of a particularly English identity (101–14).

4 Louis Wann, "The Oriental in Elizabethan Drama," *Modern Philology* 12 (1915): 166. Burton, *Traffic and Turning*, 92.

Robert Daborne's *A Christian Turned Turk* (1612). The enthusiasm for Mediterranean plays reflects burgeoning trade with the east during the Elizabethan period, which resulted in the founding of the Levant Company (1581) and the later antagonism toward Islamic traffic underscoring Jacobean foreign policy. Investigating the mercantile and theatrical exchanges between England and the Ottoman Empire, Daniel Vitkus points out that "commercial activity was accompanied by corresponding ideological changes: the culture and literature of the time were profoundly affected by the intensified international circulation of people, goods, and texts."[5] Such nodal points of transmission both material and discursive encode the Mediterranean geography within multiple registers of signification: the Mediterranean as a site of traffic in goods and people, but also an imaginary geography where models of exchange initiate modes of subjective transformation and the Mediterranean as a surrogate arena of imperial contest, where English ambition and anxiety regarding its own quest for an empire and potential conflict with Spain can be transferred to an eastern geography replete with similar imperial and hegemonic concerns. Thus, the interpellation of the geography of the eastern Mediterranean in English drama instances a space for experimenting with both the imperial project and national subjectivity. Elizabeth's attempts at political alliance with Muslim powers found imaginative reconstruction in the danger of the other close at hand, while James's rapprochement with Spain and general disdain of Islam fostered representations of ideological and military conflicts.[6]

Before turning to the symbiotic instrumentalities of nation, gender, religion, and race as they are constructed through the prism of Muslim–Christian encounter in *The Knight of Malta*, I would like to excavate the discourses investing meaning to the geographic, political, and narrative structures of the play. The decisive historical event circumscribing the action is the failed Ottoman siege of Malta in 1565. The Order of St. John, vastly outnumbered by the forces of Sultan Süleyman the Magnificent, successfully defended, withheld, and ultimately repulsed the attack on the island. The triumph over Ottoman forces was celebrated across Europe, in Catholic and Protestant nations, as an united Christian defeat over the armies of Islam.[7] The cultural and discursive displacement of imperial aggression onto a theologically mandated conflict, reminiscent of the crusades, was facilitated by the history of the Knights of St. John, who began

---

5 Daniel Vitkus, "The Common Market of All the World: English Theater, the Global System and the Ottoman Empire in the Early Modern Period," in *Global Traffic: Discourses and Practices of Trade in English Literature and Culture from 1550–1700*, ed. Barbara Sebek and Stephen Deng (New York: Palgrave Macmillan, 2008), 27.

6 Shakespeare's *The Merchant of Venice* and *Othello* both dramatize the insider/outsider dichotomy, illustrating its danger, and ultimately advocating a policy of distance and separation. However, *Othello*, like *A Christian Turned Turk*, *The Renegado*, and *The Knight of Malta*, suggests that the threat of Islam and the Ottoman Empire can only be managed militarily.

7 Helen Vella Bonavita notes that while Reformation polemicists minimized Hapsburg contributions and the Catholicism of the Order of St. John, they still celebrated the victory over the Ottomans in Manichean, Christian–Muslim terms. "Key to Christendom: the 1565 Siege of Malta, its Histories, and their Use in Reformation Polemic," *The Sixteenth Century Journal* 33 (2002): 1021–43.

their order as protectors of the Holy Land after the First Crusade. With the defeat of the Christian armies in Jerusalem, the Order moved its base of operations to Rhodes, where they continued to plague Muslim forces—the Ottomans this time.[8] Rhodes's location in the eastern Mediterranean provided an ideal base from which the knights could disrupt Ottoman trade from Egypt. However, the Knights' engagement in acts of piracy and aggression against the empire made them obvious targets, and in 1522, fresh from his successful campaign in Belgrade, Süleyman set his sights on Rhodes. The siege of Rhodes lasted five months, after which the Knights surrendered and moved to Sicily before finally settling in Malta. The Knights' successful defeat of the Ottomans on Malta evoked tropes of religious contest and conflict echoing the affective power of the crusades. Moreover, it placed Malta in the European and, particularly, English imaginary as a "bastion" of Christian resistance to Islamic hegemony.[9] Malta's or the Knights' political structure might also have provided English writers and dramatists with a multicultural, national model for the emergent British imperial identity, for the Knights formed a transnational community united by their commitment to Christianity. Thus, as native or ethnic identities are subsumed within the cultural and religious hegemony of Christendom so, too, might multiple national identities, such as English, Scottish, and Welsh be contained under the rubric of British. Malta oscillates, then, between an exotic geography far removed from England and a simulacrum of English national and imperial subjectivity.

The rise of Ottoman hegemony in the eastern Mediterranean facilitated the discursive renewal of crusade ideology. Such a resurrection compelled a return of medieval narratives, like romance, "which emerged during and after the crusades, in an effort to narrate contacts with Islam: the fictions of chivalric romance are a response to the failure of the crusades, acts of collective cultural fantasy that seek to take imaginative possession of the long and fluctuating border between Latin Christendom and Islam."[10] A genre that "enabled new ways of thinking about identity and difference," and located itself in a border zone between cultures provides the quintessential structural model for a play like *The Knight of Malta*, which also deploys radical difference as a means through which to assert nationalistic unity and cultural superiority.[11] Crucial to this narrative project is a formulation of social, religious, and gender norms around which identity can coalesce. In fact, the construction and maintenance of identity in *The Knight of Malta* is

---

8 While many early modern writers do not make distinctions between Muslims of various regions, often identifying Arabs as Turks, I point this out in order to show how the Ottoman campaign against Rhodes manipulates the ideology of religious war to advance its national/imperial agenda. Indeed, Sultan Selim I, Süleyman's father, waged such a war on the Mamluks of Egypt, who were also Muslim. The Order of the Knights of St. John moved to Rhodes in the early fourteenth century and occupied that island until 1522. Ferdinand Braudel, *The Mediterranean: And the Mediterranean World in the Age of Philip II*, vol. 2 (New York: Harper Collins, 1973), 668–69.

9 Andrea, *Women and Islam*, 251–52.

10 Robinson, *Islam and Early Modern English Literature*, 4–5.

11 Robinson, *Islam and Early Modern English Literature*, 3.

fastened to the period's nascent nationalism, which manifests in the form of an "imagined community."[12] The normative values and identity promulgated by the play are observed in "an imagined political community" that is "limited" by the physical borders of the island and by the "deep horizontal comradeship" that characterizes the Order and the nation it mimetically represents, one that is Christian, pan-European, and masculine.[13] The limiting agents of community—geography and fraternity—are, however, problematically elastic: simultaneously including, excluding, and necessitating certain kinds of identities within the nation. As we encounter in *The Knight of Malta*, the threat to national identity obtains from undesirable yet indispensable modes of difference. The play's occlusion of how these modes of difference have come to inhabit its island setting underscores the threat contact and encounter permeating its contested geography.

Even as radical difference becomes figured as deviant and unwanted in the play, lines of desire, whether imperial, martial, material, or sexual underscore the instances European-Muslim encounter prominent in early modern English drama set in the Mediterranean. I deploy the identity marker European here rather than Christian to stress that while religious markers blanketed Moorish and Ottoman identities, collapsing distinctions between them, Europeans were increasingly identified and characterized in nationalistic terms in drama.[14] Moreover, it is through the trajectories of desire between self and other and the emerging discourse of nationalism that we can locate the constellations of difference in *The Knight of Malta*. Unlike the plays mentioned above, *The Knight of Malta*'s intervention in the English cultural obsession with the Muslim-dominated eastern Mediterranean is to construct an episteme of difference that yokes race to religion as a strategy to mitigate the threat of "turning Turk,"—the *sine qua non* of contact with Islam—in order to effect a pure, European-Christian identity, which I will expose as a fraught, uneasy, and somewhat impossible effort.

The Knight of Malta coheres around symbols of purity and fidelity: the most notable of which are women and the knighthood of the Order of St. John. The drama's narrative, thematic, and ideological commitments foreground the religious and imperial antagonism between Christianity and Islam in an attempt to endow its exemplars with their symbolic signification. The religio-military conflict between Christians (pan-European members

---

12 Benedict Anderson, *Imagined Communities: Reflections on the Origin and Spread of Nationalism* (London: Verso, 1983), 15. Anderson's thesis takes as its starting point the nationalism of the Enlightenment, which created nations by "destroying the legitimacy of the divinely-ordained, hierarchical dynastic realm" (16). Nevertheless, I believe it is possible to project the notion of "imagined communities" into the early modern period because of the disparate ways in which emerging European nations and empires were coming to a recognition of their distinctness. In terms of English drama assertion of national boundaries and intra-island unity can be traced through all of Shakespeare's history plays, most especially in the two tetralogies. We can also observe anxieties about national v. imperial identity through James I's failed attempts at unification.

13 Anderson, *Imagined Communities*, 15–16.

14 The tourney that inaugurates the action of Thomas Kyd's *Soliman and Perseda* features a cast of European and non-European characters, most of whom are identified and caricatured by and because of their nationalities.

of the Order) and Muslims ("Turks") in the eastern Mediterranean structures the binaries informing the play, emplotting an identity that falls in line with its preoccupations. Negotiating this arena of cultural competition in *The Knight of Malta* is the Moor, Abdella, an insider inhabiting the physical and cultural boundaries of the island yet a racial and religious outsider. Abdella's characterization reveals the play's investment in an epistemology of difference undergirded by its somatic and religious manifestations that signal an essential, ontological quality of otherness. Abdella's presence confirms and disturbs the valourized symbols of the play: her radical difference fashions her as a foil while her sex and the ideological and affective burden it carries aligns her with other women, proclaiming her sameness. Malta's geographic location in the contested space of the eastern Mediterranean demands the construction of a nation and identity with fixed religious, racial, and sexual boundaries, yet the circulation of women, European and other, destabilizes this effort. The play's setting is quite significant, for as Bernadette Andrea indicates Malta circulated in the European cultural imaginary as "an overdetermined geographical space," because of the Knights' success at fending off Ottoman invasion.[15] The affective meanings loaded onto the island allowed for it to be a site where anxieties about imperial traffic and conquest could comfortably be executed. Thus English fears of encounter in the eastern Mediterranean could be domesticated within the island's imaginative and protective boundaries. The diffuse threat of Islam in *The Knight of Malta* is embodied by Abdella and made visible through her attacks on women, knighthood, and marriage, the foundations of Malta's cultural security; however, because of her allusive proximity with other women, the rigid boundaries that the play attempts to fix between Christianity and Islam prove permeable.

Although much dramatic attention in *The Knight of Malta* affects concern for the menacing Ottoman threat at its sea borders, the majority of the plot unfolds through various trials of virtue on the island. The main action centres on the desirability of Oriana, the sister of the grand master of the Order of St. John, and the schemes enacted by the villainous fallen knight, Mountferrat, and his conspirators, including Abdella, to facilitate her seduction. Obstacles to Mountferrat's possession of Oriana take the form of Gomera and Miranda, two men who are not knights yet fight with the Order against the Ottomans, and Oriana's own virtuous character, which succeeds in protecting her body from Mountferrat but not her reputation from his slander. The preliminary trial in the play is Oriana's, wherein she must answer the charge of treason (conspiracy with a Muslim ruler to betray her faith and Malta) with her life. Gomera acts as her champion while a disguised Miranda dupes Mountferrat into letting him fight as his proxy, thereby fixing the match, and assuring the preservation of Oriana's life and innocence. The end of the contest exposes Mountferrat's villainy and ends with Oriana given to Gomera as his bride, while Miranda, who also loves her, is offered a better prize: membership to the Order of St. John. The intermediary trial proves Miranda's commitment to chastity as he is courted

---

15 Bernadette Andrea, "From Invasion to Inquisition: Mapping Malta in Early Modern England," in *Remapping the Mediterranean World in Early Modern English Writings*, ed. Goran V. Stanivokovic (New York: Palgrave Macmillan, 2007), 246.

by a figure of temptation *par excellence*, the Muslim woman. In this case it is not Abdella, but another Muslim woman, the Ottoman captive Lucinda. Taken in a sea raid by Maltese forces led by the Danish captain Norandine, Lucinda asks to be put into Miranda's service in order to protect her virtue. The potential seduction and eventual abnegation of sexual desire establishes both characters as ready for their respective destinies: Miranda's future knighthood and Lucinda's conversion to Christianity. The terminal trial reunites Oriana and Miranda in a test of love, whereby both must renounce their physical love for each other and accept the consolation of divine love. While *The Knight of Malta* drives towards its resolution through the accession of Miranda into the ranks of knighthood, the reunion of Oriana with her husband, the conversion of Lucinda, and the security of Malta through the expulsion of Mountferrat and Abdella, the reverberations of potential failure in its strategies of unification linger through the inability of the Order to absorb all of Malta's noble fighters, the vulnerability of women who are made to bear the ideological burden of culture, and the presence of Abdella as a challenge to the assimilative impulses informing the cultural and imperial hegemonies of the play.

The Knight of Malta's dramatic intervention within romance narrative and the discourse of nationalism is its triangulation of gender, religion, and race. Women bridge the self–other binary and become the means through which the playwrights experiment with multiple forms of difference and construct a racialized religious identity whereby the sign of religious affiliation becomes visible on the bodies of adherents. This teleology is predicated upon the construction of Oriana's symbolic, normative whiteness which signals her ontological similitude to the "imagined community"—at the same time that her sex problematizes her position—and upon the non-normative blackness embodied by Abdella. The introduction of these characters in a plot involving sexual desire emphasizes the distant moral poles from which they operate. The play introduces Oriana as the victim of Mountferrat's illicit desire: his confessions of love are disgraceful because he is a knight of the Order and has taken a vow of celibacy. Her rejection occasions the appearance of Abdella, who Mountferrat will manipulate into destroying his Oriana because "she doth love" him (1.1.90).

The negotiation of difference in the play linking the dyad of European-Christian and non-European-Muslim, is conceived via the complex and overdetermined figure of the Moor. In the early modern period, the term Moor carried varied, shifting, and indeterminate meanings. Moor indicated not only dark or black skin but also suggested a Muslim religious identity.[16] Black skin, moreover, had its own set of negatively coded meanings. Black was evil and sinful: "whiteness is desired, blackness is condemned. White is the color of the regenerated, of the saved; black is the color of the damned, the lost."[17] Such stark opposition facilitated the very easy and prejudicial characterization of

---

16 *Oxford English Dictionary* definition for Moor, "Originally: a native or inhabitant of ancient Mauretania, a region of North Africa corresponding to parts of present-day Morocco and Algeria. Later usually: a member of a Muslim people of mixed Berber and Arab descent inhabiting northwestern Africa (now mainly present-day Mauritania), who in the 8th cent. conquered Spain."

17 Anthony Barthelemy, *Black Face Maligned Race: The Representation of Blacks in English Drama from Shakespeare to Southerne* (Baton Rouge: Louisiana State University Press, 1987), 2–3.

dark peoples and was complicit with the emerging colour-coded colonial discourse of the period. However, as Jack D'Amico points out, the connection between Moor and Islam problematizes constructions of identity: "No longer a pagan in need of conversion, the Moor as Mohammedan became an aggressive threat, the frightening spiritual and political counterforce to European Christianity."[18] The "Moor as Mohammedan," challenged the cultural and imperial hegemonies that Europe was attempting to establish both in the New World and in the Mediterranean: the Moor as Muslim was a rival on all fronts and perhaps less easily imaginatively contained than Moor as black man.[19] *The Knight of Malta* conflates racial and religious difference in the designation of Moor to create a figure that elicits anxiety based on the Moor's blackness while simultaneously produced by the suggestion of Islamic traits. Thus, Abdella's blackness contains shifting and multiple meanings all of which signal her alterity and difference, just as her Muslim identity points to early modern fears of Islamic sexual and military aggression.[20] I do not intended to elide Abdella's position as a black woman in this play; rather I seek to excavate the sediments of meaning attached to her blackness, which should include a Muslim religious identity.

As the embodiment of the internalized threat of Muslim difference in *The Knight of Malta*, Abdella is the Moorish maidservant who conspires with Mountferrat to destroy her mistress Oriana. Fletcher, Field, and Massinger employ the common dramatic type of the black maidservant in their construction of Abdella. Her two most obvious antecedents are Zanthia, from John Marston's *The Tragedy of Sophonisba* (1606), and John Webster's Zanche in *The White Devil* (1611).[21] Like Abdella, both women serve white women, but while Marston's Zanthia plots against her mistress, Zanche is a faithful accomplice to her mistress's murderous actions.[22] Through her various plots against Oriana and the fetishization of her blackness Abdella follows in the tradition of both Zanthia and Zanche, functioning as both literal and metaphoric dark devil to her angelic, fair mistress.[23] The archetypal connection is furthered by the fact that Abdella's name, as indicated in the dialogue of Act 1 of the play text, is Zanthia, identical to Marston's

---

18 Jack D'Amico, *The Moor in English Renaissance Drama* (Tampa: University of Florida, 1991), 75.

19 I deliberately employ gendered classification here to indicate that most studies of blackness/ Islam in the period have focused on the representation of men. I differ in my analysis by focusing on the triangulation of blackness, Islam, and gender.

20 *The Knight of Malta* does not present Islam as a legitimate theology. It engages with the religion either as a heresy or as an ethnicity.

21 Malieckal points out "black maids are often portrayed as evil and promiscuous opposites to white heroines." ("'Hell's Perfect Character'," 53).

22 A fuller discussion of Marston and Webster's maidservants can be found in Barthelemy, *Black Face Maligned Race*, 72–146. Malieckal also calls attention to the characters from the two plays, in addition to the unseen Moorish maid, Barbary, in *Othello*. "'Hell's Perfect Character'," 53–68.

23 Williams's textual notes point to a misprint in the Folio, at 1.3.1., where "Zanchia" stands for Zanthia. This mistake certainly shows that this character was fashioned from the type of the other two Moor maidservants. John Fletcher, Nathan Field, and Philip Massinger, *The Knight of Malta*, ed. Fredson Bowers, vol. 8 (New York: Cambridge University Press, 1992), 454.

character name. In fact, most editions of the play follow the 1647 Folio, which reads "Enter Zanthia alias Abdella," by referring to the character as Zanthia throughout, even though in Acts 2–5 she is called Abdella in both the dialogue and stage directions.[24] The misprision in naming extends to the folio edition of the play, which substitutes Zanchia for Zanthia. In addition to indicating a stock character, the name Zanche / Zanthia has specific Turkish and Arabic roots: the Turkish word *zenci* comes from Arabic *zanj*, both of which are used to refer to black people. In the early modern Mediterranean, where the movement of language and people was as fluid as the sea, it is seems likely that these character names had a linguistically Eastern, Islamic origin.[25]

I deviate from the common critical tradition of naming her Zanthia and use Abdella for its aural and etymological closeness to the names of earlier Moorish stage characters.[26] George Peele's *Battle of Alcazar* (1591) contains the Moorish characters Abd-el-Malik, the heroic "white Moor" and Abdelmunen, the villain Muly Mahamet's uncle.[27] Although the playwrights may or may not have been aware of the name's significance—Abdella is the feminine form of the Muslim name Abdullah, the name of the Prophet Muhammad's father, which in Arabic means the servant of Allah—they must have been aware of the characters from Peele's drama, who were quite obviously Muslim.[28] Indeed, if we posit

---

24 In the edition of the play I employ, edited by George Walton Williams (in Francis Beaumont, John Fletcher, and Fredson Bowers, *The Dramatic Works in the Beaumont and Fletcher Canon* (Cambridge: Cambridge University Press, 1966)), the character is referred to as Abdella. Williams's textual notes indicate that he favours the name Abdella because this name appears more frequently in "directions and prefixes throughout Acts II–V," 455. He notes that this name change is a "reversal" with editorial tradition (455). References to quotes from this editon will be given parenthetically in the text.

25 In Turkish the letter C is pronounced like the English J. Additionally, in this period the Mediterranean island of Zante is controlled by the Ottoman Empire and was an important source of currants, a highly valued import to England. The island's name is also aurally connected to Zanche/ Zanthia, suggesting an Ottoman geographical sphere if not origin.

26 See Barthelemy, *Black Face, Maligned Race*; Malieckal, " 'Hell's Perfect Character' "; Elliot Tokson, *The Popular Image of the Black Man in English Drama 1550–1688* (Boston: Hall, 1982); Nancy Cotton, *John Fletcher's Chastity Plays: Mirrors of Modesty* (Lewisburg: Bucknell University Press, 1973); and Carolyn Prager, " 'If I Be Devil': English Renaissance Response to the Proverbial and Ecumenical Ethiopian," *Journal of Medieval and Renaissance Studies* 17 (1987): 257–79.

27 Analyzing the naming discrepancy, Williams's text cites an unidentified "Brock," who claims that Fletcher saw the character simply as a Moor and gave her the "inevitable name of Abdella." Williams remains skeptical, finding nothing "inevitable" about the choice of name. He points out that while there were no other Abdella's on the early modern stage, there were, in Peele's *Battle of Alcazar* "Abdil," "Abdelmalec," and "Abdelmunen" (*The Knight of Malta*, ed. Williams, 454).

28 Peter Heylin's *Cosmography* (1621) contains some biographical material about Muhammad that may have had greater circulation before publication. I do not know for certain if Fletcher was aware of the close connection between the name he chose for his Moor and its very close connection to Islam's Prophet. Heylin writes, "By birth of Jathripp, an obscure village then, not far from Medina; his father called Abdalla, and Idolatrous Pagan; his mother named Hemina, as perverse a Jewess." Quoted in Byron Porter Smith, *Islam in English Literature*, ed. S. B. Bushrui and Anahid Melikian, 2nd ed. (Delmar: Caravan Books, 1977), 4.

that Fletcher, Field, and Massinger and their audience were aware of the meaning of Abdella's name, then we find that her religious identity reiterates her racial one, for as a "servant of Allah," Abdella would certainly be seen as an agent of evil, if not evil itself.

Concomitant with Abdella's Muslim lineage, *The Knight of Malta* constructs an episteme of desire and sexuality that allows for the separation of characters into the play's moral dichotomy. Abdella's openly aggressive sexuality is presented as symptomatic of her race. Unlike Oriana, who rejects Mountferrat out of deference to his vow of celibacy and her own inherent modesty, Abdella flaunts her desirability and difference in an attempt at seduction. Cataloguing her extensive physical charms—all of which celebrate her blackness—Abdella appropriates the traditional blazon:

> My tongue Sir, cannot lispe to meet you so,
> Nor my black Cheeke put on a feigned blush,
> To make me seeme more modest then I am.
> This ground-worke will not beare adulterate red,
> Nor artificiall white, to cozen love.
> These dark locks, are not purchas'd, nor these teeth,
> For every night, they are my bedfellows;
> No bath, no blanching water, smoothing oyles,
> Doth mend me up; and yet Mountferrat, know,
> I am as full of pleasure in the touch
> As ere a white fac'd puppet of 'em all
> Juicy, and firme; unfledged 'em of their tyres,
> Thir wyres, their partlets, pins, and periwigs,
> And they appeare like bald cootes, in the nest;
> I can as blithely work in my loves bed,
> And deck thy fair neck, with these Jetty chains,
> Sing thee asleep, being wearied, and, refresh'd,
> With the same organ, steale sleep off againe.

(1.1.172–189)

Abdella's anatomy of physical and erotic delights reverses the colour-coded binaries of the play, and her manipulation of genre vitiates the ascendancy of whiteness in constructions of beauty. Claiming that her blackness discloses a natural and undisguised truth, as opposed to whiteness that is subject to alteration in order to appear increasingly fair, Abdella problematizes the epistemological and ontological transparency of both terms. White, which should be transparent, becomes implicated in fraud, while the opaque black of her skin testifies to her authenticity. In fact, Abdella suggests that blackness denotes constancy by the simple fact that it cannot change—that she cannot "feign" a blush to appear "more modest" than she is. She proudly reconfigures the proverbial impossibility of whitening the Ethiop, emphasizing the indelibility of blackness, which cannot be cosmetically altered. Despite (or because) of her colour, she possesses the sexual power to enthrall men: her "jetty chains" can sooth and satiate Mountferrat's desire better than those of any "white faced puppet." Indeed, later in the play we see Abdella use similar language to convince Mountferrat of her desirability: "Am I not here / As lovely in my blacke to entertaine thee, / As high and full of heat, to meet thy pleasures?" (2.3.11–13).[29] By forging a link between her external colour and internal sexual "heat," Abdella accepts the common early modern associations of blackness and proclaims her agency through her appropriation.[30]

Abdella's subversive exaltation of her blackness and its attendant sexuality combined with her Muslim characterization corroborates early modern accounts of Moors that focused, with prurient interest, on their sexual practices.[31] Most often, we find that African men were thought to have large, bestial genitals and, therefore, animalistic sexuality.[32] Moorish women did not escape the sexualized gaze cast on them by European travellers and historians, who often remarked on their sexual availability and deviance. In *The Navigations Peregrinations and Voyages, made into Turkie*, Nicolas De Nicolay notes,

> [A]ll along the river and the shore the Moorish women and maiden slaves of Algier do go to wash their linen, being commonly whole naked, saving that they wear a piece of cotton cloth of some strange colour to cover their secret parts, (which notwithstanding for a little piece of money they will willingly uncover).[33]

Nicolay's casual observations present these women as nothing more than sexual objects. Once in Constantinople, Nicolay realizes that the women of the Sublime Porte have much more aggressive sexual proclivities. The common ritual particularly questionable for Nicolay was the *hamam* (public bath), where it seemed that the women

> Do familiarly wash one another, whereby it cometh to pass [...] sometimes [they] become so fervently in love the one of the other as if it were with men, in such sort that perceiving some maiden, or woman of excellent beauty, they will

---

29 Abdella's erotic desire for Mountferrat conforms to the dramatic trope of the black woman's desire for a white man. As Ania Loomba indicates, "the marginality of black women, [...] is routinely expressed through the folly of their desire for white men. In play after play, black women, usually servants, are sexually but never romantically linked to white men." Ania Loomba, " 'Delicious Traffick': Racial and Religious Difference on Early Modern Stages," in *Shakespeare and Race*, ed. Catherine M. S. Alexander and Stanley Wells (New York: Cambridge University Press, 2000), 215.

30 While I read these moments as articulations of strength by Abdella, they can also, as Ania Loomba notes, expose strategies of containment for "deviant" feminine energy by foreclosing them within a racialized discourse. Ania Loomba, "The Color of Patriarchy: Critical Difference, Cultural Difference, and Renaissance Drama," in *Women, "Race" & Writing in the Early Modern Period*, ed. Margo Hendricks and Patricia A. Parker (New York: Routledge, 1994), 26.

31 Moors could be both Muslim and African or Africans who were not Muslim. The elasticity of the term makes it difficult to narrow the scope of its classification. Indeed, it seems that it was deployed with great liberality in the period. See Jack D'Amico, *The Moor in English Renaissance Drama*, and also Michael Neill, " 'Mulattos,' 'Blacks,' and 'Indian Moors': *Othello* and Early Modern Constructions of Human Difference," *Shakespeare Quarterly* 49 (1998): 361–74.

32 Barthelemy, *Black Face Maligned Race*, 5–6.

33 Nicolas De Nicolay, *The Navigations, Peregrinations and Voyages, Made into Turkie*. Translated out of the French by T. Washington the younger (London: [At the cost of John Stell] by Thomas Dawson, 1585). STC (2nd ed.) / 18574. (B$_{4v}$).

not cease until they have found means to bathe with them, and to handle and grope them everywhere at their pleasures, so full are they of luxuriousness and feminine wantonness.[34]

The erotic tableau of the *hamam* becomes a recurring and fetishized image of Muslim women's sexuality not just for Nicolay but for other early modern travellers as well. George Sandys, in *Relation of a Journey* (1615), writes: "Much unnatural and filthy lust is said to be committed daily in the remote closets of the darksome bannias: yea, women with women: a thing uncreditable, if former times had not given thereunto both detection and punishment."[35] Because of its communal nature, sex-segregated public bathing, a common practice for Ottoman men and women, became a site to fix Ottoman and Muslim permissiveness and immodesty. To be sure, neither of these men would have access to the women's section of the *hamam* to confirm their suspicions of lesbian behaviour; however, as a locale free from patriarchal surveillance, where loose clothing signalled loose morality, combined with the belief that Islam encouraged all pleasure and that "any sexual act at all is not only not forbidden but allowed and praised" the *hamam* sustained the construction of Muslim women's sexuality as liberal and unnatural.[36]

While these examples provide pornographic scenes of titillation, they also reveal a concern about female sexual aggression and a resultant lack of masculine agency. As characterized in much early modern European writing, including *The Knight of Malta*, the sexual and social perversion of the Islamic world disrupts patriarchal authority and the natural order by making men irrelevant in the sex act.[37] In such formulations of Muslim societies, Muslim women's sexuality threatens Muslim masculinity and diminishes Islamic cultural and imperial potency, opening up a strategic space through which Europeans achieve discursive mastery over Islam and its peoples. Importantly, the root of such feminine degeneracy is naturalized in Muslim women. In the case of *The Knight of Malta*, we do not observe lesbianism in Abdella, but we do encounter her voracious and unbounded lust, which serves the same disruptive and socially damaging purposes. Abdella is ruled by her "mad affections" for Mountferrat, and will do anything—including betray her mistress, "for love of thee Mountferrat, (Oh! What Chaines / Of deity or duty can hold love?)" in order to "enjoy" him (3.2.7; 1.1. 215–16; 3.2.12). Like the earlier examples of sexually aggressive Muslim women, Abdella is demonized because she crosses racial and religious boundaries and because her desire threatens to destroy not only the social structure of Malta, but also a virtuous, Christian woman. Later in the play, when Mountferrat and Abdella's role in Oriana's destruction is at the point of

---

34 De Nicolay, *The Navigations, Peregrinations and Voyages*, (I₃ᵣ).

35 George Sandys, *A relation of a journey begun an: Dom: 1610 ... Containing a description of the Turkish Empire of Aegypt, and of the Holy* Land (London: Richard Field, 1615), STC: 21726 (1307).

36 Norman Daniel, *Islam and the West* (Alva: Edinburgh University Press, 1960), 144.

37 Further examples of Muslim women's sexual degeneracy and the general licentious behaviour promoted in Islamicate sexualities can be found in Leo Africanus's *General History of Africa* (1550; English translation 1600) and in Robert Burton's *Anatomy of Melancholy* (1621), which locates the haram as a site for Muslim women's insatiable sexual appetites.

being revealed, Mountferrat fears fighting while Abdella eagerly takes charge in order to save herself and shoots Gomera: "I'll just do it, / All will goe wrong else" (4.4.18–19). Appropriating a masculine position, Abdella acts decisively with a brutal instinct for self-preservation. Mountferrat's repeated inability to overpower any of the men on Malta, even to subdue and control Abdella, is indicative of his disgrace and impotence. The relationship between Mountferrat and Abdella falls in line with the claims of the travel writers discussed above, that Muslim men are emasculated and Muslim women dangerously deviant.

Abdella's articulation of sexuality and the eroticism of her blackness place her in opposition to Oriana. However, the sexualized construction of both women, Oriana as the object of Mountferrat's desire and Abdella as the object of his feigned desire—and a desiring subject herself—devises a point of intersection. Indeed, Abdella's desire and Oriana's rejection prompt Mountferrat to consider the trajectory of his own desires and whether they can be neatly satisfied through substitution:

> It is not love, but strong Libidinous will
> That triumphs o're me, and to satiate that,
> What difference twixt this Moore, and her faire Dame?
> Night makes their hews alike, their use is so.
>
> (1.1.219–25)

Sex and darkness render the two women coeval. The taxonomies of skin colour undergirding the construction of and distinction between Abdella and Oriana become irrelevant in their confrontation with sexual availability. While his later actions belie the hypothesis articulated here, Mountferrat exposes a fundamental anxiety of the play, the dissolution of difference: "What difference twixt this Moore, and her faire Dame?" The terrifying answer insinuated again and again is that there simply is none. Thus, the action that follows finds and attempts to rehearse and reinforce essential categories of distinction.[38]

The play binds Oriana and Abdella not only as mistress and servant, nor simply through the influence of Mountferrat, but also in the chiaroscuro of their composition. As the figure to which all lines of desire (sexual and imperial) orient, Oriana occupies the representational frame as a primary figure; consequently, Abdella functions as Oriana's opposite and "negative space," like a background of no apparent consequence.[39] In drawing, a cursive figure "is one whose ground is merely an accidental by-product;" even as a supplement, this unintentional result maintains a connection to the product from which it derives.[40] Thus, while the ground may be different from the main figure, it retains resemblance to its origin. Abdella as the distorted reflection of Oriana is one way

---

[38] The anxiety that women engender in their seeming changeability is remedied in this play and in other early modern drama through what Loomba calls "the linkage between deviant femininity and outsiders." "The Color of Patriarchy," 32.

[39] Barbara Johnson, *The Feminist Difference: Literature, Psychoanalysis, Race, and Gender* (Cambridge, MA: Harvard University Press, 1998), 17.

[40] Johnson, *The Feminist Difference*, 18.

that the play simultaneously hides and exposes its fears of identity slippage. The play's most explicit articulation of this is when Abdella writes a letter in Oriana's hand. The aim of the counterfeit is to besmirch Oriana's reputation so that she will either succumb to Mountferrat's seduction or be killed. Knowing that the pasha of Tripoli has solicited Oriana to love, betrayal, and marriage, "Love unto him, and treachery to the Island, / Which will she undertake, by *Mahomet* / The Turke there vowes, on his blest *Alcharon*, / Marriage unto her," Mountferrat lays the foundation of his scheme upon Oriana's universal desirability (1.1.204–7). Abdella's forged letter "so like her hand / As if it had bin moulded of" not only implicates Oriana in a plot that would deliver the island into enemy, Muslim hands, but also attacks her modesty, virtue, and "faire soul" (1.1.212–13; 1.3.142). Her appropriation of Oriana's identity exposes not only her villainy but also her likeness to Oriana, at the same time that it uncovers another modality difference evoking anxiety in the play, that of gender.

The letter and its testimony of Oriana's guilt discloses the fraught position that women occupy as both idealized objects of desire and as potential agents of disruption, always carrying the possibility of being unworthy of the symbolic cultural values placed upon them. Indeed, expounding upon the dangers women pose, Mountferrat points out that "they lurke in our bosomes would subvert / This State, and us, presuming on their blood, / And partiall indulgence to their sex?" (1.3.131–37). Mountferrat's words are heavily ironic given that he represents the insidious danger to which he alludes, yet the success of his contretemps prove that women embody the fear of duplicity and infidelity. By securing his excoriation of Oriana in the special dispensation she receives as a woman, her "partial indulgence," Mountferrat exposes the affective dimension to which women are hewn: as symbols of the community's values and culture.[41] Oriana's supposed collusion with the Muslim pasha sullies not only her "faire soul," and jeopardizes Malta, but also exposes women's symbolic function as the "boundary and metaphoric limit" of the nation.[42]

A boundary must continually be patrolled and protected, and when women inhabit that liminal zone, it is their sexuality and sexual availability that requires patriarchal safeguard. The scandal of the epistle, beyond the fact that it is a clandestine, erotic communication, is that it renders both Malta and Oriana as offerings to Islamic hegemony:

> Let your forces by the next even be ready, [...] the Keyes of the Castle, you shall receive at my hands: that possest, you are Lord of *Malta*, and may soone destroy all be fire, then which I am hotter, till I embrace you, Farewell, *Your Wife*.
>
> (1.3.156–60)

---

41 In different contexts both Anne McClintock, in *Imperial Leather: Race, Gender, and Sexuality in the Colonial Conquest* (New York: Routledge, 1995), and Geraldine Heng, in *Empire of Magic: Medieval Romance and the Politics of Cultural* (New York: Columbia University Press, 2003), indicate that nationalism and nation-building produces and represents women in metaphoric and symbolic ways, making them "carry the burden of culture," (Heng, *Empire of Magic*, 192). The result is that women's role in the community is limited at the same time that they are the limits of the community (McClintock, *Imperial Leather*, 354).

42 McClintock, *Imperial Leather*, 354.

Her appropriation of the instruments of access (knowledge of events, points of entry, and literal keys), illustrates the disruptive capacity of women, that they can use their position within the community to occasion its ruin. Moreover, the construction of her desire, its heat and illicit orientation reiterates the dangers of unbounded female sexuality. To manifest her own burning sexual needs Oriana will allow Malta to burn. Indeed, the conflation of island with woman furthers the metaphorical construction of women as a geographical space conquered and possessed by nations—men—locked in imperial contest. To be sure, the letter is counterfeit, yet the ease with which it testifies against her, challenging her "spotlesse" virtue, puts pressure on her symbolic fairness (2.5.89). Oriana's apparent collusion with the pasha uncovers the sexual power of women, the mechanics of their agency, as well as the necessity of keeping them controlled, for, the play claims, if women are unfettered from the constraints of propriety and patriarchy, society as a whole is at risk.

Oriana's ordeal and the repeated trials of virtue that follow rehabilitate her character through the generic conventions of romance, which stabilize Malta's community by projecting and transferring the anxieties engendered by women onto a more appropriate figure of radical difference. The East–West, Muslim–Christian, and Ottoman–European contact zone of the play's Mediterranean setting, creates a fluid and transformative geographical space within which romance *topoi*, such as the quest or travel motif and the "experience of the strange and remote," operate.[43] These generic features contour Oriana's role in the play: her quest and that of her protectors is to unequivocally prove her innocence and thereby reaffirm her cultural value and, consequently, that of the nation; her encounter with the strange is the ubiquitous danger of habitation in the eastern Mediterranean: contact with and potential conversion to Islam. Indeed, the pasha of Tripoli's proposal encodes this exact possibility, as it, too, draws on romance tropes, like Saracen rulers' ardent passion for Christian women and exogamous marriage.[44]

While the generic conventions of romance may call for a journey through which characters encounter and overcome obstacles, Oriana's travels and travails remain within the bounds of Malta even as her metaphorical ambit crosses the divide between life and death. Oriana's itinerary proceeds from her elevated position as the sister of the grand master, to that of traitor for her apparent conspiracy with a Muslim enemy and, later, to unfaithful wife, and terminates with the restoration of her honour, reputation, and position. Theorizing the cultural and nationalistic nodes of hagiographic, domestic romances, Geraldine Heng collates them under the rubric of the "Constance Group," since they all feature a woman (often called Constance) who is "repeatedly an object of sexual desire, the desire of men for her," and "institutes a new kind of

---

43 Robinson argues that romance "emerge[s] around moments of contact, moments of expansion, moments opening the possibility of new global or cosmopolitan identities, moments in which travel and the other place take on a renewed cultural and psychic resonance" (*Islam and Early Modern English Literature*, 3).

44 Heng, *Empire of Magic*, on Christian women and Saracen rulers, 188–91; and Robinson, *Islam and Early Modern English Literature*, on exogamous romance, 60–61.

imperialism [and] cultural hegemony."[45] Additional elements of the narrative include a journey or exile, assault on her virtue and faith, and somatic fairness that points to the transparency of body and soul.[46] Oriana operates as a Constance-type fundamentally because she is the locus of all desire on Malta; furthermore, both the destructive and constructive ends of that desire manifest the national and imperial goals of the play. Even as it deploys the conventional trope of Muslim rulers' desire for Christian women, the pasha of Tripoli's suit highlights the concern for cultural ascendancy within the eastern Mediterranean. Oriana's rejection of the pasha's proposal, the exposure of her innocence in the plot, and her restoration of status—to that of a chaste Christian woman—reveal not just her unstinting virtue but also metaphorically recast her as the bulwark of unyielding faith, a symbol not only of valorous womanhood, but also of Malta.[47]

Oriana's innocence rests in the visibility of her virtue. In order to affect the materiality of such an intangible, the play mobilizes a racial and colour-coded discourse. Addressing the gathered assembly before her trial, Oriana defends her honour and reputation by accessing the symbolism common in the early modern tropes of whiteness and blackness:

> Behold me in this spotlesse white I weare,
> The Embleme of my life, of all my actions,
> So ye shall find my story, though I perish:
> [...]
>   had I been practis'd,
> And known the way of mischiefe, travell'd in it,
> And given my blood, and honour up to reach it,
> Forgot religion, and the line I sprung on,
> Oh heaven, I had been fit then for thy justice,
> And then in black as dark as hell, I had howl'd here.

(2.5.35–48)

Oriana discursively produces her innocence through the instrumentality of colour, exposing the symbolic registers within which colour operates, and at the same time fixing colour upon bodies and allowing somatic colour, skin, to be transparent and legible. Since we are aware that the guilty party is not the fair Oriana but in fact the black Abdella, *The Knight of Malta* invites the equation of Abdella with "mischiefe" or evil that is "as dark as hell." Kim F. Hall has argued that such moments point to the increased racialization of the early modern period, for the common association of blackness with negative, radical difference—both cultural and physical—produced a "racial

---

45 Heng, *Empire of Magic*, 181–83.

46 Heng, *Empire of Magic*, 181–239.

47 Oriana's rejection of Mountferrat accomplishes much the same thing. Indeed, if we consider him as a renegade or apostate figure, then we can say that she faces an Islamic threat on all sides, and is firm in her rejection of Muslim men's desire for her.

discourse."[48] In fact, this point is reinforced throughout the play as various characters observe and point out the transparency of Oriana's fairness, which signals her honour, modesty, and virtue, and Abdella's blackness, which is persistently constructed in hellish and demonic terms. Norandine, the Danish captain of Malta's sea forces, tells Oriana that she has nothing to fear from the trial because he can read her innocence in the whiteness of her hands: "Give me your fair hands [...] / As white as this I see your Innocence, / As spotlesse, and as pure" (2.5.68–70). When confirming Abdella's guilt once all of the plots are revealed, Norandine's vicious attack relies on the negative symbolic register in which her blackness circulates, "she fears not damning: hell fire cannot parch her blacker then [sic] she is" (5.2.153–54). The polarities of colour and morality supplement those of religion, so that Oriana's fairness buttresses her purity and, consequently, her Christianity, just as Abdella's blackness confirms her Muslim identity.

Oriana's multiple trials mentioned above not only affirm the virtue and morality of the play's protagonists, but also imbue whiteness with symbolic signification. Thus, its opposite must be similarly legible. I read the mobilization of the instrumentality of race or colour as forging a definite link between blackness and Islam. The connection rests on Abdella's similarity to and difference from another woman, Lucinda, Norandine's Ottoman captive, who is undeniably Muslim, yet, significantly, marked as appropriate for conversion. Just as Oriana's journey illustrates the discursive and symbolic potential of hagiographic romance—wherein the heroine's suffering manifests ideal feminine virtue and reinforces patriarchal order—Lucinda mimics the Saracen woman who is transformed by superior religious, cultural, and imperial values. *The Knight of Malta* presents multiple scenes where men express the hope that "she will be Christian" (3.4.132). While the erotic gaze and energies of Christian men can legitimately be directed at Lucinda—Norandine does express the desire to sleep with her and convert her through sex—Abdella is always, because of her blackness, beyond the economy of conversion and licit sexuality.[49] Abdella's blackness serves two purposes at the end of the play: to emphasize her difference from Lucinda and to graft black firmly on to Muslim. Thus, Lucinda's Muslim—but fair—body can be appropriated into Malta's "imagined community," even as her conversion problematizes such inclusion.

Mediating and transgressing the borders the play establishes between Oriana and Abdella, Lucinda embodies multiple registers of radical difference, which are successively eroded in order to reverse the motif of dissolution of self into other. She is introduced as an Ottoman captive of the Maltese captain, Norandine. As booty Lucinda is nothing more than a warm, sexually available body. She manages to escape gang rape, however, through her claims of chastity, and her articulation of nobility and virtue: "My liberty, I kneele not for; mine honour, / (If ever virtuous honour toucht your heart yet) / Make deere, and precious, sir" (2.1.169–71). Noting that she "speaks finely," with a

---

48 Kim F. Hall, *Things of Darkness Economies of Race and Gender in Early Modern England* (Ithaca: Cornell University Press, 1995), 6.

49 The exchange is between Miranda and Norandine, where the pirate tells Miranda that he should send her to him, if Miranda is unwilling to have sex with her. Lucinda is seen as an available and desirable sexual partner, and someone who can be converted (3.4.17–29). For a discussion of the assimilability of other women into European cultural hegemony see Loomba, "Delicious Traffick."

"good" "tongue," Norandine agrees to let her serve "the Noble Gentleman" Miranda (2.1.172; 182; 180). Lucinda's desire to preserve her honour and her appeal to virtue presents an obvious distinction between her and Abdella. Lucinda's acceptance into the Christian fold comes through the timely revelation that Collonna, another of Miranda's servants, is actually Lucinda's presumed-dead husband, Angelo. He had been captured by the Ottomans when they overran his island home, and as a slave in Constantinople, fell in love with Lucinda, convinced her to convert, and they both escaped the capital without consummating their marriage for fear of Ottoman laws regarding inter-religious sex, a capital offence only when it concerned Muslim women and men of different faiths.[50] The deadly fear of the consequences of their inter-religious—the inter-racial implication of their marriage is never mentioned—union is quite justified, yet, more importantly, as Bindu Malieckal has pointed out, the play characterizes Lucinda's captivity and conversion to Christianity, not just as spiritual liberation, but also a literal one, for as she says "Turkish women" were often seen as "the victims of an Islamic tyrant."[51] The men of Malta, while uneasily representing the Islamic tyrant in their own erotic desire for Lucinda, free her from the oppressive Muslim society that only sees her as a sexual object.

The play consequently attempts to fix its ideological claim by advancing the ennobling effects of Christian virtue and chastity through Lucinda's interaction with Miranda. During her service in Miranda's household, Lucinda operates within the modalities of Romance, as the noble Saracen maiden already inclined toward Christianity.[52] Indeed, she even says "I am half a Christian, / The other half, I'll pray for" (3.4.159–60). However, in its acknowledgement of Lucinda's split subjectivity, the play reveals that she is still, dangerously Muslim and as such she is also a seductive, Muslim temptress. Exposing the routine orientation of inter-religious sexual desire, Ania Loomba notes that:

> The most common form of sexual transgression had in fact involved Christian men and Muslim women. In stories of Christians turning Turk that circulated in early modern times, Muslim women are temptresses who ensnare Christian men into a licentious faith [...] but such fears are theatrically allayed by either the destruction of such women or their own conversions to Christianity and marriages to Christian men.[53]

---

50 We see a similar fear enacted in *The Renegado* when Donusa and Vitelli are sentenced to death for their liaison. Moreover, early modern travelogues are quite clear in warning readers about the dangers of having sex with Muslim women: that it is a lethal offence. See William Lithgow's *The totall discourse of the rare adventures, and painful peregrinations...*, where he discusses the punishment of death given to women who engage in adultery and to Christian men who are caught having sex with Muslim women.

51 Malieckal, " 'Hell's Perfect Character'," 61.

52 Warren discusses the narrative of a Muslim princess who convert to Christianity under the guidance of French captives held by her father in his article on Orderic Vital's *Historia Ecclesiastica*, Book 10. See F. M. Warren, "The Enamoured Moslem Princess in Orderic Vital and the French Epic," *PMLA* 3 (1914): 341–58. for a fuller discussion. See also Heng, *Empire of Magic*.

53 Loomba, "Delicious Traffick," 214.

When Miranda tests her virtue, there is an opaque moment in the text where his motives and desires, whether he will succumb to her allure, become difficult to determine. Indeed, during his trial of her virtue *he* comes perilously close to losing his own: "I'le try you a great deale further: prethee to bed; / I love thee, and so well: come kiss me once more; / Is a maidenhead ill bestow'd o' me?" (3.4.118–20). The modalities of difference animating *The Knight of Malta* require that women circulate within the erotic economy as objects of exchange and use; however, Lucinda complicates this telos because she represents the alluring but always dangerous other woman, who can prove fatal to the Christian man.[54] The sexuality that draws men to her exposes her connection with Abdella, yet her claims to honour, virtue, and pseudo-Christianity allow her to operate in a register congruent with the morality valourized by the Maltese and symbolized in Oriana.

Despite her Ottoman heritage and Islamic religion, Lucinda possesses a spiritual and literal fairness which Abdella lacks. In fact, after Miranda has assured himself of her chaste nature, he calls her his "fair, and vertuous maid" (3.4.156). I have, above, uncovered the multiple valences of the rhetoric of fairness, and I believe the play's ideological investment in the taxonomy of colour, its racial calculus, illustrates that Miranda's use of fair as a descriptor for Lucinda indicates not only her moral character but also her somatic whiteness, which contributes to isolate Abdella as the sole symbol of radical difference at the same time that it makes Lucinda a "sister in the skin" to Oriana.[55] The skin as a legible sign, confirms the appropriateness of the sexual desire that has been oriented toward Lucinda by the Christian defenders of Malta, since her whiteness makes her a worthy target of their erotic inclinations. The skin, simultaneously, belies her nature by proving her to be treacherous and disloyal to her *natural* religion and people. Lucinda's conversion validates the religious and cultural superiority of Malta/Christianity over the Ottoman Empire/Islam; however, it is problematized by her aggressive sexuality and defiance of patriarchal and cultural authority.[56] Unlike Oriana, whose white skin and spotless nature form a cultural mirror of transparency, Lucinda

---

54 Again, I see Lucinda being a character similar to Donusa, drawn to the shape and discourse of European manhood. Lucinda is warned by Collonna to not go to Miranda, but she does, because she wants to test herself and be close to him. While both parties remain innocent throughout the scene, the temptation to act and to experience sexual desire charges this scene with the dangers of close contact with the other and contains the threatening potential of Miranda "turning" Turk.

55 Citing the work of Jacqueline de Weever, Geraldine Heng notes that "the whitening of the Muslim beauties, who are often explicitly depicted as white- or light-skinned [...] aimed at reducing the other to the same," and reflected "one modality of colonization" in such narratives (*Empire of Magic*, 187).

56 On noting the distinction between the Constance figure and the renegade Saracen princesses, Heng writes: "Utterly inconstant to their religious and political communities, and often slyly treacherous to their families, these Saracen princesses tend to be written by cultural fantasy as desiring, sexually aggressive agent, whose religious conversion is part of their bold enactment of their erotic attraction to particular Christian men. Part of the fantasy of empire, as colonial and conquest literatures of later periods will amply teach us, is that the colonized, in the form of their women, desire the colonizers" (*Empire of Magic*, 187).

reflects a paradox that the play carefully conceals through the overdetermined discourse of colour. In other words, Lucinda's fair skin simultaneously belies and testifies to her nature. It hides her Muslim identity even as it positions her as available to Christian conversion. In many ways, then, Lucinda suggests a greater danger to the society of Malta, because she can freely move in it without her somatic difference calling attention to her real or imagined religious and cultural difference. I conceive of the function of colour here not to be unlike that of circumcision, the literal inscription of religious identity that marks the bodies of Muslim men but is absent from those of Muslim women.[57] Thus, the spotless and necessarily fair bodies of Muslim women can be baptized and their former religion washed away. I read Abdella's blackness as serving the same function as circumcision. Just as circumcision excludes Jewish and Muslim men—in early modern drama—from baptism, so, too, does Abdella's blackness imprint religious difference and inassimilability on to her. Consequently, at the end of *The Knight of Malta* we have a celebration of the marriage between Lucinda and Angelo (previously Collonna) and the condemnation of the monstrous alliance between Abdella and Mountferrat. The contrast exposes the play's ideological commitments while one woman is blessed because her union constructs a cultural and imperial victory over Islam, the other, despite her own union with a Christian man, is rejected and ousted from the community since her blackness circulates as a sign of the trenchant radical difference of a kind of Islam (militant and destructive) that cannot be transformed or converted.

The Knight of Malta concludes with the reunion of Oriana and Gomera, the revelation of Lucinda's conversion and marriage, and Miranda's ascension to knighthood as a member of the Order of St. John, in a triumphant assertion of Christian valour, virtue, morality, and chastity. In addition to negating the anxiety attached to the triangular relationship between Oriana, Gomera, and Miranda, the play preserves the symbols of the community, the chaste, white woman and the knighthood, through strategies of transfer, substitution, and obfuscation. The cohesive triumph of order is alternately marred and reinforced by Norandine's fixation on Abdella's blackness. The taxonomy of colour and its alignment with religious difference must become the issue upon which to terminate the multiple examinations of difference within the play because it creates the illusion of visible and stable cultural borders. The resolution requires the expulsion of the agents of disruption; thus, Abdella, is rewarded for her crimes by being given the object of her sexual desire—Mountferrat—and both are commanded to leave the island. By ending with an allusion to the possible monstrous miscegenated offspring of this union, "Away

---

57 Judaism and Islam share the ritual of circumcision; indeed, in other early modern plays, such as Shakespeare's *The Merchant of Venice* and Marlowe's *The Jew of Malta*, where we find Jewish women converting, we observe that the absence of such a mark on the body facilitates the conversion. Loomba also points the absence of a physical marker on Muslim as Jewish women as a sign of their fitness for conversion, and the connection between the uncircumcised and fair of white body ("The Color of Patriarchy", 17–34). For a more complete discussion of circumcision and early modern drama, see Julia Reinhard Lupton, "*Othello* Circumcised: Shakespeare and the Pauline Discourse of Nations," *Representations* 57 (1997): 73–89.

complig ? transpers- unlel. that he true for Malto?

French stallion, now you have a Barbary mare of your own, go leap her, and engender young devillings," the play sublimates the inter-racial and inter-religious anxieties contained in the marriage of Lucinda and Angelo (5.2.279–80), in addition to negating the anxiety attached to the triangular relationship between Oriana, Gomera, and Miranda. The simultaneous assimilation and expulsion of Muslims emplots a discursive trajectory that will construct Muslims who challenge and defy the cultural hegemonies asserted by the English and Europeans as racialized. The ambit of Islam's disruptive energies is, seemingly, contained within the figure of Abdella and her ejection from the "imagined community." Nevertheless, Malta remains at risk; the Ottoman Empire continues to threaten and trespass on its boundaries as is evidenced by the need for the Order of St. John. In 1618 it was certainly possible to imagine and stage the successful rout of Islamic aggression; however, that construction remained just that, a fantasy of victory in the eastern Mediterranean where the power of and force of the Ottoman Empire seemed virtually unstoppable. *The Knight of Malta* writes its imperial and cultural anxieties, its fears of the fluidity of the Mediterranean and its economy of traffic, travel, exchange, and conflict on the body of a black, Muslim woman, showing that managing the threat of Islamic hegemony requires strategies that will make it legible and thus racialized. The black body, because it is constructed as inassimilable, resists the episteme of conversion, movement, and translation that encode the cultural investments of English imaginative writing about the Mediterranean.

Chapter 12

EXPERIENTIAL KNOWLEDGE AND THE LIMITS OF MERCHANT CREDIT

JULIA SCHLECK

ABSTRACT

Although significant knowledge of the Islamic world came to Christendom through the transmission and translation of written works, the first-hand experiences of European travellers served as another major source of information about contemporary Muslim societies. The transmission and reception of such knowledge was notoriously problematic, however, as travellers were routinely dismissed as exaggerators or simple "travel liars." Some experiential knowledge was valued and some derided, depending largely on the source of the account and his or her standing in the home community. This paper will explore the credit given to one of the most organized and experienced set of travellers from early modern England to the Persian and Mughal Empires and other points around the Indian Ocean: the English merchants of the nascent East India Company. Despite the growing wealth and influence of these merchants in English society, their status as commoners and their devotion to business served to diminish the epistemological value of their knowledge claims. These same traits thus ironically served to enhance their knowledge base, and degrade its reception as truth in England. By focusing on an offer made by the Persian ambassador Robert Sherley to King James in 1622 for a direct trade in silks with Shah Abbas I, this paper will display the paradoxical role that the experiential knowledge of merchants played in the development of English familiarity with Islamic lands and peoples.

Keywords: East India Company, travel, trade, Persia, Sherley, credibility, witnessing

ALTHOUGH SIGNIFICANT KNOWLEDGE of the Islamic world came to Christendom through the transmission and translation of written works, the first-hand experiences of European travellers served as another major source of information about contemporary Muslim societies. The transmission and reception of such knowledge was notoriously problematic, however, as travellers were routinely dismissed as exaggerators or simple "travel liars." Some experiential knowledge was valued and some derided, depending largely on the source of the account and his or her standing in the home community. This paper will explore the credit given to one of the most organized and experienced set of travellers from early modern England: the members of the nascent East India Company. Despite the growing wealth and influence of these merchants in English society, their status as commoners and their devotion to business served to diminish the epistemological value of their knowledge claims. The same traits which served to enhance their knowledge base thus simultaneously impeded its reception as truth in England. By examining a contentious offer made to King James in 1622 for a direct trade in silks with Shah Abbas I of Persia, and the East India Company's efforts to oppose it, this paper will display the paradoxical role that the experiential knowledge of merchants played in the development of English familiarity with Islamic lands and peoples.[1]

***

In her book *The Witness and the Other World: Exotic European Travel Writing*, Mary Baine Campbell wrote that "neither power nor talent gives a travel writer his or her authority, which comes only and crucially from experience."[2] Subsequent studies have made clear, however, that this confident assertion of the supremacy of empirical knowledge better reflects our current reality than that of the sixteenth and seventeenth centuries. In the early modern period, empirical knowledge had only a partial claim to credibility in European societies, and it shared that space with the powerful contender of received tradition, often tellingly referring to in the period simply as "authority."[3] Furthermore, the legal status of witnessing, including eyewitnessing, was also in flux in the period, shifting from older medieval precedents of what Andrea Frisch has called "socio-ethical" witnessing to a more modern "epistemic" witnessing.[4] To take the latter term first, "epistemic" witnessing refers to our modern understanding of the act, wherein, as Campbell articulated, the witness's credibility relies upon their ability to say that they were there during the event in question, and that they saw or heard something that anyone in the same place would have seen or heard. Their credibility relies upon their transparency and objectivity. A given individual happened to occupy the place of the witness through their positioning in time and space.

The early modern period had a different idea of the function of the witness. Their legal protocols did have a place for "epistemic" eyewitnesses, but as Frisch notes,

---

1 Sincere thanks are due to the American Philosophical Society, which provided the support necessary to complete the research for this article.

2 Mary B. Campbell, *The Witness and the Other World: Exotic European Travel Writing, 400–1600* (Ithaca: Cornell University Press, 1988), 3.

3 This point has been made quite compellingly in relation to travel writing by Anthony Grafton and Nancy Siraisi in *New Worlds, Ancient Texts: The Power of Tradition and the Shock of Discovery* (Cambridge, MA: Harvard University Press, 1992).

4 Andrea Frisch, *The Invention of the Eyewitness: Witnessing and Testimony in Early Modern France*, North Carolina Series in the Romance Languages and Literatures 279 (Chapel Hill: University of North Carolina Department of Romance Languages, 2004).

the narrow terms of the modern, epistemic paradigm simply do not account for the range of discourses that form and inform early modern testimony. The eyewitness constituted but one subtype of witness among many in sixteenth-century Europe, and as such, was subject to the norms governing early modern witnessing and testimony quite broadly construed.[5]

The broader understanding of witnessing Frisch alludes to here is what she describes as "socio-ethical" witnessing. In this regime a witness's credibility related directly to their standing in the community.

> In order to be eligible to give testimony, a folklaw witness had to be recognized as a legitimate deponent in the eyes of his community. This legitimacy was not based on a witness's epistemic capacities, but rather on his socio-ethical status [...] a witness's social status retained priority over his potential knowledge in determining his juridical legitimacy and thus, his credibility.[6]

So the primary qualification governing the ability of a person to testify in a case of doubtful knowledge was their social standing within the community. Someone of lesser status or known to be of dubious morality would have less credit as a witness, regardless of whether they happened to be in a position to see or hear the events in question first hand. Barbara Shapiro sums this up nicely in her book *"Beyond Reasonable Doubt" and "Probable Cause": Historical Perspectives on the Anglo-American Law of Evidence*. She writes:

> The credibility of witnesses was related to social and economic status as well as to the opportunity to observe first hand the fact in question. Thus the testimony of nobles counted for more than that of commoners, ecclesiastics for more than that of laypersons, men more than women, and Christians more than Jews. The value system of the medieval era was thus incorporated into the system of proof.[7]

This has obvious ramifications for travellers, and for the claims they made about foreign lands and peoples. Such claims were frequently doubtful, given the general lack of knowledge about foreign cultures and the challenges that their practices and beliefs offered to European ideologies and ways of life. The socio-ethical standing of the traveller-witness thus played a large role in the reception of the testimony they offered about foreign lands. A traveller's credit, in other words, depended heavily on their place within the home community and less on the fact of their travels. This dynamic shifted significantly across the course of the seventeenth century, but it still held force in the Elizabethan and Jacobean eras, the point at which the great English trading companies began their regular ventures to the Middle East, India and Indonesia. Although the members of these

---

5 Frisch, *The Invention of the Eyewitness*, 23.

6 Frisch, *The Invention of the Eyewitness*, 38, 44.

7 Barbara Shapiro, *"Beyond Reasonable Doubt" and "Probable Cause": Historical Perspectives on the Anglo-American Law of Evidence* (Berkeley: University of California Press, 1991), 188.

companies were the most frequent and knowledgeable travellers to the east during this time, their status as commoners rendered their knowledge less worthy of credit than that acquired by members of the nobility or clergy. Their empirically derived information sat uneasily beside their lower social status throughout the period, a process best displayed in moments when the two were placed in tension. At those moments, the place occupied by merchant trading companies became an odd one indeed, at least to modern eyes.

The rest of this article will focus on one such event, centred on a silk trading proposal made by an ambassador for Abbas I, the Safavid shah of Persia to James I, king of England and later his son Charles I in the mid-1620s. This episode will highlight the ways in which empirically generated knowledge of the Persian economy and political landscape was considered and then rejected, in spite of what today we would consider authoritative claims made by the East India Company based on their extensive experience in the country. Although the dominance of the epistemic witness and empirically derived knowledge of foreign lands was soon to come, at the dawn of the British mercantile age, the reception and acceptance of such knowledge was still tempered by the social structure. Much ink has been spilled on the role that racial or ethnic prejudice played in the generation and acceptance of knowledge about the Middle East in Europe in the early modern era, but relatively little on the impact of social status. Here I will argue that domestic prejudices surrounding rank and social status are just as, if not more, important to consider when studying the reception in Europe of knowledge from and about the Islamic world.[8]

***

As a merchant collective, the East India Company was in a different position than the many individual travellers who wrote about their adventures in foreign lands. They did not publish accounts of the travels made by company agents, and usually had no need of public display or public acceptance of the truth of their experiences in the East. A return on investments was sufficient for the joint stock holders, who did not demand further explanations of events overseas. This was not true for most individual travellers, whose published accounts register both a need to justify (and/or promote) their actions abroad and anxiety about how their stories will be received. These individual traveller-writers sought to establish their credit on the basis of first-hand experience. They emphasized the authority that came from being an eyewitness in the written accounts they published upon returning to their homelands. But in so doing, they also anxiously highlighted the skepticism with which such travellers were met when providing empirical information about foreign places. William Parry, for example, travelled through the Ottoman Levant into Persia and then following a brief stay at the court of the shah, he went north along the Caspian Sea and Volga Rivers through Russia and back to England. He made this journey as part of the entourage of Sir Anthony Sherley, and published an account of his

---

8 For further consideration of this argument see Julia Schleck, *Telling True Tales of Islamic Lands: Forms of Mediation in English Travel Writing, 1575–1630* (Selinsgrove: Susquehanna University Press, 2011).

travels upon returning to London in 1602. Although a minor gentleman and thus part of the noble estate, Parry is clearly anxious about the reception of his narrative, and he begins his account by recognizing the difficulties faced by travellers such as himself in getting their stories believed. He begins his narrative with the observation that "It hath beene, and yet is, a proverbiall speech amongst us, that Travellers may lie by authority." He is uncertain whether this proverb arose from travellers taking advantage of the authority eyewitnessing gives by lying to their countrymen with complete abandon, or whether it comes from the narrow minds of English readers who "wil beleeve nothing that falles not within their owne ocular experience, or probabilitie of truth." But he is sure that there are many "honest and true Travellers" who "for speaking the truth of their owne knowledge (for in the world are many incomprehensible miracles of Nature) yet, because it exceeds the beliefe of the unexperienced and home-bred vulgars, they are by them concluded liers for their labour."[9] He proclaims himself to be such an honest and true traveller, and clearly hopes that this introduction will have eased the reception of his narrative sufficiently to avoid being considered a liar.

As someone publishing a traveller's account and hoping thereby to gain credit from his readers—something he no doubt hoped to translate into employment or preferment—Parry was in a particularly delicate position. In contrast, the merchants of the East India Company and other great trading companies of England had no need to print their tales, and therefore submitted their travellers' tales to no public censure. Company captains, agents and factors were required to submit detailed accounts of their travels to the governing committee back in London, but there they encountered readers well familiar with the wonders of these distant lands, and who had already testified to their trust in the traveller by hiring him. It was only when the Company had publically to account for their travellers' knowledge that the dynamics highlighted so vividly in Parry's account came strongly into play.

Such an occasion arose in 1623 when the king sought their advice on an unusual trading arrangement offered by the Safavid shah, Abbas I, through his ambassador, Sir Robert Sherley. As his name might indicate, Robert Sherley was not your usual Persian ambassador. An English-born subject of King James, Sherley had travelled to Persia on the same voyage as Parry, accompanying his brother Anthony to the shah's dominions. When Anthony was sent back to Europe as a Persian ambassador, attempting to secure an alliance between Persia and the princes of Christendom against the Ottomans, Robert was left behind as security for Anthony's good behaviour and ultimate return. When Anthony neither behaved nor returned, Robert was stranded in Persia, left to the displeasure of the shah.[10] Robert nevertheless managed to survive, and to regain the shah's

---

9 William Parry, *A new and large discourse of the trauels of sir Anthony Sherley Knight, by sea, and ouer land, to the Persian Empire Wherein are related many straunge and wonderfull accidents: and also, the description and conditions of those countries and people he passed by: with his returne into Christendome. Written by William Parry gentleman, who accompanied Sir Anthony in his trauells* (London: Printed by Valentine Simmes for Felix Norton, 1601), A3r–v.

10 Accounts of the lives of Robert and Anthony Sherley brothers include Richard Raiswell, "Sherley, Anthony, Count Sherley in the nobility of the Holy Roman empire (1565–1636?)," *Oxford*

good opinion of him sufficiently to be sent like his brother on an ambassadorial mission to Europe (it is worth noting that both brothers were sent as *ilchi*, or "messengers," who were usually considered the most dispensable of the classes of messengers sent to foreign princes, and so the Western title "ambassador" is somewhat misleading here).[11] Robert began his first tour as the shah's *ilchi* in 1608 and returned to Isfahan in 1615. The shah was so pleased with his work that he immediately returned him to Europe, over Robert's protestations, and it is during this second journey that Robert presented to King James what seemed like an extraordinary arrangement for Persian silk imports. In brief, the ambassador offered a direct trade between the two monarchs, in which James would be permitted to import the entire Persian silk market for resale in England and Europe at large. He was also invited to export enough English woollens to Persia to balance the trade, so that no bullion need leave the kingdom, as it did under the current trade managed by the East India Company.[12] The Shah promised to provide soldiers sufficient to protect the merchandise if the English provided the ships for long-distance

---

Dictionary of National Biography (online), Oxford University Press, 2004; Richard Raiswell, "Shirley, Sir Robert, Count Shirley in the Papal Nobility (*c.*1581–1628)," *Oxford Dictionary of National Biography* (online), Oxford University Press, 2004; D. W. Davies, *Elizabethans Errant: the Strange Fortunes of Sir Thomas Sherley and His Three Sons, as Well in the Dutch Wars as in Muscovy, Morocco, Persia, Spain, and the Indies* (Ithaca: Cornell University Press, 1967); and E. Denison Ross, *Sir Anthony Sherley and his Persian Adventure, Including some Contemporary Narratives Relating Thereto* (London: Routledge, 1933). The Sherleys, including Robert's Circassian wife, Teresa, have also attracted recent critical attention: see Jonathan Burton, "The Shah's Two Ambassadors: The Travels of the Three English Brothers and the Global Early Modern," in *Emissaries in Early Modern Literature and Culture: Mediation, Transmission, Traffic, 1550–1700*, ed. Brinda Charry and Gitanjali Shahani (Burlington: Ashgate, 2009), 23–40; Sanjay Subrahmanyam, *Three Ways to Be Alien: Travails and Encounters in the Early Modern World* (Waltham: Brandeis University Press, 2011); Schleck, *Telling True Tales of Islamic Lands*; Bernadette Andrea, "Lady Sherley: The First Persian in England?," *Muslim World* 95 (2005): 279–95; Jane Grogan, *The Persian Empire in English Renaissance Writing, 1549–1622* (New York: Palgrave Macmillan, 2014), 150–79; and Kaya Şahin and Julia Schleck, "Courtly Connections: Anthony Sherley's *Relation of his travels into Persia* (1613) in a Global Context," *Renaissance Quarterly* 69 (2016): 80–115. There are also several contemporary literary works based on Sherleys, analyzed most notably by Laurence Publicover, "Strangers at Home: The Sherley Brothers and Dramatic Romance," *Renaissance Studies: Journal of the Society for Renaissance Studies* 24 (2010): 694–709; Anthony Parr, "Foreign Relations in Jacobean England: The Sherley Brothers and the 'Voyage of Persia,'" in *Travel and Drama in Shakespeare's Time*, ed. Jean-Pierre Maquerlot and Michèle Willems (Cambridge: Cambridge University Press, 1996), 14–31; Ralf Hertel, "Ousting the Ottomans: The Double Vision of the East in The Travels of the Three English Brothers (1607)," in *Early Modern Encounters with the Islamic East: Performing Cultures*, ed. Sabine Schülting, Savine Lucia Müller, and Ralf Hertel (Farnham: Ashgate, 2012), 135–51; and Nedda Mehdizadeh, "Translating Persia: Safavid Iran And Early Modern English Writing" (PhD dissertation, George Washington University, 2013).

11 For a discussion of the cultural mistranslation of Sherley's status as "ambassador," see Burton, "The Shah's Two Ambassadors." For the term *ilchi*, see Mehdizadeh, "Translating Persia," 89–92.

12 The amount of bullion exported by the East India Company and other long-distance trading enterprises was a bitter point of debate. A series of pamphlets were published on the issue in early

transport. The deal would produce an extraordinary amount of revenue for the king's customs, as well as enrich the wool trade in England. It was a deal that was too good to ignore.

The East India Company was familiar with Robert Sherley through its agents in Persia and India. He had been a dubious ally on a few occasions but was generally regarded with suspicion, since he acted, as befitted a servant of the shah, to forward the interests of his Persian master and not necessarily those of England or its merchants. When he arrived in England with trading proposals for James, the Company immediately took notice, discussing his history with the company in their Court of Committees on the third of February, 1623:

> it was remembred that S:r Rob[er]te Sherly came out of Persia 7 yeares since, that his Commission was Immediately for Spayne, and not for England, that in his former Ambassag[e] he came first for Spayne, next offered the trade to the Hollanders, and when his proposic[i]ons tooke no effect, he last came into England, and had wrested from the Company divers sommes of money besides his passage into thindies notwithstanding w[hi]ch he had done ill s[er]ruices for the Company, and rayled against them.[13]

Given this state of affairs, the Company put itself on the defensive, preparing to combat whatever proposals might emerge from the embassy that would affect its business. They directed one of their members to look out for arriving letters from the region that might give them information on their own recent efforts to establish a regular trade in Persia, and they directed another member to consult the court records and familiarize himself with the past history of the Company in relation to Sherley and the Persian trade. In short, they "armed themselves with reasons to putt of[f] the charge like to acrew to the Company."

---

the 1620s, including Thomas Mun, *A discourse of trade, from England vnto the East-Indies answering to diuerse obiections which are vsually made against the same* (1621); Edward Misselden, *Free trade, or, The meanes to make trade florish. Wherein, the causes of the decay of trade in this kingdome are discouered and the remedies also to remooue the same are represented* (1622); Edward Misselden, *The circle of commerce. Or The ballance of trade in defence of free trade: opposed to Malynes little fish and his great whale, and poized against them in the scale. Wherein also, exchanges in generall are considered: and therein the whole trade of this kingdome with forraine countries, is digested into a ballance of trade, for the benefite of the publique. Necessary for the present and future times* (1623); and Gerard Malynes, *The center of The circle of commerce. Or, A refutation of a treatise, intituled The circle of commerce, or The ballance of trade, lately published by E.M. By Gerard Malynes merchant* (1622). For a general history of the East India Company, see K. N. Chaudhuri, *The English East India Company: The Study of an Early Joint-Stock Company 1600–1640* (London: Routledge, 1999). For one focused more specifically on the company's finances see William Robert Scott, *The Constitution and Finance of English, Scottish and Irish Joint-Stock Companies to 1720*, 3 vols. (Cambridge: Cambridge University Press, 1910). See also Robert Brenner, *Merchants and Revolution: Commercial Change, Political Conflict, and London's Overseas Traders, 1550–1653* (Princeton: Princeton University Press, 1993).

13 "A Courte of Comittees houlden the 3:d of February 1623," EIC IOR-B-8: Court Book VI, 2 July 1623–30 June 1624. F. 394.

The weapons the Company sought to arm themselves with were twofold. First, they sought ways to diminish Sherley's socio-ethical status so that his credit as a witness to conditions in Persia and future trading predictions would be weakened. Sherley had been by this time absent from Persia for a number of years. How could he be properly acquainted with the state of the Company's affairs there, especially since they had only very lately concluded upon certain trading capitulations with the shah? And how could he have received more recent instructions from his master, given the distance and the fact that reliable overland routes between Persia and Europe had recently been closed?[14] "There is litle probabilitie," they concluded, or rather "allmost no posibility that S:r Rob[er]te Sherly should have any authentique power out of Persia to negociate as an Embassador, the circumstances of time, and the shutting of all passage overland into or out of those partes Considered."[15]

Indeed, from the very first mention of Sherley in the 1623 accounts, "the Courte conceived that he was an Ambassador, but had vsurped the title, yet because his Ma[jes]tie tooke notice of him as An Ambassador it became not this Company to make shewe of the Contrary."[16] The Company would recognize Sherley's status as ambassdor since the king saw fit to do so, but they considered it an illegitimate, or "usurped" title.[17] Accordingly, in addition to questioning the currency of his mission and knowledge in the area, they sought to discredit Sherley's place as ambassador in a rather novel way: by seeking out and bringing to London what they considered to be a more legitimate ambassador, setting the two ambassadors against each other in James's court.

The Persian Naqd Ali Beg arrived in England in 1626 and was promptly greeted by the Company as a more legitimate representative of the Persian shah than their erstwhile countryman. Upon the first meeting of the two rival ambassadors at a private house, Sherley attempted to show the Persian his letters of credit from the shah, but Naqd Ali Beg tore up the letters and physically attacked Sherley.[18] When the gentlemen

---

14 Paraphrase from "A Courte of Comittees houlden the 3:d of February 1623," EIC IOR/B/8: Court Book VI, 2 July 1623–30 June 1624, F. 394 and "A Courte of Comittees houlden the 13th of August 1624." British Library, IOR/B/9: Court Book VII, 2 July 1624–14 April 1625. F. 70.

15 "A Courte of Comittees houlden the 13th of August 1624." British Library, IOR/B/9: Court Book VII, 2 July 1624–14 April 1625. F. 70.

16 "A Courte of Comittees houlden the 3:d of February 1623."

17 Although the Company's reasons for this opinion are unclear, they rather interestingly align with modern critical assessment on this point. There was no commensurate role in Europe for the lower-valued "messengers" often sent from Middle Eastern and Indian courts. "Ambassador" was an inappropriate cultural translation for this position, in that it accorded too much status and importance to the individual concerned. The title thus was in a sense "usurped" by both of the Sherley brothers while carrying the shah's messages to European princes. See Burton, "The Shah's Two Ambassadors."

18 An account of these events was later published by a court official involved in the Sherley negotiations. My summary here draws directly on this source: John Finett, *Finetti Philoxeni: Som choice observations of Sr. John Finett Knight, And Master of Ceremonies to the two last Kings, Touching the Reception, and Precedence, the Treatment and Audience, the Puntillios and Contests of Forren*

of the court who had accompanied Sherley broke up the fight, they queried the violence of the Persian ambassador, who excused his rage by claiming that the letters were fake and Sherley an imposter who falsely played the role of ambassador. He could tell, he said, because the Shah's signature was on the back rather than at its proper location on the front of the document. Robert defended himself by claiming that the letters carried by "strangers" like himself were signed on the back, in comparison to those carried by native-born Persians. But this defence served only to highlight Sherley's less-than-regular status as a Persian representative, implying somehow that the East India Company's claims were true, and that Sherley had "usurped" the role of ambassador. Furthermore, Sherley's behaviour during the assault, in which he dodged away and hid behind the other English noblemen attending the meeting, damaged his status as a nobleman. In addition to not standing his ground and fighting back at the time, in the aftermath of the event Sherley defensively offered explanations and justifications rather than taking offence and accusing the Persian of impugning his honour, and subsequently demanding restitution. In the end, Sherley's status as an ambassador from a king had been shaken, and his status as a member of the English nobility had been decidedly tarnished. The Company's effort to damage Sherley's socio-ethical status with the noblemen who were to advise the king on this trading deal was both creative and effective.

The Company furthermore sought to tar Sherley's character by means of his acquaintance. A former Company employee, Richard Steele, was supporting Sherley's trading proposal at court. Steele had previously claimed to have "discovered" and opened up the trade for Persian silks, but the Company directors wryly noted that he "arrogated those thinges to himself, w[hi]ch were in question, and thought on long before."[19] And indeed, the Persian silk trade had been a target of English merchant activity since the 1550s, when the Muscovy Company sent agents down the Volga River to the Caspian Sea. Steele had also previously run afoul of the Company by both personal transgression and professional incompetence. Against explicit Company policy, he had smuggled his wife on board their outgoing fleet, disguised as a lady's maid, only admitting their relationship when she revealed herself to be pregnant somewhere around the Cape of Good Hope. Once in India, Steele had insisted on presenting a plan to develop a waterwork on the Yamuna River to the Mughal emperor Jehangir I, despite the warnings of the Company's main agent on the ground, Sir Thomas Roe.[20] The plan showed little knowledge of the

---

Ambassadors in England. Legati ligant Mundum (London: Printed by T. R. For H. Twyford and G. Bedell, and are to be Sold at their Shops in Vine-Court Middle Temple, and the Middle Temple Gate, 1656), 135–37, 172–77.

19 "A Court of Comittees held: Novembris. 8°. 1619," EIC IOR-B-6: Court Book IV, 19 Sept. 1617 – April 1620. F. 446.

20 Upon his return, the Company investigated Steele's behaviour in India, and their conclusions were scathing: "In w[hi]ch his vndertakinges he wrongd the Compa[ny] excedeinglye, as Sr Thomas Roe made it appeare, first, because the Riuer Gemini was vnfit to set a Myll vppon, raging wth vyolence of watrs 3 mo together, over flowing his boundes a myle from his bankes, so that it app[ear]ed impossible to settle such a worke either at the highest or lowest tyme therof, when he falls wthin his bankes againe Secondly the Bamans [Brahmins] in Agra (who are the greatest p[ar]t of the inhabitantes) will

cultural and hydrographical realities on the ground, including the fact that the river flooded regularly and that the Mughal court already possessed an excellent waterwork system tapping into another river in the area. That Sherley's proposals were backed up by Richard Steele, the Company stated, only made them less likely to be grounded in truth. All told, the East India Company launched a remarkably effective multi-pronged campaign to tarnish Sherley's socio-ethical position in England, destabilizing his rank and status as a royal ambassador in an effort to compensate for their own comparatively low status as commoners and level the playing field somewhat.

The second form of weapon the Company used in their fight against Sherley's proposal had to do with their instructions to their two members, to seek in their records for past accounts of their dealings with Sherley and the area, and to look out for current letters arriving with the fleet. With the help of these two committee members, the Company amassed empirical details of the past and current state of affairs in Persia, using their carefully kept records and correspondence networks. In so doing they leaned upon their collective status as eyewitnesses, claiming authority by virtue of their continuing travels to the region. Their business was to know the state of affairs in the nations of the East, including Persia, and they did so through agents who sent regular reports back to England by multiple routes to ensure its delivery. Letters arrived frequently throughout the year from East India Company servants on the ground in Persia and India, and they clearly hoped to claim authority based on their awareness of the most current news from the region. The company thus based their claims on a complex combination of epistemic and socio-ethical witnessing. The committee members in London who ran the Company had mostly never travelled to the region, so they were not themselves eyewitnesses. They were, however, commoners of quite high status in London, and well known at court. In their position as company directors, they had multiple eyewitness accounts given to them, which they trusted due to their personal knowledge of the author of each account. The socio-ethical standing of the author within the Company meant a great deal as to the credit extended a given account. Large amounts of money were committed based on such information, and so the need for accurate and reliable eyewitness accounts were critical to the Company. They would stand behind the authority of the accounts their agents sent, just as they did every time they made a business decision based on those accounts. This internal vetting system meant that the Company itself could collectively claim to be the possessor of the most reliable eyewitness accounts at the time, even though its directors had never travelled. The social status of the directors—commoners, but very wealthy London citizens—in turn boosted the credibility of the reports sent them by lower-status agents. The Company hoped to use this collective witnessing of conditions in Safavid Iran to make their case against Sherley's trade proposal and the expenses it would entail.

---

not touch nor medle w[i]th any wat[e]r that is brought or handled by any other then them selues. 3. The king and Nobilitie haue as excellent and artificall watrworkes of ther owne as can be desired." "A Court of Comitrees held Nouembris: 10. 1619." British Library, IOR/B/6: Court Book IV, 19 Sept. 1617–April 1620. F. 449.

The Company reminded the king's agent, Secretary Conway, of their authority in questions of trade multiple times within the long series of exchanges on this matter. "[T]he vent of Clothes in Persia is better knowne to the Company, then it cann be either to S:r Robert Sherly or Steele, the Company Factors having endeavored to vent of Clothes all the Country over," East India Company directors stated bluntly to Conway. Since their "experience & knowledge of the Trade in that Country, farr excee[s] Sr Robert Sherlys," their skepticism regarding the deal he proposed should be heeded. They recognized the authority of the king to make this decision, and respected the noble counsellors who advised the king on this matter, but they were insistent that experience should trump social status in this instance. Indeed, their own status as commoners, as those who *worked* in trade, should in this case, weigh in their favour: "[i]f there were any possibility of doeing good by otherwyes then have bene allready found, the marchant would for his gayne find it out." It is their business, they insisted, to seek profit, and if a more profitable deal were available in Persian silks, they would already have sniffed it out, or would, shortly. And they not only had a strong motive to do so, they had means. Citing the formidable intelligence network set up through the company agents' regular, often coded, correspondence with the governing committee in London, the directors continued that

> neither is it probable that either S:r Rob[er]te Sherely or Steele whose hande is in this p[ro]iect cann come nere the Companie, in getting intelligence from those partes. For as much as the Company do employ thither the ablest men they cann gett, and are well furnisht of such whoe could neither give hope either of such a vent of English Commodities, or such retournes in exchange.[21]

The Company had both motive and means to seek out the most reliable information available in Persia on this matter, and their conclusion was that Sherley had no idea what he was talking about. His proposal was deemed "inconvenient" and contained "such matter, as seemed [neither] fitt nor feisible."

The Company also sought to back up this rather insulting conclusion with logical explanations for their judgement. They went into the details of the trade with the noblemen tasked by the king with handling the issue, Secretary Conway, Sir John Coke, and a committee from the House of Lords. First of all, they began, the numbers involved were unrealistic. It was said, they claimed,

> [t]hat Sr Robert Sherley hath possessed the State That such a proporc[i]on of silk may bee brought from thence, as will give the King 450 thousand poundes yearely for Custome, whereas the proporc[i]on that the Companies Factors have advertised will not produce above 40,000li Custome if it were all to bee brought hither.

Furthermore, the Company "Governour satisfied the boord that where the proiect speakes of silke to the vallue of many millions, the silke of Persia that vends in [all]

---

21 "A Courte of Comittees houlden the 13th of August 1624."

Christendome doth not amount to one Million."[22] Similarly, Sherley claimed that the Company would be able to sell 30,000 English woollens each year in Persia and India, which would allow them to bring back the silks after a simple barter. In other words, they would not have to export bullion from the realm, a point of some contention in England, as it was believed to make the country poorer, and certainly made it cash poor.[23] But the Company scoffed at such a number, noting that they had never been able to sell anywhere near that amount of English cloth in Persia. The proportion cited, they claimed, was simply "frivolous."

Besides, the Company argued, the shah himself had refused exactly such a trade in the near past. They had made efforts, through letters sent from King James and negotiated through an agent residing in Isfahan, to get Shah Abbas to agree to the Company purchasing 4,000 bales of silk on credit and storing it in a factory near the waterside. This was a critical part of mercantile practice, as it allowed agents to store up stocks of local goods and send them back to England at the ideal time when the proper fleet arrived. The merchants would pay back debts accrued during the year once further ships from England arrived with bullion and with English goods to sell in Persia, the latter of which they would also store and sell at a time considered most advantageous price-wise. There was considerable flex in this system, and the Company needed to be trusted that it could and would always pay back debts accrued during the course of the year. The shah simply refused to trust them to do that. As the Company records stated, he denied these requests "refusing at all tymes to trust out more then there was estate in his Country to satisfy for."[24] Given the consistently distrustful attitude displayed by the shah towards the English merchants, how was it credible that he should suddenly offer such free and advantageous trading terms through Robert Sherley? The answer of course, was that it was not credible, and neither was Sherley.

From a contemporary perspective, the Company's arguments sound quite logical and persuasive. They mistook Robert Sherley, who was in fact sent by the shah with a number of military and trade proposals to Europe, but they were likely correct about the state of things on the ground in Persia. Sherley had indeed been away from the shah's court for eight years (1615–1623) by the time he arrived in England, and was unlikely to know the shah's current mind on the proposals he had sent so many years before. Alliances had been shifting rapidly in the Gulf as the Portuguese were ousted from Ormuz with English help, and the Anglo-Dutch rivalry in the Far East heated up. The Company's skepticism was well justified.

James, however, appears to have been less convinced by the Company's claim to expertise in the Persian trade, or rather, he considered it less important than other factors in the decision. Regarding the matter of Sherley's status as ambassador, Robert had been received by James in the past under such a title, and to admit that he was wrong, and had

---

22 "A Court of Comittees holden the 20th of December 1624." British Library IOR/B/9 Court Book VII, 2 July 1624–14 April 1625. Ff. 271–76.

23 See note 12 above.

24 "A Courte of Comittees houlden the vj[th] of December 1624 Afternoone." British Library IOR/B/9 Court Book VII, 2 July 1624–14 April 1625. Ff. 236–37.

honoured one of his own subjects with a status he did not deserve, was not an attractive idea. Both James and his son Charles, who succeeded his father in 1625, handled the matter by alternately ignoring it and refusing to receive either of the two ambassadors while ordering various of their secretaries to look into the details of the matter, who met with both Sherley and the Company directors. For James at least was enamoured with silk, and would dearly have loved to have put such an arrangement in place. He had infringed on the Company's charter rights to trade exclusively in the area at least once before in the Company's history, and clearly had no qualms about doing so again.[25] It was the king's prerogative. He hoped, therefore, to bring the Company to agreement with the proposal, and sought to reconcile all parties to the idea. The Company's arguments about its knowledge and experience in the trade, therefore, were likely all the more irritating for being logical. James also clearly relied most heavily on the socio-ethical status of the ambassador as a messenger from another king, regardless of Sherley's status as a member of the lower nobility in England, for when the Company made objections to the probability of the numbers proposed by Sherley, the reply from the king's side was "that the probability was the more because the moc[i]on comes from an Embassador of a great Prince."[26] And not, it was implied, from mere merchants.

In the end, the king sided with Sherley, deciding to pursue the trade offered with or without the Company's help. The Company was informed that

> [T]he King having duely Considered the overtures made by Sr Robert Sherley concerning the Persian Trade, and the important Consequences depending therevpon, and having likewise with the advise of the Lords of his Councell weighed the severall answers given by the Merchants of London vnto those proposic[i]ons, hee was now resolved with the assistance of his Nobility and such others as wold ioyne with him to pursue that trade his owne way hoping to bring the whole Trade of the Persian silk vpon freight hither into England by Contract between the 2 Kings.[27]

James was no merchant, but the idea of bringing tons of bales of silk into England by direct agreement with another king appealed to him. The Persian trade would now be the purview of the English nobility, who would reap its rewards, dealing directly with their counterparts in the Persian court.

We are not, unfortunately, able to see the results that such an effort might have produced, because the king died shortly after this pronouncement in 1625. His son Charles

---

25 In 1604, only a few years after the incorporation of the East India Company, King James disregarded the Company's privilege of exclusive trade in the east by granting his pensioner, Sir Edward Michelborne, a licence to trade to Cathaia, China, Japan, Corea, Cambaia and nearby lands. For more details, including the outcome of the voyage and the company's response, see *The Register of Letters &c. of the Governour and Company of merchants of London trading into the East Indies, 1600–1619*, ed. Sir George Birdwood and William Foster (London: Bernard Quaritch, 1893), 134n2.

26 "A Court of Comittees holden the 20th of December 1624," f. 70.

27 "A Courte of Comittees houlden the vj[th] of December 1624 Afternoone." IOR/B/9 Court Book VII, 2 July 1624–14 April 1625. F. 236.

I was less enthused about silk, and less convinced of Sherley's proposals or identity. The entire matter was postponed until the questions surrounding Sherley's status as ambassador and the legitimacy of his offer could be ascertained. The rival ambassadors were put on an East India Company fleet, along with agents from the king tasked with finding out the truth of the matter from the Persians themselves. The Persian ambassador, Naqd Ali Beg, committed suicide shortly before the fleet arrived at the port of Surat, and Sherley, as a member of a nation which had recently fallen out of favour with the shah, was brusquely treated and cast aside upon arriving at Isfahan in 1628. The shah would likely have repented and brought Sherley back to court in a relatively short time, as he had in the past, but Sherley pre-empted him by dying as well, mere months after his return to Isfahan (July 1628). The idea of the silk trade was abandoned by the English king and court, and the merchants were left to pursue their trade in peace, no doubt to their great satisfaction.

***

Although we tend to treat the early modern period as the dawn of an empirically based exchange of knowledge directly between formerly isolated European locations like England and the great empires of the Middle East and Asia, we would do well to hold off according the era any accolades for empiricism. Aside from the many familiar problems of translation and prejudice that Said so aptly highlighted in his work on later periods, there are additional issues surrounding the reception of empirically derived knowledge about the Islamic world in Europe. Merchants are arguably good sources for such information, given their professional need for accuracy and their pragmatic approach to navigating social and cultural difference in their pursuit of profit. But their networks of informers and long experience on the ground in the Ottoman Empire, Egypt, Persia, and India were still regarded as only one factor in the assessment of knowledge by their social superiors. As commoners, the merchants necessarily lacked the socio-ethical credit of the nobility. Their claims to expertise were taken into consideration, but were not decisive when placed against contradictory accounts by higher-ranking individuals such as royal ambassadors. The oddity of Sherley's status as a Persian ambassador and his shaky reputation as an English nobleman gave the East India Company merchants an excellent opportunity to assert their case and potentially to triumph over the desires and solidarity of the aristocracy. Yet even with these favourable conditions, King James ruled against their knowledge and experience, and only his sudden death and the caution of his successor allowed the Company to continue its trade undisturbed. The episode stands as a cautionary tale to those who would argue for the growing empiricism of the period, and a reminder that the reception and acceptance of knowledge from the East was mediated not only by European prejudice against Muslims, but by domestic regimes of rank and status as well.

SELECTED BIBLIOGRAPHY

Primary Sources

Benjamin of Tudela, Benjamin of. *The Itinerary of Benjamin of Tudela (Sefer ha-Masa'ot)*. Translated by Nathan Adler. Malibu: Joseph Simon, 1987.

Daud, Abraham ibn. *The Book of Tradition*. Edited and translated by Gerson D. Cohen. Philadelphia: Jewish Publication Society, 1967.

Ferdowsi, Abolqasem. *Shāhnāma*, eds. Djalal Khaleghi-Motlagh, Mahmoud Omidsalar, and Abū al-Faẓl Khaṭībī. 12 vols. New York: Bibliotheca Persica, 1987–2008.

——. *Shahnameh: The Persian Book of Kings*. Translated by Dick Davis. New York: Penguin, 2016.

Al-Ghazzali, *The Mysteries of Worship in Islam*. Translation of al-Ghazzali's *Book of the Ihya on the Worship* by Edwin Elliot Calverley. Lahore: Muhammad Ashraf, 1925. Reprint, 1977.

Ibn Jubayr. *The Travels of Ibn Jubayr*. Translated from the original Arabic with introduction and notes by R. J. C. Broadhurst. London: Jonathan Cape, 1952.

Ibn Qudâmah al-Maqdisi, Muwaffaq ud-Deen Abdullah ibn Ahmad. *Fiqh of Worship: Commentary on 'Umdat al-Fiqh (The Reliable Source of Fiqh)*. Translated by Hatem al-Haj. Riyadh: International Islamic Publishing House, 2011.

Josephus, Flavius. *The Jewish War: Revised Edition*. Edited by Betty Radice and E. Mary Smallwood, translated by G. A. Williamson. Harmondsworth: Penguin, 1981.

Khāqānī, Shīrvānī. *Maṣnavī-i tuḥfat al-'Irāqayn*. Edited by Yaḥyā Qarib. Tehran: Shirkat-i Sahāmī-i Kitābhā-yi Jībī bā hamkārī-i Mu'assasah-'i Intishārāt-i Amīr Kabīr, 2537/1978–79.

Leo Africanus, *A Geographical Historie of Africa, written in Arabicke and Italian by John Leo, a More borne in Granada and brought up in Barbarie*. Translated and collected by J. Pory. London: George Bishop, 1600.

Tafur, Pedro. *Andanças e viajes de Pero Tafur* in *Viajes medievales II*. Edited by Miguel Angel Pérez-Priego, 211–379. Madrid: Biblioteca Castro, 2006.

William of Rubruck (Willem van Ruysbroeck). *The Mission of Friar William of Rubruck: His Journey to the Court of the Great Khan Möngke, 1253–1255*. Translated by Peter Jackson. Indianapolis: Hackett, 2009.

Secondary Works

Akbari, Suzanne Conklin. *Idols in the East: European Representations of Islam and the Orient, 1100–1450*. Ithaca: Cornell University Press, 2009.

Alam, Muzaffar and Sanjay Subrahmanyam, eds. *Indo-Persian Travels in the Age of Discoveries, 1400–1800*. Cambridge: Cambridge University Press, 2007.

Allsen, Thomas T. *Commodity and Exchange in the Mongol Empire: A Cultural History of Islamic Textiles*. Cambridge: Cambridge University Press, 1997.

Atasoy, Nurhan and Lale Uluç. *Impressions of Ottoman Culture in Europe: 1453–1699*. Istanbul: Turkish Cultural Foundation, Armağan, 2012.

Barthelemy, Anthony. *Black Face Maligned Race: The Representation of Blacks in English Drama from Shakespeare to Southerne*. Baton Rouge: Louisiana State University Press, 1987.

Bartlett, Robert. *The Making of Europe: Conquest, Colonization and Cultural Change, 950–1350*. Princeton: Princeton University Press, 1993.

Biglieri, Aníbal A. *Las ideas geográficas y la imagen del mundo en la literatura española medieval*. Madrid: Iberoamericana, 2012.

Borm, Jan. "Defining Travel: On the Travel Book, Travel Writing and Terminology." In *Perspectives on Travel Writing*. Edited by Glenn Hooper and Tim Youngs. Aldershot: Ashgate, 2004.

Brancaforte, Elio. *Visions of Persia: Mapping the Travels of Adam Olearius*. Cambridge, MA: Harvard University Dept. of Comparative Literature; distributed by Harvard University Press, 2003.

Brancaforte, Elio, and Sonja Brentjes. *From Rhubarb to Rubies: European Travels to Safavid Iran (1550–1700)*. Cambridge, MA: Houghton Library, Harvard University, 2012.

Braudel, Ferdinand. *The Mediterranean: and the Mediterranean World in the Age of Philip II*. 2 vols. New York: Harper Collins, 1973.

———. *The Wheels of Commerce*. Translated by Siân Reynolds. New York: Harper & Row, 1982.

Brenner, Robert. *Merchants and Revolution: Commercial Change, Political Conflict, and London's Overseas Traders, 1550–1653*. Princeton: Princeton University Press, 1993.

Brockey, Liam Matthew. *Journey to the East: The Jesuit Mission to China, 1579–1724*. Cambridge: Belknap, 2007.

Brotton, Jerry. *Trading Territories: Mapping the Early Modern World*. Ithaca: Cornell University Press, 1997.

Brotton, Jerry, and Lisa Jardine. *Global Interests: Renaissance Art between East and West*. Ithaca: Cornell University Press, 2000.

Burton, Jonathan. *Traffic and Turning: Islam and English Drama, 1579–1624*. Newark: University of Delaware Press, 2005.

Campbell, Mary B. *The Witness and the Other World: Exotic European Travel Writing, 400–1600*. Ithaca: Cornell University Press, 1988.

Canby, Sheila R. *Shah 'Abbas: The Remaking of Iran*. London: British Museum Press, 2009.

———. *The Shahnama of Shah Tahmasp*. New York: Metropolitan Museum of Art, 2014.

Carrizo Rueda, Sofía. *Poética del relato de viajes*. Kassel: Reichenberger, 1997.

Casale, Giancarlo. *The Ottoman Age of Exploration*. Oxford: Oxford University Press, 2010.

Charry, Brinda, and Gitanjali Shahani, eds. *Emissaries in Early Modern Literature and Culture: Mediation, Transmission, Traffic, 1550–1700*. Burlington: Ashgate, 2009.

Cohen, Jeffrey Jerome. "Pilgrimages, Travel Writing and the Medieval Exotic." In *The Oxford Handbook of Medieval Literature in English*, edited by Elaine Treharne and Greg Walker. 611–28. Oxford: Oxford University Press, 2010.

Cosgrove, Dennis. *Apollo's Eye: A Cartographic Genealogy of the Earth in the Western Imagination*. Baltimore: Johns Hopkins University Press, 2003.

Cumming, Owen F. *Prophets, Guardians, and Saints: Shapers of Modern Catholic History*. New York: Paulist, 2007.

Dawson, Christopher. *The Mongol Mission: Narratives and Letters of the Franciscan Missionaries in Mongolia and China in the 13th and 14th Centuries*. London: Sheed Ward, 1980.

De Lorenzi, James. "Red Sea Travelers in Mediterranean Lands: Ethiopian Scholars and Early Modern Orientalism, Ca. 1500–1668." In *World-Building in the Early Modern Imagination*, edited by Allison Kavey, 173–200. New York: Palgrave Macmillan, 2010.

Della Valle, Pietro. *The Pilgrim: The Travels of Pietro Della Valle*. Translated by George Bull. London: Hutchinson, 1990.

Desing, Matthew V. "Luciana's Story: Text, Travel, and Interpretation in the *Libro de Apolonio*." *Hispanic Review* 79 (2011): 1–15.

Dunn, Ross E. *The Adventures of Ibn Battuta: A Muslim Traveler of the 14th Century*. Berkeley: University of California Press, 1986.

Eickelman, Dale, and James Piscatori, eds. *Muslim Travellers: Pilgrimage, Migration and the Religious Imagination*. Berkeley: University of California Press, 1990.

Elsner, Jan, and Joan-Pau Rubiés, eds. *Voyages and Visions: Towards a Cultural History of Travel*. London: Reaktion, 1999.

Euben, Roxanne L. *Journeys to the Other Shore: Muslim and Western Travelers in Search of Knowledge*. Princeton: Princeton University Press, 2006.

Evans, Robert John Weston, and Alexander Marr, *Curiosity and Wonder from the Renaissance to the Enlightenment*. Burlington: Ashgate, 2006.

Faroqhi, Suraiya. *A Cultural History of the Ottomans. The Imperial Elite and its Artefacts*. London: I. B. Tauris, 2016.

Frankopan, Peter. *The Silk Roads: A New History of the World*. London: Bloomsbury, 2015.

Freedman, Paul. *Out of the East: Spices and the Medieval Imagination*. New Haven: Yale University Press, 2008.

Frisch, Andrea. *The Invention of the Eyewitness: Witnessing and Testimony in Early Modern France*. North Carolina Series in the Romance Languages and Literatures 279. Chapel Hill: University of North Carolina Department of Romance Languages, 2004.

Grabar, Oleb. "Patterns and Ways of Cultural Exchange." In *The Meeting of Two Worlds: Cultural Exchange between East and West During the Period of the Crusades*, edited by Vladimir P. Goss. 441–554. Kalamazoo: Medieval Institute Publications, 1986.

Green, Nile, ed. *Writing Travel in Central Asian History*. Bloomington: Indiana University Press, 2013.

Harney, Michael. *Race, Caste, and Indigeneity in Medieval Spanish Travel Literature*. New York: Palgrave Macmillan, 2015.

Harrigan, Michael. *Veiled Encounters: Representing the Orient in 17th-Century French Travel Literature*. Amsterdam: Rodopi, 2008.

Herbert, Thomas. *A Relation of Some Yeares Travaile*. London: William Stansby and Jacob Bloome, 1634.

Jackson, Peter. *The Mongols and the West, 1221–1410*. Harlow: Pearson, 2005.

Jacobs, Martin. *Reorienting the East: Jewish Travelers to the Medieval Muslim World*. Philadelphia: University of Pennsylvania Press, 2014.

Jardine, Lisa. *Worldly Goods. A New History of the Renaissance*. New York: Norton, 1996.

Juynboll, G. H. A. *Muslim Tradition: Studies in Chronology, Provenance and Authorship of Early Hadith.* Cambridge: Cambridge University Press, 2008 [1983].

Kafescioğlu, Çiğdem. *Constantinopolis/Istanbul: Cultural Encounter, Imperial Vision, and the Construction of the Ottoman Capital.* University Park: Penn State University Press, 2009.

Khair, Tabish, Martin Leer, Justin D. Edwards, and Hanna Ziadeh, eds. *Other Routes: 1500 Years of African and Asian Travel Writing.* Bloomington: Indiana University Press, 2005.

Khanmohamadi, Shirin A. *In Light of Another's Word: European Ethnography in the Middle Ages.* Philadelphia: University of Pennsylvania Press, 2014.

Lach, Donald F., and Edwin J. Van Kley. *A Century of Advance: Trade, Missions, Literature.* Asia in the Making of Europe 3. Chicago: University of Chicago Press, 1993.

Lach, Donald. *Asia in the Making of Europe.* 3 vols, with multiple books per volume. Chicago: University of Chicago Press, 1965-98.

Legassie, Shayne Aaron. *The Medieval Invention of Travel.* Chicago: University of Chicago Press, 2017.

Lestringant, Frank. *Mapping the Renaissance World: The Geographical Imagination in the Age of Discovery.* Oxford: Oxford University Press 1994.

MacLean, Gerald, ed. *Re-Orienting the Renaissance.* New York: Palgrave McMillan, 2005.

Matar, Nabil. *An Arab Ambassador in the Mediterranean World: The Travels of Muhammad ibn 'Uthmān al-Miknāsī, 1779–1788.* New York: Routledge, 2015.

———. *Europe Through Arab Eyes, 1578–1727.* New York: Columbia University Press, 2009.

———. *In the Lands of the Christians: Arabic Travel Writing in the Seventeenth Century.* New York: Routledge, 2003.

Matthee, Rudolph P. *The Politics of Trade in Safavid Iran: Silk for Silver, 1600–1730.* Cambridge: Cambridge University Press, 1999.

Micallef, Roberta, and Sunil Sharma, eds. *On the Wonders of Land and Sea: Persianate Travel Writing.* Cambridge, MA: Harvard University Press, 2013.

Müge Göçek, Fatma. *East Encounters West: France and the Ottoman Empire in the Eighteenth Century.* Oxford: Oxford University Press, 1987.

Necipoğlu, Gülru. *Architecture, Ceremonial, and Power: The Topkapi Palace in the Fifteenth and Sixteenth Centuries.* Cambridge, MA: MIT Press, 1991.

Netton, Ian Richard. *Golden Roads: Migration, Pilgrimage and Travel in Medieval and Modern Islam.* London: Routledge, 2005.

Pérez-Priego, Miguel Angel, ed. *Viajes medievales II.* Madrid: Biblioteca Castro, 2006.

Phillips, Kim M. *Before Orientalism: Asian Peoples and Cultures in European Travel Writing, 1245–1510.* Philadelphia: University of Pennsylvania Press, 2013.

Prawer, Joshua. "The Roots of Medieval Colonialism." In *The Meeting of Two Worlds: Cultural Exchange between East and West during the period of the Crusades,* edited by Vladimir P. Goss. 23–38. Kalamazoo: Medieval Institute Publications, 1986.

Richard, Jean. *Les Récits de voyages et de pélerinages.* Turnhout: Brepols, 1981.

Rose, Susan. *The Medieval Sea.* London: Continuum, 2007.

Roth, Norman. *Conversos, Inquisition, and the Expulsion of the Jews from Spain.* Madison: University of Wisconsin Press, 1995.

Roux, Jean-Paul. *L'Asie centrale, histoire et civilisation*, Paris: Fayard. 2007.

Rubiés, Joan-Pau. "Travel Writing as a Genre: Facts, Fictions and the Invention of a Scientific Discourse in Early Modern Europe." *Journeys* 1 (2000): 5–35.

Rubiés, Joan-Pau. *Travel and Ethnology in the Renaissance: South India through European Eyes, 1250–1625.* Cambridge: Cambridge University Press, 2002.

Rubio Tovar, J. *Libros españoles de viajes medievales.* Madrid: Taurus, 1986.

Ryan, Maria del Pilar. *El Jesuita Secreto: San Francisco de Borja.* Valencia: Biblioteca Valenciana, 2008.

Said, Edward W. "Orientalism." In *The Edward Said Reader,* edited by Edward W. Said, Moustafa Bayoumi and Andrew Rubin, 73–74. New York: Vintage, 2000.

———. *Orientalism.* New York: Vintage, 1979.

Schleck, Julia. *Telling True Tales of Islamic Lands: Forms of Mediation in English Travel Writing, 1575–1630.* Selinsgrove: Susquehanna University Press, 2011.

Smith, Pamela H., and Paula Findlen, eds. *Merchants and Marvels: Commerce, Science, and Art in Early Modern Europe.* London: Routledge, 2002.

Snyder, John P. *Flattening the Earth: Two Thousand Years of Map Projection.* Chicago: University of Chicago Press, 1993.

Speake, Jennifer, ed. *Literature of Travel and Exploration: An Encyclopedia.* 3 vols. New York: Fitzroy Dearborn, 2003.

Subrahmanyam, Sanjay. *Three Ways to Be Alien: Travails and Encounters in the Early Modern World.* Waltham: Brandeis University Press, 2011.

Taylor, Christopher. *In the Vicinity of the Righteous: Ziyara and the Veneration of Muslim Saints in Late Medieval Egypt.* Leiden: Brill, 1999.

Touati, Houari. *Islam and Travel in the Middle Ages.* Translated by Lydia Cochrane. Chicago: University of Chicago Press, 2010.

Youngs, Tim. *The Cambridge Introduction to Travel Writing.* Cambridge: Cambridge University Press, 2013.

Zemon-Davies, Natalie. *Trickster Travels: A Sixteenth-Century Muslim Between Worlds.* New York: Hill and Wang, 2006.

Zubillaga, Carina. *Poesía narrativa clerical en su contexto manuscrito: Estudio y edición del Ms. Esc. K-III-4.* Buenos Aires: Dunken, 2014.

Zumthor, Paul. "The Medieval Travel Narrative." *New Literary History* 25 (1994): 809–24.

INDEX